THE
ENGLISH LANGUAGE
IN AMERICA

THE
ENGLISH LANGUAGE
IN AMERICA

GEORGE PHILIP KRAPP

Volume II

FREDERICK   UNGAR   PUBLISHING   CO.
NEW YORK

Copyright 1925
by The Modern Language Association of America

Copyright renewed 1952 by Elisabeth Krapp

Republished 1960
by arrangement with the author's estate

Second printing, 1966

Printed in the United States of America

Library of Congress Catalog Card Number 60-9103

CONTENTS

THE
ENGLISH LANGUAGE
IN AMERICA

PRONUNCIATION

(1) *Introduction*

The history of the pronunciation of English in America may be studied either for the light which it throws on the general history of the English language, or for the interest which American pronunciations have within this special division of the English language. The second would seem to be the more weighty reason, from the point of view of this book, for entering into the subject. Though the facts of American pronunciation may be made to serve as the occasion for an exhaustive inquiry into a complete history of English sounds, to treat them so might seem like making the tail wag the dog. Certainly a more economical and convenient method of approach to the general history of English sounds may be devised. To the dog, however, the tail is a somewhat important, even essential part of his being, and the interest which students of American speech have in their present linguistic habits and in the history of their habits is not only legitimate, but pious. Its common speech is one of the most important of the distinctive social possessions of the American people, and only by sympathetic study can they hope to understand it or themselves.

The knowledge to be attained of the history of English pronunciation in America must be pieced together from a variety of fragmentary sources. Among these may be mentioned local documents and records, especially the records of New England town communities; numerous grammars and spelling books, the latter being also guides to pronunciation, and often containing lists of improprieties in speech; dictionaries and the comments of dictionary makers;

naïve spellings in diaries, letters and similar documents, which often indicate pronunciation by their departure from conventional spellings; the rimes of the poets; literary transcriptions of dialects; and a few early attempts at spelling reform, especially Benjamin Franklin's scheme for a phonetic alphabet and, to some slight extent, Noah Webster's reformed spelling as employed in his *Essays* (1790).

These authorities, the most important of which will be found listed alphabetically in the bibliography, are of unequal value. The grammars soon exhibit the tendency common to most authors of grammars of copying one from another, and it is therefore sometimes difficult to tell when a criticism of speech is a genuine observation and when it is merely an echo. Some of the early grammars printed in America are also only American reprints, without acknowledgment, of British books. The various writings of Noah Webster, on the other hand, are authorities of prime importance. Webster set it down as an axiom that it is the student's "business to find what the English language *is*, and not, how it *might have been made*," *Dissertations*, p. ix. And in all his studies Webster conscientiously endeavored to observe the facts and to base his interpretations upon the facts as he viewed them. His head, to be sure, was full of Yankee theories, about language as about other things, but at the same time he was a man of practical wisdom who knew the realities of the world in which he lived. When at times he forgets his good intentions and exalts theory, even fantastic theory, above fact, it is not difficult to separate these errors of judgment from the good wheat.

No doubt Franklin was equally honest and independent, but the value of his phonetic alphabet as a record of American speech is rendered somewhat uncertain through the fact that when it was written out in 1768, Franklin was living in England, where he had passed a good part of his time since 1757, serving as colonial agent for Pennsylvania. In preparing his alphabet, Franklin pretty certainly had no notion of describing a kind of speech which was distinctive for America as contrasted with the speech of Great Britain. Perhaps there was no such distinction in his day. In his mind, standard American English probably differed not at all from standard

British English. Nor can Franklin's phonetic records be taken as intentionally representing Boston speech, in which city he was born in 1706, or Philadelphia speech, in which city he had lived since the time of his early manhood. If any local characteristics of American speech are indicated in Franklin's phonetic scheme, they are not there intentionally, but by inadvertence.

A word should be said concerning the rimes of the poets. A large body of distinctively American verse was written during the latter years of the eighteenth century, especially in Connecticut, and one readily turns to it in the expectation of finding some definite indications of how words sounded in the ears of the rimesters of the time. In interpreting the meaning of rimes, the main difficulty lies in the fact that one cannot always tell whether or not a poet's ear was exact, or if it was exact, whether or not the poet really tried to rime exactly. Now it is well known that the conventions of riming were loose in the eighteenth century, even among poets who followed the regular metrical patterns standardized by Pope. One cannot, therefore, accept their rimes at face value. On the other hand, the rimes need not be altogether discounted or discarded. If cautiously interpreted, they may serve a useful purpose as providing confirmatory evidence for points in pronunciation which are more or less established by other evidence. They have a value, also, when they are not literary echoes, as being fairly direct evidence of real speech, thus betraying to some extent the variety of usage in living speech, whereas the statements of grammarians, dictionary makers and theorists are likely to disregard the varieties of practice in usage either for the sake of simplicity or brevity of statement, or in the interest of some ideal conviction of what pronunciation ought to be as measured by a fixed standard.

Local records as a source of information are of exceptional importance because in many instances they go back almost to the very beginnings of colonization in America. This is especially true of the local records of town affairs in the towns of Massachusetts, Connecticut, and New York. A not inconsiderable number of these town records have been published through the patriotic interest of the towns themselves. The publication has been done in the main in a careful and scholarly way, with scrupulous fidelity to the letter of the original documents. Since these documents were often naïvely written by persons of little conventional training, they provide rich stores of information in the way words sounded to the ears of persons who felt no compunctions in writing down words as they sounded. To be sure, even the most illiterate town clerk was not wholly illiterate. Before one can conceive oneself as embarking upon the adventure of written expression, one must be to some extent literate. The main interest of these naïve records consists in just those lapses from literary convention which show that at the moment the writer had his mind fixed upon something other than literary convention, or at least was unsettled in his mind as to literary convention. When, for example, the spelling of the *Norwalk Records* gives *drumne*, p. 76 (1681), or *drumb*, p. 71 (1678), for *drum, weight*, p. 76 (1681), for *wait*, one realizes that the clerk who wrote these records had notions about spelling and pronunciation which were not altogether those of the conventionally trained record keeper. From such spellings one can make several pretty certain inferences. Such departures from convention are more frequent and illuminating in the local town records than they are in the records of more important courts and assemblies. In the more dignified bodies the records were usually kept, even in the seventeenth century, by persons of some experience and training in this occupation, and in consequence they are all written in the accepted and generalized forms of what may be called the standard official language of their period. This language was approximately the same, whether used to record the acts of the General Court at Boston, of the House of Burgesses in Virginia, or of the House of Commons in London. It offers little, therefore, which is distinctive, and on the whole gives much less information concerning the pronunciation of English in the early periods of America than the more crudely written records of town meetings. For it is one of the commonplaces of the historical study of English that the conventional spellings of literary English since the close of the Middle English period do not give a faithful picture even of standard cultivated speech. Certainly the gap between the written expression of the literary and the naïve writer in the seventeenth and eighteenth centuries must have been much greater than that between the spoken language of the same persons. It is unfortunate that these naïve records are abundant only for New England. Southern institutions provided nothing equivalent to the town meeting of New England, and indeed it is generally characteristic of the difference between New England and the South that in the latter region the plain and unlettered citizen, who must have been just as numerous as he was in the North, had little to do with controlling the details of the life of the community in which he lived, and consequently there was little that made demands upon his powers of written expression.

If one considers all the varieties of English speech which are in existence in any community, at any given moment, one becomes aware of the utter impossibility of giving a complete picture of this speech in all its shades and levels of dialect. Limitation becomes an obvious necessity. For the purpose of this study, the specially limited section of American speech chosen as the basis and point of departure for investigation is that which is commonly called standard speech. It is scarcely necessary to enter into the troubled question of what constitutes standard. A sufficient definition of the term standard will perhaps be found in the statement that speech is standard when it passes current in actual use among persons who must be accounted as among the conservers and representatives of the approved social traditions of a community. In American life such persons have always been distinguished by a certain amount of literary culture. They have been aware of a language with written and printed as well as spoken associations, and have on the whole been impressed with a certain sense of obligation and honor in preserving the decencies and proprieties of the language. Among them differences of opinion and practice have always existed, but these differences are not the same as those which distinguish the illiterate from the literate users of language. Among the former, differences are likely not to be felt, or if felt, likely not to be considered of importance, whereas among the latter, differences are likely both to be keenly appreciated and vigorously defended or repudiated.

It does not follow that the feeling determining standard speech in America would be the same as that active in other languages. "If pressed to say definitely what good American English is," remarks R. O. Williams, *Our Dictionaries*, p. 111, "I should say, it is the English of those who are believed by the greater number of Americans to know what good English is." Williams does not assume that the same test would suffice to determine good English in England, but thinks there is more respect in America for those who are supposed to "know" than in England. "Language there [in England] is more generally a matter of family usage than it is here; it is the speech one grows up with, and to change it would smack of affectation and a desire to ape one's betters."

Good English in America has always been a matter of the opinion of those who know, or think they know, and opinion on this point has always been changing. In a New England village or town of the latter seventeenth century, the feeling for standard would obviously be different from that which prevails in the same village or town to-day. A very respectable townsman might not be able to sign his own name in the seventeenth century, as the town records of the period amply prove. But it is inconceivable that a respectable townsman to-day should not be able to sign his own name. Formerly more was forgiven in the way of conventional accomplishment to the one whose circumstances had not made it practicable to acquire these accomplishments. Or perhaps it would be truer to say that the elementary accomplishments were not then so highly prized, not so eagerly sought as they have been in later days. They were both less important and less necessary than they have become in these times of universal education. The final impression that one derives from the historical study of American English is that differences of practice among standard speakers, that is, among members of good standing in the community, were formerly much more numerous than they are to-day, and that they continue to show an increasing tendency to disappear in an all-embracing uniformity. As conven tions spread they become more exacting and at the same time less significant. When all must speak alike, manifestly there can be no distinction in speaking like one's fellows. The conventional language then ceases to be an accomplishment and becomes merely an elementary necessity. For this reason, perhaps, students are sometimes inclined to esteem too highly popular and illiterate habits in speech as being supposedly more genuine and picturesque than others. Though the present writer has no intention of excluding from attention popular forms of speech when they throw light on the developments of cultivated speech, as they frequently do, the popular and illiterate dialects of American speech will not be made the center of interest, nor will it be acknowledged that they are in themselves historically either more important or interesting than those forms of English speech which have passed current in respectable sections of American society.

The method followed as the point of departure in ordering the materials of this chapter has been to take sounds as they appear in groups of words containing the several sounds, the sounds under which the words are organized being those of present American English. The purpose of the chapter has been to present an historical description of those sounds only which have in their history something distinctive in the records of American speech, or something specially interesting because of American association. Many words and their sounds in present American speech are the same as those of present British speech, and all along have had the same history. As this study is not an attempt to examine the whole history of English pronunciation, with American English as a starting place, it has not been widened to include all sounds of American English, whether or not they have had anything distinctive or significant in their history.

It has seemed best to proceed from the present sounds of American speech, for under them can most conveniently be ordered the words of the language. Thus under the sound *o* as in *note*, that is [oː], the history of all words with present [oː] that have had other sounds in American speech will be considered, for example, New

England *stone*, *Holmes*, and similar words, or the pronunciation *going* as *gwine* [gwaɪn], now current only as a Southern illiterate pronunciation, but formerly present also in cultivated speech. This organization of the material under sounds is followed merely for the sake of practical conveniency. Some order indeed is necessary to prevent the discussion from falling into a medley of chatty remarks on pronunciation. It is true that no one's interest in pronunciation lies merely in sounds considered as sounds, but in sounds exemplified in words. The diphthongal quality of long *u* is not in itself a matter of practical importance, but it is important to know the facts about the pronunciation of words like *duty*, *duke*, *tutor*, etc., the present facts if one is concerned with present usage, the historical facts if one is concerned with the history of pronunciation. But the only way in which words can be systematically classified according to pronunciation is by the sounds which occur in them. Since the vocabulary of English has remained practically unchanged during the whole American period, the sounds in words of present English will necessarily carry one back over the whole range of the English vocabulary.

Another practical convenience and necessity is the use of a phonetic alphabet. Phonetic transcriptions may at times seem grotesque to one unfamiliar with them, but they are not nearly so grotesque as the painful efforts often made to indicate sounds in literary transcriptions of dialect speech. Thus Holmes in *Elsie Venner* writes *mahn*, *tahvern*, *mahterr*, the purpose of the *h* being to indicate a vowel like that of *father*, the purpose of the second *r* in *mahterr* apparently being merely to indicate that the *r* was actually heard and was not silent as normally in the cultivated pronunciation that Holmes was familiar with. One can guess what these spellings mean, but it is often difficult, sometimes impossible, to tell with any exactness what Holmes meant by his spelling, for example, *aäfter* for *after*, *haälp* for *help*, *threugh* for *through*, etc. It is impossible to tell what Holmes meant because he has not told his reader the value he would have him give to such spelling as *aäfter*. In the interest of economy, one must settle upon a set of symbols for recording sounds, and must give some descriptive statement of the meaning of these symbols, before one engages to talk about sounds. This is all that a phonetic alphabet, at least as here employed, is expected to do. The alphabet used is one of only medium precision, therefore is not complicated by the presence of a large number of symbols. It is essentially the alphabet of the International Phonetic Association, and is the one employed by the author in his *Pronunciation of Standard English in America* (1919). All phonetic transcriptions are placed within square brackets. A long vowel is indicated by a colon following the vowel symbol, as in [ɑː], and main stress is marked by the acute, secondary stress, by the grave accent, as in *bookshelf* [ˈbʊkˋʃɛlf]. Otherwise the remaining symbols that call for comment may be briefly described, and those about which nothing is said are to be taken with the value they have in present English. The symbol [ɑː] means the vowel of *father*, and the same vowel short, [ɑ], occurs often in America in words like *hot got, rob*, etc. The terms short and long refer only to quantity, and a short vowel does not differ in quality from a long vowel. The symbol [aː] indicates a vowel not quite as "broad" as [ɑː]. Many speakers do not like to say *past* [pɑːst], and compromise on a vowel halfway between the vowel of *father* and the vowel of *fat*, and this compromise sound is symbolized here by [aː], as in *past* [paːst]. The very common vowel of *hat, sat, that*, etc., is symbolized by [æ]. The vowels [eː], [iː], [oː], [uː], have their so-called Continental values, and as longs appear respectively in *bate* [beːt], *beat* [biːt], *boat* [boːt], boot [buːt]. The vowels [eː] and [oː] may become noticeably diphthongal, especially when final or before voiced consonants, in which case they are written [eɪ], [oʊ], as in *play* [pleɪ], *go* [goʊ]. In standard southern British speech, these long vowels are said to be always diphthongal, and they are certainly more markedly diphthongal there than they ever are in American speech. The symbol [ɛ] indicates the vowel of *get* and [ɛː] the vowel of *there, fair*, etc., [ðɛɪr], [fɛɪr]. For the unstressed vowel of *about* [əˈbaʊt], and generally for nearly all unstressed vowels, the symbol [ə] is used. The symbol [ɚ] indicates the general American pronunciation of *e, i, u*, and sometimes *o*, before *r* in the speech of those persons who are said to pronounce their *r's,* as in *pert* [pərt], *shirt* [ʃərt], *hurt* [hərt], *worth* [wərθ]. The tongue position for *r* is already almost completely assumed while the preceding vowel is being pronounced, and careful analysis is necessary to make clear the distinction between a vocalic [ə] and a genuinely consonantal [r]. In the speech of those persons who are said not to pronounce their *r's,* and who consequently do not revert the point of the tongue while pronouncing the vowel preceding *r,* the vowel sound present is the one indicated by [ʌɪ], as in the New England pronunciation of *pert* [pʌɪt], *shirt* [ʃʌɪt], *hurt* [hʌɪt], *worth* [wʌɪθ], etc. With [iː] the vowel of *free* [friː], etc., should be compared [ɪ] the vowel of *sit* [sɪt], *rich* [rɪtʃ], etc.; with [oː], the vowel [ɔ], [ɔː] as in *auditory* ['ɔdɪ'tɔrɪ], *awe* [ɔː]; and with [uː] the vowel [ʊ] as in *bush* [bʊʃ], *put* [pʊt], *bull* [bʊl], and [ʌ], as in *bunt* [bʌnt], *luck* [lʌk], etc. Besides those already mentioned, the important diphthongal sounds are [aɪ], the vowel of *ride* [raɪd], *sky* [skaɪ]; [ɑʊ], the vowel of *house* [hɑʊs], *now* [nɑʊ], etc.; [ɔɪ], the vowel of *boil* [bɔɪl], *coin* [kɔɪn], etc.; and [juː], the sound of *mute* [mjuːt], *few* [fjuː], which is not strictly speaking diphthongal, since the first element is consonantal. The genuine diphthong would be [ɪuː], a sound now only heard in dialectal speech. For practical convenience, however, [juː] may be grouped among the diphthongs. For the consonants, [j] represents the initial sound of *ye* [jiː], *yawl* [jɔːl], etc.; [ŋ] is the final consonant of *sing* [sɪŋ], *long* [lɔŋ]; [s] is always voiceless, as in *best* [bɛst], *price* [praɪs], and [z] is voiced, as in *rise* [raɪz], *rouse* [rɑʊz]; [ʃ] is the consonant of *wish* [wɪʃ], *dash* [dæʃ], which appears in combination with [t] in *rich* [rɪtʃ], *such* [sʌtʃ], *witch* [wɪtʃ]; [ʒ] is the voiced equivalent of [ʃ], as in *pleasure* ['plɛʒər], *rouge* [ruːʒ], and it appears in combination with [d] in *judge* [dʒʌdʒ], *gem* [dʒɛm], etc.; [θ] is the voiceless consonant of *thin* [θɪn], *thank* [θæŋk], etc., and [ð] the voiced sound of *that* [ðæt], *oathes* [oːðz], etc.; [w] is a voiced sound as in *wet* [wɛt], *wing* [wɪŋ], and [ʍ] is the voiceless sound of *what* [ʍat], *whine* [ʍaɪn], etc.

One aspect of importance in the matter of pronunciation, that is the cadence of speech, it is impossible to treat historically because it has never been historically recorded, in fact, even now is not adequately recorded for any form of present British or American speech. Distinctions of cadence are often more subtle and intimate as colors in speech than are the shadings of quality in sound or of significance in the meanings of words. Only rarely on the printed page does one discover positive marks of speech which enable one to place the writer in his local setting, but scarcely a dozen spoken words will frequently determine not only whether or not the speaker is British or American, but even the particular region of England or America in which his habits of speech were formed. Since cadence is such a subtle test of difference, it is the more regrettable that means have not been discovered for practically recording this element in speech. But obviously it is just because cadence is so subtle that it escapes mechanical record. Instead we have descriptive adjectives which may be full of meaning, or at least of feeling, to the persons who use them, but which can rarely convey a definite meaning to another. Two of these terms must be considered, however, since they have long been current in accounts of American speech. These terms characterize American speech, especially in contrast to British speech, as being marked by a drawl and a twang. What is meant by the American drawl and the American twang?

Now the word drawl usually implies slow and dragging speech. In the *Grammatical Institute*, Part I, 1783, p. 6, Webster says that "in New England we hear a flat, drawling pronunciation." This is the earliest mention of the New England drawl. Lowell, *Introduction to the Biglow Papers*, Second Series (Boston, 1885), p. 43, says, "No one is more painfully conscious than I of the contrast between the rifle-crack of an Englishman's *yes* and *no*, and the wet-fuse drawl of the same monosyllable in the mouths of my countrymen." Dickens in his *American Notes* evidently means to indicate the American drawl as a slow, drawn out speech when he records the words of an American as follows, *American Notes*, chapter IV: "There is a clever town in a smart lo-ca-tion, where he expects you have con-cluded to stop." Similar observations were made by other travelers in America from the time travelers began to take notice of the peculiarities of America and the Americans in the latter part of the eighteenth century. The nasal twang was usually combined with the drawl in these descriptions of American speech. The presence of these characteristics is not denied by Americans themselves, and Webster, in his *Dissertations*, gives an explanation of the facts which will be noted later. Something which may be, and often is, described in the same terms is still present in American speech, and probably these traits of contemporary speech are not widely different from those observed by earlier critics and students. A slow and deliberate speech is one of the marks of the Brother Jonathan type of character, a speech relaxed and deliberate, with implications of a philosophically humorous and amused, not to say quizzical, view of the incidents of life. The contrasting speech would be rapid and explosive, high stresses and high pitch at certain points, falling to very low at others. The typical native American speech is more level, the voice rising and falling but little. The American manner of speech because of its level stressing permits a fuller pronunciation of unstressed or secondarily stressed syllables than the kind of speech represented in the British pronunciation of *medicine* as ['mɛdsɪn], of *library* as ['laɪbrɪ], in which a very heavy expiratory stress on the first syllable seems to exhaust a large share of the energy which might be devoted to the later syllables of the word.

Nasalization of vowels is also present not infrequently in this slow or level type of contemporary American speech. Whether or not the nasalization should be called a twang, depends very much upon what one means by twang. Nasalization is not all of the same kind, and some persons who would pass one kind of nasalization unnoticed, would designate another kind as a twang. Since the word as it is commonly used has a very vague content, it would be futile to attempt to give it an exact meaning. The word "twang" often means nothing more than merely "flavor." Moreover, these terms drawl and twang, as applied to American speech, have to a considerable extent become vaguely traditional. In the beginning they were intended to describe certain aspects of the speech of New England which impressed observers as being characteristic for that region, but they have often been loosely applied since to any features of American speech which seemed to call for a distinguishing epithet. The terms were also limited in their earlier application to rustic American speech. Thus Pickering, *A Vocabulary*, Boston, 1816, p. 42, notes the remark of Lambert, in his *Travels*, London, 1814, II, 505, that "the country people in Vermont and other New England states use many curious phrases and quaint expressions . . . which are rendered more remarkable by a sort of nasal twang which they have in speaking"; and Pickering adds this comment of his own: "This *nasal twang*, as Mr. Lambert observes, is very common in New England, among the '*country*-people.' In the seaport towns also people of all classes undoubtedly have a slower and more deliberate manner of speaking than the English; and, in some instances, they fall into a drawling pronunciation. An American, however, is not likely to be sensible of this, unless he has been absent from his country for some time, and his ear has been familiarized to the pronunciation of Englishmen."

Timothy Dwight, *Travels*, I, 465 ff. observed, as he thought, a distinctive quality in the cadence of Boston speech which separated it from the speech of other regions in America. He notes that the people of Boston "with a very small number of exceptions . . . speak the English language in the English manner," and also that the Bostonians exhibit greater ardor and vivacity of temperament than other Americans. "From this ardor springs," he continues, "in the inhabitants of this town, especially in the middle and lower classes, a pronunciation unusually rapid . . . the rapidity of their pronunciation contracts frequently two short syllables into one, and thus renders the language, in itself too rough, still rougher, by a violent junction of consonants, which in the spelling were separated. Dissyllables, accented on the first, and terminating the last with a liquid, particularly with *l*, *n*, or *m*, they pronounce in such a way as to leave out the sound of the vowel. Thus *Sweden, Britain, garden, vessel*, are extensively pronounced *Swed'n, Brit'n, gard'n, vess'l*. By this contraction, also, the harshness of the language is increased." From these comments one may infer that, in Dwight's judgment at least, the "drawl" was general in American speech, and that rapid utterance was peculiar to Boston. In his own speech, words like *garden, vessel,* etc., were distinctly and fully dissyllabic.

The remarks of Cooper, *Notions,* II, 130–131, on this point are not altogether clear, but should be noted. "The peculiarity of the New England dialect (the term is almost too strong) is most discernible," he observes, "in the manner in which they dwell on the last word of a sentence, or the last syllable of a word. It is not properly drawling, for they speak very quick in common, much quicker than the English; so quick, indeed, as to render syllables frequently indistinct; but in consequence of the peculiar pause they make on the last word, I question if they utter a sentence in less time than those who dwell more equally on its separate parts. Among men of the world, and of education, this peculiarity is, of course, often lost; but education is so common, and the state of society so simple in New England, as to produce less apparent distinction in speech and manners than it is usual to find elsewhere." As an illustration of this manner of speech, Cooper cites the phrase *I wonder if he did,* and says, "it is usually uttered 'I wonder if he de-e-e-ed,' with a falling of the voice at the last word, to nearly an octave below the rest of the sentence. Sometimes there is more than one resting point, in a sentence of any length." Just what this means in precise terms it is difficult to say. Cooper found New England speech unusually rapid, and Dwight, except in Boston, unusually slow. But perhaps we may infer that Cooper at least preferred a relatively slow speech, one which would not "render syllables frequently indistinct." In the sentence *I wonder if he did,* Cooper apparently heard the last word, as pronounced in New England, unusually long and with a circumflex, that is a rising-falling inflection. Similar observations were made by Samuel Worcester in his reading books. He remarks, *Fourth Book,* p. 418, that "the final syllables of words, and the final words of sentences, must not have a long, descending, tapering tone. The people of the United States, and especially those of New England, continue these syllables and words much longer than good speakers in England."

Worcester insistently corrects what he regards as the faulty but prevalent use of the "wave," "double slide," or "circumflex" in the colloquial accent and the local reading accent of New England, "a fault which even well-educated persons often unconsciously display on the gravest occasions," *Fourth Book*, p. 12. "This tone," he adds, "is strikingly exemplified in every emphatic word of what are popularly termed 'Yankee stories,' but may be traced, in a reduced form, in the current tones of New England, whether in speaking or in reading." As an example of faulty New England intonation, he gives the sentence, p. 33, *Abel was a keeper of sheep, but Cain was a tiller of the ground*, with circumflex intonation on *Abel* and *sheep*, and on *Cain* and *ground*, producing an effect which he calls "peculiarly unhappy." One whose ears are accustomed to the cadences of contemporary New England rustic speech will have no difficulty in calling to mind the kind of intonation which Cooper and Worcester attempted to describe. It was this intonation which led more than one earlier observer to declare that American speech "more resembles singing than speaking." [1] This sing-song cadence was undoubtedly a part of what many critics felt impelled to name the American drawl, or whine, or twang.

Granting then that there have been in certain types of American speech these characteristics which are loosely designated as drawl and twang, it becomes of interest to inquire whether they must be taken to be of native American development, or like most elements in American speech, are inheritances from a British original. Unfriendly critics were formerly sometimes led to see in American speech that native tendency toward degeneration which, according to Buffon and some other early naturalists, the general low state of development of the country illustrated, whether in climate, land, insects, quadrupeds, or mankind. This blanket accusation, however, manifestly puts an unfair burden of justification upon the country, as did later Oscar Wilde's opinion that the contours of the American hills and mountains were vulgar. If American cadences in speech were a native development, some more specific cause must

[1] *Monthly Mirror*, March, 1808, in Cairns, *British Criticisms*, p. 37.

be found for them. Such a cause Webster, *Dissertations*, p. 106, attempted to give. "It may surprise those who have not turned their thoughts to this subject," he remarks, "that I should ascribe the manner of speaking among a people, to the nature of their government and a distribution of their property. Yet it is an undoubted fact that the drawling nasal manner of speaking in New England arises almost solely from these causes.

"People of large fortunes, who pride themselves on family distinction, possess a certain boldness, dignity and independence in their manner, which give a corresponding air to their mode of speaking. Those who are accustomed to command slaves, form a habit of expressing themselves with the tone of authority and decision.

"In New England, where there are few slaves and servants, and less family distinctions than in any other part of America, the people are accustomed to address each other with that diffidence, or attention to the opinions of others, which marks a state of equality. Instead of commanding, they advise; instead of saying, *you must;* they ask with an air of doubtfulness, *is it not best?* or give their opinions with an indecisive tone; *you had better, I believe.* Not possessing that pride and consciousness of superiority which attend birth and fortune, their intercourse with each other is all conducted on the idea of equality, which gives a singular tone to their language and complexion to their manners.

"These remarks do not apply to the commercial towns; for people who are conversant with a variety of company lose most of their irregularities, and hence well-bred people resemble each other in all countries. But the peculiar traits of national character are found in the internal parts of a country, among that class of people who do not travel, nor are tempted by an intercourse with foreigners, to quit their own habits.

"Such are the causes of the local peculiarities in pronunciation, which prevail among the country people in New England, and which, to foreigners [Englishmen were foreigners to Webster], are the objects of ridicule. The great error in their manner of speaking proceeds immediately from not opening the mouth sufficiently. Hence words are drawled out in a careless, lazy manner, or the sound finds a passage thro the nose."

Webster with all his fondness for native traits in language could not approve the one here discussed, and he concludes the subject by remarking that "nothing can be so disagreeable as that drawling, whining cant that distinguishes a certain class of people; and too much pains cannot be taken to reform the practice. Great efforts should be made by teachers of schools, to make their pupils open the teeth, and give a full clear sound to every syllable."

Webster's engaging picture of New England equality one may accept without being convinced that this equality adequately explains the character of New England speech. It is true, as Webster points out, that New England to his day had been in the situation of an island; "during 160 years, the people, except in a few commercial towns, have not been exposed to any of the causes which effect great changes in language and manners." But this would seem to be rather an argument proving the retention of something which they already had than the invention or development of something new. Social contacts undoubtedly have an influence upon one's manner of speech, but the psychology of the relations between superior and inferior, as here presented by Webster, is too dubious to serve as a firm ground upon which inference so far-reaching can be built. Franklin, in his *Autobiography*, defended at length the habit of expressing oneself with "modest diffidence," and he advised speakers never to use the words *certainly, undoubtedly,* "or any others that give the air of positiveness to an opinion." This superlative caution, whether admittedly or not, was manifestly the counsel of perfection, for it can scarcely be supposed that even in New England did men so completely subdue human nature in all the walk of their familiar daily life where speech is formed as never to express themselves strongly or feelingly.

Another explanation was offered by Marsh in his *Lectures on the English Language*, New York, 1860, p. 670. These lectures were delivered in 1858. "We are said to drawl our words by protracting the vowels," says Marsh, "and giving them a more diphthongal sound than the English. Now, an Englishman who reads, will habitually utter his vowels more fully and distinctly than his countryman who does not; and, upon the same principle, a nation of readers, like the Americans, will pronounce more deliberately and clearly than a people, so large a proportion of whom are unable to read, as in England. From our universal habit of reading, there results not only a greater distinctness of articulation, but a strong tendency to assimilate the spoken to the written language." Of this tendency, Marsh gives *dictionary* and *military* as examples, with strong primary and secondary stress in American speech, but only one stress in British speech. As to diphthongization of long vowels, he observes that "this tendency will, of course, be strengthened by any cause which produces greater slowness and fulness of articulation." He then proceeds to show, still less successfully, that climate has affected American speech, American climate being relatively southern as compared with that of England, and articulation being, in southern latitudes, "generally much more distinct than in northern regions." "Participating, then," he concludes, "in the physical influences of a Southern climate, we have contracted something of the more distinct articulation that belongs to a dry atmosphere, and a clear sky."

Here again a small grain of truth may be separated from a good deal of vague theorizing. In one detail, Marsh's remarks are directly contradicted by the observations of exact students of speech. The long vowels in American speech are not more diphthongal, but ordinarily much less diphthongal than the long vowels of that southern British English which is usually taken as the type of standard British speech. In this respect American speech is more like northern British, in which the long vowels are so slightly diphthonged, if diphthonged at all, as scarcely to be perceived as such.

But the influence of the visual forms of language upon speech has undoubtedly been real, both in America and in England. This influence has always been exerted, but probably has been greater since the relatively modern expansion of democratic education, an expansion which has been going on in England as well as in America in the last two centuries. Whether or not the people of America have been more given to reading than the people of England is a question not to be determined by a facile generalization. A system of universal elementary education does not necessarily produce a nation of readers. It is probably true, however, that speech in America has been less subject to checks and restraints imposed upon it by social tradition than it has in England. A recognized class system carries with it the self-justification of what is done by the favored class. Such a court of appeal has never existed so effectively in America as it has in England, and lacking the firm support of an established social opinion, users of American English have doubtless tended to substitute something for it which seemed equally firm and stable, that is, judgments based upon the visual forms of the printed and written speech. In other words, the standard of speech has tended to become more literary in America than in England. This is very obvious in the treatment of proper names. The discrepancy between the written and the spoken forms of many British proper names has long been one of the standing jokes in American humor. But *Cholmondeley*, pronounced *Chumly*, seems humorous to the American because the word is mainly to him an eye-word. If the word had established itself in his mind first through oral tradition, no humorous associations would have attached themselves to the word, no matter how inadequately it was spelled. In this situation the American, if he makes any change at all, can do one of two things. He can change the spelling to accord with the pronunciation, as when he changes *Worcester*, the older name of the town in Massachusetts, to *Wooster*, the town in Ohio, or he can change the pronunciation, as when he pronounces *Tottenham* with three distinct syllables, as contrasted with the British ['tɔtnəm]. In making such changes, the American does not show that he is more practical, more utilitarian than the Englishman, but merely that he has accepted the control exerted by an eye-standard in preference to that exerted by a traditional social or ear standard. But the main question at present under consideration is whether this difference has been so extensive as to account for the differences in the general types of cadence exhibited by American and British English. If this question is phrased somewhat differently, the mere phrasing supplies the answer to it. If one asks whether American speech as a whole has been transmitted from individual to individual, from generation to generation, at any given time, prevailingly through oral or prevailingly through literary tradition, the answer is self-evident. The traditions of American speech, like those of British speech, have always been overwhelmingly oral, and not literary traditions. One notices the effects of literary tradition mainly because they are so exceptional. Taking the speech at large, however, it is impossible to suppose that its general character has been determined by a relatively insignificant part of the activity in speech, a part moreover which also covers relatively only a short chronological period.

Allowing all the weight reasonably to be granted to the notion that the democratic habit of social intercourse in America and the democratic and literary system of popular education have had influence in determining the character of American speech so far as its cadences are concerned, one must look further for an explanation more fundamental and far-reaching. An explanation there must be, whether immediate or remote, for general tendencies in methods of articulation do not arise without cause. Ultimate causes of facts of this kind, however, are likely to be extremely remote and of so undeterminate a character that formulating them seems little different from theorizing. One may attempt to account for the difference between two dialectal types of articulation on the ground of climate, occupation, physiological traits, social and political institutions, economic pressures, or a dozen other grounds, but rarely can the connection between the supposed cause and the phenomena themselves be made close enough to become convincing. Especially in speech covering short chronological periods, as is the case in comparing British and American speech, one may more hopefully look to inheritance than to ultimate causes in seeking to account for the traits which present themselves. Inheritance obviously will not explain everything, since what is inherited must ultimately have had a determining cause, must have had an origin; but if one cannot discover ultimate origins, the historian, at least, can content himself with transmissions.

It is one of the illusions resulting from distance that the speech of England should seem to Americans to be uniform for all the country. But such is not now and pretty certainly has never been the case. If one seeks for origins for American traits of speech, one need not limit one's attention to the present type of southern British English, now fashionable in England, or to its antecedents. In this matter of cadences, it is quite obvious to one familiar with various types of British speech, that the cadences of speech in the north of England are on the whole much closer to those of American speech than are the cadences of the speech of the south of England. If one avoids extreme types on either side, it is not difficult to discover educated Englishmen and Americans whose rhythms in speech are so near alike that the differences are easily negligible. But even the extremer aspects of American speech find their parallels and their possible sources in British speech. The term nasal twang is by no means exclusively appropriate to Americans. It is one of the features of the Puritans as they were described by Macaulay in a well-known passage of his essay on Milton, and students of British speech today still find it flourishing, Ripman, *Sounds of Spoken English*, p. 14. Butler's *Hudibras* (1663), Part I, Canto III, ll. 1149–1160, describes the "Puritan" nasal twang as follows:

> "'Synods are whelps o' th' Inquisition,
> A mongrel breed of like pernicion,
>
> .   .   .   .   .   .
>
> Whose business is, by cunning sleight
> To cast a figure for men's light;
> To find in lines of beard and face
> The physiognomy of Grace,
> And by the sound and *twang of nose*
> If all be sound within disclose;
> Free from a crack or flaw of sinning
> As men try pipkins by the ringing."[1]

[1] See also *Cambridge History of English Literature*, VIII, 79.

And Shelley's *Peter Bell the Third*, Part I, Stanza II, reasserts a connection between religiosity and nasality:

> "His eyes turned up, his mouth turned down;
>   His accent caught a nasal twang;
> He oiled his hair; there might be heard
> The grace of God in every word
>   Which Peter said or sang."

The testimony of an observer who by the verdict of the ear found a very close resemblance between the speech of Eastern Massachusetts and a clearly defined region in England is worth noting. Essex County, Massachusetts, was, as Remarkable Pettibone says with pride, in Cooper's *Pioneers*, Chap. XV, "provarbal for pronounsation," and it was the speech of this region that the observer found so similar to the dialect of the old Essex in England (H. T. Armfield, *The Essex Dialect and its influence in the New World*, in *Transactions of the Essex Archæological Society*, Vol. IV, pp. 245–253, New Series. Colchester, 1893). He is convinced that the New England nasal twang came from Essex in England. "The American twang was somehow," he remarks, "a natural growth of the Old Country—of that I felt sure. But where? I had learned to speak several different dialects of North as well as South [of England]; but I never heard this. Till at last I landed in the valley of the Colne and the mystery was solved. In my own parish of Colne Engaine I heard it on all sides of me. One man says to another, 'where are you a-gooin together?' 'I'm gooin to Colne,' was his sing-song reply. I heard it in the way that he says 'wal' for 'well' and 'twalve' for 'twelve'; and I thought that we had probably a trace of the same influence in the word which we satirize as the most characteristic word of the New Englander in the word 'reckon' for 'think,' 'suppose'—which is so common about here." His conclusion is that "the speech of the New Englander is largely indebted to the county of Essex, and specially to the valley of the Colne." As confirmatory evidence, he cites an article by Col. J. L. Chester, *Transactions of the Essex Archæological Society*, Vol. III, p. 37, and Vol. IV, p. 189, in which Chester gives a list of thirty-two New

England towns that bear Essex names, and declares that "in the foundation of New England, Essex exerted more influence than all the rest of England combined." "These views," continues Armfield, "have received recent confirmation in the impressions made upon one of the members of our society, Mr. D. Gurteen, of Haverhill. He told me that the resultant impression left upon his mind by a visit to the namesake town of Haverhill in America, was that the State of Massachusetts was simply peopled from East Anglia, and in the town of Haverhill itself the people had preserved the old pronunciation of the name as it still prevails here. They call it Ha-verhill [i.e., heɪ-] while if you go twenty miles away the pronunciation is Hav-erhill." Lowell's *Biglow Papers* seemed so familiar to this observer that he declared "we might almost say that he has written them in the dialect of Essex"; and he closes his discussion with a list of supposed New Englandisms taken from Lowell which find in a surprising way parallels in the dialect of Essex in England. All this, to be sure, is not scientific proof that the dialect or the cadence of New England or any part of New England was derived directly from Essex in England, nor is it even scientific proof that any dialect of New England is the same as the dialect in Essex. It is as near, however, as popular studies of dialectal relations ever come to scientific proof, and at least suggests the proper method of attack if one were to try to account for the origin of the characteristic features of American speech, especially in this matter of cadence, in which the testimony of a sensitive ear is the best proof to be had.

A good deal of evidence is available to show that formerly the general style of American enunciation was more relaxed, that is, more drawling, especially as shown by the pronunciation of certain consonants, than it is now in approved American English. The somewhat lazy manner of speech of the South and of negro speech is not improbably, however, merely a survival from an earlier more general habit. Thus in Duncan Mackintosh, *Essai Raisonné*, p. 67, we find *t* described as silent in *fact, respect, afflict, distinct, precept, postscript,* but not silent in the preterites of verbs ending in *pt*, as in *kept, crept,* or in *receipt*. As Mackintosh agreed with Dr. Johnson that the best speech was that nearest to the written word and as his own rules often illustrate this belief, there can be no doubt that pronunciations of words like *respect* and *precept* without a final *t* were respectable at the end of the eighteenth century, and that even *kept, crept*, etc., were not infrequently pronounced [kɛp], [krɛp], as they of course still are in popular speech.   Mackintosh, p. 55, also records *d* as silent when followed by another consonant, as in *bands, hands, handmaid, friendship, handsome*, and in *almond, diamond* (*l* also is silent in *almond* and *a* in *diamond*), *riband, Wednesday*, and in *and* before a consonant, as in "Cesar and Pompey."   In one of these words pronunciation and spelling now agree in discarding the *d, riband* now being spelled *ribbon*.   In several the *d* is retained in spelling, though not in pronunciation.   In the main, however, when *d* appears in the spelling, pronunciation of the type which Mackintosh has described would now have an audible *d*.   A pronunciation ['daɪmən] for *diamond* would not now occur in cultivated speech, certainly would not be advocated by any observant critic. On p. 54 of the *Essai, c* is likewise described as silent in *indict, verdict, victuals, perfect, arctic;* and two of these words have persisted with a *c* silent in present English.

The spelling of the early New England town records confirms the statements of Mackintosh, and shows that the lax articulations which he described were merely stray examples of a general style of speech.   For *fifth, sixth, eighth* pronunciations *fift, sixt, eight* are frequently indicated.   For *artist*, the *Groton Records* have *artis, artise*, p. 122 (1702); for *grant*, one finds *gran*, p. 122 (1702), and so often.   In the *Plymouth Records*, for *next* occurs *nex*, I, 199, 224 and often; for *against* occurs *agans*, I, 234; for *request* one finds *reques*, I, 240; for *select* occurs *selleck,* I, 317, and this form of the word is very frequent in other records.   For words like *grand, sufficient, land, vacant, front, account, right, convenient*, one finds the spellings *gran*, I, 275; *suffician*, II, 17, 46, 47; *lan*, II, 29; *vacan*, II, 33; *fron*, II, 34; *accoun*, II, 44; *righ*, II, 45; *convenien*, II, 120.   For the proper name *Gardner* occurs the spelling *Garnner, Garner*, II, 30, which survives as a separate name.   In the *Easthampton Records*,

II, 85 (1679), occurs the phrase *uppon ornarie times*. This form of the word *ordinary* has also persisted, but only in popular use. In the *Dedham Records*, V, 67 (1677), occurs the word *grousels*, for *groundsills*, and again as a verb, V, 79 (1678), *timber to grousel a barne*. This stands close to Milton's *grunsel*, in the line *In his own temple, on the grunsel-edge*, Paradise Lost, I, 460. In the *Huntington Records* for *patent* one finds *patten*, p. 440 (1686), and so often; for *Strickland* occurs *Stricklan, Sticklon*, etc., see p. 37 (1661), p. 54 (1663), etc. The loss of *r* after a consonant indicated by the spelling *Sticklan* is met with in the spellings of other records, as in the *Watertown Records*, where the name *Briscow* is sometimes spelled with *r*, as in *Brysko*, p. 21 (1650), but very frequently without, as in *Bisco, Biscoo, Bysco, Bisko*, etc.; on p. 91 (1667) of these records, *abreast* is spelled *abeast*. A similar pronunciation with *r* omitted after consonants may occasionally be heard in contemporary speech, where it impresses one as being a survival from infantile speech. The *Watertown Records* contain many other examples of lax articulation, as for example, *Arnall*, p. 11 (1647) and often, for *Arnold; Line*, p. 77 (1663), for *Lynde?; Jeames Hollon*, p. 113 (1672), for *James Holland; Garfill*, p. 128 (1676) and often, for *Garfield; Parkis*, p. 136 (1678) and often, for *Parkhurst; Townsin*, p. 118 (1673), for *Townsend; compos*, p. 69 (1660), for *compost; seleckmen*, p. 103 (1670), for *selectmen*. Sometimes the spellings indicate merely a general looseness of articulation not of the definite types illustrated above, as in *Pickram*, p. 79 (1663), for *Pickering*, surviving apparently in the contemporary proper name *Pegram; Pembleton*, p. 1 (1634), for *Pendleton; Mihill*, p. 55 (1657), for *Michael; winesenite*, p. 42 (1651), for *Whitsun-night; carepindur* ['kærpmdər], p. 119 (1674) for *carpenter; debuty*, p. 131 (1677) and often, for *deputy*. With these lax articulations should also be grouped the pronunciation of *carry* in its various forms in ways which are differently represented in spelling, as in *cared* for *carried*, Huntington Records, p. 25 (1660); *carring* in Hanover Records, p. 66 (1786), *caring*, in Suffield Records, p. 309 (1749), for *carrying;* and the grammarians frequently note for correction a pronunciation of *carry* which seems to have been almost monosyllabic. In the *Braintree Records*, p. 5 (1652) and frequently, *with, without* are spelled *uth, uthout*. Occasionally a consonant is added where it does not historically belong, as in *proft*, p. 83 (1664), for *proof; Simont*, p. 22 (1651) and often, for *Simon*. But the general tendency was to omit, not to add final consonants. With the increase of popular education a familiarity with the printed or written aspect of words established them in their conventional forms, and thus pronunciations with consonants omitted where they historically belong, or added where they do not, have tended to be regarded more and more as the marks of an uncultivated "drawling" speech, or of those types of speech, like Southern American English, which have been unusually conservative in the retention of older habits.

Some other general conclusions arising from the detailed study of the sounds of American speech which constitutes the material of this chapter may be briefly summarized at this place. To the question whether the distinguishing features of American pronunciation are in general of indigenous growth or are merely survivals from older usages of the language, the evidence affords a very positive answer. If one did not fear to affirm a universal positive, one might say that in every case the distinctive features of American pronunciation have been but survivals from older usages which were, and in some instances still are, to be found in some dialect or other of the speech of England. Certainly wherever evidence is available, it supports this general conclusion, a conclusion which the scientific student of language would expect on purely theoretical grounds. For though of course change must at times originate in language, in highly developed languages, such as English was in the seventeenth and eighteenth centuries, such changes as present themselves to critical notice are much more likely to be due to the emergence into general or into prominent use of forms which were current in some unobserved dialectical division of the speech than to direct and new origination. It may not be possible always to trace the direct line of transmission from earlier British to American use, for here, as frequently in the study of language, one has to do with circumstantial evidence which justifies only probable conclusions. Yet if one finds numerous correspondences between American and British English, one soon begins to realize that the long arm of coincidence must be unduly stretched to reach them all. So the loss of [r] and the presence of [r] before consonants and finally in different localities are both features of British as of American speech. The pronunciation of *a* before [f], [s], [θ], [ns], etc., has always been as varied in England as in America. The value of *o* as [ɑ] in *hot, got, not*, etc., is not only to be found in present British dialects, but it has undoubtedly been there as long as it has been in American speech. British speech today is no more uniform than American speech—perhaps always has been less so. The student who would explain American speech as derived from British speech has an inexhaustible store of variations to draw upon, and it is only when the probabilities in all directions have been exhausted that one may turn to the theory of independent and original development of speech sounds in America.

A further somewhat definite conclusion is possible, that is, that the so-called Eastern type of American English stands nearer to the southern type of British English, and the Western or General type of American English stands nearer to northern British English. The question whether northern or southern British English is to be preferred as a social custom must be left for Englishmen themselves to decide, though one may point out in passing that the question is open to debate, see Zachrisson, *Northern English or London English as the Standard Pronunciation*, in *Anglia* (1914), XXXVIII, 405–432, where references to other expressions of opinion will be found. But it is interesting to note that the most important of the marks of difference between London and northern British English pointed out by Zachrisson indicate a clear parallel between American and northern British, and more specifically, between Western or General American English and northern British English. Thus the long vowels of words like *rate, rote*, are given as [eː], [oː] in northern British, as contrasted with southern British, which makes the vowels distinctly diphthongal and gives to the first element a lowered character, approximately [ɛ] and [ɔ]. In America the character of [eɪ] and [oɪ] as long vowels is in the main fully preserved, and though they may sometimes become slightly diphthongal under certain circumstances, when final and before voiced consonants, as they do also in northern British, yet they rarely become like the characteristic diphthong of southern British English. Secondly, the consonant r is more distinctly sounded in northern British and Western American than it is in London and Eastern American English. A glide vowel after r is "less marked, or altogether missing in Northern English," and the same is also true of American English. Again, certain words written with o, ou, before r final or r and a consonant are pronounced with the vowel [ɔː] in London English, e.g., *force* [fɔɪs], *pork* [pɔːk], etc., and so they tend to be pronounced in the Eastern type of American English. In northern British, however, as in Western American, many of these words tend to be pronounced with [oː], *course, cord, port, forge, pork, force*, etc., being pronounced [koːrs], [koːrd], [poɪrt], [foːrdʒ], [poɪrk], [foɪrs], etc. With the r lost, this pronunciation appears not infrequently in Southern American English, as in [koɪt] for *court*, [boɪd] for *board*, etc. Fifthly, the characteristic [aɪ] of London and Eastern American English, as in *pass* [paɪs], *path* [paɪθ], *dance* [daɪns], etc., appears more generally as [æ] or [a] in northern British and Western American English. Finally the lengthening of [ɔ] to [ɔː] before [f], [s], followed by consonants, as in *soft, moss*, etc., said to occur in London English, is not found in northern British or in American English, except occasionally in rustic dialects. The remaining differences between northern and London English pointed out by Zachrisson are of slighter significance and not clearly paralleled in American speech.[1]

[1] Perhaps attention should be called to the fact that the term northern British as here used, and as the term is now employed by British phoneticians, does not mean the descendant of the northern dialect of Anglo-Saxon and Middle English, this older northern dialect being more faithfully represented in Lowland Scotch than in the dialect of the north of England. It would seem that in England, the northern dialect occupies relatively somewhat the same position as the Western or General type in America, that the approved southern or public school standard of present English use in England is a special class and local speech which special conditions have raised to

Fascinating but difficult is the question whether American speech in the course of time has at all adapted itself to British speech, that is, whether the parallelisms which exist between the two speeches are due to some extent not to inheritance from a common stock, but to the cultivation of British speech habits upon American soil. The reverse might also be true, that the British have cultivated American speech habits on British soil, thus bringing the two speeches closer together, but this hypothesis is so manifestly improbable that it calls for no discussion. On the other hand, considering the respectful attitude America has always assumed toward European culture, one would not be surprised to find that even the forms of speech in an admired and near relative like English have been assimilated. Yet when one pauses to think, obviously one can with much greater readiness find very characteristic forms of British speech which do not find parallels in American speech than those which do. If the attitude of America towards England was that of admiring imitation, why have not the more striking features of fashionable British English been adopted in America? The answer is that there has been no attitude of admiring imitation in America on the part of a sufficient number of speakers to affect the whole, and that not a single instance in speech can be discovered in which the usage in America was determined by conscious imitation of the usage in England. The most striking apparent exception is the loss of [r] before consonants and finals. This of course is not universal in American speech, nor is it universal in British speech. It does occur, however, in the Eastern and Southern types of American speech in exactly the same way as in the commonly accepted standard southern British speech. Now according to the statement of practically all the earlier grammarians and dictionary makers, this [r] was still heard, and always heard well into the nineteenth century. There is no more positive statement among the grammarians than

a place of eminence, as might have happened, for example, with the speech of New England in America. But beyond the limits of the public school type of speech in England, the prevailing type everywhere seems to be close to the northern type, just as the Western or General type prevails in America everywhere beyond the limits of natural or cultivated eastern Massachusetts speech.

the common assertion that *r* always has the same sound and is never silent. Yet *r* has come to be silent both in the approved British standard based on the speech of southern England, and in two of our local approved American standards based upon Eastern and Southern American speech. Did this happen because Eastern American speech adapted itself to the changing character of British speech? It is impossible to think so. We must believe that when the early grammarians said that *r* was never silent, they were making a statement which was not true, and which many of them who took the pains to examine their statements knew was not true. As early as the year 1791, Walker had described explicitly and fully a state of affairs in the cultivated pronunciation of London with respect to *r* which would be applicable to standard British and Eastern standard American today. What Walker described as an accomplished fact of cultivated speech must have been long present in other, perhaps lower, forms of British speech. Indications of this weakening of *r* begin to appear in critical statements as early as the first quarter of the eighteenth century, see Jespersen, I, 360, though complete recognition of its loss was slow. Even now it is a curious fact that so-called illiterate spellers rarely omit their *r's* in. spelling, even when they regularly omit them in speaking. Obviously, however, there can be no such thing as spelling which is altogether illiterate, and it has always been true that anyone who had sufficient confidence to attempt to write at all, in the main had sufficient knowledge of the consonantal structure of words to enable him to write *r* where it etymologically belonged. The lack of full and explicit recognition of the loss of *r* need not prevent one from supposing that this manner of pronunciation in all probability was present in the speech of certain of those emigrants who in the seventeenth century carried with them the traditions of their old homes to New England and to Virginia. There these traditions continued to develop, and such similarity as one now finds in the pronunciation of *r* between Eastern and Southern American on the one hand, and British English on the other, is most reasonably to be explained as due to common origin. It is, moreover, an accident, a genuine coincidence, that the general social habits of New England, through the early development in that region of a relatively high literary and civil culture, acquired a position of eminence in American life similar to that occupied in English esteem by the social life of the south of England, and that in consequence the approved Eastern type of American speech should in many respects coincide with what is in England the most generally respected and accepted type of standard British speech.

On the other hand, the pronunciation of words like *future, nature, creature*, etc., as it has now become established in both America and England with [tʃ] as the middle consonant, may indicate that this pronunciation finally prevailed in America because it had the support of a British custom generally accepted by the end of the eighteenth century, this support being so strong that the older pronunciation with [t] was compelled to yield even in New England. Yet the most that one can say here is that the speech of New England adapted itself to the general custom, though perhaps not because of British example but because the rest of the country was in this respect less provincial than New England. And again the pronunciation of *a* as [ɑɪ] in *half, dance, path*, etc., though never general outside New England and never universal within New England, probably has been able to maintain itself more or less as a local New England pronunciation because it has the support of an admired type of British speech. In short, it will be found in all instances that questions of direct and determining influence of British upon American speech since the period of migrations must always be stated with many qualifications and limitations.

Another general conclusion of some interest abundantly illustrated by the detailed study of American pronunciation is that very many of the pronunciations which now seem peculiarly Southern are merely survivals of earlier pronunciations which were formerly more general and found in the North as well as the South. Though material for the study of colloquial speech in Virginia and other Southern states in the seventeenth and eighteenth centuries, such as is provided for New England by the local town histories, is unfortunately not abundant, one can safely hazard the guess that the speech of Virginia and the speech of New England at the period of colonization were essentially the same. Why should they not be? The colonists were contemporaries, they came from the same regions of England, in the main from London and Midland and Southern regions, and they represented the same social classes, a sprinkling of gentry in a large body of artisans, farmers and laborers. The differences which now characterize the two speeches probably entered in most instances after the time of colonization and were not imported as established general habits in the first years of the several colonies. The prime cause of differentiation has been that New England speech, especially in Boston and in highly cultivated communities, has yielded to many outside influences, some perhaps exerted from England, some from other regions of America, some from educational ideals, whereas in the South many older pronunlations still linger in respected local practice. Thus the pronunciation of *garden, carpet,* etc., with a glide sound between the initial consonant and the succeeding vowel was once a general fashionable pronunciation. The pronunciation of words like *court, board,* etc., with what is scarcely more than a long *o,* survives from an earlier time when the vowel had not been lowered as it commonly is in present speech before *r.* The value of the diphthong of words like *house, cow, about, south,* as [æʊ], [ɛʊ] is so general as to be almost universal in the South, and so it was also in earlier periods in the North. The pronunciation of *e* before *n* as *i,* that is *men, pen, tennis,* as *min, pin, tinnis,* prevalent in Georgia, Alabama, and other regions of the South, is but a survival of a colonial pronunciation that probably passed current on all levels of society. When one turns from cultivated local Southern speech to the speech of a more rustic and dialectal character, one finds still more numerous instances of survival. Thus *watermillion* for *watermelon* was once proper English in the North as well as South; the negro pronunciation of *head, dead* to rime with *laid,* has earlier historical justifications; even the so-called lazy or relaxed general tone of Southern speech, its slow tempo and its loose articulation of final consonants, often explained as the result of climate, is an inheritance from the general colonial English of the seventeenth century. It is remarkable how many details of a popular dialect in the South may be paralleled by similar details in present or earlier New England speech. The inference to be drawn is not that the parallels are coincidences, but that they are to be explained as having a common origin. Thus in the popular speech of Scott County, Virginia, a secluded region in the mountainous part of southwestern Virginia,[1] one notes, in a brief and partial summary, the following details all of which might have been taken from a description of New England speech in the seventeenth and eighteenth centuries:

(a) Unstressed *a* at the end of a word becomes obscured, as in *Sarah*, written in dialect stories as *Sairy* to indicate this pronunciation.

(b) For orthographic *e* the pronunciation [ɪ] occurs in many words, as in *kettle, get, stead*, pronounced *kittle, git, stid;* also -*es* of plurals, pronounced [ɪz] as in *horses* ['hɔrsɪz], ['hɔːsɪz].

(c) Before *m* and *n* in the same syllable, *e* and *i* are pronounced exactly alike, *empty, general*, etc., being *impty, gineral*. The same applies to [ɛ] written *a* in *many*.

(d) The final unstressed syllable of words like *potato, widow, fellow, tobacco* is pronounced as though written -*er*.

(e) For *au* in some words [æ] occurs, as in *haunt, jaunders*.

(f) For *oi, oy*, the pronunciation [aɪ], occurs, as in *pennyroyal, boil, hoist*, etc.

(g) For *p*, the voiced consonant [b] sometimes appears, as in *Babtis* for *Baptist*.

(h) After a liquid or nasal, *d* is regularly lost, as in [læn] for *land*, [waɪl] for *wild*, etc.

(i) Final unstressed [ŋ] becomes [n], as in *morning, nothing, running*, etc.

(j) In *burst, parcel, curse*, sometimes *horse, r* is not heard.

(k) Final *t* is lost, as *post, toast*, pronounced [poɪs], [toɪs].

[1] See *A Word-List from Virginia*, by L. R. Dingus, *Dialect Notes*, IV, 177–193.

Many similar details could no doubt be found, not only in pronunciation but also in vocabulary and syntax, though they are not needed to support the conclusion that the archaisms and provincialisms of Southern popular speech are in very many instances merely survivals from what were earlier more general habits of speech in America.

(2) [ɑː] as in *father*

This is the sound which has long been commonly described in works on English pronunciation as "Italian a." Unfortunately this description apparently has not always meant precisely the same sound. To the modern ear accustomed primarily to English speech the sound is typically represented in the vowel of *father,* or of *calm, palm,* and similar words. But the range of sounds which must be considered in the discussion of [ɑː] varies through all degrees between the two extremes of [æː] and [ɔː]. Thus in a word like *launch,* at least three distinct types of pronunciation are represented in contemporary cultivated speech, as in [læːntʃ], not a frequent but also not an unknown pronunciation; in [lɑːntʃ], which is fairly common; and in [lɔːntʃ], which is the most general pronunciation. All of these may also have short vowels. So also *haunt* may be heard in popular speech as [hæːnt], as [hɑːnt], and as [hɔːnt]. In a word like *bath,* one hears [bæθ], [bæːθ] and [bɑːθ] as the most general pronunciations, and occasionally as an extreme pronunciation, [bɔːθ]. This last pronunciation is, or at least used to be, one of the marks of the grotesque pronunciation of the haw-haw type of comic Britisher on the stage. It is elaborately described by Richard Grant White, *Words and Their Uses* (1870), pp. 60–62. But a fourth variety of pronunciation is also sometimes employed in cultivated speech, with a vowel intermediate between [æː] and [ɑː], represented by [aː]. We have, then, at the least, four shades of sound to be kept in mind in the consideration of the words in which [ɑː] may occur, the sounds represented by [æː], [aː], [ɑː], and [ɔː].

The groups of words, arranged according to their organic and historical character, in which [ɑː] may occur in Modern English are as follows:

   (1) The sound [ɑː] may occur in words in which it is a distinct and often conscious retention of "Continental a." These words are necessarily few in number in comparison with the main body of the vocabulary and usually of a learned or otherwise specialized kind. Thus *lava* may be ['lɑːvə], though of course it may also be Anglicized to ['lævə]. For *massage, garage,* occur [mə'sɑːʒ], [gə'rɑːʒ]. For the note *fa* in singing the sound is [fɑː]. A refined pronunciation of *tomato* is [tə'mɑːto]. The "Continental a," or "Italian a" is now commonly heard as [ɑː], but formerly the characteristic color of this vowel was taken to be [ɔː]. A discussion of "Continental a" as [ɔː] will be given in a later paragraph.

   (2) For *a,* before *r* final or *r* and a consonant and sometimes for *ea* before *r* and a consonant the value is [ɑː]. In one instance in American speech, the word *sergeant,* e followed by *r* and a consonant has [ɑː]. In England this pronunciation occurs in other words, e.g., *clerk* [klɑːk], *Derby* ['dɑːbɪ], etc. In American popular speech the service berry bush often has the pronunciation [sɑːrvɪs]. What has happened in words of this latter type is that early Middle English *e* followed by *r* or *r* and a consonant tended to become the same as *a* followed by *r* or *r* and a consonant, Middle English *ferr(e)* becoming *far* [fɑːr], *derk* becoming *dark* [dɑːrk], *herte* becoming *heart* [hɑːrt], and so with large numbers of similar words. The orthography was not changed in all cases, however, to agree with the change in pronunciation, hence spellings like *sergeant,* etc. This phonetic change took place at the end of the Middle English period, but it did not affect all words with *e* before *r* in the same way. For besides developing into [ɑː], in some words *e* followed by *r* went through a different series of changes resulting in the modern pronunciation of *herd, pert,* etc., as [hərd], [pərt] or [hʌɪd], [pʌɪt], etc. The same word sometimes illustrates both possibilities, as in

person and *parson, Berkeley, Barclay, clerk, Clarke, further, farther.*

(3) A Modern English [ɑː] appears in a large number of words historically containing the possibility of a variant diphthongal development which gave [ɔː]. These words are of several different origins, but are best grouped together because in them usage has from time to time oscillated between [ɑː] and [ɔː] according as the undiphthongal or the diphthongal development predominated.

(a) Words with a silent *l* before *m, f,* appear with [ɑː] as in *calm, palm, alms,* and *calf, half.* When this *l* was vocalized, it disappeared entirely as a consonant, either assimilating to the preceding vowel which thus became [ɑː] or surviving as a vowel element [u] which united with the preceding vowel to form the diphthong [ɑu]. The first of these possibilities would give Modern English *calm* [kɑːm], *calf* [kɑːf], the second would give [kɔːm], [kɔːf], pronunciations not now current in standard speech, but which are recorded for earlier periods and for dialects other than that of present standard English. In all these words the general English tendency to treat *a* in a closed syllable as [æ] might also appear, giving [kæm], [kæf], etc. A pronunciation of *balm, psalm,* etc., as [bɔːm], [sɔːm] is recorded by some of the early historians and is mentioned by Sheridan, I, 59, as one of the features of Irish pronunciation. Its presence in Ireland merely means that it was an archaic survival there.

(b) For *a* followed by an earlier *h, gh, ht, ght,* Modern English may have [ɑː]. The *h, ht* in these words ordinarily still appears in spelling, but has either disappeared entirely from pronunciation or persists as [f]. An example of this latter development is the word *draught,* from Middle English *drauht,* the word sometimes being now spelled *draft,* though, however spelled, it is pronounced [drɑːft], or following the general tendency of *a* in a closed syllable, as [dræft]. That this combination might develop also as a diphthong [au] into [ɔː] is illustrated by the word *slaughter*, from Middle English *slaghter*. A diphthongal pronunciation of *draught* no longer persists, but it is mentioned as a popular pronunciation by Worcester, *Fourth Book* (1834), p. 419, who corrects *drawts* for *draughts* (drafts). With this may be compared the word *daughter*, which has had historically and dialectally a number of pronunciations, including ['dɔːtər], ['daːtər], ['daːftər], ['dæftər].

(c) Words from French with *a* or *au* before a nasal and consonant, especially before *nt, nce, nch* have either [aɪ] or [ɔː] in English according as the vowel developed as a simple vowel or as a diphthong. Thus we may have *haunt* as [haɪnt] or [hɔɪnt], *chant, chaunt* as [tʃaɪnt] or [tʃɔɪnt], *chance* as [tʃaɪns] or [tʃɔɪns], though the pronunciation [tʃɔɪns] has disappeared from present standard English. In these cases as in others, the vowel in the closed syllable may be [æ], giving [hænt], [tʃænt], [tʃæns]. The variation between *a* and *au* before nasals goes back to a difference in French dialects, the tendency to *au* being characteristic of the Norman dialect, and the tendency to *a* of the Central French dialect.

(4) For *a* before *f, ft, s, st, th* [θ] Modern English may have [aɪ], as in *chaff* [tʃaɪf], *shaft* [ʃaɪft], *grass* [graɪs], *last* [laɪst], *path* [paɪθ]. As there was no diphthongal development in these words, pronunciations with [ɔː] do not occur.

(5) After *w, wh*, the value of *a* is either [aɪ], [a], or this sound further rounded by the influence of the labial to [ɔː], [ɔ], as in *swan* [swaɪn] or [swɔɪn], *what* [ʍat] or [ʍɔt].

(6) Finally and exceptionally, Modern English has [aɪ] in *father*, which differs from all other words in that *a* in this word occurs in an open syllable, followed in the next syllable by a voiced *th* [ð]. The word *rather* is sometimes treated in the same way, but it does not have [aɪ] universally as *father*

does, and other similar words, *gather*, *lather*, *slather*, regularly have [æ].

Some general consideration of the possible historical origins of [ɑː] is necessary to clear the ground for further discussion of the complicated history of this sound. Of course, Old English long *a* [ɑː] is not the source of any words with [ɑː] in Modern English, since Old English long *a* [ɑː] regularly became Middle English *o* [ɔː] and Modern English *o* [oː]. Old English short *a* [ɑ] in the open syllable became Middle English long *a* [ɑː] which in turn became Modern English *a* [eɪ], as in Old English *nama* ['nɑmɑ], Middle English *name* ['nɑːmə], Modern English *name* [neːm]. The Old English sources of Modern English [ɑː] must therefore be sought for in Old English short *a* [ɑ] in closed syllables. Now ordinarily Old and Middle English short *a* [ɑ], in closed syllables has become Modern English [æ], as in *cat*, *bad*, *black*, *nap*, *dab*, and hundreds of words like these. This pronunciation of *a* as [æ] in the closed syllables may be said to have been the common tendency of the language. Exceptionally, however, before certain continuants, especially *f*, *ft*, *s*, *st*, and *th* [θ], all of these being voiceless, *a* in the closed syllable may become [ɑː] instead of [æ], though of course it may also follow the general tendency and become or remain [æ]. The rise of [ɑː] in these words is most probably to be explained on the basis of the lengthening of the vowel before a voiceless continuant. This development in the case of *a* should be compared with such words as *lost*, *frost*, *cough*, *cloth*, etc., where a similar tendency towards lengthening of the vowel preceding the continuant consonant is present. Whether or not *a* [ɑ] as it lengthened in these combinations passed through the stages [æ], [æː], [ɑː] is a debatable and doubtful question. Critical opinion throughout the eighteenth century certainly favored the sound [æː] in all the words in question, and when Sheridan, Walker, and other orthoepists began to write about English pronunciation in the latter eighteenth century, they showed considerable agreement in the opinion that [ɑː] in many words in which they approved [æː] was the mark of what they called an antiquated and vulgar pronunciation.

These opinions may reflect, however, merely the changing currents of sophisticated opinion, and [ɑɪ] or [æ], [æɪ] may have existed side by side in these words from the beginning of the Modern English period. In short, before the voiceless continuants, [ɑ] of Middle English may have become directly [ɑɪ], or it may have gone the way of other [ɑ]'s in closed syllables and have become [æ]. But this [æ] before the voiceless continuants may also have lengthened, giving [æɪ]. One would thus have a tendency towards lengthening before the voiceless continuants which might as readily affect [ɑ] as [æ], but there seems no convincing reason to prove that [ɑ] always passed through the stages [æ], [æɪ].

For [ɑɪ] before r or r and a consonant, the explanation is to be sought in the influence of the r. The same tendency which brought e followed by r, through the lowering stages of [ɛ], [æ], [ɑ] into the same class as original a followed by r would obviously operate to keep a as [ɑ]. It should be remarked, however, that the quantity of the vowel in a word like arm is open to debate. If the r is not pronounced, there can be no question but that the vowel is long and that the word is pronounced [ɑɪm]. If the r is pronounced, however, the vowel certainly would be shorter, and the more consonantal the r, the shorter the vowel. It may be, therefore, that the lengthening of the vowel a before r and r followed by a consonant depends upon the gradual loss of the consonantal quality of r.

Finally the remaining examples of a [ɑɪ] in Modern English are to be explained as lengthenings in which a consonantal or vocalic element has united with the preceding vowel, causing either a long vowel or producing a new diphthongal combination, which resulted in [ɔɪ].

Summarizing, one may say that [ɑɪ] as the sound developed in Modern English, in practically all cases is the result of the lengthening of a short vowel in a closed syllable as the result of certain combinative circumstances, the main exceptions being found in words in which [ɑɪ] is a direct retention of "Continental a." As the common tendency of [ɑ] in closed syllables was to become [æ], it is apparent that an extraordinarily fertile situation was here present

for the rise of divergent practices in usage. In certain of the [ɑː]
words, [æ] and [ɔː] might also appear, in others [æ], [ʌː], [ə] might
appear, and in others, the simplest group of all, the variation was
only between [æ] and [ɑː]. But in no other sound of the English
language has there been present the possibility of such varied historical complication.

The pronunciation of "Continental *a*" as [ɔː] is a special case
affecting a number of words which may be discussed before the
general situation with respect to [ɑː] is presented. English phoneticians in the eighteenth century, when the sound [ɑː] had not yet
become established in general cultivated use, the common sound
being [æ], very frequently equated English [ɔː] with French and
German long *a*. Walker, p. xvi, for example, speaks of the "broad
German *a*, as in *fall, wall, water*," and "as in French *âge, Châlons*."
The author of the *British Grammar*, p. 17, says that "*au* and *aw*
sound broad (a), i.e., as Foreign Nations sound *a;* or that (a) has in
all, call." In Bachmair, *A German Grammar*, Philadelphia, 1788,
p. 1, the name of the first letter of the alphabet in German is given
as *aw*, of *h, k*, as *haw, kaw*. On p. 2, German *kahl, fahl, war* are
given as pronounced like English *call, fall, war*, and German *kan,
hat, narren*, as having the vowel of English *want, watch, warren*.
Bachmair's *Grammar* was an English publication, the first edition
of which appeared in London, about 1750, the Philadelphia edition
being merely an American reprint. In *Eine nuetzliche Anweisung*,
Germanton (sic), (Pa.), 1762, long German *a, aa* is very distinctly
defined as [ɔː], as in *all, call, walk, talk, malt, war, dwarf*, etc., and
short German *a* is defined as [ɔ], as in *on, fox, otter, blossom, body, ox*,
etc. In the phonology of this writer there is no [ɑ] or [ɑː], either in
German or English. Whether or not these statements of the grammarians are correct, whether or not the "Foreign Nations" mentioned
by the author of the *British Grammar* actually sounded their *a* as
[ɔ], [ɔː], is a question that must be left to the special students of
French and German. It is well known of course that certain dialects did so. In Follen's *Practical Grammar of the German Lan-*

guage, Boston, 1837, p. xi, the first edition of which appeared in 1828, the comment is made that "English students of the German language, as well as German students of English, may be surprised to find, that the only sound which Walker, in his *Critical Pronouncing Dictionary*, characterizes as a German sound (I mean the *broad German a*, as he calls it), does not exist in the German language; that the sound is confined to some dialects, and is never heard from the mouth of a well-bred German." The real German *a* Follen describes, p. 5, as "an intermediate sound between *a* in *father*, and *a* in *water*." Fosdick, *Introduction to the French Language*, Andover, 1840, says, p. 14, that the sound of French *a* "is not, as is commonly stated, exactly that of *a* in the English word *father*, but intermediate between that and the sound of *a* in the English word *call*." And he adds, p. 15, that "well-educated Frenchmen could in nearly all cases readily detect the foreign origin of an American or Englishman by his manner of sounding the French letter *a*, even supposing there was no other indication within their notice. The grammars of the French language commonly mislead the learner on this point."

Fashion seems to have been changing in the early nineteenth century, at least in English instruction in French and German, but there can be no doubt that by English ears in the eighteenth century, this foreign sound of *a* in French and German words was felt to be the sound which perhaps stood nearest to it in the English speech of the time, that is, the sound [ɔ], [ɔː]. Thus Sheridan gave the pronunciation in English of the borrowed French word *eclat* as [eˈklɔː], and Walker spelled the word *eˈklaw* to indicate its pronunciation. This pronunciation also appeared in *vase*, and in this word has persisted almost to the present day as one of the several pronunciations permissible. Nares, *General Rules* (1792), p. 8, characterizes [vɔːz] as a frequent but affected pronunciation. Formerly the pronunciation [gɔːz] for *gas* occurred, as is shown by Barlow's rime *laws: gaz*, in the *Columbiad*, p. 156. Walker pronounced *la*, "behold," as [lɔː], a pronunciation still surviving in popular speech, though in cultivated or literary usage the word has been replaced by *lo*. But the pronunciation [lɔː] was still recorded approvingly as late as

Cummings (1822), p. 141. It is interesting to note that Cummings, p. 157, gives *baa* and *bay* as likely to be confused in sound. This confusion could possibly have occurred if *baa* were pronounced [bæː], but not if it were pronounced either [baː] or [bɔː]. Sheridan gave this word *baa* as having the vowel of *hate*, but Walker gave it as having the vowel of *father*.

For the words *papa*, *mama* an abbreviated form *pa*, *ma*, is general in popular American English, pronounced [pæː], [mæː], or [paː], [maː], or most commonly [pɔː], [mɔː], this last pronunciation being merely a survival of the eighteenth-century equivalent for [aː]. For the unabbreviated form of the word, a pronunciation with [ɔː] is recorded by De Vere, *Americanisms*, p. 152, who says that the name for a negro nurse, or mammy, in South Carolina and some of the Gulf States is "sounded and written *Maumer*." With the stress on the first syllable, *mamma* would readily assume the several forms ['mæmɪ], ['maːmɪ], ['maːmə], ['mɔːmə]. Longstreet, *Georgia Scenes*, p. 110, note, says that " 'aunt' and 'mauma,' or 'maum' its abbreviation, are terms of respect, commonly used by children to aged negroes. The first generally prevails in the up country, and the second on the seaboard."

The distinctively American word *boss*, an adaptation from Dutch *baas*, also has in it the sound [ɔ], [ɔː] because of the eighteenth-century fashion of equating foreign *a* with English [ɔ], [ɔː]. The word is recorded as early as the first quarter of the nineteenth century and undoubtedly was already in general use in the eighteenth.

Another characteristic American word from Dutch, which like *boss* has been taken over to a considerable extent into British English, is *Santa Claus*. This is derived, according to the *New English Dictionary*, from a Dutch dialect form *Sante Klaas*, for standard Dutch *Sint Klaas*, both being forms of the name St. Nicholas. The phonetic form of *Claus* is of course [klɔːz], with the customary English [ɔː] for Continental *a*.

In New York and vicinity, a word for Easter of Dutch origin is still in current but disappearing use. It is commonly spelled *Paas*, and appears in this form on the packages of Easter egg dyes offered annually for sale. De Vere, *Americanisms* (1872), p. 86, says that

Paas (Paasch) is "still used in many families in New York, Easter eggs being called Paas-eggs." The word is now most commonly pronounced with a voiceless consonant, [pɔs] or [pɔɪs], and perhaps always has had a final [s]. It is used by Cooper, *The Water-witch*, Chap. I, in the phrase "Paus merry-making," and the spelling here indicates a pronunciation [pɔs], or [pɔɪs]. In Irving's *History of New York by Diedrich Knickerbocker*, Book VII, Chapter II, Peter Stuyvesant is described as a great promoter of merry-makings, and "under his reign there was a great cracking of eggs at Paas or Easter; Whitsuntide or Pinxter also flourished in all its bloom; and never were stockings better filled on the eve of blessed St. Nicholas." The word *possblummies* (Dutch Paas-bloeme) is recorded by Quick, *Vandemark's Folly*, p. 111, for Rondout Valley in New York.

The word *cole-slaw* is another borrowing which has become almost universal in American popular usage. It stands close to Dutch *kool sla*. The earliest citation in Thornton, *American Glossary*, I, 190, is for 1794. The word *slaw* [slɔɪ] is now also used as an independent word for salad.

The common American pronunciation of the name of the festival elaborately celebrated at New Orleans, the Mardi Gras, is ['mɑɪrdɪ grɔɪ], though the dictionaries record only [grɑɪ]. The word has been extended to apply to town celebrations held at other places than at New Orleans.

In Alexander's *Columbian Dictionary* (1800), the words *belleamie*, *belleamour* are given as pronounced ['bɛlɔɪmi] and [bɛlɔɪ'muɪr], with [ɔɪ] for French *a*.

For Spanish *papayo*, *papaya*, the word *papaw*, *pawpaw*, has come into general American use. The common popular form gives the word two stresses, ['pɔɪ'pɔɪ], the vowel almost always being [ɔɪ]. The spelling *aw* in this word, as in a number of others, has resulted from the endeavor to bring the spelling into harmony with the pronunciation.

For *jalap*, from Spanish *jalapa*, probably through a French form, the name of a Mexican climbing plant from the roots of which a drug is prepared, Nares, *General Rules*, p. 9, gives a pronunciation with [ɔɪ] in both syllables. Sheridan prescribed [ɔɪ] or [ɔ] in the first syllable, the quantity not being indicated, and Walker preferred [æ], remarking that "the pronunciation of this word, as if written *jollop* which Mr. Sheridan has adopted, is, in my opinion, now confined to the illiterate and vulgar." Later authorities pretty generally prefer [æ] for the vowel of the stressed syllable.

For *aa*, frequent in Biblical names, the usual pronunciation is now [eɪ], and this pronunciation was specifically prescribed by many of the earlier grammarians and lexicographers. The pronunciation [ɔɪ], however, also occurred, as in the *Anarchiad*, p. 100:

> "Till their own saints before 'em fall,
> As once the Jews bow'd down to Baal."

For *canal*, when the word was new, a pronunciation with [ɔɪ] was current, as shown by the rime in Halleck, *Poems*, p. 312, of *balls* with *canals*. The old pronunciation survives in the facetious phrase "the raging canawl." Quick, *Vandemark's Folly*, p. 30, gives some lines of a song on the Erie Canal about 1850:

> "Come, sailors, landsmen, one and all,
> And I'll sing you the dangers of the raging canawl."

For *vase* the two most general pronunciations now are those which make the word rime with *face* or *phase*. A third and more limited pronunciation gives the vowel the value of [ɑɪ], as in [vɑɪz]. Still another pronunciation was formerly used in which the vowel was [ɔɪ], as in [vɔɪz]. In James Jeffrey Roche's poem *The V-A-S-E*, these four pronunciations are described in an ascending scale of elegance. A speaker from the West rimes *vase* with *place*, one from New York rimes it with *praise*, one from Philadelphia with *grandpapas*, and the pinnacle of culture is reached when the speaker from Boston rimes *because* and *vaws*. *Dies erit praegelida, Sinistra quum Bostonia*, remarks the poet, the American Latin of which would be in American English, "It will be a cold day when Boston gets left." So far as *vase* is concerned, however, Boston and [vɔɪz] have long since been left behind.

In New England, and specially in Boston, a restaurant is called a *spa*, pronounced [spɔɪ].

A word in local use in Pennsylvania and surrounding regions, and undoubtedly of German origin, is familiar to the ears of many Americans, but has no accepted spelling. Phonetically it is ['pɔɪn 'hɔɪs], and it may be written *pawn-hoss*. It means scrapple, a kind of meat pudding, and it is derived from German *pfanne-hase*, see *Dialect Notes*, I, 422, with the same vowel for German [aː] as in other similar words of foreign origin. The phonetic form of the word in Pennsylvania German seems to have varied. De Vere, *Americanisms*, p. 144, gives it as *pawnhost*. Mr. M. B. Lambeth of Allentown, Pennsylvania, says that the vowel of the first syllable is now short, the word being pronounced [pænhɔɪs]. The analogy of the English word *pan* would obviously suggest itself, and the name is sometimes jocosely anglicized into *panrabbit*. Was it originally a facetious compound, like Welsh rabbit for a dish made with cheese, or Marblehead turkey for cod?

The exclamation *hurrah* is not of altogether certain origin etymologically, nor does it have a single phonetic form in present use. The most common pronunciation is [hu'rɔː] with a heavy stress on the second syllable and a lighter stress on the first syllable. When the first syllable is cut off, as in college yells, the word becomes simply [rɔː]. But the pronunciations [hu'raɪ], [raɪ] are sometimes heard, especially in the pronunciation of women, and still less commonly, and often facetiously or jocosely, the pronunciation [hu'reɪ], sometimes written *hooray*. It is not improbable that this word came into wide English use through the influence of German. It was "the battle cry of the Prussian soldiers in the War of Liberation (1812–13), and has since been a favorite cry of soldiers and sailors, and of exultation," see *New English Dictionary*, under *hurrah*. Though forms similar to *hurrah* are recorded as early as the beginning of the eighteenth century, the word as it is now known appears not to have been widely used until the beginning of the nineteenth century. The date of its first dictionary record is 1818, but since then, especially in America, the word has passed into universal popular use. It has been suggested that *hurrah* is merely a variant of *huzza*, a word which it has now displaced. The final vowel of *huzza* had all the values of the vowel of *hurrah*, that is [ɑː], [ɔː], and [eɪ], and it had also a parallel in German *hussa*. Some connection between English *hurrah*, *huzza* and the German words *hurra*, *hussa*, can scarcely be doubted, though the precise line of it cannot be traced. In time *huzza* came to be substituted sometimes for *hurrah* as a literary equivalent of the latter, though even when written *huzza* it was usually pronounced *hurrah*.

In his first spelling book, 1783, p. 35, Webster gives the word *huzza*, but appends a footnote, stating that the form of the word should not be *whorra*. Later he reversed his position, for in the Dictionary of 1828, he gives the word *hoora*, *hooraw*, with other spellings *hurraw*, *hurrah*, and remarks that "this is the genuine English word, for which we find in books most absurdly written *huzza*, a foreign word never or rarely used." Webster cites a Swedish *hurra*, which he says "appears to be the English word." Since Webster knew the word *hurrah* as early as 1783, it is quite possible that it came to America with the German mercenary soldiers of the Revolution. Webster's statement that the word should not be *whorra*, that is, *hurrah*, seems to be but a bit of pedantry which proves that it was something like that.

"My soul becomes indignant," says Carlton, *The New Purchase*, p. 42, "when I find printed, instead of that spirit-stirring, frank-hearted '*Hurraw!*' that pitiful, sneaking, soulless, civilized, '*Huzza.*' Dare any man say *that* sounds like the thing? No more than it looks like it. Freemen let nice, pretty, mincing, lady-like dandies huzza! by note—do you ever cry out Hurraw! ex-tempore."

The name *America* is of course mainly stressed on the second syllable. This stressing, however, leaves it possible to put a secondary, therefore relatively heavy stress on the last syllable, a possibility which is often utilized when the word is employed in verse. Nowadays the final vowel of *America* if stressed would be [ɑː] as in [ə'mɛrɪ'kɑː], but formerly usage was unsettled. Waller, *On a Wcr with Spain*, ll. 31–32, has the following rime:

> "Meanwhile the Spaniards in America,
> Near to the line the sun approaching saw."

Walker, p. 9, says that "the sound *a*, when terminating a syllable not under the accent, seems more inclined to the Irish than the English *a*, and that the ear is less disgusted with the sound *Ah-mer-i-cah* than of *A-mer-i-cay*." The Irish sound to which Walker refers seems to be [ɔː] or at least a sound nearer to [ɔː] than to [ɑː]. He finds the same sound in Scotch, and represents it by the spellings *Sawtan, sawcred*, for *Satan, sacred*. He points out, indeed, that *a* final and unaccented "has an obscure sound, bordering on *u*," that is [ə], but of course his concern here is with an *a* that bears some stress, and this *a* in *America* he regards as preferably [ɔː], not [eː], though apparently best of all [ɑː]. In *Eine nuetzliche Anweisung*, p. 4, it is put down as a general rule that final *a* in an English word of foreign origin is pronounced [eː], and as an example *huzza* [hʌˈzeː] is given. In the *Huntington Records*, the various spellings of *America* employed indicate that great difficulty was felt in determining the proper way of recording this word. Besides *America*, it is spelled *Americae*, p. 462 (1686), *Americai*, p. 449 (1686) and so often; *Americaie*, p. 486 (1687); and *Amaracah*, p. 434 (1685?). The pronunciation which these spellings were intended to represent was most probably *Americay*, the one Walker reprehends. This pronunciation is often indicated also by the rimes of the ballads and songs of the American Revolution, and the spelling of the Huntington Records show that it was then of long standing. Samuel Low's *Ode on the Arrival of Washington in New York*, *Poems* (1800), p. 104, begins as follows:

> "Hail, bright, auspicious day!
> Long shall America
> Thy praise resound."

Many Indian place names in America with *a* pronounced [ɔː] retain the eighteenth-century value of *a* as [ɔː], perhaps through the influence of the early French pronunciation of Indian names, or perhaps through a desire to give to these names a sound which was felt to be appropriate to a foreign word. Thus we have *Omaha* [ˈoːməˈhɔː], *Chicago* [ʃɪˈkɔːgo], though also often [ʃɪˈkɑːgo], *Arkansas* or *Arkansaw* [ˈarkənˈsɔː], *Altamaha* [ˈæltəməˈhɔː], *Utah* [ˈjuːˈtɔː],

Ouachita [ˈwɑʃɪˈtɔɪ], [ˈwɔʃɪˈtɔɪ].   This last word, the name of a town
and river in Arkansas, contains three survivals of French spelling,
ou for *w* [w], *ch* for sh [ʃ], and *a* for [ɔɪ].   In some of these proper
names there seems to be at present a strong tendency to substitute
[ɑɪ] for [ɔɪ] wherever possible.   Thus *Omaha* is often pronounced
[oˈːməˈhɑɪ] and *Utah* is pronounced [ˈjuːˈtɑɪ].

Some family names also contain survivals of an eighteenth-century pronunciation of continental *a* as [ɔ].   Thus French *Des Champs*
has given *Scomp*, *Banta* has given *Bonta*, *Bonty*, see Dunlap, pp.
7–8.   Kuhns, *German and Swiss Settlements of Colonial Pennsylvania*, p. 242, puts it down as a general rule that German names of
the eighteenth century with *a*, as they become anglicized, changed
a to *au*, *o* [ɔɪ], as in *Groff* from *Graf*, *Ault* from *Alt*, *Aughey* from
Ache, *Rawn* from *Rahn*.   Many similar names will be found by going
through the long lists contained in *Names of Foreigners who took
the Oath of Allegiance to the Province and State of Pennsylvania*, 1727–
1775, ed. Egle, Harrisburg, 1892.

When we go back to the descriptions of American pronunciation
in the eighteenth century, we find that many of them do not recognize the existence of a sound [ɑɪ] at all in standard English, and that
those who record it limit its occurrence very narrowly.   Thus
Franklin has symbols only for the sounds [ɔ], short and long, as in
John, *folly*, *awl*, *ball*, and [æ], which with him seems always to be
short, as in *man*, *can*.   His record for the word *far* is [fær], p. 301,
for *hardly* is [ˈhærdlɪ], p. 302.   The vowel of *are* he records as having
the same quality as the vowel of *get*, that is [ɛ], a sound so close to
[æ] that it is doubtful if Franklin really discriminated clearly between the two, p. 301.   For *passed* his record is [pæst], p. 300, for
blast he has [blæst], for *calm* he has [kælm] with the *l* sounded, for
lasting, he has [ˈlæstɪŋ], p. 301, and for *hereafter*, he has [hirˈæftər],
p. 303.   He records the vowel in *what*, *whatever*, as [æ], p. 303, where
it varies in present English between [ɑ] and [ɔ].   The unescapable
conclusion is that Franklin had no vowel [ɑɪ], [ɑ], at least in his
theoretically approved pronunciation, and even the vowel of *father*

he must have pronounced as [æ]. Words like *not, on, of, along, perform, storm,* Franklin always records with [ɔ], and for the first element of the present English diphthong [aɪ] or [ɑɪ] as in *ride,* he uses a sound which may have been either [ə] or [ʌ] but certainly was not [a], [ɑ] or [æ]. For the first element of the present diphthong [aʊ] as in *house* he uses the sound [ɔ].

With Franklin's practice may be compared the description of Mackintosh (1797). In his key of vowels, Mackintosh recognized four values of *a*, and so in his discussion throughout. The first of these is [æ], long and short, the second is [e] with its "grave" variant [ɛ], the third is [ɔ], and the fourth is [ə] Mackintosh's examples in his key are for (1) *arc, fat, arm;* for (2), *date, hate, care, any;* for (3) *hall, haul, bald;* for (4) *above, liar.* All these are quite clear except perhaps the examples for (1), long and short. Mackintosh says that he uses accented as equivalent to long and unaccented as equivalent to short. The question is whether his long, or accented, *a* was the same in quality as his short or unaccented. Now his short vowel is certainly [æ], and there is nothing to show that his long vowel differed in quality from this sound. Mackintosh has no discussion of any [aɪ] or [ɑ] sound, and apparently recognized nothing between [æ] and [ɔ]. He marks the following words, p. 21, as having the same vowel except for difference in length or accent: "*arc, art* (verb)*, art, bag, bar, cat, car, dab, dart, fat, far, hat, hard, jam, jar, lacerate, land, macerate, mandate, pacify, part, patch, quaff, quart, ram, ramble, sang, sanguine, start, sand.*" These words are grouped more or less in pairs, *start* supposedly having a short vowel, and *sand* a long one; so the vowel of *ram* is short but that of *ramble* is long. Mackintosh's distinctions of length, or accent, in vowels are hard to follow, but it seems quite clear that they did not imply in his mind any differences of quality. This same sound [æ] appears also, he says, p. 21, in *badge, dance, trance, large, parse, farce,* but not in *scarce,* which has [eɪ]. On p. 23 he gives another list of words having this same sound, among which are *Athens, eradicate, family, famine, father, gradual, gratis, gratify, imagine, la, Latin, lavish, magic, navigate, Patrick, papa, quadrant, rather.* In all of these there

can be little doubt that Mackintosh pronounced [æ]. On p. 45 he
gives *darn, hearken, heart, hearth*, as all having [æ]. On p. 25 he
records *aunt, vaunt*, etc., as having [ɔ] and on the same page *balm,
qualm, salt* as having [ɔː]. He apparently therefore felt no need
for a symbol representing a sound [ɑ], [ɑː].

The presence of [æ] or [æː] in cultivated American speech of the
eighteenth century in words where later use had always [ɑː] is indicated clearly by the rimes of the poets. These rimes do not give a
complete picture of pronunciation, but as far as their evidence goes,
it supports the inferences one would draw from Franklin's transcriptions. Thus one finds rimes like *arms: terms, Anarchiad*, p. 43,
which would mean [ærmz]: [tɛrmz] or [tærmz]; *heart to: virtue, Anarchiad*, p. 67; *guard: prepar'd*, Humphreys, p. 62, 135, 183; *research:
arch*, p. 38; *harness'd: earnest*, p. 229. In Timothy Dwight's verse
we find *glare: star, Conquest of Canaan*, p. 32; *air: afar*, p. 142, 293;
spears: cars, p. 289, *desert: heart*, p. 57; *part: desert*, p. 196; *wand:
hand, Greenfield Hill*, p. 71; *despair: bar*, p. 35; *car: air*, p. 71; *glass:
space*, p. 44; *waist: passed*, p. 44. These last two rimes in any case
seem to be inexact, but [glæs], [pæst], form at least more reasonable
rimes for *space* and *waist* than [glɑːs], [pɑːst]. In general the rimes
furnish little evidence for the pronunciation of *a* except when *a*
stands before *r*, or *r* and a consonant. But if one finds *a* pronounced
[æ] in these positions, one may pretty safely infer that it was also
pronounced [æ] in the other positions in which it later appears as
[ɑː]. The following further rimes may be noted in Barlow: *air:
star, Columbiad* (p. 304); *there: star*, p. 333; *search: march*, p. 339,
344. In Trumbull the following are illustrative of the same point:
alarming: chairman, I, 104, cf. *vermin: chairman*, I, 67; *guard: prepar'd*, I, 112; *hair: tar*, I, 165; *air: care*, II, 115, *air: there*, II, 124,
cares: stars, II, 174; *person: farce on*, I, 18; *alarming: sermon*, I, 33;
observe: starve, I, 37; *infernal: Arnold*, I, 153; *researches: marches*, I,
155; *verse: farce*, II, 13; *desert: heart*, II, 53. In Ladd occur *bear:
tar*, p. 37; *are: fair*, p. 116; *bard: heard*, p. 118, 151, 160. The following rimes from Hitchcock are indicative of the same pronunciation: *theirs: stars*, p. 25; *heart: desert*, p. 54; *far: air*, p. 88; *shar'd:*

debar'd, p. 91; *averse: farce*, p. 140; *art: assert*, p. 162; *rehearse: farce*, p. 72.

The naïve spellings of the early town records also often indicate a pronunciation [æ], [ɛ] for *a* followed by *r* and a consonant, as in *Gearffields* for *Garfields*, *Watertown Records*, p. 16 (1648), *Bairsto* for *Barstow*, ibid., p. 17 (1648), *fearm* for *farm*, *Dedham Records*, III, 21 (1636), *fairm* for *farm*, *Lunenburg Records*, p. 107 (1740); and the interchange of *e* and *a* in such spellings as *persels* for *parcels*, *Plymouth Records*, I, 197 and often; *parsonably* for *personably*, i.e., *in person*, ibid., I, 333; *marchantable* for *merchantable*, ibid., I, 58; *afarmative*, *afermitive for affirmative*, *Dedham Records*, IV, 34 (1660). Numerous spellings like the above may be found throughout the town records of the seventeenth century, though they became less frequent as the records take on the conventional spellings of standard speech. As late as 1834, however, Worcester, *Fourth Book*, p. 298, says that many people pronounce *farmer, hardly, carding, largely* as ['færmər], ['hærdlɪ], ['kærdɪŋ], ['lærdʒlɪ].

For this omission of the sound of [ɑː] in the early records of American pronunciation, one could have found abundant authority in the statements of British students of pronunciation who wrote at the time. It will be remembered that Franklin was himself living in London when in 1768 he wrote his scheme for a phonetic alphabet and reformed spelling, and doubtless he looked upon his scheme as faithful both to British and American pronunciation. Mackintosh was of Scotch ancestry, and though he gives abundant evidence that he was a careful observer of speech at first hand, we can be sure that he would not have presented for approval a description of American speech that separated it widely from what he regarded as good British use.

In his treatment, or lack of treatment, of [ɑː], Franklin's scheme corresponds closely to the statements of Sheridan, the first edition of whose *General Dictionary* was published twelve years later, in 1780, so soon after Franklin wrote out his scheme that, so far as pronunciation goes, Franklin and Sheridan may be regarded as conemporary. Sheridan had begun to publish books in English as early as 1762. Sheridan allows for only three qualities of *a*, as exemplified in *hat*, *hate*, and *hall*. It is true that Sheridan distinguishes between a long and short quality of the vowel in *hat*, but there is no indication that his long sound differs otherwise than in length from the short sound. Thus he records the three vowels in *pap*, *papa*, as exactly the same in quality and there can be no question that Sheridan pronounced *papa* as [pæ'pæ], with the second vowel probably long. "When *a* precedes *r*," says Sheridan, p. 22, "the accent is on the vowel, which is thus made long, though it retains the same sound," as in *car*, *bar*, *far*, evidently pronounced [kæːr], [bæːr], [fæːr]. When *a* is followed by *r* and preceded by *w*, Sheridan gives it the sound [ɔː], as in *war*, *ward*, *warm*, etc. When preceded by *w* and followed by a consonant other than *r*, it has the sound [ɔ], as in *wash*, *watch*, except the two words *waft*, *wasp*, which are given as [wæft], [wæsp] The combination *au* is usually given the value of [ɔː], but *aunt* is recorded as [ænt], the same as *ant*. Though one must hesitate at times to accept such statements as these of Sheridan in their literal sense, in this instance there seems no escape from the conclusion which Sheridan's words so explicitly warrant, that the sound [ɑ], [ɑː], found no place in the pronunciation of standard English *as Sheridan viewed it*. Anyone who is inclined to be sceptical of the statement that words which now have [ɑ], [ɑː], formerly had [æ], [æː], may perhaps have his scepticism in some measure reduced by reflecting that even now many speakers say [æ], where others say [ɑː], not only in words like *path*, *laugh*, *dance*, *glance*, etc., but even in *father*, which is still dialectally current as ['fæɪðər] in rustic pronunciation; or *papa*, *mamma*, which are still common in the cultivated speech of Philadelphia, Baltimore and other parts of the South as [pə'pæː], [mə'mæː]; or in *palm*, *calm*, *psalm*, which can still be heard occasionally in cultivated old-fashioned speech as [pæɪm], [kæɪm], [sæɪm].

In the one word *scarce* the older pronunciation of *a* as [æ] before *r* and a consonant apparently survives in a slightly modified form. In the words of similar form *sparse*, *farce*, only [ɑː] occurs. The word *scarce* is sometimes explained as derived from a form in Middle English which had already in that period a long vowel [ɑː], this vowel regularly developing into later [eː], giving as the early Modern English form of this word [skeːrs], the vowel [eː] later lowering before [r] into [ɛː]. There seems to be no more reason, however, for assuming an original long vowel in Middle English for *scarce* than for *sparse*, *farce*.

When one examines other evidence, however, it is obvious that Sheridan, so far as actual practice is concerned, gave only a partial view of the situation in his own day. His description is too simple and regular to be altogether a faithful account of living speech. He undoubtedly describes what he considered to be the best English speech, though there can be no question that other widely used pronunciations were current side by side with Sheridan's theoretically best pronunciations. In William Perry's *Royal Standard English Dictionary*, the first edition of which was published in 1775, Sheridan is taken to task for omitting certain vowel sounds, "and particularly the sound of *à*, as heard in the words *part, dart*, etc.," Preface, p. 5. This sound of *à* in Perry which can have been only [ɑː], he records not only for *a* before *r*, but also for *a* before *f, s, st, nce*, etc. as in *chaff, grass, mast, dance*, and for *au* in *daunt, haunch, haunt*, etc. Perry says on the title page to his *Royal Standard English Dictionary* that the pronunciations he has given are "according to the present practice of men of letters, eminent orators, and polite speakers in London." His *Only Sure Guide* preceded his *Dictionary*, and the same principles of pronunciation were advocated in that work. All of Perry's work was well known to Webster and other early American dictionary and spelling-book makers, and undoubtedly it exercised considerable influence on their own expressions of opinion. How far back this sound recorded by Perry should be carried, it is uncertain; but the spelling *arst* for *asked*, in *Groton Records*, p. 130 (1706), seems to be pretty certain evidence of its existence in dialect speech in Massachusetts as early as the beginning of the eighteenth century. Still earlier is the spelling *pausters* for *pastures*, in the *Hempstead Records*, I, 93 (1660). With this spelling should be compared the pronunciation recorded by R. M. Johnston, *Mr. Absalom Billingslea*

(1888), p. 21, for central Georgia. The word is spelled *parscher* and as [ɑɪ] is unknown ordinarily in this dialect for *a* before [f], [s], [θ], etc., it is extremely likely that we have in *parscher* a stray survival from an older use generally lost in the Georgia dialect. The spelling *parscher* would be similar to such spellings as *darter* for *daughter*, *arfter* for *after*, *marster* for *master*, etc., which are occasionally met with in literary transcriptions of popular dialects, and which leave one in some doubt so far as the presence of the *r* is concerned, as to their meaning. But if one does not quite know whether or not to take the *r* in these spellings at its face value, one can at least be sure that the quality of the vowel must be taken as [ɑɪ], not as [æ], or [ɔɪ]. The spelling of *pastures* as *pausters* might possibly be taken as meaning [pɔɪstərz], but this is not probable. It should be observed that if a writer wished to indicate a sound [ɑɪ] as distinguished from the more common [æɪ], [æ], the natural spelling to use would be *au*, since for the sound [ɔɪ] the spelling *o* would be available. It is not improbable therefore that other seventeenth-century spellings with *au* indicate [ɑɪ], as in *cauelfes* for *calf's*, *Southold Records*, I, 15 (1652), *caulves* for *calves*, I, 248 (1661), *Auter* for *Arthur*, I, 276 (1678), *drauft* for *draft, draught*, II, 481 (1719); in the *Hempstead Records*, besides *pausters* noted above, occur *caulfes*, I, 93 (1660), *haulf* for *half*, I, 102 (1661). On the other hand the presence at the same time of the [æ] pronunciation in this Long Island community is evident from such spellings as *feather* for *father*, *Hempstead Records*, I, 171 (1665), also *ffeather*, I, 202 (1665), *peath* for *path*, I, 198 (1679), *eare* for *are*, I, 164 (1665), *piert* for *part*, I, 34 (1660). The quality of this sound is indicated by the spelling *pearsens* for *persons*, I, 204 (1665).

The presence of forms like *marse* [mɑɪs], *marster* [mɑɪstə] in old-fashioned Southern negro speech justifies certain chronological inferences. Since *a* is not ordinarily [ɑɪ] before *s* or *s* and a consonant in Southern speech, a word like *marse, marster* seems best explained as an archaic survival in negro speech of a pronunciation of this word which was formerly general and probably as early as the seventeenth or early eighteenth century. In conjunction with forms like *pausters*, *parscher*, it suggests the inference that *a* became [ɑɪ] before [s] earlier than before the other continuants.

In the year preceding that in which Franklin's scheme was promulgated, Granville Sharp, well known to students of history as a friend to those principles of liberty for which the colonists in America were soon to make their final defense, published a *Short Treatise on the English Tongue: being an attempt to render the Reading and Pronunciation of the same more easy to Foreigners*. This first edition of Sharp's work in 1767 appeared again in 1786 under the title *An English Alphabet for the Use of Foreigners*. There were various other editions of the work, the one used for the present purpose being designated as the sixth, printed at London in 1812. Sharp also published an elementary work, called *The Child's First Book*, which is useful as confirming the statements of his other work. Though a native of the north of England, where his youth was spent, Sharp went early in life to London, and consequently was familiar with several types of English speech when he wrote his *Short Treatise*. His value as an observer is also increased by the fact that he was not endeavoring to establish a standard but was merely trying to describe English pronunciation for the benefit of foreigners. Besides [eɪ] as in *danger, manger*, Sharp distinguishes three values for *a*, two being long and one short. The short sound is [æ], as in *add, bad, lad, mad*, etc., *English Alphabet*, p. 14, and to these illustrations others may be added from *The Child's First Book*, pp. 5, 10, showing that *a* remained [æ] even after *w* or before *r*, e.g., *bar, far, war, mar, wan, wad*. Of the two long sounds of *a*, one was the sound [ɔɪ] for *a* before *ld, lt*, and *ll* (except *shall, mall*). The same sound appears for *a* in the open syllable after *w* in *water*, *English Alphabet*, p. 12. These two sounds, [æ] and [ɔɪ], may be characterized as the common sounds of *a*, in Sharp's usage, when it was not [eɪ]. The remaining sound is described by Sharp as "a medium sound between *aw* [ɔɪ] and the English *a* [eɪ]," *English Alphabet*, p. 12. The sound is most probably [ɑɪ], and it is illustrated by the *a* in *father*, and the last syllable of *papa, mamma*. This sound occurs by rule, according to Sharp, for *a* before *lf, lm, lve*, "and before *nd* in words derived from the Latin word *mando*," *English Alphabet*, p. 15.   Here it is "sounded like the Italian *a*, only somewhat shorter, as in *half, calm, salve, command, demand*, etc."   It is also recorded by Sharp, p. 15, for *a* "in *han't* (for *have not*), *master*, and *plaster*"; but not for *grass, past, last*, etc.   The common sounds of *a* are therefore, according to Sharp, [eɪ], [æ] and [ɔɪ], and though he recognizes a value [ɑɪ], he limits this sound, in its occurrence in English words, very narrowly. With others the following words, *wash, bath, wrath* (also a form *wroth* is given), *gasp, hasp, wasp, cast, mast, ask, bask, task, dance, chance, prance, ant, barb, bard, hard, ward, barge, marl, farm, harm, warm, barn, carp, harp, warp, art, cart, dart, hart, mart, part, quart, tart, wart*, are all listed, *Child's First Book*, pp. 13–17, as having [æ].   Though *a* is "pronounced rather broad like the foreign *a*" in words derived from Latin *mando*, in other words before *nd* it is pronounced [æ] according to rule, as in *and, band, wand, Child's First Book*, p. 18.   In *hearken, heart, hearth*, the sound of *ea* is also given as [æ], *English Alphabet*, p. 28.   At the end of his *English Alphabet*, Sharp has given some twenty pages of English texts with pronunciations indicated, and these are important as providing abundant illustrations and confirmation of the principles laid down in his general rules.

The *British Grammar*, by one who seems to have been a competent observer and a man of independent mind, was first published at London, 1762.   An American reprint appeared at Boston in 1784, the latter being the edition to which reference has been made. The writer of the grammer declares that the letter *a* has three sounds, "the long slender sound, as in *came*, by which the writer means [eɪ], "the short sound of *a*," as in *bad, bat*, which is evidently [æ], and "the broad sound," as in *all, call, ward, war, warm*, etc., which is evidently [ɔɪ].   But in a footnote he adds: "A has really five different sounds; for besides the three above mentioned, it has a more slender Sound still than long (a), which is like French (e) masculine, and is expressed in *late, plate, rate*, etc.   It has also an open Sound, which approaches to its broad Sound, and is expressed in *Wrath, rather, Father, Glass*, and some others.   But as these two sounds occur but seldom, the former has been confounded with the slender long (a), and the latter with the less open short (a)," p. 7. The observation which the author of the *British Grammar* makes with respect to the vowel of *late* as compared with that of *came* is probably the familiar one that this vowel is slightly higher and tenser before a voiceless stop than it is before either a voiced stop or a continuant. He sets aside [aɪ], however, not because it seems a slight variation in sound from [æ] but because the sound actually did not occur frequently enough to call for much attention in what he regarded as good pronunciation. So he describes, p. 18, words like *hearken, heart, hearty, heartless*, as being pronounced with "(a) short," that is, with [æ], and this was evidently the pronunciation which he commonly heard in words which later generally took the sound of [ɑ] or [ɑɪ].

In Walker's *Critical Pronouncing Dictionary*, the first edition of which appeared in 1791, the situation is described as being somewhat further developed, and one infers either that usage was changing and [ɑɪ] was becoming more general, or what is more probable, that Walker merely included in his description elements of speech which had been current in practice for some time but which other students had seen fit to exclude from their descriptions as not belonging to what they regarded as approved forms of speech. Walker recognized four values for the letter *a*, the first of which, "long *a*," we may exclude from present consideration as being really [eɪ] and therefore not entering into the discussion of words in which [ɑɪ] may occur. The other three sounds he describes as (1) "the long Italian *a*," as in *far, father*, and the second syllables of *papa, mama*, and further describes this sound as equivalent to "French *a*," in *fable, rable;* (2) "the broad German *a*," as in *fall, wall, water*, equivalent to French *â*, as in *âge, Châlons;* and finally, (3) "the short sound of this Italian *a*," as in *fat, mat, marry*, equivalent to French *a* in *fat, matin*. This identification of the vowel of *fat, mat*, with the vowel of *far, father*, the latter being described as long Italian *a* and the former as short Italian *a*, immediately raises the question of the quality of Walker's "long Italian *a*." Did he pronounce the vowel of *far*, *father* as Franklin did, or did he really have here the sound of [aɪ]? His words, taken literally, would plainly lead one to suppose that he said [fæɪr], ['fæːðər] for *far*, *father*, and for his other two type words, *papa*, *mamma* [pə'pæɪ], [mə'mæɪ]. On the other hand, one would not be surprised to find a writer of Walker's day equating his vowels as the long and short quantities of the same quality, although the vowels were in fact qualitatively quite different. Thus one finds the vowel of *get* often described as the short sound of the vowel of *seat*, or the vowel of *pin* as the short sound of *pine*. It would be no more incorrect to speak of [æ] as being the short sound of [aɪ], and when all the evidence is considered, one must conclude that this was what Walker did. The precise quality of Walker's long Italian *a*, however, is not thus determined, and perhaps all one can say of it is that his vowel in *far*, *father*, *papa*, *mamma*, stood closer to [ɑ] than to [æ]. One might question, of course, whether his [ɔ], which is described as being the third sound of *a*, as in *fall*, *wall*, and the third sound of *o*, as in *nor*, *for*, *or*, the sounds being alike according to Walker's explicit statement, may not really have been an unrounded [ɔ] sound, that is approximately an [ɑ], and in consequence, what we have designated as his [aɪ] may not have been [aɪ], or even a sound still closer to [æɪ]. If this were so, Walker's descriptions of these sounds would stand much closer to Sheridan's than they do if we take his second sound of *a* as being [aɪ], and his third sound as [ɔɪ]. But in view of the identification of the sound of the vowel of *foll* with that of *for*, it seems impossible to conclude otherwise than that the pronunciation indicated as the third value of *a* was a genuine [ɔ], and this being granted, that the second value of *a* was a genuine [ɑ].

As to the distribution of [aɪ] in usage, Walker has some interesting remarks which go to show that practice, as he observed it, in the pronunciation of words in which the sound might occur, was very much divided. "We seldom find the long sound of this letter in our language," he says, p. 10, "except in monosyllables ending with *r*, as, *far*, *tar*, *mar*, etc., and in the word *father*." But he then goes on to say that [aɪ] is "regular" before *r* in monosyllables; before *lm*, as in *calm;* "sometimes before *lf*, *lve*, as in *calf*, *half*, *calve*, *halve*, *salve*"; and "before the sharp aspirated dental *th*, in *bath*, *path*, *lath*, etc., and in the word *father*," which last word would be exceptional in having [ɑː] in an open syllable before a voiced *th*. "This sound of the *a*," he continues, "was formerly more than at present found before the nasal liquid *n*, especially when succeeded by a *t* or *c*, as *grant*, *dance*, *glance*, *lance*, *France*, *chance*, *prance*, etc." "The hissing consonant *s* [i.e., voiceless *s*] was likewise a sign of this sound of the *a*, whether doubled as in *glass*, *grass*, etc., or accompanied by *t*, as in *last*, *fast*, etc., but this pronunciation of *a* seems to have been for some years advancing to the short sound of this letter, as heard in *hand*, *land*, *grand*, etc., and pronouncing the *a* in *after*, *answer*, *basket*, *plant*, *mast*, etc., as long as in *half*, *calf*, etc., borders very closely on vulgarity." In the body of the *Dictionary*, under the word *plant*, Walker remarks that "There is a coarse pronunciation of this word, chiefly among the vulgar, which rhymes with *aunt* [which Walker would pronounce ɑːnt]. This pronunciation seems a remnant of that broad sound which was probably given to the *a* before two consonants in all words, but which has been gradually wearing away, and which is now, except in a few words, become a mark of vulgarity." The only pronunciation Walker records as standard for this word is [plænt.] When he speaks of the broad sound as probably occurring before two consonants in all words, this statement seems to be based on the supposition that *a* would regularly be [eɪ] in open syllables, as in *fatal*, *natal*, *pagan*, etc., and equally regularly, some other sound in the closed syllable. This principle Walker occasionally applies, as in the pronunciation of *satire* with [eɪ], but it was a rule that obviously must have been open to a great many exceptions. The main point is, however, that the classes of words in which [ɑː] was permissible were not clearly defined in Walker's day. He declares that "it would be gross to a degree to sound the *a* in *castle*, *mask*, and *plant*, like the *a* in *palm*, *psalm*, etc.," p. 22, yet elsewhere his condemnation of this pronunciation in similar words is not so severe, and one is led to conclude that a dogmatic statement, such as Walker makes, was to a certain extent personal, and not a faithful and impartial record of the usage of the day. Yet one can infer at least that to many speakers of the time the sound of [ɑɪ] suggested a broad popular variety of pronunciation rather than a cultivated one.

In a note added to one of the Principles in a later edition of his *Dictionary*, Walker remarks that "Mr. Smith in a Scheme of a French and English Dictionary," has expressed different views from his own, especially concerning the pronunciation of *a* followed by *ss*, *st*, or *n* followed by another consonant. In these words Smith gave the sound of *a* as [ɑɪ]. "That this was the sound formerly," continues Walker, "is highly probable from its being still the sound given it by the vulgar, who are generally the last to alter the common pronunciation; but that the short *a* in these words is now the general pronunciation of the polite and learned world, seems to be candidly acknowledged by Mr. Smith himself; and as every correct ear would be disgusted at giving the *a* in these words the full long sound of the *a* in *father*, any middle sound ought to be discountenanced, as tending to render the pronunciation of a language obscure and indefinite." [1] This is one of the earliest references to an attempt to inculcate a compromise sound between [æɪ] and [ɑɪ]. Discussing the sound [ɔɪ] in *broth*, *froth*, *moth*, etc., instead of [ɔ], the sound which Walker approves, Walker again calls attention to the effort to establish a compromise sound, neither the one nor the other, and adds that "no middle sound ought to be admitted, as good orators will ever incline to definite and absolute sounds, rather than such as may be called *non-descripts* in language." [2] It may be noted in passing that the pronunciations indicated by Perry in his dictionary and spelling book must have seemed extremely old-fashioned to Walker. For Perry recognized the second [ɑɪ] not only in those positions in which Walker recommended it, but also in words like *ask*, *branch*, *cast*, *grass*, *dance*, *grant*, etc., *Sure Guide*, pp. 18–19.

That contemporary opinion was not altogether in harmony with

---

[1] From Coxe's *Dictionary* (1813), pp. 11–12. Coxe reprints Walker's *Principles* from an edition not specified, but later than the first.

[2] *Ibid.*, p. 23.

Walker is shown also by the remarks of Stephen Jones, the first edition of whose *General Pronouncing and Explanatory Dictionary* appeared in 1798. In his Preface, Jones declared that Walker had been too sparing in the use of [ɑː], that he employed it with too much timidity. Jones indicated the sound not only in *half, calf, psalm, ah, father,* but also in such words as *lass, last, past,* etc., and he adds that "giving to those and similar words the flat dead sound of *a* in *lack, latch, pan,* etc., is encouraging a mincing modern affectation, and departing from the euphonical pronunciation of our language." "I consider it," he says, "as a legitimate English sound; and believe its unmerited degradation and disuse to be of very recent date."

In his *Dissertations,* published 1789, two years before the appearance of Walker's first edition, Webster clearly indicated the presence of [ɑː] in certain groups of words in New England pronunciation.

But still earlier, in the first edition of the *Spelling Book,* which appeared as the first part of Webster's *Grammatical Institute* in 1783, we find full records of the occurrence of [ɑː] in New England speech. The statements of the first edition of 1783 were carried over into the later editions with practically no alterations. In the edition of 1783, Webster remarks, p. 16, that the sound of *a* in *ask* "seems commonly to arise from the following consonant, but it is really a sound by itself. It is really as long as *a* in *name,* but a very different sound; for which reason I have considered it as a distinct vowel." In his table of vowels, p. 21, he distinguishes four sounds of *a,* (1) *a* as in *name,* (2) *a* as in *man,* (3) *a* as in *bald,* (4) *a* as in *ask.* The groups of words in which the fourth sound of *a* is said to occur are words of the type of *artist, arm, clasp, after, balm, grant, advance,* etc.

In the *Dissertations,* p. 137, Webster says that *sauce,* "with the fourth sound of *a,*" this being the sound as he uses it in *ask, path,* etc., "is accounted vulgar; yet this is the ancient, the correct, and the most general pronunciation." "The *aw* of the North Britons is much affected of late: *sawce, hawnt, vawnt;* yet the true sound is that of *aunt, jaunt,* and a change can produce no possible advantage." Webster's ascription of the pronunciation [ɔɪ] to North Britons in the words spelled with *au* followed by *n* and a consonant may be set down as a haphazard guess. Such words are uniformly recorded with the sound [ɔɪ] by Sheridan, but with [ɑɪ] by Walker, who expressly repudiates Sheridan's pronunciation, permitting it only in the words *vaunt, avaunt,* which he says "are chiefly confined to tragedy" and "may be allowed to 'fret and strut their hour upon the stage' in the old traditionary sound of awe," Walker, p. 27. On the other hand, the use of [ɑɪ] in *daughter, sauce, saucer, saucy,* "as if written *darter, sarce, sarcer,* and *sarcy,*" instead of [ɔɪ], Walker designates as "corrupt," and one that "cannot be too carefully avoided." He reprehends *sausage,* with [æ] as vulgar for correct [ˈsɔɪsɪdʒ]. In the body of the dictionary, under the word *haunt,* Walker says this word was "in quiet possession of its true sound till a late dramatic piece made its appearance, which, to the surprise of those who had heard the language spoken half a century, was, by some speakers, called the Hawnted Tower. This was certainly the improvement of some critick in the language; for a plain common speaker would undoubtedly have pronounced the *au,* as in *aunt, jaunt,* etc., and as it had always been pronounced in the *Drummer,* or the *Haunted House.*" From this it appears that though Walker and Webster were at one in the pronunciation given to *aunt, jaunt,* and similar words, this state of harmony did not extend to the words *sauce, saucy, saucer,* which Webster regularly pronounced with [ɑɪ].[1]

Webster has nothing to say in the *Dissertations* about the other possible occurrences of [ɑɪ] in words like *half, past, path,* etc., except that in remarking upon the British pronunciation of *wrath* as [rɔθ], he notes, p. 124, that "the Americans almost universally preserve the analogous sound, as in bath, path." "This is the correct pronunciation," he declares, "and why should we reject it for *wroth,* which is a corruption?" Another occurrence of [ɑɪ] is noted, *Dis-*

---

[1] Grandgent, p. 214, through some misconception, says that Webster in the *Dissertations,* "prefers ǣ in *aunt, jaunt, sauce,* although the English use ɔ." But Webster ascribes [ɔɪ], not [ɔ] to the North Britons, not to the English in general, and he certainly did not pronounce *aunt, jaunt, sauce,* as [æɪnt], [dʒæɪnt], [sæɪs].

sertations, p. 105, in the "very common error, and particularly in New England," of pronouncing *e* before *r*, as *a*, e.g., *marcy* for *mercy*. "This single mistake," says Webster, "has spread a false pronunciation of several hundred words among millions of people." The character of this sound as [ɑ:] is further determined by Webster's remark that to avoid this mistake, "some fine speakers have run into another extreme, by pronouncing *e* before *r*, like *u* in *murcy*," whereas the "true" sound is that of short *e*, as in *let*, this being the "correct and elegant pronunciation of the letter in all words of this class." Now if this reprehended pronunciation was not *murcy* or the "correct and elegant" pronunciation ['mɛrsɪ], it can scarcely have been anything other than ['mɑ:rsɪ].

Webster also calls attention to what he considers "an error of great consequence" on the part of Sheridan, "in marking the two qualities of sound in *bard* and *bad* with the same figure," *Dissertations*, p. 379. The only distinction which Sheridan makes in the vowels of these two words, it will be remembered, was one of length. Webster notes that Sheridan distinguishes "the different qualities of sound in *pool* and *full*, and in *not* and *naught;* and why he should omit the distinction of sound in *bard* and *bad, ask* and *man*, is to me inconceivable. The last distinction is as obvious as the others which he has marked; and the defect of his scheme must lead a foreigner into mistakes. His scheme is singular; Kenrick, Perry, and Burn all make a distinction in the time of pronouncing *a* in *ask* and *at;* and even Scott, who copies Sheridan's pronunciation almost implicitly, still makes the same distinction." It is not easy to determine just what Webster means by quantity and quality in these criticisms, but the most reasonable supposition is that he meant words like *bard* and *ask* to be pronounced with [ɑ:].

And yet elsewhere, for *a* after *w*, Webster shows an unexpected preference for [æ], which probably indicates nothing more, however, than the fact that usage was unsettled in his day. "The words *shall, quality, quantity, qualify, quandary, quadrant*," he remarks, *Dissertations*, p. 114, "are differently pronounced by good speakers. Some give *a* a broad sound, as *shol, quolity*, and others, its second sound, as in *hat*." In the first four of these words, Webster thinks that usage strongly favors [æ], and this usage Webster approves, "that being the proper sound of the English *a* which is heard in *hat* or *bar*." Authorities vary as to the last two, but "in such a case, we can hardly hesitate a moment to call in analogy to decide the question, and give *a* in all these words, as also in *quash*, its second sound." The rimes of the poets who wrote in Webster's day show clearly enough that pronunciations like [bær] for bar, [kwæʃ] for *quash* were very common, yet as these were not the pronunciations which Webster advocated a few years later in his spelling books and dictionaries, the inference is that Webster was at different times of different mind on a point which was unsettled in usage.

Carrol, *The American Criterion* (1795), gives *a* the value of [aɪ] when it precedes "ft, ff, r single, and r, s, or followed by any other consonant"; also when *a* precedes "ch or th, not followed by *e* final"; and for *a* before nce, nt, h, lf, lve, lm. Exceptions occur when *w* precedes *a*, the vowel then having its "broad sound," and in the word *valve*, which has its short sound [æ].

The sound [aɪ] or [a] appears also in Elliott and Johnson's *Selected Pronouncing and Accented Dictionary*, Suffield, Connecticut, 1800. The authors distinguish what they call two short sounds of *a*, as represented respectively in the accented vowel of *abandon*, and in *ask, past*. The vowels are marked in the same way in the somewhat crude system of indicating pronunciation which the compilers of the dictionary employ, but there is an evident attempt to indicate two different sounds here and the distinction intended can scarcely be any other than that between [æ] and [aɪ] or [a]. In their *Preface*, the authors declare that their standard in pronunciation has been "the practice of men of letters and Gentlemen of the first abilities, and experience, in school education in modern times." The work, though slight, shows evidences of independent judgment and is interesting otherwise as one of the earliest attempts at dictionary making by Americans for Americans.

In Alexander's *Columbian Dictionary*, Boston, 1800, the quality of [aɪ] is indicated with clearness, and the sound is described as occurring not only for *a* before *r*, and before *lm*, but also in *glass*, *path*, *dance*, *half*, *daunt*, *gaunt*, *haunt*; in short, its occurrence is as general as in Perry.

The distribution of the sound as its use was recommended by Webster appears more fully in his spelling book. Here Webster recognizes five values for the letter *a*, see *American Spelling Book*, p. 25, which repeats essentially the statements of the first edition of 1783, as represented in the words *name*, *man*, *bald*, *ask*, and *what*. Of these he calls number four "flat *a*," "the sound of *a* in *father*." Number five, the vowel of *what*, is merely the short sound of the vowel of *bald*. The fourth sound of *a* he records (1) in words in which *a* occurs before *r* final or *r* followed by a consonant, as in *debar*, *depart*, *disarm*, etc., see *American Spelling Book*, p. 36; (2) before *lm*, as in *embalm*, etc., p. 36, 49; (3) before [s], [f], [θ], as in *pass*, *mass*, *ask*, *staff*, *half*, *calf*, *path*, *bath*, *wrath*, see pp. 49, 53; (4) before *lv*, as in *calve*, *salve*, see p. 49; (5) before *n* followed by *t, c, ch*, as in *pant*, *grant*, *ant*, *dance*, *glance*, *blanch*, see p. 49; (6) in words spelled *au* before [s], as in *saucer*, *saucy*, see p. 59; (7) in words spelled *au* before *n* followed by *t, ch*, as in *aunt*, *daunt*, *haunt*, *jaunt*, *vaunt*, *launch*, *staunch*, *craunch*, etc., see p. 49; (8) for *au* before *n* followed by *d* in *jaundice*, see p. 60; and (9) for several words which do not fall in any of these classes, as in *chamber*, p. 54; in *slander*, p. 60, and *gape*, p. 49. He also gives *bracelet*, p. 59, with [aː], though in the dictionary of 1807 it appears with [eɪ]. As exceptional to class seven, he records *gaunt* as [gænt], see p. 47. Before [l] final or [l] followed by a stop consonant, *a* of course becomes [ɔ], as in *all*, *bald*, etc., and after [w] it becomes the same sound, as in *wasp*, *warp*, *want*, etc., see p. 49. As to the length of this vowel, Webster expresses doubt whether the vowel of *cost*, *born*, *warm*, should be given as long or short, but adds that "the liquids that follow them have such an effect in lengthening the syllables, that it appears more natural" to suppose a long vowel, and that "a similar remark applies to *a* in *bar*," p. 49, note.

The rules thus laid down in the *American Spelling Book* passed over into Webster's dictionaries, the first of which was the *Com-*

pendious Dictionary, Hartford and New Haven, 1806. In the Preface, p. xii, Webster remarks that "Sheridan, the first author whose work engaged public attention, took the liberty to omit in his scheme, the Italian sound of *a*, which we hear in *ask, demand, father*," and he adds that "outrageous as this innovation was, extending perhaps to thousands of words, whose pronunciation was thus perverted, it was followed in some parts of this country, producing that mincing, affected pronunciation of *dance, psalm, ask, father*, etc., which is observed by strangers among the people of the middle States." As a matter of fact, though Sheridan omitted the Italian *a* from his scheme, he cannot be said thereby to have prevented the true pronunciation of the words in which Webster thought [ɑː] should be heard. Usage evidently was divided in England in the latter eighteenth century, just as it was in America, and all that one can infer from Webster's remarks is that in New England, as Webster heard the speech of New England, which was probably with a considerable degree of accuracy, the sound of [ɑː] had established itself in several large groups of words, whereas elsewhere in America the sound [æ] or [æː] prevailed in these words. But the "stranger" from New England who explained the [æ], [æː] of the Middle States as due to Sheridan's dictionary would have accorded that book an incredible degree of influence. It is probably true, however, that social custom had generalized upon the sound [æ], [æː] in the Middle States rather than upon [ɑː] because the population of that region was more mixed and more cosmopolitan than the population of New England, and consequently was more likely to be influenced by a general polite custom, such as the pronunciation of *a* as [æ], [æː] undoubtedly was in the late eighteenth century, and to a considerable degree, even in the early nineteenth century. In New England, on the other hand, the independent and self-determining population of which Webster always speaks with pride would very readily generalize upon its own local custom, even if that custom was a somewhat rustic one.

That the pronunciation of *a* as [ɑː] in some of the words in question was at least open to the charge of being a somewhat rustic one may be inferred from Webster's characterization of the sound [æ] [æɪ] as mincing and affected. He evidently regarded [ɑɪ] as the good home-spun pronunciation, and [æ], [æɪ] as the refined pronunciation. The situation was reversed in later American speech, and now whenever the question of choice between [ɑɪ] and [æ], [æɪ] occurs in words like *laugh, dance, branch*, etc., it is the second sound which is likely to be preferred as more refined or elegant. This change, however, has been brought about only by the gradually increasing influence of Webster's various books, and still more by the predominant position of New England culture in American life during the middle quarters of the nineteenth century. But at the most the change was mainly one of sentiment or theory, and the pronunciation of words like *laugh, dance, branch*, etc. with [ɑɪ] has established itself nowhere as a popular custom outside of New England.

The preference of the other sections of the country for [æ] or [æɪ] in words which in New England had [ɑɪ] is established by other evidence than that of Webster. Of course the influence of Walker is very plainly to be seen in many of the statements of students of speech who do not follow the system of Webster, but it seems scarcely probable that Walker would have been accepted and approved if his prescriptions had not been in harmony with what was considered to be the best practice. Various American editions of Walker appeared in the early years of the nineteenth century. It will be remembered that Walker gave wholehearted assent to [ɑɪ] only for *a* before *r* final, or followed by a consonant, as in *mar, mart*, and for *a* before *lm*, as in *psalm, calm*, and it is only in these words, with one or two exceptions like *father*, that [ɑɪ] seems to have been generally used in early nineteenth-century speech outside of New England.

The *New Critical Pronouncing Dictionary of the English Language*, by An American Gentleman, published at Burlington, N. J., in 1813, was the work of Richard S. Coxe, a native of New Jersey and a graduate of Princeton. The book was based upon Johnson for spelling and Walker for pronunciation, and Walker's *Principles of English Pronunciation* was printed as part of the introductory matter of the volume. Now Coxe, though he makes occasional annotations on Walker's statements and by no means follows his model slavishly, in this detail of the pronunciation of [ɑː] follows Walker without a word of dissent, and in the body of his dictionary regularly indicates [æ] for *a* in words like *pass, last, chance,* etc. Webster's ruling on this point must have been well known to Coxe, but he evidently preferred a statement which was more in accord with the practice of his own community. Since many speakers in Coxe's community used [æ] not only in *pass, last, chance,* etc., but probably also in *far, part, calm,* etc., one might have expected to find the same sound recorded for these latter words. So great a departure from standard as prescribed by Walker called for more boldness, however, than one might reasonably look to find in an American lexicographer of the early nineteenth century.

The *American Standard of Orthography and Pronunciation and Improved Dictionary of the English Language,* by Burgiss Allison, Burlington, N. J., 1815, also professes to have followed Walker's pronunciation, "with a very few exceptions," but the exceptions are so few as to be negligible. *The New York Expositor,* New York, [1825], by Richard Wiggins and John Griscom, said to be "chiefly on the authorities of Johnson and Walker," on the other hand, makes no provision at all for a sound [ɑː], using the same symbol for the vowel in *ardent, faster, calm,* for example, as for the vowel in words which unquestionably had [æ.] A word like *dauntless* is marked with the *u* silent and the *a* as having its short value, that is the same sound as it would have in *hovoc.* If the authors' description means anything, therefore, it means a pronunciation ['dæntləʃ], which would not be an unexpected form for this and other possible [ɑː]- words in New York speech of the first quarter of the nineteenth century.

Lyman Cobb (1821), p. 57, Webster's great adversary, gives [ɑː] in *daunt, flaunt, gaunt, jaunt, laugh, launch, salve, taunt, vaunt,* p. 114, in *bath, lath, path, hearth;* but [æ,] pp. 58–59, in *class, clasp, fast, flask, glass, ask, asp, bass, branch, dance, cast, chaff, raft,* etc., and in *wrath,* p. 114.

The *Speller's Guide*, Buffaloe, Va., 1824, by Joseph Shreve, acknowledges the existence of a vowel [ɑː] but limits it almost exclusively to the pronunciation of *a* before *r*. The author's prescriptions are inconsistent, however, and indicate probably a lack of harmony between literary authorities with which he was familiar and the practice of his own speech. In the latter he probably said [æ] even for *a* before *r*, and on p. 47, *remark, discard, enlarge, embark,* are given as having the same vowel as *attract, relax, attack,* etc., and though *psalm, qualm* are given, p. 85, as having [ɑː], on p. 46, *embalm* has [æ]. On p. 35, *calf* has [æ], on p. 85 it has [ɑː]. In the main, however, the author favors [æ], both before [r] and before [f], [s], [θ], etc. Cooper, *North American Spelling Book*, Philadelphia, 1830, a resident of Philadelphia, had no [ɑː] in his recorded pronunciation. He records the sound of "ă short as in *măt, flăt,*" p. 36, not only in words like *ask, clasp, calf, salve, branch, chance,* etc., but also in *qualm, balm,* with *l* silent, in *guard, snarl, starch, parse, charge, sharp, scar,* etc., and in *daunt, launch, gaunt, haunt, taunt, aunt, flaunt,* etc. It is somewhat surprising to find all these pronunciations approved as late as 1830, but other evidence makes it certain that they were current good pronunciations in Philadelphia at that time.

The remarks of Duponceau, written in 1817, and evidently based upon a close observation of the language of the Middle States, are interesting in this connection. Duponceau was born in France, but had been a resident of the United States for some thirty years when his essay on *English Phonology* was read before the Philosophical Society at Philadelphia. He was familiar with the lexicographical work of Sheridan, Walker, and others, and with the phonology of various other languages besides English and French. His purpose in this essay was to describe the sounds of the English language as those sounds actually impressed the ear, and to this end he endeavored to free the auditory impressions of the sounds as completely as possible from the visual images with which they are likely to become confused through the influence of spelling and writing. Though the effort cannot be said to have been completely successful,

the part played by the tongue, for example, in the organic formation
of sounds being inadequately represented, the study is nevertheless
notable as the work of one who realized the nature of correct method
in the study of speech sounds and who was himself a competent
observer of wide experience.   Duponceau distinguishes seven main
vowel sounds in English, which he names Aulif, [ɔː], [ɔ]; Arpeth
[æː], [æ]; Airish, [ɛː], [ɛ]; Azim, [eː], [e]; Elim, [iː], [i]; Oreb, [oː], [o],
and Oomin, [uː], [u].   The distinction between long and short Arpeth,
Duponceau considers to be only one of quantity.   When long he
finds it to be represented by *a* in the noun *art; aa* in *baa,* "the cry
of a sheep"; by *ae* in *Haerlem;* by *agh,* in *Armagh;* by *ah,* in *ah;* by
au, in *aunt;* by *ea* in *heart.*   The same sound short he finds represented by the *a* of *art,* third singular of the verb, *man, carry,* etc.;
by *e* in *herd, merchant;* by *ea* in *learn;* by *i* in *fir, sir, third, bird.*   He
notes that according to Sheridan, *merchant* is to be pronounced
martshant, and according to Walker, *mertshant.*   "Neither of these
writers," he continues, "seems to be aware that the only difference
between these modes of pronunciation is in the quantity given to
the vowel *e,* and not in the sound that it receives.   Those who follow
Sheridan, lengthen the sound of the first vowel, and the disciples
of Walker make it short," p. 251.   But the quality of Duponceau's
Arpeth is brought out still more clearly in the comparison he makes
between it and Airish.   "There is," he says, p. 253, "a real difference between the two sounds which I call Arpeth and Airish, though
some have confounded them together as if they were the same; a
Frenchman will hardly be persuaded that they are different sounds,
he will call Airish an *e* ouvert, and Arpeth, an *e* plus ouvert."   "The
Virginians," he goes on to say, "in almost every case employ the
sound of Arpeth, instead of Airish, as in *there, where, stairs,* which
they pronounce as if they were written *thahr, whahr, stahrs.*"   Now
it is extremely unlikely that a man of Duponceau's phonetic experience would have called attention to the similarity between Arpeth
and Airish if the former stood for [ɑː] and the latter for [ɛː].   These
two latter sounds are so dissimilar that even a crude observer would
perceive the difference between them.   But [æː] and [ɛː], though

not the same, as Duponceau points out, are nevertheless sufficiently alike to call for some exactness of analysis in discriminating between them. The whole point of his discussion turns therefore on the value of Arpeth as [æɪ], [æ], the only vowel he recognizes between Aulif [ɔɪ], [ɔ] and Airish, [ɛɪ], [ɛ].

It is significant also to note that Duponceau heard Arpeth, short, in words like *fir, sir, third, bird, firkin, firmament*, etc., in all of which he describes a vowel different from the [ɛ] of *get*, and the vowel of *fur*, which latter was probably [ə]. To prove that the vowel of *bird* is Arpeth, short, he instances this word "in which I find the sound of *i* to be the same with that of *a* in *bard*, except that the first is short and the last is long." "Again, in the words *thou art*, accent the word *thou*, and the *a* of the word *art*, pronounced short, will produce the sound of *i* in *bird*," p. 252. These descriptions of the sound of *i* followed by *r* final, or *r* and a consonant could apply only if Duponceau's Arpeth was a genuine [æɪ], [æ].

The fact, on the other hand, of the tendency for [aɪ] to run into a broad popular pronunciation, at least in New England, is also indicated in several ways. For one, it is in point to note that [aɪ] was extended in New England to words of rustic speech outside the groups in which [aɪ] occurred in cultivated speech. Thus Lowell, in the Introduction to the *Biglow Papers* (1848), says that the "genuine Yankee" gives to *a* in *handsome* the broad sound it has in *father*. Holmes in the *Autocrat*, a collection of essays first published in the form of a volume in 1858, groups *sahtisfahction, sahtisfahctory, a prahctical mahn*, with other reprehended examples in broad New England speech. One may still hear, says Grandgent, p. 215, writing in 1899, from elderly New England rustics, [ˈɑpl], [ˈhɑmə], [ˈmɑtə], [ˈpɑntrɪ], [ˈsɑtdɪ], for *apple, hammer, matter, pantry, Saturday*. The prevalence of [aɪ] Grandgent thinks was at its height between 1830 and 1850. The sound is mentioned by Willard, *General Class Book*, p. vii, who speaks of the short sound of *a* in *father*, that is [ɑ], as the sound "which the people of New England formerly gave, and the vulgar still give to such words as *fathom, ladder*, or *matter*." In *Elsie Venner*, first published in 1859, Holmes indicated [ɑ] in the rustic speech of New England in a number of words like *tavern, man, matter, Abner, Sabbath, handsome,* etc., which he writes *tahvern, mahn, mahterr, Ahbner,* etc. Samuel Worcester, *Fourth Book* (1834), p. 296, says there is "a very disgusting error, prevalent in many towns of New England, in pronouncing such words as *calf, half, staff, laugh, haunt,*" with the vowel of *care* instead of the vowel of *father,* a statement which at least indicates as yet no shadow of dissatisfaction with [ɑː.]

As early as 1830, however, it is clear that some meticulous speakers were beginning to look with suspicion upon [ɑː] even in New England. In that year was published the first edition of Joseph E. Worcester's *Comprehensive Pronouncing and Explanatory Dictionary.* Though a native of New Hampshire and a graduate of Yale, Worcester early took up his residence in Cambridge, and in the rivalry which the differences between Webster's and Worcester's dictionaries brought about, he came to be regarded as the special spokesman for the culture of the Hub of the Universe. Worcester was the first to introduce into American discussions of [ɑː] the particular shade of sound which is designated by [aː]. This sound he called the intermediate sound of *a,* "between its short sound, as in *fat, man,* and its Italian sound, as in *father, far.*" The distinction will be found after 1864 in the later editions of Webster's dictionaries. The words in which this sound was prescribed by Worcester were those in which *a* stood before [f], [s], [θ], or before *n,* followed by [t], and in some words by [d]. For *a* before [r] final or [r] followed by a consonant, and for *a* before *lm,* Worcester gives the sound as unequivocally [aː]. Now the interesting point here is that Worcester's hesitation with respect to the sound of *a* in words like *ask, dance, chaff,* etc., was due not to the fear that the sound [aː] which he advocated in these words might seem too near the sound [æː], but too near the sound [ɑː]. In other words, the vulgar extreme which was to be avoided was the sound [ɑː] and not the sound [æː]. In his Revised Edition (1859), Worcester quotes with approval the words of Smart, a British lexicographer, whose first edition had appeared in 1836 and who noted a tendency to "broadness" in the pronunciation of *grass, graft, command,* the sound [ɑː] in words like these being reprehended as a "decided vulgarism." The "exact sound," according to Smart, lay between the vowel of *hat* and the "vulgar corruption" which appears in [grɑːs.]

It is extremely doubtful if Worcester had heard a sound [aː] which was established by custom in actual speech and upon which he based his advocacy of this particular refinement of pronunciation. It is more probable that his [aː] was an invention of theory than that it was an established custom in practice. It has never become a genuine and popular pronunciation, even in New England, though it is occasionally heard in the speech of persons who make an endeavor to steer a middle course between the two genuinely popular sounds, [ɑː] and [æː]. It early appeared in the school books, as in Fowle, *Common School Speller,* Boston, 1842, who remarks, p. 23, that when *r* follows *a,* "the sound is fuller than when it is followed by other letters; the latter sound being intermediate between *a* in *fat* and *a* in *far.*" The relative significance of the sound, however, has now changed and those speakers who cultivate the sound [aː] do so not as a safe escape from a possibly vulgar [ɑː] but from a possibly vulgar [æː]. The prime cause of this change of theoretical front has been instruction in the schools. The New England school book and also the New England school and school teacher exerted an enormous controlling influence over American education during the second and third quarters of the nineteenth century. Webster's books alone circulated by the millions of copies. This occupation of the field of education, and to a considerable extent also of literary effort, by New England, naturally induced on the part of those who were eager to appropriate some of the cultural life of the more highly favored region a lofty respect for so significant a social custom as speech. And since [ɑː] in *grass, calf,* etc., was one of the distinctions of New England speech, as contrasted with [æ], [æː] elsewhere, it came about that many speakers cultivated the sound [ɑː] in certain words, though it did not occur normally in these words in the speech of their communities, and did so just at the time when critical New England was trying to escape from this sound as having become broadly popular or rustic.   Grandgent places the sound [ɑɪ] in New England at its point of widest use between 1830 and 1850, and writing in 1899, he adds that "at present it seems to be declining, both in urban and rural speech."   The period of highest esteem of [ɑɪ], or [aɪ], outside New England, perhaps falls in the two decades from 1870 to 1890.   It was not generally prescribed in the various writings of William Russell, an able professional teacher of elocution who was born in Scotland but who came to America at about the age of twenty.   Russell published a number of text books on speech in the second quarter of the century and was a prominent and popular teacher of speech.   He lived in various parts of America and was thus familiar with several types of speech.   It is interesting therefore to note that though he recommends [ɑɪ] for words like *aunt, gaunt, saunter*, etc., he gives [ɑɪ] as an error for [æ] in *blast, laughing, fastened, masthead, Sequel to the Primary Reader*, Boston, 1845, pp. 32, 81, 104; and he gives the following, p. 19, as a list of words with [æ]: *bat, cat, hat, mat, pat, sat, have, has, glass, class, mass, grass, asp, grasp, clasp, vast, past, fast, waft, raft, graft, grant, craft, shaft, slant, gland, latch, dance, lance, glance, trance, France, chant, branch, crash, man, can, gather, rather, alas, advance*.   A few years later, however, the position of [ɑɪ] as an elegancy of speech is well indicated in the remark of Richard Grant White, *Words and Their Uses* (1870), Chapter III, a native of New York, that "the full, free, unconscious utterance of the broad *ah* sound of *a* is the surest indication, in speech, of social culture which began at the cradle."   "The tendency among uncultivated persons," he observes, "is to give *a* either the thick throaty sound of *aw* . . . or, oftenest, to give it the thin, flat sound which it has in 'an,' 'at,' and 'anatomy.'"   Though not extinct as a test of social culture, both [aɪ] and [ɑɪ] in words of the type of *grass, calf*, etc., are now coming to be regarded as marks either of a local New England pronunciation, or of a somewhat professional elocutionary pronunciation.   Professor Lounsbury remarked, *English Spelling Reform*, New York, 1909, p. 101, that the sound of [ɑɪ] "shows every sign of steady though slow disappearance," that it was once heard generally in many classes of words "where it is now never heard at all." "Such, for instance," he continues, "was the case when *a* was followed by *n*, as in *answer, chance, dance, plant;* by *f*, as in *after;* by *s*, as in *grass, glass, pass; st*, as in *last* and *vast*. . . . Before *lf* and *th*—which can be illustrated respectively by *calf, half*, and by *path, bath*—the original sound, once generally heard, has given way largely and is still giving way. . . . In the case of some of these, as a result of diminishing use, the sound, when heard, is already looked upon by many as an affectation."

Something further must be said concerning the group of words spelled *au* before [s], [nt,] [ntʃ], as in *sauce, haunt, daunt, launch, haunch*, etc. From the end of the Middle English period doubtless varying pronunciations of these words have existed, according as they developed from a diphthongal vowel [au], or a simple vowel [ɑ] of Middle English into Modern English, the former giving [ɔː] the latter [ɑː].

By Sheridan words of this type were pretty uniformly recorded with the sound of [ɔː], but by Walker they are pronounced with [ɑː]. Now the probable inference from this is that both [ɔː] and [ɑː] occurred in general use in cultivated speech at the end of the eighteenth century, that these two dictionary makers, following that habit of those who make standards of speech, which fixes upon a single custom and disregards all others, have in this instance chosen to accept two quite different customs of the time as their standards. Perry, p. 39, is a little more divided, giving only *aunt, daunt, flaunt, jaunt, craunch, haunch, scraunch, paunch, draught* and *laugh*, as having [ɑː]; but though he gives *gaunt* as having only [ɔː], he marks *daunt, haunt, haunch, paunch*, as having a double pronunciation, either [ɔː] or [ɑː]. Perry gives only [ɔː] for *sauce*.

In his various writings on pronunciation, Webster agreed with Walker in recording the pronunciation [ɑː] in almost all the words of this group, and Worcester is in accord with Webster. In the *American Spelling Book*, p. 47, however, Webster gives *gaunt* as [gænt]. In the dictionary of 1828 he gives two spellings for the word, *gaunt*, pronounced [gɔːnt], and *gant*, pronounced [gænt]. But otherwise words of this type are all pronounced with [ɑː] in the dictionary, including the words *sauce, saucy, jaundice*. Many of these words have developed and maintained popular pronunciations with [æ], e.g., *staunch*, pronounced [stæntʃ], *taunt* pronounced [tænt], and most general of all *sauce, saucy*, pronounced [sæs], ['sæsɪ]. The pronunciation of *sauce, saucy* as [sɑːs], ['sɑːsɪ] seems never to have been general outside New England, but students and recorders of New England dialect often take great pains to indicate it as one of the characteristic features of New England pronunciation. Webster, *Dissertations*, p. 137, says that "sauce with the fourth sound of *a* [the vowel of *ask* [ɑːsk], *path* [pɑːθ], etc.] is accounted vulgar; yet this is the ancient, the correct and the most general pronunciation. The *aw* of the North Britons is much affected of late; *sawce, hawnt, vawnt;* yet the true sound is that of *aunt, jaunt*, and a change can produce no possible advantage." The pronunciation of *jaundice* as ['dʒɑːndɪs] has also been modified in popular speech and the word is commonly pronounced ['dʒændərz]. This pronunciation of *au* as [æ] seems to be parallel to [æ] in *path, bath*, etc., Middle English [ɑ] in both cases developing as a short vowel into [æ].

The later American dictionaries for all these words give only the pronunciation [ɑː], or if they record [ɔː], it is as a second choice. Indeed if one were to gather one's information concerning the sound [ɔː] in words like *daunt, haunt*, etc., from the American dictionaries, one might easily be led to believe that the sound did not occur at all in the American pronunciation of these words, or that if it did occur, it was only as an exception. As a matter of fact, the most cursory observation of present American English and English during the past generation shows that usage with respect to these words is extremely divided, that only a very elaborate statistical examination would enable one to say whether ['lɔːndrɪ] or ['lɑːndrɪ], [dɔːnt] or [dɑːnt] was the more common pronunciation. This division in usage, it is extremely probable, has always existed in American speech. The almost complete uniformity of American dictionaries upon the point is probably due to the influence of Walker, but the very great influence of Walker upon the making of dictionaries must not be taken as implying an equal influence upon the actual practice and life of speech. The growing tendency in the pronunciation of these words appears to be in favor of [ɔː] and this is the sound usually preferred by the *New English Dictionary* and by English writers on pronunciation in their descriptions of British speech. The drift towards [ɔː] was already indicated by the remarks of Willard, p. 16, who was a judicious observer, to the effect that "*au* is sometimes pronounced like *a* in father, as in *aunt*, *gaunt* (lean, hungry, etc.). In most words, however, *au* and *aw* have exactly the same sound with *a* in *wall*, or *o* in *north*, as in *sausage*, *awful*." An extreme opinion is that of Mackintosh, p. 25, who records *aunt*, *vaunt*, *augment*, as having [ɔ] and *balm*, *qualm*, *salt* as having the same sound long.

If the discussion in the preceding paragraphs gives a truthful record of the facts, if we may believe that in the middle quarters of the eighteenth century, the letter *a* before [f], [s], [θ], etc., and before [r] was pronounced as [æ] [æː] very generally, and probably prevailingly in standard speech in America, and that earlier, perhaps even in the seventeenth century, [ɑː] began to make its way into good use, becoming general in New England in all the positions indicated, but elsewhere in America, only in those groups of words in which *a* stood before *r* final, before *r* and a consonant, and before *lm*, one is led to inquire for the reason for this clear division in the groups of words concerned. It should be observed first of all that a similar development has taken place in British speech. Before *r* final, before *r* followed by a consonant, and before *lm*, in England as in America, [ɑː] is practically the universal pronunciation for *a*. But for *a* before [ns], [nt], [ntʃ] and before [f], [s], [θ], etc., usage varies in England as in America. It is true that the British books on pronunciation usually record only the vowel [ɑː] in words of these latter groups as well as for words in the former, and this is the sound which has become established in the so-called "public school" pronunciation of England, which locally belongs to the south of England, and socially has come to be regarded as one of the marks of academically approved speech. Yet [ɑː] is by no means universal, even among cultivated Englishmen, in words containing *a* before [f], [s], [θ], etc.   Whether [æ], [æɪ] in such words is relatively as common in England as in America, it would be difficult to decide in the absence of any statistical evidence; yet it certainly would be as wrong to assume, as one might very well do, on the evidence of the books on British pronunciation, that the sound was a rare one in England, as it would be to make a similar assumption with respect to American speech on the evidence of the American dictionaries and guides to pronunciation, practically all of which record either [ɑː] or [aː] as the sound of *a* in words of all these several groups.   The inference to be drawn from this parallelism is not, however, that American speech has followed where British speech has led.   There is no evidence to indicate that any single pronunciation which has become general in America has become so through imitative influence of British pronunciation.   The inherent probabilities are all against the notion that such an influence could have been exerted.   A more reasonable explanation is to be found in the supposition that British and American speech possessed by inheritance a common fund of dialectal possibilities which might have developed divergently as readily as in parallels.   In this particular instance the parallelism was caused by the accident that the sound of [ɑː] became established as a popular speech sound in that very section of America which came to be recognized as our first seat of culture, and that in England, by a curious similarity, the situation is exactly the same.   This is, however, merely a coincidence of history, and if Philadelphia had won for itself the admiration which the nation accorded to Boston in the second and third quarters of the nineteenth century, it is not probable that an observer today would be struck by a great appearance of similarity between the standard of American speech as recorded in the current dictionaries and the dictionary standard of British speech.

In the case of the words with *r*, a physiological explanation suggests itself.   One immediately thinks of the parallel situation in the lowering of Middle English *e* [ɛ], probably through the stage of [æ] to [ɑ], in words like Middle English *derk* becoming *dark, person*

becoming *parson*, etc.[1]   One thinks also of the change of *i* [ɪ] before
r to the distinctly lower sound which now appears in *fir*, *sir*, *shirt*,
etc. and of the similar development which affects other vowels before
r.   From these parallels one might be led to the statement that *r*
in the development of Modern English has tended to cause a lowering of the vowel that preceded it, and in this physiological fact,
one might find the explanation of the lowering of [æ] to [ɑː].   The
changes would thus be similar to the change of [o] to [ɔ] in words
like *store*, *more*, etc.   The length of *a* in these words in which it
occurs before *r* is extremely variable, depending upon the extent to
which the consonantal quality of *r* persists.   Thus a word like *far*
when pronounced with a strongly consonantal *r* may have as short
a vowel as a word like *fat*.   But when *far* is pronounced without the
final consonant, as in Southern [faː], the vowel is very long and
may even be diphthongal, as in [faːə].   Between these two extremes
all stages of length exist, according as the *r* is more or less vocalized.
In words of the type of *calm*, *alms*, etc., the consonant *l* has been
completely eliminated as a sound, or perhaps it would be better to
say, has been absorbed by the preceding vowel.   Here again, therefore, it seems that the character of the vowel [ɑː] in *calm*, *alms*, etc.,
has been determined by physiological causes dependent upon the
presence of an original [l] following the vowel, just as the vowel of
chalk [tʃɔːk] has been caused by similar physiological causes.   That
the [l] did not produce the same result in *calm* and *chalk*, giving
either [kɔːm], [tʃɔːk], or [kɑːm], [tʃɑːk], must be accounted for by
further physical elements in the situation, for example, the character of the consonant by which the *l* is followed.   It is not possible

---

[1] A similar variation between *e* and *a* before *r*, with consequent confusion in usage
is recorded in the history of French pronunciation.   "Quand *r* était suivi de consonne
ou double," says Brunot, *Histoire de la Langue Française*, II, 249, "l'hesitation était
toujours extrême, et l'incertitude des grammairiens témoigne des contradictions de
l'usage.   Si l'on ne savait comment écrire, c'est qu'en réalité l'*a* qu'on entendait était
si ouvert qu'on ne le distinguait pas de *è*; Ronsard, faisant rimer *armes* et *termes* (IV,
243), *ferme* et *m'arme* (V, 413), le dit en propres termes.   Il justifie de telles rimes en
déclarant que 's'en offusquer c'est être ignorant de sa langue, ne sentant point que *E*
est fort uoisine de la lettre *A*, uoire tel que souuent, sans i penser, nous les confondons
naturellement' (II, 481, M-L)."

to state precisely how these physical causes operated, producing results as regular as if they had been realized in response to an unescapable command. It is in these physical causes, however, that one must seek for the explanation of the agreement between the British and American branches of the English language in this particular set of words, and not in any of the imitative or social aspects of the psychological side of language.

But if the loss of *l* in *calm*, *alms*, etc., has resulted in a universal pronunciation [kɑːm], [ɑːmz], etc., in standard speech, why has not the similar loss of *l* in *calf*, *half*, etc., resulted in a similar generalized habit with respect to these words? It obviously has not, for only those speakers who say *dance* [dɑːns], *grass* [grɑːs], etc., would also say [kɑːf], [hɑːf], etc., while those Americans west of the Atlantic sea-board who commonly say [dæns], [græs] would not, except in very rustic speech, say [kæm], [æmz]. The explanation of this divergence is to be sought in the special character of the words with *lm*. They are all words of Latin origin and all of somewhat learned connotation. They were therefore not subject to the leveling influence of analogy to the same degree as purely popular and native words like *half*, *calf*, which were readily attracted in pronunciation to other words like *chaff*, *laugh*, etc., which never had an *l* in spelling. On the other hand a vowel [ɑː] has always been felt, in the past as in the language today, to be more appropriate in a foreign or learned word than in a familiar word, and therefore has always managed to establish itself more firmly there than elsewhere.

For *a* after *w*, the earliest American critical students of speech indicate a rounded sound similar to the sound which they usually represented by the spelling *aw*. This sound would be [ɔ], [ɔɪ], and undoubtedly this was the direction in which the vowel in the combination *wa* was developing. It was recorded by Webster, *American Spelling Book*, p. 49, in words like *war*, *swarm*, *warm*, *warn*, *wart*, *quort*, *dwarf*, *warp*, *wasp*, *want*. It is indicated also by such spellings in the *Plymouth Records* as *swomp* for *swamp*, I, 185 (1686); *whorfe* for *wharf*, I, 204 (1686); *worn* for *warn* II, 120 (1714); *quontity* for *quantity*, II, 94 (1713); *quorter* for *quarter*, I, 223, 245, and so often;

and the spelling *Wodsworth* for *Wadsworth*, I, 239. For *war* the spelling *wor* occurs in Green, *Three Military Diaries*, p. 94, and similar spellings are to be found not infrequently in naïve writings of the seventeenth and eighteenth centuries. But the rimes of the poets of the third quarter of the eighteenth century, and of some even in the early nineteenth century, indicate that the older pronunciation [æ], [ɑ] still persisted in America, as indeed it did in England (see Gabrielson, *Rime as a Criterion of the Pronunciation of Spenser, Pope, Byron, and Swinburne*, p. 157), and of course pronunciations like *wash* [wɑʃ,] *water* [wɑtər], *want* [want], *wasp* [wasp] are still very common in American speech. The rimes of the Connecticut poets of the eighteenth century indicate clearly a pronunciation with [æ] for this period. One might question whether these rimes were not merely traditional rimes of eighteenth-century verse, but they are too numerous and too general to be taken as anything other than reflections of spoken usage, at least of New England speech, at that time. Similar rimes occur, though sporadically, in the verse of the early nineteenth century; but these rimes by this time were probably only occasional old-fashioned pronunciations which had persisted after the tendency toward the rounding of *a* [æ] preceded by *w* had become general. Even among the poets of the eighteenth century, one finds here and there a rime which indicates a rounded vowel for *a* after *w*, though these rimes are very much less numerous than those which call for [æ]. In the poems of Dwight, the following may be noted: *warm'd, charm'd, Conquest of Canaan*, p. 4; *dare: war*, pp. 6, 206; *care: war*, pp. 55, 125, 184; *war: car*, p. 22; *bear: war*, p. 22; *reward: regard*, p. 22; *arm: warm*, p. 121; *war: air*, pp. 176, 303; *glare: war*, p. 252; *forbear: war*, pp. 102, 116, 190; *guard: reward*, pp. 11, 17; *wand: hand, Greenfield Hill*, p. 71; *war: mar*, p. 71; *far: war: spare: bare*, p. 103; *charm: warm*, pp. 66, 69, 74, 164. In Barlow's *Columbiad*, these rimes occur: *air: war*, pp. 70, 104, 118, 178, 218; *spare: war*, p. 75; *share: war*, pp. 84, 96, 98, 180; *care: war*, pp. 94, 128, 217; *prepare: war*, pp. 98, 118; *blare: war*, pp. 100, 232; *glare: war*, p. 184; *snare: war*, p. 204; *despair: war*, p. 206; *bear: war*, p. 248; *bare: war*, p. 261; *afar: war*, p. 63;

war: jar, p. 116; *unbar: war*, p. 355; *scars: wars*, p. 195; *warm: charm*, p. 141; *warm: arm*, p. 194; *warms: farms*, p. 223. In the verse of Trumbull, the following have been noted: *war: air*, I, 72, 103; II, 101; *share: war*, I, 82; *despair: war*, I, 146, II, 98; *spare: war*, II, 97; *land: wand*, I, 21, 170; *wand: command*, I, 171; *hand: wand*, II, 33, 114; *wand: strand*, II, 206; *war: far*, I, 44; *car: war*, I, 57; *tar: war*, I, 68; *star: war*, I, 78; *jarring: warring*, I, 98; *swarms: arms*, I, 128; *warm: harm*, I, 153; *warms: charms*, II, 71, 172; *regard: reward*, II, 153. In the *Anarchiad* occur the following: *despair: war*, p. 37; *bear* (verb): *war*, p. 62; *mar: war*, p. 22; *far: war*, p. 22; *car: war*, p. 54; *bar: war*, p. 57; *grant: want*, p. 52; *wand: land*, p. 76. The following are from the poems of Humphreys: *afar: war*, p. 8; *war: star*, p. 9; *war: scar*, p. 10; *mar: war*, p. 37; *warm: arm*, p. 57; *swarms: arms*, p. 139; *scanted: wanted*, p. 197; *rewards: bards*, p. 185; *guard: reward*, p. 187; *errant: warrant*, p. 185; *pants: wants*, p. 109.

In the poems of Ladd, a native of Rhode Island, one notes *air: war*, p. 34; *bard: reward*, p. 42; *afar: war*, p. 54; *war: car*, p. 55; *declare: war*, p. 69; *prepare: war*, p. 73; *charms: warms*, p. 110. The rime *calm: warm*, p. 149, probably means that both the *l* and the *r* were silent, and that the vowel in both words was [æ].

Similar pronunciations were current in the Middle States, as evidenced by the following rimes from Freneau, a very careful rimester: *charms: warms*, pp. 20, 83; *afar, war*, pp. 141, 318; *car: war*, p. 144; *tars: wars*, p. 183; *trash: wash*, p. 222; *stars: wars*, p. 240; *bar: war*, p. 303; *jar: war*, p. 308; *declare: war*, p. 313; *regard: reward*, p. 316; *grant: want*, p. 61. The following rimes from Freneau are also interesting as indicating his pronunciation [æ] for *a* before *r*: *star: air*, p. 22; *far: her* [her], p. 23; *were: are*, p. 70; *air: far*, p. 113; *afar: there*, p. 142; *prepare: are*, p. 208; *air: fair*, p. 353. In Foster's poems, published at Salem, New York, in 1805, the vowel [æ] for *a* after *w* is indicated by the rime *share: war*, p. 76, and similar unrounded vowels are found in the riming of *war* with *mar*, pp. 24, 45, 66, with *afar*, pp. 36, 58, with *prepare*, p. 45, with *scar*, p. 47, with *star*, p. 58, and of *bard* with *reward*, p. 99. On the other hand, the rime *more: war*, p. 6, occurs once In *Heroes of the Lake*, pub-

lished at New York in 1814 and written in the autumn of 1813 by
one who does not give his name, one finds the following similar
rimes: *far: bear*, p. 20; *far: war*, p. 12, 21; *declare: war*, p. 71; *warm:
charm*, pp. 10, 11.   In Charles Reid's *Mississippian Scenery*, published at Philadelphia in 1819, besides rimes of the older type, such
as *war: air*, p. 112; *car: war*, p. 110; *repair: war*, p. 110, one finds also
the fully rounded vowel indicated by the rimes *more: war*, p. 106,
low'r: war, p. 112, and this was undoubtedly at this time the growing
and perhaps prevailing pronunciation.

The word *wrath* is pronounced [rɔ θ] in England, but [ræθ] or
[raɪθ] in America.   The division in usage goes back far.   Walker
recorded both pronunciations, noting that the first is "by far the
more usual, but the last is more analogical."   The theoretical objection to [rɔɪθ], as Walker points out, is that *w* does not cause a
rounding of a following vowel when the consonant *r* intervenes in
wrap, *wrangle*, and consequently should not do so in *wrath*.   Here
again American pronunciation, having the choice between two
forms, has chosen the one most in accord with analogy.   Webster
noted, *Dissertations*, p. 124, that the English pronounce *wrath* with
the sound which he represents by *aw*, "but the Americans almost
universally preserve the analogous sound, as in *bath, path*."   Webster's sound in *bath, path* was [aɪ], but in regions outside New England, the sound would be [æ] in this word, as well as in *bath, path*.
Since the English practice is erroneous, says Webster, "let it remain
so; we have no concern with it."   Benezet, p. 147, gives *wrath*
(anger), and *wroth* (to be angry) as pronounced alike.

The similar pronunciation of *wrap* as [rɔp] occurs in present
English mainly as a Southern provincialism, but it was used by
Seba Smith in the Jack Downing papers as a New England pro-
vincialism of the early nineteenth century.   For occurrences in
present dialect use, see the indexes to the several volumes of *Dialect
Notes*.

For *tassel* ['tæsl] of standard speech, a dialect from *tossel* ['tɔsl]
is current in various localities in America (see the citations in *Dialect
Notes*).   This is evidently a survival from an earlier seventeenth

and eighteenth century pronunciation, the earliest examples with *o* recorded in the *New English Dictionary* being for the end of the seventeenth century. It is mentioned by Nares, *General Rules* (1792), p. 9, as an exceptional but not improper pronunciation of *a*. Sheridan has only the pronunciation ['tɔsl] but Walker has only ['tæsl]. Webster (1828) gives *tossel* as a variant spelling and pronunciation of *tassel*, but does not condemn it. The origin of the [ɔ] in this word is not clear. It has been suggested that the word came to be associated in thought with the verb *toss*, and by popular etymology, took the vowel of *toss*. But it seems improbable that this should happen so late in the history of the word, even granting that the connection in sense between *tassel* and *to toss* was sufficiently close to cause such an analogy to operate. It seems more probable that the word being from its first meaning an ornamental bunch of silk, a fashionable rather than a popular word, came to be associated in the eighteenth century with the polite value of *a*, which, as was pointed out above, in many other words of similar character was taken to be [ɔ]. In America this polite word then was applied to the tassel of the Indian corn, the word thus becoming a genuinely popular word and continuing to the present in popular dialect speech in the form *tossel*, the form in which it was originally taken over from polite into popular use.

(3) [ɛ] as in *set*

If one could accept the descriptions which some of the earlier phoneticians give for their equivalent of this sound, one would have to assume that in the course of time a considerable change had taken place in the pronunciation of a very large number of words in which it occurs. Webster insists that "*late* and *let* being pronounced with the same aperture of the mouth, and with the same disposition of the organs, as nearly as the consonant *t* will permit, must contain the same vowel," *American Spelling Book*, p. 13. If this statement were interpreted literally, it would mean that the vowel of *let*, as Webster heard it, differed only in quantity from the vowel of *late*.

Yet Webster himself soon after speaks of *late, let; ask, hat; here, fit,* etc., as illustrating "different qualities of the same sound." But how could *late* and *let* have "the same sound" if the vowels in the words were different in quality? The same point is labored in the *Dissertations*, pp. 83, 377, with the same inexplicable confusion between quantity and quality. "Thus *i* in *fit* has the same quality of sound as *ee* in *feet*, for both are pronounced with the same disposition of the organs; but the first is the shortest articulation of the sound, and the last, a long or grave articulation." "The other vowels," he continues, "have also their short or abrupt sounds; *a* in *late* has its short sound in *let*; *a* in *cart* has its short sound in *carry*; *a* in *fall* has its short sound in *folly*; *oo* in *fool* its short sound in *full*." Now when Webster says that the vowel of *carry* is the short vowel of *cart*, this statement is a physical absurdity, unless one pronounced *carry* as ['kɑrɪ], a pronunciation which Webster certainly did not have in mind. If the vowel of *cart* [kɑːrt] was [ɑː], the equivalent short vowel would be [ɑ], and [æ] would be, both by the test of the ear and by the test of the manner of its organic formation, quite a different sound. It seems strange that an observer of Webster's keenness should have been guilty of such confusion of statement. His error, however, was one to which phoneticians of his time were quite generally subject. It arose from the notion that a vowel, or rather a letter, had a sound which expressed its inherent and natural character, a character as definitely fixed by the quality of the sound as the character of iron and lead were fixed by their respective qualities. Thus if the "natural" value or "power" of the letter *a* were taken to be [eː], its peculiarly English sound, as it was often described, one might then be led to speak of other sounds, for example [ɛ,] as variants of the essential sound. This was what Webster did, and therefore when he declares the vowel of *let* to be the same as the vowel of *late*, only short, one cannot assume that the vowel of *let* was [e.] The same applies to the vowels of *sit* and *full*, which, according to Webster's statement, would be [i] and [u], but which, in actual speech, were probably [ɪ] and [ʊ]. To be sure it is not impossible that the vowels of words like *let, sit, full* were really higher and nearer like the long sounds in quality in the eighteenth century than they now are, but Webster's description of these sounds gives no trustworthy proof that this was so.   What he says is so obviously not to be taken at its face value that it rather proves the opposite than the positive of what it affirms.   This faulty statement of the case was one that Webster never corrected.   The *Elementary Spelling Book* (1843), p. 8, is not so insistent on the identity in quality of the vowels of *late* and *let*, but the statement there made, that "the long sound of *a* in *late*, when shortened, coincides nearly with that of *e* in *let*," is not less absurd from the point of view of the science of phonetics than the earlier statement.   If the sound of *a* in *late* is shortened and then coincides with the vowel of *let*, it ceases to be the same vowel.

The rimes of the earlier poets do indeed in some instances indicate a vowel [e] or [eɪ] in words which now have [ɛ] and which were ordinarily recorded with [ɛ] in the dictionaries and other descriptions of pronunciation of the eighteenth century.   Most of these words are such as had by origin a long vowel, e.g., *spread, head, breast, tread*, which later became shortened, just as the vowel of *deaf*, which Webster defends as correctly pronounced [diːf], became shortened to [dɛf].   Thus the following rimes occur in Barlow's *Columbiad*: *shade: spread*, pp. 170, 175, 182, 317; *spread: trade*, pp. 173, 341; *outspread: pervade*, p. 66; *breast: waist*, p. 83; *head: maid*, p. 125; *spread: glade*, p. 175; *tread: shade*, p. 191; *paid: head*, p. 239; *spread: bleed*, p. 258; *taste: breast*, p. 375, and many others like these.   In the *Conquest of Canaan*, by Dwight, similar rimes occur, e.g., *display'd: o'erspread*, p. 2; *array'd: head*, p. 5; *dread: shade*, p. 7, etc. Dwight rimes *said* and *maid*, but *said* long continued with some speakers to be pronounced [seɪd], even after it had ordinarily been shortened to [sɛd].   The pronunciation with [eɪ], [eɪ], is still heard in the north of England, see Jespersen, I, 325.   If one may trust his rimes, this was Freneau's regular pronunciation.   The shortening of [eɪ] to [ɛ] in the forms of this verb, as in *says* [sɛz], *said* [sɛd], resulted probably from their frequent use in unstressed positions. In Ladd, *head* rimes with *made*, p. 67, and *spreads* with *shades*, p. 119.   On p. 37 *spreads* rimes with *meads*, but as *mead* rimes with *stray'd*, p. 118, and *shades*, p. 155, and as Ladd ṣeems frequently to have had [eː] where standard pronunciation now has [ɛ], it seems probable that he pronounced *mead* as [meːd]. In Honeywood, p. 120, *evade* rimes with *head*. These rimes offer fairly convincing evidence that many words which in Old and Middle English had long vowels, but which acquired shortened vowels in early Modern English, were still pronounced at times with long vowels in the eighteenth century. In his *Greenfield Hill*, Dwight rimes *spread: display'd*, p. 39, and *spread(s)* with *shades*, p. 40, *made*, p. 43, *survey'd*, p. 71, and *cascades*, p. 152. He rimes *head* with *display'd*, p. 47, *shade*, p. 51, and *dead* with *unpaid*, p. 89. In several instances he rimes words with an historically short vowel with words having a long vowel, e.g., *led: shade*, p. 104, *decay'd: fled*, p. 129, *shame: them*, p. 154, but rimes like these are rare and are best explained as inexact rimes. In Trumbull's poems, one finds *head* riming with *aid*, II, 44, *afraid*, II, 61, *parade*, II, 65, *display'd*, II, 94, *glade*, II, 115, *shade*, II, 178; *spread* rimes with *shade*, II, 215; and there are many similar rimes.

These original long vowels were shortened under conditions not clearly known, conditions also which operated with a singular irregularity, *dead, breast*, for example, and *deed, east*, now having different vowels, though they started with the same form in early Modern English. So also we have *breath* with a short vowel, and *heath* with a long vowel, both going back to the same vowel in Old English. That *heath* has the same vowel as *breath* in some dialectal uses is indicated by the spelling *heth* for *heath* in Hardy's *Return of the Native* in the dialect speech of Devonshire characters. The explanation sometimes given of this change, that the vowel was shortened before point consonants, is an explanation that neither explains nor fits all the examples. But whatever the explanation, it seems probable that older pronunciations of some of the words still persisted in the eighteenth century and are recorded in the rimes of the poets given above. These pronunciations have completely disappeared, except for a few popular survivals, like [deːd], [heːd], written *daid* and *haid* in dialect stories, for *dead, head*.

An interesting picture of the extent of this former divergence and confusion in usage is afforded by the comments of Mackintosh. On p. 45 of his essay he gives *bread, dead, head, knead, lead* (verb), *meadow* as having only [eː], and *read* (pret. of *to read*), *spread, ready, stead, steady, thread, weapon, early, beat* (pret. of *to beat*), *leaven, steak, break*, only [ɛ]. He also remarks that *ea* followed by two consonants generally has the value [eː], as in *beard, cleanse, dealt, death, earl, earn, earth, hearse, learn, search, treacherous*, but that the sound is [ɛ] in *feather, leather, neather, heard, meant*, and adds that though one pronounces [eː] in *breath, death*, one says [ɛ] in *health, stealth, wealth*, and in *dearn* or *darn, hearken, heart*, one has [æ]. That the distinctions in sound intended are as Mackintosh has described them is evident from his key of sounds. In his key he gives *bread, yet, great, bear, ere*, as exemplifying a sound [e], long and short, and *bell, bent, bend*, as exemplifying [ɛ], long and short. For *e* with the value of [i], long and short, his examples are *seen, scene*, and for *a* with the value of [e], long and short, his examples are *ale, date, hate*, and as a long grave sound, the vowel in *care, day*, as a short grave, the vowel in *any*. This last pronunciation is either a spelling pronunciation, or it may reflect the earlier value of the first syllable of *any* as derived from Old English *ǣnig*. Mackintosh's distinctions of length of vowels are hard to follow; for example, he gives the vowel of *date* as being [e] short, and the vowel of *hate* as [e] long, but it is quite clear that he meant no distinction of quality between the vowels of *date* and *hate*, or between those of *ace* and *bread*. To some extent Mackintosh's descriptions were influenced by formal standards, especially spelling, but they scarcely could have departed widely from practice as he observed it in the careful speech which he approved.

In dialect speech, as was pointed out above, some of these pronunciations with long vowels may still be heard, e.g., *dead, head*, pronounced [deːd], [heːd] or *deaf* pronounced [diːf]. In his *Dissertations*, p. 128, Webster says that *deaf* "is generally pronounced deef." This he declares to be "the universal practice in the eastern states" and to be "general in the middle and southern;

tho some have adopted the English pronunciation *def*." On the grounds of analogy to such words as *leaf*, *sheaf*, etc., Webster defends [diːf] and long continued to support it. Staniford, p. 66, writing in 1797, records the pronunciation *def* as a vulgarism for *deef*. But *def* was the only pronunciation recorded by Walker, and very probably Webster's ear, in the case of this word, was tuned more in harmony with analogy than with the real speech of his day. Even in the dictionary of 1828 he continued to defend [diːf], declaring that "the true English pronunciation of this word is *deef*, as appears from the poetry of Chaucer, who uniformly makes it rhyme with *leaf;* and this proof is confirmed by poetry in the works of Sir W. Temple. Such was the pronunciation which our ancestors brought from England . . . *Def*, from the Danish and Swedish pronunciation, is an anomaly in English of a singular kind, there being not another word like it in the language." Of course the pronunciation [dɛf] owes nothing to Danish and Swedish pronunciation, and when Webster says that this is the only pronunciation of the kind in English, the statement is true only in so far as an earlier long vowel has been shortened before *f* in this word; the same shortening has occurred, however, before other consonants in many words, sometimes in violation of what would seem to be obvious analogies, as in *breath* [brɛθ], but *heath* [hiːθ], both from words with the same long vowel in Old English.

The pronunciation [dɛf] is the only one authorized by Worcester, 1830, and from Worcester it passed into the later editions of Webster.

A similar shortening took place in the word *weapon*, which in present standard speech is always ['wɛpn], but which persists in dialect speech (see *Dialect Notes*, I, 69) as ['wiːpn] and is frequently recorded as *weepun* in literary transcriptions of Wild West speech. Walker, under the word *weapon*, says that the word "is not infrequently pronounced with *ea* long, as in *heap*, *reap*, etc.," but he rejects this pronunciation as contrary to the statements of the orthoepists, and in his opinion, to the best usage. The earlier American dictionaries regularly record the word only with a short vowel.

The pronunciation *weepons* is indicated for central Georgia by R. M. Johnston, *Mr. Absalom Billingslea*, p. 12.

In the word *wreck* [rɛk] usage is now uniform, but an older pronunciation [ræk] formerly competed for favor with [rɛk]. The older form still survives in the alliterative phrase, *rack and ruin*, in which the spelling *wreck* has been modified to accord with the pronunciation. A similar modification presumably appears in the title *Castle Rackrent*. In poetic or literary usage, as in "the wrack of a storm," the archaic pronunciation survives. The form [ræk] is occasionally mentioned by the early grammarians as an impropriety, e.g., by Dearborn, *Columbian Grammar* (1795), p. 137, by Staniford (1797), p. 72, and as late as 1828 in the fourth edition of Jaudon's *Union Grammar*, p. 214. The pronunciation [ræk] accounts for the rime *attack: wreck* in the *Anarchiad*, p. 37, and *back: wreck*, Hitchcock, p. 137. The only pronunciation recorded by Sheridan for *wreck* is [ræk], but by the end of the century this pronunciation seems to have given place pretty completely to [rɛk], which is the only pronunciation recorded by Walker. In England as in America the spelling spoke decisively for the form [rɛk].

A variation between [ɛ] and [æ] occurred also in the word *catch*, though the situation was here reversed, since [kætʃ] was the defended and [kɛtʃ] the reprehended pronunciation. The form [kɛtʃ] has by no means died out of the English language, and may be heard frequently on the lower colloquial level and occasionally even on the higher colloquial level. The variant [kɛtʃ] goes back at least as far as the seventeenth century, and it has given rise to the word *ketch*, a kind of vessel. Early plays on the name of the hangman, Jack Ketch, also indicate the prevalence of the two pronunciations of *catch* (see the *New English Dictionary*, under *catch, ketch, Jack Ketch*). The presence of [kɛtʃ] in standard eighteenth-century speech is attested by the rime *fetching: catching*, Trumbull, I, 57. The form [kɛtʃ] is usually included in the lists of vulgar pronunciations which began to appear in the grammars of the late eighteenth and early nineteenth century. The inference from this is that the pronunciation was in pretty general use. As in the case of *wreck*, however, the influence of spelling was so strongly in favor of [kætʃ] that the form [ketʃ] could not maintain itself in cultivated use, though it is still widely used in popular speech. Walker in his "Rules to be observed by the Natives of Ireland in order to obtain a just Pronunciation of English," p. 10, gives [ketʃ] for *catch* as one of the pronunciations to be corrected. The pronunciation was a common inheritance to both Irish and American English from British English. But at another place Walker, p. 12, speaks of "a corrupt but received pronunciation" of *a* as [ɛ] in *any, many, catch, Thames,*" a remark which shows that in 1791, [ketʃ] still moved in good company. Nares, *General Rules* (1792), p. 10, gives *catch, gather, January, jasmin, many, radish, thank* as all having [ɛ] for *a*, and remarks that of these *gather* and *thank* with [ɛ] are confined to familiar use. Elliott and Johnson, in their *American Dictionary*, 1800, give *ketch*, a ship, and *catch* as sounding alike, p. 23, but a little later, p. 30, they stigmatize [ketʃ] as a vulgar error. It was probably one of those errors that were reprehended at one moment and practised at the next. In popular speech, *radish* is now frequently pronounced ['rɛdɪʃ], and this pronunciation was recognized as early as Benezet, pp. 147–154, who gives the adjective *reddish* and the noun *radish* as having the same pronunciation. Cobb, pp. 168–172, corrects *redish* for *radish*, also *gether* for *gather*, and *rassle* for *wrestle*. For *have, has*, Franklin's transcriptions show that his pronunciation was [hɛv], [hɛz]. Lowell, *Biglow Papers*, p. 33, gives *hev* and *hed* as common New England rustic usage for *have, had*, and it is not probable that [ɛ] was very general in cultivated speech in *have, has, had* after the close of the eighteenth century. It is still occasionally recorded in literary transcriptions of rustic New England speech.

For the vowel of *yellow*, a popular dialect pronunciation with [æ] still exists, and one finds this pronunciation among those contained in the earliest lists of pronunciations to be corrected. Walker notes that Sheridan, Nares, Scott and Fry all pronounce this word to rime with *tallow*, but Walker disapproves this pronunciation and thinks it borders "closely on the vulgar." Here again the influence of spelling has spoken decisively against a pronunciation ['jælo] both in England and America.

For *keg*, two pronunciations were formerly generally current and both may still be heard, [kɛg] and [kæg], though the latter is now rare except as a local dialect pronunciation. The spelling *kag*, *cag* is also recorded in the earlier dictionaries and spellers, and is defended by Webster in the dictionary of 1828 as the better form of the word. Walker has both *keg* and *cag*, but he has only one pronunciation, *keg* being given as pronounced [kæg]. But the spelling *keg* seems always to have been the more general and to have determined the ultimate preference in favor of [kɛg].

Variant pronunciations ['sɛlərɪ] and ['sælərɪ] also occurred formerly for *celery*, but the second has now disappeared. Elliott and Johnson correct the pronunciation [flɛks] for *flax*, to [flæks], p. 30. They also record *mash* for *mesh*, p. 24, and this form of the word is given in Webster's early dictionaries and even in the dictionary of 1828, though he remarks here that *mesh* is the common spelling. The etymology of this word, which is probably of Dutch origin, is uncertain (see *New English Dictionary*, under *mesh*), and it is recorded in English only from the sixteenth century. Earlier spellings like *meishe, meash*, however, indicate a long vowel which has been shortened, like the vowel of *flesh* from Old English *flœsc*, giving the form *mesh*. But from the time of this shortening probably a variant form *mash* existed by the side of *mesh*, and only in fairly recent times has usage finally settled on *mesh* as the only correct form of the word. With *mesh* pronounced with a long vowel should be compared *freesh*, *Southold Records*, I, 5 (1651), also II, 6 (1665), for *fresh*, and *leese* for *less*, I, 127 (1665). A pronunciation of *fresh* with a long vowel seems to be indicated for the dialect of the Tennessee Mountains in Charles Egbert Craddock's literary version of that dialect, as in *The Young Mountaineer*, p. 17, *a fraish start*.

For [θræʃ] Webster records both the spellings *thresh* and *thrash*, but remarks that the common pronunciation is that which accords with the second spelling. Both spellings persist but the pronunciation remains almost universally [θræʃ], especially as applied to grain or to whipping. As the name of a bird, *brown thrasher* occurs. This seems to have been the older established pronunciation, since Walker has only the form *thrash* for the word.

Nares, *General Rules*, p. 20, gives [æ] as the proper pronunciation for *e* in *celery, clerk, mesh, sergeant, terrier, yellow*. In common usage, *e* in *errand, errant* were also pronounced [æ], says Nares, but "are more becomingly pronounced with the proper short sound of e." But the older pronunciation of *errant* still survives in the form of the word written *arrant*, as in "an arrant knave." Shreve, *Speller's Guide*, Buffaloe, Virginia, 1824, gives *exle-tree* as the proper spelling, but pronounces *exle* as though it were written *axle*.

The spellings of the early town records show numerous occurrences of the spelling *e* for [æ] and also of *a* for [ε], and examples of both will be given here. Thus we find frequently spellings like *Jenery* for *January, Watertown Records*, p. 39 (1654), *mege* for *Maggie*, ibid., p. 41 (1654), *Rendall*, also *Randoll, Randall*, ibid., p. 42 (1655) *Fleg* for *Flag*, ibid. p. 73 (1661), and so very often, though also sometimes *Flag*. In *Springfield Records*, I, 228 (1653), occurs *mester* for *master*, and ibid., I, 232, *mestr* for *master*. In *Groton Records, January* is written *genewar*, p. 68 (1681), and so often, *Jeniwary*, p. 91 (1685), *salary* is written *sellerie*, p. 67 (1681), *slant* is written *slent*, p. 74 (1682). The spelling *hev, heve* for *have* occurs, *Plymouth Records*, II, 156 (1700); *Easthampton Records*, II, 104 (1681); and elsewhere not infrequently. Unusually frequent in the *Groton Records* is the spelling *a* for *e*, as in *salackt* for *select*, p. 71 (1682), and often, *whather* for *whether, atand* for *attend*, p. 71 (1682), *wast* for *west*, p. 75 (1682), *panc* for *pence*, p. 92 (1685), *matt* for *met*, p. 103 (1691), *fach* for *fetch*, p. 103 (1691), *cradit* for *credit*, p. 104 (1692), *prascot* for *Prescott*, p. 126 (1705), *capt* for *kept*, p. 127 (1705), *racun* for *reckon*, p. 125 (1704), *salf* for *self*, p. 127 (1705), *satel* for *settle*, p. 127 (1705), and dozens of other spellings like these. They are so numerous that one questions whether they may not have been merely orthographic substitutions of *a* for *e*, without a corresponding substitution in the scribe's speech of a pronunciation [æ] for [ε]. But the spellings are found in the records of different recorders and therefore are not to be explained as an individual habit of spelling. Similar spellings are also found in the records of other towns and unquestionably reflect a very general characteristic of pronunciation. They are, for example, unusually abundant throughout the *Hempstead Town Records*, as at I, 161 (1665), where one finds *fance* for *fence*, *nack* for *neck*, *mande* for *mend*, *manchened* for *mentioned*, *panlty* for *penalty;* *had* is written for *head*, I, 174 (1665); on p. 163 (1665), occurs *lankth* and *brath* for *length* and *breadth;* I, 100 (1661), *Lanck* occurs for *length*. In *Plymouth Records*, II, 96, and often elsewhere, *sexton* is spelled *saxton*, a form of the word which still persists in the proper name *Saxton*. In the same records, II, 215 (1721), the name *Wrestling Brewster* is spelled *Wrastling Bruster*, and [ræsl] is still a popular pronunciation for *wrestle*. In *Watertown Records*, p. 128 (1677), occurs *raddy* for *ready*, p. 115 (1673), *selackt* for *select*. Kruisinga, *Grammar of the Dialect of West Somerset*, § 151, gives numerous examples of this interchange of [ɛ] and [æ] in the dialect of West Somerset.

In a great many words which now have [ɛ] usage formerly vacillated between [ɛ] and [ɪ]. This is usually considered nowadays as one of the marks of Irish-English pronunciation, and is often explained as having made its way into American speech through the extensive Scotch-Irish immigrations of the late seventeenth and eighteenth centuries. It was formerly current, however, as a general feature of popular American speech. Thus Seba Smith, in the Jack Downing papers, uses freely such pronunciations as *inemy*, *gineral*, *Sinnet*, for *enemy*, *general*, *Senate*, as features of Down East dialect in which the possibility of Irish influence is excluded. Cooper, in his Leather Stocking Tales, especially in the first, *The Pioneers* (1823), and the last, *Deerslayer* (1841), of the series, uses abundantly such pronunciations as *ind* for *end*, *inemy* for *enemy*, *sintence* for *sentence*, *gin'rous* for *generous*, *rigiment* for *regiment*, *endivours* for *endeavours*, *frind* for *friend*, *chist* for *chest*, *invy* for *envy*, not only in the specifically Irish dialect of Irish characters, such as Mrs. Hollister and her husband in *The Pioneers*, but also in the speech of characters like Natty and Hurry Harry, who are supposed to speak a genuine vernacular in keeping with their typically representative Americanism in thought and feeling. It was certainly not Cooper's intention that these pronunciations were to be taken as Irishisms in American speech, but as established habits in the pure native dialect. It is true that Irish immigration was greater into Pennsylvania and the North Central States generally than into New England, and conceivably Cooper might have used dialect characteristics of the locality with which he was most familiar without discriminating very clearly with respect to their appropriateness to the characters in whose speech they are found. In *The Pioneers*, the main current of interest of the characters in the outside world, as of Cooper himself, flows westward and south to Philadelphia. On the other hand, Cooper is so obviously attempting to be realistic in dialect in the tale, with his British English of Ben Pump, his French English of Le Quoi, his German English of Major Hartmann, his negro English of Agamemnon, his New England English of Remarkable Pettibone and Elnathan Doolittle, his Irish English of Mrs. Hollister and her husband, to say nothing of the impossible elegant English of his genteel characters, that one hesitates to think that in his native homespun American he has included traits of mixed historical origin. Here, if anywhere, one ought to be able to trust Cooper's correctness of intuition and observation. And as a matter of fact, this particular detail of the change of [ɛ] to [ɪ] in words spelled with *e* can be shown to have been so old and so general in American speech as to make it unnecessary to call in the aid of the Irish immigrant to explain its presence. That Irish English in America and American English should have many traits in common is entirely to be expected, and is to be explained by the fact that the English spoken in Ireland by those Ulsterites who formed so large a part of the early Irish immigration to America was merely a transferred form of seventeenth and eighteenth century British English. American English had the same source, and for this reason characteristics common to Irish and to American English are often to be explained simply on the ground of common origin.

In the naïve spellings of the early town records, *i* for etymological *e* occurs with great frequency, and the spelling undoubtedly reflects a very general habit in pronunciation.   Thus in *Watertown Records* we find *alphabitical*, p. 13 (1647), for *alphabetical*, *gitt*, p. 17 (1648), and often elsewhere for *get; Ginery, Ginrie*, and other spellings for the proper name *Chenery; ginerall*, p. 89 (1666), for *general; middooes*, p. 114 (1672), for *meadows; aginst*, p. 114 (1672), for *against*.   In the *Groton Records* we find *trible*, p. 27 (1669), *git*, p. 41 (1672), *ginnrall*, p. 64 (1681), and so often, *midow*, p. 75 (1682), *hilld*, p. 75 (1682), for *held, ind*, p. 91 (1685), for *end, comminsment*, p. 104 (1692), *frinds*, p. 108 (1693), *represintiue*, p. 124 (1703).   In the *Dedham Records* occur *frind*, IV, 67 (1663) and so often; *intered*, IV, 57 (1662), for *entered, git*, IV, 54 (1662), *gineraly*, V, 80 (1678), *intire*, V, 100 (1680), for *entire*.   In the first volume of the *Plymouth Records* occur *prigudice*, I, 186, for *prejudice; Insine*, I, 192, and so often, for *Ensign; rigements*, I, 214; *Rid oake*, I, 55, 57, and so very often, for *red oak*, though sometimes also *red ook* is the spelling found; *primises*, I, 110, for *premises*.   In *Springfield Records*, II, 401 (1716), occurs *instid* for *instead*.   In *Huntington Records* occur *hild*, p. 47 (1663), for *held, crives*, p. 318 (1681), for *crevice; primises*, p. 408 (1684), for *premises, kicham*, p. 415 (1685), and so often, for the proper name *Ketcham*, often also spelled *kecham, pible*, p. 517 (1688), for *pebble*.   In Green, *Three Military Diaries*, 1775–1779, occur *rigiment*, p. 83, *yit*, p. 85, *git*, pp. 86, 91, *domistick*, p. 96, *yisterday*, p. 99, *frinds, p.* 88.   In the *Hempstead Records* [ɪ] for [ɛ] occurs frequently, as in *oursilves*, I, 16 (1657), *fichte* for *fetched*, I, 17 (1657), *gineral*, I, 18 (1657), *Hinery* for *Henry*, I, 18 (1657), and so commonly, *alphabit*, I, 19 (1657), *finse* for *fence*, I, 25 (1657), *lingthe* for *length*, I, 26 (1657), *watermillion*, I, 134 (1663), *hild* for *held*, I, 135 (1694), *Livetenant*, I, 145 (1663), etc.   In the *New Haven Records* occurs *chist* for *chest*, p. 26 (1639), and elsewhere; *thridd* for *thread*, p. 176 (1656); also *watermelon*, spelled *-million*.   In Puritan days, as later, the watermelon must bear the blame for occasioning certain moral delinquencies.   In 1647 "Wm. Pert was warned to the court [the General Court at New Haven] for taking water-myllions one Lords Day out of Mr. Hook's lott"; he confessed that "he tooke 2 watermillions, he said it was the first act of his in this kind and hoped it should be the last." For the "unrighteousness and profannesse of his sperit and way" he was sentenced to be publicly corrected, "although moderately because his repentance did appeare," *New Haven Records*, p. 325. On another occasion Margaret Cadwell, Elizabeth Downinge and Joseph Guernsie "went forth . . . to eat watermjllions, about one a'clock at night, and were fownd by the watch," *New Haven Records*, p. 327 (1647), an adventure which caused idle tongues to wag. At Norwich, Connecticut, September 19, 1720, before a justice of the peace, Lettice Minor and Hannah Minor were charged with taking "about 30 water milions which is contrary to law," but the court after considering the evidence "don't find matter of fact proven," therefore gallantly acquitted the defendants and placed the charges on the plaintiff, Barber, *Connecticut Historical Collections*, New Haven, 1836, p. 302. Considering the latitude in which these depredations on water milion patches are placed, one wonders if the melons were really watermelons and were not muskmelons. The pronunciation of *melon* as ['mɪljən] persists now mainly in Southern negro dialect, but as the above citations show, it was formerly common in the North as well as South. In Seba Smith's *My Thirty Years Out of the Senate*, New York, 1859, p. 32, *water million* occurs as a Maine dialect pronunciation of the third decade of the nineteenth century.

Some further proof of the earlier respectable pronunciation of present *e* as [ɪ] is afforded by Franklin's transcriptions, which show that he said [frɪnd] for *friend*, p. 303, and also [gɪt] for *get*, p. 301. In *Eine nuetzliche Anweisung*, p. 19, *friend* is given as pronounced with the same vowel as *field*, which would seem to mean [iː]; on p. 33, *yes* is given as pronounced with [ɪ.] The rime *friend: wind* in Freneau, p. 279, indicates a pronunciation of *friend* with [ɪ]. Other rimes of the same kind are *sin: agen* (Dwight's spelling for *again*), in *Greenfield Hill*, p. 135; *cleanse: sins* in Trumbull, I, 26, *engines: Indians*, ibid., I, 50, *again ye: ninny*, ibid., I, 51; *forgetting: Britain*, ibid., I, 164. In the *Anarchiad*, p. 108, the rime *instance: against us* was possible only with the pronunciation [əgɪnst]. In Ladd, p.

130, occurs the rime *mince: sense;* Hitchcock, p. 153, rimes *wit* with *yet*.

Indication of the extent of the pronunciation of words containing *e* with [ɪ] in New England, is afforded by the grammars and dictionaries of the late eighteenth and early nineteenth centuries which universally legislate against it. This means of course that the practice was one of long standing and that the books were attempting to correct an error only after it had established itself. Their main reason for objecting to the pronunciation of *e* as [ɪ] was the violation which this pronunciation committed against the analogies of spelling. So powerful has been this objection that scarcely any of the words in question can now be heard with [ɪ] except occasional old-fashioned survivals, like ['kɪtl] for *kettle*, or familiar colloquialisms, like [gɪt] for *get*. The old lists indicate, however, a wide range in usage. Dearborn (1795) notes for correction *ginnerally* for *generally*, p. 135, *sildom* for *seldom*, p. 138, and *frind* for *friend*, p. 135. Staniford (1797) corrects *chist* for *chest*, p. 66, *dint* for *dent*, p. 67, *innimy* for *enemy*, p. 67, *gineral, ginerous, git* and *ginesis* for *general, generous, get* and *genesis*, p. 67, *instid* for *instead*, p. 70, *trible* for *treble*, p. 71, *yit* for *yet*, p. 72. Johnson and Elliott (1800), pp. 30–31, give [əgɪn] as the correct pronunciation for *again*, marking [ə'geɪn] as an incorrect pronunciation, but they note the following for correction: *benificence* for *beneficence, chist* for *chest, divil* for *devil, frind* for *friend, git* for *get, gineral* for *general, instrip* [sic] for *instep, muskmillion* for *muskmelon*, and *yit* for *yet*. Ussher, pp. 95–96, gives *frind, invy, stiddy*, as improprieties for *friend, envy, steady*. Many of these pronunciations continue to appear in later lists of improprieties, but by the second quarter of the nineteenth century most of them seem to have sunk to the level of sheer vulgarisms. Yet in Jaudon's *Union Grammar* (Fourth Edition, 1828), prepared as a guide for the young ladies in a fashionable girls' school by their "Late Ladies Preceptor," one still finds *kittle, sildom, ginnerally, Jinnewary, watermillion, mushmillion, yisterday*, and *yis* (for *yes*), listed as sins to be avoided. This condemnation of *yis* for *yes* is the first instance the writer has met with of the specific rejection in America of the pronunciation of *yes* with [ɪ]. The early dictionaries show a remarkable agreement in preferring the pronunciation with [ɪ], and this is one of the points on which Walker holds the same opinion as Sheridan. Under the word *yet* Walker remarks that "the *e* in this word is frequently changed by incorrect speakers into *i*," and then adds that "though this change is agreeable to the best and most established usage in the word *yes*, in *yet* it is the mark of incorrectness and vulgarity." The pronunciation *yis* was approved by Lindley Murray, and on his authority and that of Walker, it passed into many American grammars and guides to pronunciation. It is recorded without comment in Coxe's *New Critical Pronouncing Dictionary*, and in Allison's *American Standard*, but since both of these works are avowedly based upon Walker, their pronunciation cannot be accepted without question as current usage in America. On the other hand, Webster in his first two dictionaries, 1806 and 1807, records only *yes*, without comment, nor has he discussed this subject in his *Dissertations*, as he surely would have done if a pronunciation *yis* were generally current in his day. Moreover since neither the form *yes* nor *yis* is criticized in any of the early lists of improprieties that the writer has met with, such as Dearborn's or Staniford's or Elliott's, it seems probable that the appearance of the word in later lists, as in Jaudon (1828), who rejects the form *yis*, and in Kelley, *The American Instructor* (1825), p. 10, who approves it, was due to literary influence and not to direct observation of speech. For these reasons it seems reasonable to suppose that *yis* was never a general pronunciation for *yes* in America, though it may have been cultivated by some few people on the authority of Walker and Sheridan as a British refined pronunciation, and on the other hand may have been current as a popular pronunciation of the same class as *git* and *yit* for *get* and *yet*. Lowell, in the *Biglow Papers*, p. 36, records *yis* for *yes* as rustic New England usage in his day, together with other similar pronunciations, e.g., *instid* for *instead*, *yit* for *yet*, and *git* for *get*. In a Connecticut tale published in the *Yale Literary Magazine*, Vol. IX (1844), p. 75, etc., an old hunter uses the form *yis*. Mackintosh, p. 27, gives not only [jɪs] for *yes* as correct, but also [blɪs] for *bless.* Alexander, *Columbian Dictionary*, gives *yes, yester(day), yest (yeast), yet*, all as having [ɪ] but ordinarily, as in *bless, get*, he gives [ɛ].

The pronunciation of *Jenny* as ['dʒɪnɪ] is now heard in America only in low colloquial and popular speech, but it persists in England as a frequent cultivated usage. Undoubtedly the spelling has crowded out the pronunciation with [ɪ] in America.

These instances of the change of [ɛ] to [ɪ] fall into two main groups, those in which the vowel is preceded by a palatal consonant, and those in which it stands before a nasal. The change in the first group may be characterized, therefore, as a kind of palatization, the vowel being raised and fronted under the influence of the preceding consonant. The physiological cause for the change of [ɛ] to [ɪ] before nasals, especially [n], may not seem so apparent, but the change has been noted so often at different times and in different languages that its physiological character can scarcely be doubted. Being an alveolar lingual sound, [n] would readily cause the fronting of a sound that preceded it. When the change took place in early stages of English, the spelling was modified to accord with the pronunciation, as in *string, wing* from Middle English *streng, weng*. In *England, English*, however, the phonetic change has taken place, but the spelling has not been made to conform. These two words are exceptional, however, in being proper and official names about which conservative traditions have clung with unusual tenacity.

In connection with the pronunciation [frɪnd] for *friend* [frɛnd], it is interesting to note that in his first two dictionaries Webster gives the pronunciation [fɛnd] for *fiend*, the word being spelled *fiend*, with the *i* marked as silent and the *e* without the customary accent which, in these books, indicates length. In the dictionary of 1828, Webster seems to have changed his mind, for there he records only [fiːnd]. That the pronunciation [fɛnd] was a current eighteenth-century pronunciation in America is evident from Freneau's verse, in which one finds *fiend* always riming with words that have [ɛ], e.g., *fiend: bend*, p. 101; *end: fiend*, p. 139, *intends: fiends*, p. 166, *contend: fiend*, p. 186, *sends: fiends*, p. 195. In Alexander's *Columbian*

Dictionary, the only pronunciation given for *fiend* is [fɛnd], and for *friend* is also [frɛnd].

The word *chemist* and related forms is universally spelled with *e* in America, and pronounced ['kɛmɪst]. In England it is commonly written *chemist*, but is pronounced either ['kɛmɪst] or ['kɪmɪst]. Formerly the spelling *chymist, chimist,* was also current, the spellings with *e* and *y, i* being reflections of two different conceptions of the proper etymology of the word, for the details of which see the *New English Dictionary* under *alchemy, chemist,* etc.   Most of the older dictionaries preferred the form of the word with *y, i,* including Johnson, Perry, Sheridan, Walker and even Webster as late as 1828, who settled the whole question with his usual dictatorial certainty, though wrongly from the point of view of modern scholarship.   Worcester (1830), however, exhibits his usual good luck in picking out the winning form and records his preference for *chemist*.   In America the written form with *e* has been the determining influence in pronunciation, causing the pronunciation with [ɪ] completely to disappear.   As the word has always been more or less learned, it has responded readily to the changes of learned opinion.

In another group of words which now uniformly have [ɛ] one finds that earlier usage vacillated between [ɛ] and [iː].   Examples of these recorded for correction are *leest, neest, jeest* for *lest, nest, jest,* by Webster (1783), p. 30.   We find also the correction *least* for *lest,* and *neest* for *nest,* in Dearborn, p. 137, and besides these two words Staniford gives also *geast* for *jest,* p. 68.   In the *Letters of J. Downing, major, to his old friend, Mr. Dwight,* New York, 1834, p. 87, one finds this sample of Down East dialect: "if some on 'em hain't siled their own neests, I'm mistaken."   Cobb, pp. 168–172, gives *jeste,* meaning [djiːst], as an impropriety for *jest*.   The word *deaf* has already been mentioned.   Nearly all the lists give *eend* for *end,* and Lowell, p. 39, gives this pronunciation as one that he was familiar with in New England.   It is frequently indicated in Haliburton's *Connecticut Clockmaker*.   That it was a common characteristic of early American speech is clearly indicated by the fact that it is frequently employed by Longstreet, *Georgia Scenes*, p. 163, and elsewhere, as one of the marks of Georgian colloquial speech. On the other hand, in the word *yeast*, modern usage has only [iː], but earlier had both [iː] and [ɛ]. Walker records only the pronunciation *yest*, though he spells the word *yeast*. Both *yeast* and *yest* are given in Elliott and Johnson and in Webster's first two dictionaries. In the dictionary of 1828, however, Webster has only [jiːst], and by that time [jɛst] had probably disappeared from general cultivated speech. Yet Cobb, pp. 168–172, gives *yeste*, meaning [jiːst], as an impropriety for *yest*.

For the proper name Esther ['ɛstər], Cooper, *The Prairie* (1827), chapter 118, indicates the pronunciation ['iːstər], spelled Eester, the name of Ishmael Bush's wife, characterizing this as "the provincial pronunciation of America for the name." The word *tester* is recorded as having only the pronunciation ['tiːstə] in Charleston, South Carolina, Primer, *Phonetische Studien* (1888), I, 231, and this can still be heard elsewhere as an old-fashioned pronunciation. Bradford, pp. 19–28, gives *Easter* and *Hester* (a woman's name), as having the same pronunciation. Mennye (1785), p. 91, gives *Easter* and *Esther* as sounding alike.

In Barlow's *Hasty Pudding* one finds *jest* riming with *beast*, which seems to indicate a pronunciation [dʒiːst]. On the other hand, one finds *feast* riming with *prest*, *drest* and *breast*, which would indicate, if one accepts the rimes as exact, a pronunciation [fɛst], or a pronunciation [priːst], [driːst] for *pressed*, *dressed*, neither inference, therefore, being certain. The spelling *reast* for *rest*, *Groton Records*, p. 115 (1695), indicates a pronunciation [riːst]. In *Huntington Records*, p. 317 (1681), *cheasts* for *chests* indicates [tʃiːsts]. Similar spellings occur frequently in the *Hempstead Records*.

The word *retch* is commonly pronounced [retʃ] in America, but occasionally in popular pronunciation it is heard as [riːtʃ]. The word is said by Walker to be derived "from the same Saxon original as the verb to *reach* and seems to signify the same action; the one implying the extension of the arm; and the other, of the throat or lungs." Walker concludes that no good reason exists either for spelling or pronouncing the word differently, and though he does accept the spelling *retch*, he declares that "the pronunciation of both continues the same." Walker's etymology is not correct, but it is true that the vowels in *retch, reach*, both go back to the same vowel, *æ*, in the Old English originals of these words, and that consequently both should have by regular development [iː] in Modern English. The short vowel in *retch* may be due to the vowel of *stretch*, in which the short vowel is etymologically correct. Cummings, p. 145, gives *retch* and *reach* as sounding alike.

Cummings, p. 156, also says that *age* and *edge* are likely to be confused, meaning of course that *edge* is likely to be pronounced [eɪdʒ]. This pronunciation appears dialectally in present English, not only before [dʒ] but also before [g] in the words *egg, beg, leg*, etc. Cobb, pp. 168–172, gives *aje* as an impropriety for *edge*. Fowle, *Companion to Spelling Books*, Boston, 1843, p. 118, gives *aigs, baigs, laigs* as vulgarisms for *eggs, begs, legs*. R. M. Johnston, *Mr. Absalom Billingslea*, p. 128 and often, writes *aige* for *edge* in early nineteenth-century Georgia speech.

(4) [ɛɪ] as in *there*

This sound occurs in present American English in many words with *e, ea, ai* before *r*, as in *there, bear, fair*. In present British speech the vowel in such positions is marked short by the phoneticians, who give a pronunciation ['ðɛə], ['bɛə], ['fɛə], for these words. In American English, however, even when *r* is not pronounced, the vowel seems to be ordinarily long, the two current pronunciations being ['ðɛɪər], ['bɛɪər], ['fɛɪər] and ['ðɛɪə], ['bɛɪə], ['fɛɪə].

By origin, Modern English [ɛɪ] usually represents a Middle English sound of similar character, that is a long open *e*-vowel. Ordinarily Middle English open *e* [ɛː] and close *e* [eː] have had the same result in development, both becoming Modern English [iː]. This applies both to native words and to French and Latin borrowings with [ɛː], [eː], which entered before the regular transition of these sounds into Modern English [iː]. Two words like present *deed* and *heed* therefore no longer reflect their diverse origins from West Saxon *dǣd* and West Saxon *hēdan*, though in Middle English they might have been distinguished, and were distinguished in the rimes of Chaucer, by the fact that the first word had an open vowel [ɛ:,] the second a closed vowel [e:]. In words of the first type, however, considerable diversity of dialectal usage existed even in Old English times. The vowel which appeared in West Saxon as *æ* [æ:] was in Mercian and Anglian *e* [e:], and this [e:] would appear in Middle and Early Modern English as [e:]. This diversity did not affect the final result since in the end Middle English [ɛ:] ordinarily became [e:] before the transition of [e:] into Modern English [i:]. Old English short *e* in open syllables underwent the same changes, first lengthening into [ɛ:] and then, according to the ordinary rule, becoming [e:] and finally [i:]. Thus Old English *stelan, etan, wefan*, etc., became Modern English *steal, eat, weave*, etc.

The distinction between Middle English [ɛ:] and [e:] becomes historically important, however, in words in which these sounds appear before [r]. In this position [e:] consistently becomes [i:] as in *here, deer, hear*, etc., and [ɛ:] also in most instances follows the rule and becomes [i:] as in *ear, spear, tear* (noun), *fear, rear*, etc.; but on the other hand it often also remains as [ɛ:], as in *tear* (verb), *bear* (verb and noun), *share, where*, etc. This situation was obviously one that would result in divergences of usage, *sheer*, for example, by the side of *share, keer* by the side of *care, cheer* by the side of *chair*, and many others indicated by similar spellings in the writings of the early grammarians. Middle English *a* [ɑ:] in the open syllable, which would ordinarily become Modern English [e:], persists as a lowered vowel [ɛ:], before r, as in *fare, prepare, declare*, etc.

Starting from a Middle English [ɛ:] vowel before *r*, one must therefore always keep in mind the possibility that in any word under question, this vowel may have remained unchanged, or may have followed the ordinary development to Middle English [e:], may then have persisted as this sound, or have developed as one expects Middle English [e:] to develop, into [i:]. The three shades of sound which one would then have to consider, on this side, would be [ɛ:], [eɪ] and [iɪ]. But on the other hand the vowel quality of [ɛ], before r has very generally shown a tendency to lower still further, as for example in the change of early Middle English *fer, derk* into *far, dark,* and later changes such as *merchant* to *marchant, person* to *parson,* etc. A similar change may be noted in the case of [ɛɪ], and the stages of this change would be [ɛɪ], [æɪ], [ɑɪ], the final stage being represented by the familiar dialect pronunciation of *there* as *thar, bear* as *bar,* etc. This has been described as "the most conspicuous instance of a Southern mode of pronunciation," and as having "turned *affair* into *affarr, declare* into *declar, hair* into *har, stairs* into *stars,* etc.," Thornton, *An American Glossary,* I, 40. It is, however, by no means peculiar to Southern American English in its origins, but is merely one of those variants in words of this type which formerly was much more general, occurring in New England as well as in the South. In the North it has been practically exterminated by popular education, and in the South it lingers only as a colloquialism verging on the illiterate.

The descriptions which the earlier phoneticians give of the sound which corresponds to [ɛɪ] in present English are extremely unsatisfactory because of the difficulty of telling just what the descriptions mean. Thus Walker has no special designation for a sound [ɛɪ], but marks the vowels of *fair, fare,* and of *fate* in the same way. Yet one hesitates to believe that these words all had [eɪ]. Nor has Webster in the *American Spelling Book* a separate symbol for a sound [ɛɪ], or any indication that such a sound existed, *air, chair, fair, hair, pair,* being listed in the same class as *haste, taste,* and numerous other words with [eɪ], p. 45. Even in the dictionary of 1828 Webster did not make formal recognition of the difference between [ɛɪ] and [eɪ], and *fair, fare,* and *fate* are still marked in the body of the dictionary as having the same vowel. In the prefatory *Directions for the Pronunciation of Words,* however, he does remark that the presence of r "occasions a slight change of the sound of *a,* which can be learned only by the ear." There is no reason to suppose that this change was of recent occurrence. It was without a doubt present in speech long before the phoneticians had devised a

means for recording it. Once recognized, the distinction between
[ɛɪ] and [eɪ] was seen to be necessary and is now found even in the
most elementary works on pronunciation.

Franklin's record is not clear, but he seems to have made a slight
attempt to record the sound. Ordinarily he indicates the vowel in
words like *fair, their, compared,* by the same method as the one used
for vowels in words which undubitably had [eɪ]. For the word
there, however, he has recorded a pronunciation, p. 301, which in
modern transcription would be ['ðæər], and this certainly was a step
in the right direction, though it seems strange that Franklin did
not use the same pronunciation in *fair, their, compared.* In Alexander's *Columbian Dictionary* (1800), a great deal is made of the
sound in *fare, their, were, wear,* etc. It is described as the circumflex sound of *a,* p. 8, and so distinct from all other values of *a* that
the author had intended to distinguish it by a special new character
and only refrained from doing so, using the ordinary long *a,* as in
bake, hate, etc., instead, because the printer could not supply him
with an appropriate type. The nature of the sound he describes
more fully, p. 10: "The sound of *a* in *bare,* though long, is really
distinct from the sound of *a,* in *bate.* In forming the sound of *a,*
in *bate,* there is an aperture of the mouth, without any contact of
the organs. But the aperture is greater in sounding *a,* in *bare,* and
approximates near to the aperture of sounding *ă,* in *ball.*" The
exact sound that Alexander means to describe is not clear, but it
would seem to be even lower than [ɛɪ] and approximately [ɑɪ] or [ɔɪ].

One of the earliest American phoneticians who made clear the
distinction between [eɪ] and [ɛɪ] was Duponceau. He names [ɛɪ]
Airish, and [eɪ] Azim, and not only distinguishes sharply between
[ɛɪ] and [eɪ] but also between [ɛɪ] and [æɪ], p. 253. Duponceau also
states that the Virginians "in almost every case" substitute [æɪ]
for [ɛɪ], pronouncing *there, where, stairs* "as if they were written
thahr, whahr, stahrs." "This vicious pronunciation," he adds, "is
striking to those who are not accustomed to it, and shows the essential difference which exists between the two sounds," that is, between
[ɛɪ] and [æɪ].

Willard's remarks, p. vii, may also be noted. He explicitly rejects the sound of the vowel of *care* as [eɪ], as given by Walker, and says it is "precisely that of *can*, or *carry*, drawn out to a greater length or duration. . . . Again Mr. Walker speaks of the *a* in *carry* as having the short sound of *a* in *father;* a sound essentially the same [according to Walker] and differing only in duration. To my ears, the difference between these two sounds is essentially the same with the difference between the *a* in *care* and *a* in *car*."

In the absence of any exact earlier descriptions of the shades of sound which occurred in words containing *a, ea, ai* before *r*, one is enabled to make only such inferences from indirect evidences as seem probable. Many of the rimes of the New England poets indicate not only that modern [ɛɪ] was pronounced as [æɪ], the preliminary stage to what later became Southern and Northern dialectal [aɪ] in *there, bear, bare*, etc., but that even some words which have [iː] in present English, for example, *ear, year*, were formerly pronounced with a very open vowel, [ɛɪ] or [æɪ]. Thus in the *Anarchiad* one finds the rime *ear: Registrar*, p. 35, which can mean only a pronunciation [ɛr] or [æɪr], for *ear*. With *war*, pronounced [wæɪr], one finds the rimes *despair*, p. 37, and *bear*, p. 62, and *bears* is made to rime with *appears*, p. 16. Dwight, *Conquest of Canaan*, rimes *glare* with *star*, p. 32, and *air* with *afar*, pp. 142, 293. On the other hand, he rimes *ear* with *declare*, pp. 15, 32; *year* with *care*, pp. 20, 160, *there*, p. 39; *fear* with *prayer*, p. 25, *wear*, p. 5; *fear'd* with *despair'd*, p. 24; *tear* (noun) with *care*, p. 219; *rear'd* with *declar'd*, p. 136; *spear* with *air*, pp. 144, 278, *hair*, p. 188. The rime *drear: care*, p. 127, might be interpreted as calling either for a pronunciation [dreɪr] or a pronunciation [kiːr]. The latter was undoubtedly current in Dwight's day and is frequently reprehended in the early grammars. Dwight also rimes in this poem *peer* with *fair*, p. 77, and *appear* with *there*, p. 146, and it seems most probable that these last three rimes, if not inexact rimes, are to be taken as illustrations of the attraction of words with [eɪ] into the group of those with original [ɛɪ]. Other rimes in Dwight's *Greenfield Hill* are *dear* with *air*, p. 14; *ear* with *prepare*, p. 98; *near* with *there*, p. 110; *fear* with *care*, p. 111, *bear*, pp. 40, 132; *tears* with *prayers*, p. 112; *rear* with *care*, pp. 136, 143, *glare*, p. 157; and *years* with *cares*, p. 45, *wares*, p. 50. As to the word *rear*, it may be noted in passing that the pronunciation [ræɪr] or [rɛɪr] is still very general in American popular pronunciation. Further rimes which indicate [æɪ] for [ɛɪ] are the following from Barlow's *Columbiad: there* riming with *star*, pp. 304, 333; and *air, spare, share, care, prepare, blare, glare, snare, despair, bear, bare*, all riming with *war*. Words which now have [iː] in present standard speech, but which according to Barlow's rimes formerly had [ɛɪ], [æɪ], are *year* riming with *air*, p. 57; *rear* riming with *war*, pp. 74, 222, *declare*, p. 131, *repair*, p. 151, *compare*, p. 379, *dare*, p. 382, *there*, p. 232; *ear* riming with *there*, p. 88; *near* riming with *air*, p. 113. In Trumbull's verse, *air, share, despair, spare* rime with *war; scarce* rimes with *farce*, I, 46; *chairman* with *alarming*, I, 104; *prepar'd* with *guard*, I, 112; *hair* with *tar*, I, 165; *air* with *car*, II, 115; *cares* with *stars*, II, 174. On the other hand, *spears* rimes with *shares*, I, 137; *sneer* with *there*, II, 52; *fear* with *there*, II, 101; *rear* with *war*, II, 94. In Freneau, whose manifest care in riming makes his evidence of special importance, the following have been noted: *air* riming with *star*, p. 22, *far*, p. 113; *fair* riming with *are*, p. 353; *were* riming with *are*, p. 70; *there* riming with *afar*, p. 142; *prepare* riming with *are*, p. 208; *declare* riming with *war*, p. 313. Of words with [iː] in present English, we find *year* riming with *there*, p. 24, *affair*, p. 276; *near* riming with *care*, p. 52; *rear* riming with *there*, p. 142; *clear* riming with *air*, p. 156; *ears* riming with *bears*, p. 257. The rime *prepar'd: beard*, p. 332, indicates the frequent eighteenth-century pronunciation of *beard* as [beɪrd], and the rime *heard: appear'd*, pp. 151, 320, indicates either a pronunciation [hiːrd], very general in the eighteenth century, or more probably a rime [hɛrd]: [əˈpeɪrd].

In the poems of Ladd the following are to be noted: *spear: there*, p. 13; *appear: war*, p. 43, and *appear(ed)* riming with *heard*, p. 63, *care*, p. 67, *herd*, p. 74, *wears*, p. 84, *cymar*, p. 77; *spear(s)* riming with *hair*, p. 56, *bears*, p. 84; *steer: share*, p. 75; *here: care*, p. 68; *fear(s)* riming with *wear*, p. 120, *dares*, p. 128, *are*, p. 139; *severe: there*, p. 138; *tear* (noun): *Falconer*, p. 146; *fear it: merit*, p. 150;

bears: rears, p. 52. In the verse of Honeywood, New York, 1801, *ear* rimes with *share*, p. 88, and *rear* with *wear*, p. 52. In *Heroes of the Lake*, New York, 1814, *appear(s)* rimes with *swears*, p. 46, *bars* [bærz], p. 52, *far* [fær], p. 64; *forbear* rimes with *here*, p. 60, and *bear* with *year*, p. 48.

These rimes taken together indicate with sufficient clearness that there was a tendency in the eighteenth and early nineteenth century to pronounce many [ɛɪ]- words with a still lower quality of the vowel than [ɛɪ], probably [æɪ]. As the vowel [æɪ] had not in general in the eighteenth century developed into the present English [ɑɪ] even in words of the type of *car, bar, war*, etc., one would not expect at this time to find an [ɑɪ] in words like *where, there, hair, bear*, etc. In fact, there is no evidence to show that [ɑɪ] was ever very general in New England cultivated speech in words of this type. By the time [æɪ] might have developed into [ɑɪ] the leveling tendencies of popular education seem to have established finally the vowel [ɛɪ] in New England, at least in standard speech. In the South the leveling out of [æɪ] for the standard [ɛɪ] took place more slowly and later, and in fact the sound may still be heard in the cultivated speech of localities. The lowering of [iɪ] before *r* also persists as a Southern localism, *tear* (noun) and *tear* (verb) having approximately the same sound, and *gear, deer, dear, appear, spear, here*, all being pronounced with the same vowel as *chair, stair*, etc., according to Primer, "Charleston Provincialisms," in *Phonetische Studien*, I, 233. In Fredericksburg, Va., the following words are listed as having a vowel "nearly like the sound in the French *père, faire*": *ear, here, pare, tare, bear, there, pear, tear* (noun and verb), *swear, wear, fair, hair, their, scarce, pair, prayer, stair, chair, cheer, spear, dare, gear, dear, deer, appear*, Primer, "Pronunciation of Fredericksburg, Va.," *Publications of the Modern Language Association*, V, 196 (1890). The pronunciation [ɑɪ] is also heard in many of these words, "among the uneducated," as in *where, there, stairs, bears*, etc., pronounced [wɑɪr], [ðɑɪr], [stɑːrz], [bɑɪrz]. "One person was heard to say, 'I'm goin' up the stars (meaning *stairs*, pronounced [stɑɪrz]) to see the *stairs* (meaning stars, pronounced [stærz])."

Both of these pronunciations were survivals of eighteenth-century pronunciations in good standing.

In *Recollections of a Southern Matron* (1837) by Caroline Gilman several of these pronunciations are mentioned in Chapter V as prevalent in Southern speech:

"I was called up to read a part of Collins's Ode on the Passions, and commenced with,

'First fare his hand its skill to try—

'Fare,' said Mr. Bates, 'how do you spell it?'

'F-e-a-r *fare*,' said I.

'How do you pronounce these words?' said he, pointing to *appear, ear, tear*, etc., in the spelling book.

"I answered *appare, are, tare*, etc.

"With equal impropriety I pronounced the words *day, play*, etc. almost like *dee, plee*, and my southern brethren must excuse me when I tell them, ay, very intellectual ones too, statesmen and belles, that many of them pronounce in this style unconsciously, and not only so, but often call fair *fere*, and hair *here*.'

"For instance,

> 'The tare down childhood's cheek that flows,
> Is like the dewdrop on the rose.'

Or,

> 'Wreath'd in its dark brown curls, her *here*
> Half hid Matilda's forehead *fere*.'"

The early grammarians call attention to several of these divergences in usage. Dearborn reprehends *cheer* for *chair, keer* for *care, keerds* for *cards, shear* for *share, skeer'd* for *scar'd*, pp. 134–138. He also notes as improprieties *war* for *were*, p. 139, and *carr'd* for *carried*, p. 114, *car* for *carry*, p. 134. Just what is meant by *carr'd, car* for *carried, carry*, is not clear, though the spellings suggest the same kind of monosyllabic guttural pronunciation that Whittier has indicated in *Skipper Ireson's Ride*:

> "Here's Flud (Floyd) Oirson, fur his hoord horrt,
> Torr'd and futherr'd an' corr'd in a corrt
> By the women o' Morble'ead."

Staniford, p. 66, also gives *cheer, keer* as incorrect pronunciation for *chair, care,* and one example of the reverse, *shares* for *shears,* p. 70. Johnson and Elliott, p. 28, give *sheer, shear, shire* as pronounced alike, and *share* as often incorrectly pronounced in the same way. They also correct a pronunciation *care* for *carry,* p. 30. Jaudon, pp. 213, 214, gives *cheers, kear, skeert* as improprieties for *chairs, care, scared,* and *skase* for *scarce.*

The spelling *stears* for *stairs, Lunenburg Records,* p. 82 (1732), indicates a pronunciation with [iː] in this word. The analogy here was the same as that which made *shares* like *shears.* In *Southold Records,* I, 218 (1666), *share(s)* is spelled *shears, sheirs,* and also *sheere,* II, 19 (1678), II, 40 (1697). Spellings like *yaere* for *year* in the *Hempstead Records,* I, 164 (1665), *aers* for *years,* I, 165 (1665), *aire* for *ear,* I, 166 (1665), *nare, aer* for *near, ear,* I, 164 (1665), *aears* for *ears,* I, 173 (1665), *ayer* for *ear,* I, 193 (1666), *eyer* for *ear,* I, 218 (1695), seem to indicate beyond a doubt the pronunciation [ɛː] in these words. This is in fact one of the most distinctive features of language in these records.

The word *weir,* for catching fish, is now commonly spelled with *ei,* and is pronounced with a vowel [iː]. But the dictionaries also record a spelling *wear,* which is more in accord with the etymological origins of the word and the analogy of words of similar type, such as *bear, tear, pear,* etc. Many spellings of the early town records indicate a pronunciation with the same vowel as that which appears in *bear, tear* (verb), *pear,* etc. Thus in the *New Haven Records,* p. 2 (1638), occurs the phrase *fish out of any ware.* In the *Plymouth Records,* I, 5, and so very often, the word is spelled *ware,* but sometimes, as I, 114, it is spelled *weire.* In other town records also the word appears in a form which indicates a pronunciation like that of *bear, pear,* etc.

(5) [ɪ] as in *sit*

No general change that is clearly traceable has affected this sound in any large group of words. It may be that the vowel was formerly pronounced with a higher value, approximately as [i].

This would make *sin* [sin] a fairly close rime to *seen* [siːn], and rimes like this occur not infrequently in the verse of the later eighteenth century.   Webster treats the vowel of *sin* as he treats the vowel of *let*, that is *sin* is said to contain the short vowel present in *seen*, as *let* is said to contain the short vowel present in *late*.   Though Webster insists that the difference between the sounds in these two pairs is merely one of quality, as was pointed out in the discussion of [ɛ], it is extremely doubtful if Webster meant what he seems literally to say.   But even if he did mean what he says, it is also uncertain whether or not his statement truly described the facts of even his pronunciation.   In this instance, as he not infrequently did in others, Webster may have formulated his statement to accord with his sense of seemliness and order, rather than with direct observation of speech.   Certainly at any period since the science of phonetics has been sufficiently advanced to make the statement of phoneticians precise and trustworthy, the value of *i* in words like *sit, sin, hid, with*, etc., has always been [ɪ].

In the early lists of improprieties, one finds among the words with [ɪ] for [ɛ] occasional instances of the opposite to this, that is, words with [ɛ] where on all counts one would expect [ɪ], e.g. *sense* for *since*, Dearborn, p. 138, *chentz* for *chintz*, Staniford, p. 66, *hender* for *hinder*, Staniford, p. 68, *American Spelling Book*, p. 34, *rense* for *rinse*, Staniford, p. 69, and Lowell notes, p. 34, *red* for *rid*, *tell* for *till*, *rense* for *rinse*.   These pronunciations are probably reflections of the confusion with respect to [ɪ] and [ɛ] which resulted from such double pronunciations as [frɪnd] and [frɛnd] for *friend*, and [gɪt] and [gɛt] for *get*.   The rime *stint: went*, Honeywood, p. 38, indicates a pronunciation [stɛnt] for *stint* which may still be occasionally heard.   Hitchcock rimes *since* with *defence*, p. 72, and *dispense*, p. 145.   Cobb, pp. 168–172, corrects *peth* for *pith*, a form still in general popular use.   He also corrects *resk* for *risk*, *red* for *rid*, *rens* for *rinse*, *sens* and *sen* for *since*, *stent* for *stint*, *ben* for *bin*, *klentsh* for *clinch*, *dent* for *dint*, *hender* for *hinder*, *led* for *lid*.

The pronunciation [ɛ] for etymological *i* is not infrequently indicated by the naïve spellings of the early town records.   Thus in the

Watertown Records we find *defference*, p. 11 (1647), and so often; *Kemball*, p. 13 (1647), and so often, for *Kimball; Whetney*, p. 13 (1647), and often, for *Whitney; henges*, p. 29 (1651), for *hinges; sells*, p. 91 (1667), for *sills; begen*, p. 98 (1669), for *begin*, and this spelling recurs frequently; *bredg*, p. 98 (1669), for *bridge; medle*, p. 99 (1669), for *middle; hendered*, p. 102 (1670); *convenced*, p. 103 (1670); *tell*, p. 110 (1671), for *till; enventory*, p. 110 (1671), for *inventory; enstant*, p. 110 (1671), for *instant; geven*, p. 118 (1673), and so often, for *given; phezick*, p. 124 (1675), for *physic; leburty*, p. 134 (1677), and often, for *liberty; Decks*, p. 135 (1678), for *Dix; fenished*, p. 144 (1679). In the *Braintree Records, hether* occurs, p. 302 (1750), and so frequently, for *hither*. In the *Lancaster Records, Whetcomb* for *Whitcomb* occurs, p. 231 (1725). In the *Plymouth Records, e* for *i* occurs very frequently, as in *hender*, I, 204, 336, etc., *lettle*, I, 185, 209, 248, etc., for *little*, also the proper name, spelled *Lettle*, I, 251, but *Little* a few lines below; *rever*, I, 198, for *river*, and so frequently; *detch*, I, 203; *bredge*, I, 215, and often; *betwext*, I, 237; *sence* for *since*, I, 252, etc., spelled *sience*, I, 295; *contrebute*, I, 254 and often; *hether*, I, 1, 77, for *hither; Prence*, I, 3, for *Prince*, and *Prence* is the common form for this family name in the *Records; wedth*, I, 324, spelled *weadth*, II, 154; *redg*, I, 272, and often, but also often *ridg(e); Medlebery*, I, 283 and often, for *Middlebury; drefts*, II, 198, for *drifts*. The word *been* is often spelled *bin, bine*, in the *Plymouth Records*, but also often *ben*, I, 252, 285, 294, etc. In the *Dedham Records*, occur *breng*, III, 29 (1636), and so often, for *bring; hether*, III, 47 (1638), for *hither; wedowe*, III, 50 (1638), and often, for *widow; commeted*, III, 141 (1656), for *committed; stenting*, III, 144 (1656), for *stinting; retmitick*, IV, 67 (1663) for *arithmetic; Endin*, V, 101 (1680), and often, for *Indian*. For *been* the spelling *ben* frequently occurs, as in III, 31. In the *Groton Records* occurrences of *e* for *i* are very numerous, e.g. *Whetney*, p. 11 (1664); *Skener*, p. 11 (1664), for *Skinner; leburty*, p. 14 (1665), p. 72 (1682); *indeferent*, p. 15 (1665); *wretten*, p. 16 (1665), for *written; prohebeted*, p. 16 (1665); *melle*, p. 16 (1665), and so often, for *mill; consedering*, p. 26 (1669); *mester*, p. 67 (1681), for *Mr.; Smethe*, p. 68 (1681); *nek*, p. 69 (1681), for *Nick; begen*, p.

72 (1682), for *begin; leueng*, p. 72 (1682), for *living; reuer*, p. 72 (1682), for *river; bredg*, p. 74 (1682); *untele*, p. 78 (1683), and often, for *until; bells*, p. 104 (1691), for *bills; Screptur*, p. 125 (1704), for *Scripture*, and so often; *menister*, p. 126 (1702); *letell*, p. 129 (1706), for *little; sexs shellings*, p. 126 (1705); *begening*, p. 127 (1705), for *beginning; geves, thes*, p. 127 (1705), for *gives, this*. In the *Huntington Records* occur *mell*, p. 24 (1660), for *mill; betterly*, p. 119 (1668), for *bitterly; Letell*, p. 406 (1684), a proper name; *untele*, p. 37 (1661); *betwext*, p. 37 (1661). In Green, *Three Military Diaries*, 1775–1779, occur *sperital*, p. 87, for *spiritual, speret*, p. 96, *incested*, p. 99, for *insisted*. In *Lunenburg Records*, p. 109 (1740), *under Pend* for *underpinned*, and *wedth* for *width* occur. The usual spelling for *district* in the *Hanover Records* is *destrict*, as on p. 90 (1790), and often elsewhere. In the *Southold Records*, I, 215 (1675), occurs *skelet* for *skillet*. In the *Hempstead Records* one finds *devesions* for *divisions*, I, 19 (1657), *mell Rever* for *Mill River*, I, 99 (1660), *pener, penner*, for *pinner*, a variant of *pinder*, "*pounder*," I, 100 (1661), *meddle* for *middle*, I, 34 (1660), *snep, hes*, for *snip, his*, I, 169 (1665), *engen* for *Indian*, I, 212 (1665). In the *Plymouth Records*, II, 198 (1710), we read that "Thare Is a high Way Reserved . . . for parsons to Travel In The Winter seson When The snow Leys in drefts." The spellings occur also in more dignified documents, as in Hazard, II, 109 (1648), *Cambredg;* II, 113, *Contrebute, enterest;* II, 243, *sence*. The reverse, *whither* for *whether*, occurs II, 110 and often; *kittles* for *kettles*, II, 243; and *frinds* for *friends*, II, 168, 408, and elsewhere frequently in these documents of the seventeenth century.

In some scattering words variations between a sound [ɪ] and other sounds long survived. For the word *been* the weight of authority as well as of practical use in America seems always to have been in favor of [bɪn]. According to the testimony of Franklin's phonetic transcription, p. 303, he pronounced the word as [bɪn]. Walker, under the word *been*, says it "is scarcely ever heard otherwise than as the noun *bin*." Webster consistently favors the pronunciation [bɪn], see *American Spelling Book*, p. 104, *Elementary Spelling Book*, pp. 146, 154, and his dictionaries. Elliott and Johnson, p. 18, spell it *bin* as an indication of their pronunciation, and the same pronunciation is indicated by various other grammarians. A pronunciation [bɛn] is occasionally reprehended by the early grammarians, for example, Jaudon, p. 213. It appears often in the naïve spellings of the early town records, and is frequently utilized in early nineteenth century plays to characterize rustic New England speech. *Southold Records*, I, 168, 395 (1681), has *ben*, but also *bine*, I, 278 (1667). This pronunciation persists in some local dialects, and it is the pronunciation which Whittier's rimes, as in the last stanza of Maud Muller, establish for him. The pronunciation [biːn] which is occasionally heard in present English in America is due either to the influence of the spelling, or of British pronunciation, in which [biːn] for *been* is widely current. The pronunciation [bɛn] is the only one recorded for *been* in Alexander's *Columbian Dictionary* (1800).

As derived from Old English *bēon*, with a long vowel, the form [biːn] for *been* is the one which corresponds to the regular development of Old English *ē, ēo*. The forms with shortened vowel, as in [bɪn], [bɛn], are variant developments of the word arising from its relatively unstressed sentence position. The tendency of conventional use in America has been to generalize upon the unstressed form [bɪn], but in England, upon the stressed form [biːn]. The same applies to the preterite *were*.

The early grammarians frequently reprehend the pronunciation ['spɛrɪt] for *spirit*. This pronunciation still survives in popular speech, but that it formerly occurred not infrequently in cultivated speech may be inferred from such rimes as *merit* with *spirit*, Humphreys, p. 230, Trumbull, I, 148, II, 41, Freneau, pp. 284, 343, Foster, p. 87, Hitchcock, p. 130, *inherit* with *spirit*, Trumbull, I, 86.

Another word which the grammarians frequently include in their lists of mispronunciations is *miracle*, according to report mispronounced as *meracle* or *maracle*, the two spellings probably indicating approximately the same pronunciation, that is ['merəkl]. Walker comments on this word and says that Sheridan "adopted a vulgar pronunciation" which made no distinction between *i* followed by *r* and a consonant and *i* followed by *r* and a vowel. Thus for this word

Sheridan gave a pronunciation *mer-* or *mur-*, as though it were a word like *birth*, or *virtue*, or *sir*, *stir*. Walker follows the rule which present English accepts and gives only [ɪ] for *i* followed by *r* and a vowel. The pronunciation of *miracle* with [ɛ] is thus similar to that of *spirit* with [ɛ]. In certain forms of present American dialect speech this vowel would be replaced by [ə], words like *very, America,* etc., also becoming ['vərɪ], [ə'mərɪkə], etc. Lowell, p. 39, records *meracles* as still surviving in his day in New England speech, and the early correctors of speech who mention *sperit* for *spirit*, also correct *meracle, maracle* [mær-] for *miracle*. The pronunciation was without doubt formerly more current in standard speech than is its present equivalent. Staniford, p. 67, gives also *surringe* as an impropriety for *syringe*, an illustration of the same tendency in pronunciation as that which changed *spirit* and *miracle* to their popular forms.

For *since*, the early grammarians sometimes note the pronunciation [sɛns] for correction. This still persists in dialect pronunciation, and its presence formerly in standard speech is attested by such rimes as *since: nonsense*, Freneau, p. 276, *since: defence*, Hitchcock, p. 72, *since: dispense*, Hitchcock, p. 145. Elliott and Johnson, p. 31, list *sen* as an impropriety for *since*. This is an archaic survival of a form that was frequent in Middle English but which has lived on only in the dialects. In *Southold Records*, I, 33 (1682), occurs the archaic form *sythence* for *since*.

For *hinder* an incorrect pronunciation [hɛn-] is frequently recorded, e.g., by Webster, *American Spelling Book*, p. 34. This persists as a dialect pronunciation.

For *stint* present dialect pronunciation has a form [stɛnt]. The pronunciation [stɛnt] was once in better standing, and a spelling *stent* even made its way into the dictionaries, see Webster's dictionary of 1828 and the *New English Dictionary* under *stint, stent*. But the word was probably often pronounced [stɛnt] even when spelled *stint*, as in the rime *stint: went*, Honeywood, p. 38. The word *stunt*, as a noun, meaning an assigned part in a common undertaking, often of amusement, appears to be a derivation from the word *stint*. It is not recorded in any of the older dictionaries, nor has it yet made its way as an accepted word in the modern dictionaries. For citations of its various uses, see the index to the several volumes of *Dialect Notes*.

For *rinse*, Staniford, p. 69, and other grammarians record a mispronunciation [rɛns] or [rɛnz]. This pronunciation of the vowel is the one given as correct by Nares, *General Rules* (1792), p. 23, and it still persists as a very frequent popular pronunciation, though the word is also often modified by analogy to *wrench* in such a way as to make the two words exact homonyms. Sherwood, *A Gazeteer* (1837), gives *rench* as a Georgia provincialism for *rinse*.

The pronunciation [sɛt] for *sit* has long been current in popular speech, but here also analogy has entered, the strong verb *sit, sat, sat*, being made to accord with the weak verb *set*. In the weak verb the preterite and past participle are like the infinitive, and in popular speech the strong verb also has commonly only the form *set* for all three parts.

In various other words [ɪ] has been replaced by [ɛ] in popular speech, e.g., *chintz* pronounced [tʃɛnts] Staniford, p. 66, and Lowell, p. 34, notes [rɛd] for *rid*, [tɛl] for *till*, and many other similar pronunciations may be observed in transcriptions of dialect speech. In cultivated speech, however, the influence of spelling has regularly restored [ɪ].

Cummings, p. 160, notes that *itch* is sometimes pronounced like *each*, but the vowel here is historically short. In the *Southold Records*, II, 301 (1694) *bedticking* is spelled *bed-teeking*.

Numerous examples of the pronunciation [ɛ] for *i* in the speech of southwestern England are given by Kruisinga, §154, also of [ɪ] for *e*, §168.

For *hymn* [hɪm] a dialectal pronunciation [haɪm] survives, and it is recorded as a Georgia provincialism by Sherwood, *A Gazeteer* (1837).

(6) [eː] as in *fate*

No general change has affected any group of words containing the vowel [eː], though divergent usages were formerly current in

several individual words.   One of these is the word *angel* ['eɪndʒəl].
Franklin records the word, but as he does not distinguish in his
script between [e] and [ɛ], one might interpret his writing as meaning
either ['endʒəl] or ['ɛndʒəl].   It is not probable, however, that
Franklin had any notion of indicating a short [e] vowel, and as he
says that he intends to indicate [eɪ] by doubling, i.e., by writing it
ee, and as he follows this rule consistently in the passage in which
angel occurs, one may conclude that his writing of *angel* with one *e*
is intended to indicate a vowel ['ɛndʒəl].

Sheridan and Walker both give the pronunciation ['eɪndʒəl], but
under the word *change*, Walker remarks that this word and others
like it, e.g., *range, strange, mange*, etc., are "in the west of England,
pronounced with the short sound of *a* in *ran, man*, etc."; and he
declares further that the same pronunciation exists in *angel, ancient*,
etc., "which, in that part of the kingdom, sound like the article *an;*
and this, though disagreeable to a London ear, and contrary to the
best usage, which forms the only rule, is more analogical than pronouncing them as if written *chainge, strainge, aincient, aingel*, etc.,
for we find every other vowel in this situation short, as *revenge,
hinge, spunge*, etc."

The practice of his own country, as well as analogy, convinced
Webster that the only justifiable pronunciation was ['ændʒəl].   Noting that the British pronunciation is sometimes anomalous where
the American is "regular or divided," as in the word *deaf*, pronounced
[dɛf] in England but [diːf] in America, he rejects the British pronunciation of *angel, ancient* as *anegel, anecient*, and maintains that
there is "no shadow of reason why *a* in *angel, ancient*, should have a
different sound from that in *angelic, antiquity, angle, anguish*."
"In these and many other words," he concluded, "the pronunciation
in this country is more correct than that of the English; and it
would be reprehensible servility in us to relinquish a correct practice
and adopt an English corruption," *Compendious Dictionary*, 1806,
p. xv.   Webster had previously defended the pronunciation ['ændʒəl]
in his *Dissertations*, p. 93, where he remarks that the British pronunciation with [eɪ] "is followed in the middle and southern states;

but the eastern universities have restored these words to the analogy of the language, and give *a* its second sound," that is [æ]. Cooper, *Notions*, II, 131, observes that a student from a middle state returning to his home from Yale exposed himself to ridicule by using the pronunciation "'virtoous an-gel,' pronouncing the first syllable of the last word like the article."

It is doubtful, however, if the restoration by the Eastern universities, by which Webster means Harvard and Yale, was as complete as Webster thought it to be. His love of New England localisms and his passion for analogy seem to have led him in this respect, as often in others, to a more dogmatic statement than usage warranted. But if Walker's statement that [æ] in *angel* was characteristic of the west of England and Webster's that the same pronunciation prevailed in New England, are true, we may look upon this coincidence as an authentic instance of the influence of the west of England pronunciation upon New England pronunciation. The fact, however, that present standard English has given up [æ] in *angel*, *ancient*, and has only [eɪ], need not be regarded as evidence of "reprehensible servility" to British usage, but as another indication that the general standard of pronunciation in America has been determined more by Webster's "middle and southern states" than by his New England. Webster did not advocate [æ] in words like *change, range, strange*, though probably it existed in rustic New England speech. Franklin records *changing* as ['tʃendʒɪŋ], and in his transcription of Lowell's rustic New England speech, Grandgent, p. 239, gives *changed* as ['tʃændʒd]. Webster held on to the pronunciation ['ændʒəl] as long as he could, but in the dictionary of 1828 he sadly gives it up, remarking that the word is "usually pronounced *angel*, but most anomalously."

In the *Easthampton Records*, II, 104 (1681), occurs the spelling *exchenge* for *exchange*, doubtless one of a number of survivals from southwestern British dialect in these early American documents. Kruisinga, §202, gives *angel, danger, stranger, change, range*, as having [æ] in West Somerset.

The word *chamber* has had a somewhat similar history. Sheridan

records only [æ] as the vowel of the stressed syllable, Walker prefers
[eɪ], and says that "about thirty years ago the first syllable of *chamber*
was universally pronounced so as to rhyme with *Palm, Psalm,* etc."
but that the vowel is now "fully established" as [eɪ]. He regrets
this but accepts it as a fact. As Walker pronounced *palm, psalm*
with [ɑɪ] the older pronunciation of *chamber* here described would
be ['tʃɑːmbər]. This is the pronunciation which Webster recommends in his *Dissertations*, p. 94. "It is necessary to remark this,"
he says, "as there are many people in America who give *a* its first
sound [i.e. eɪ] which is contrary to analogy and to all the Englisl
authorities." It was not, however, contrary to Walker, whose
dictionary appeared in 1791, two years after Webster's *Dissertations*.
In the dictionaries of 1806 and 1807, it is impossible to tell whether
Webster meant to indicate a pronunciation with [ɑɪ] or with [æ],
though it is quite clear that he did not mean [eɪ]. In the dictionary
of 1828 he gives both ['tʃeɪmbər] and ['tʃɑːmbər] and remarks that
"the first pronunciation is most common; the last, most analogous
and correct"—a sad capitulation of principle in one who always
maintained that usage determined correctness. Lowell wrote
chămber for this word, but whether he meant to indicate ['tʃæmbə]
or ['tʃɑɪmbə] as the rustic New England pronunciation of his day
is not clear, probably the former. He plainly did not mean a vowel
[eɪ]. The only form of the word now current is the one with [eɪ].
Ussher records *charmber* as an impropriety for *chamber*. By this
spelling with *r* he seems to have meant to indicate a vowel [ɑɪ], but
it is impossible to tell whether the vowel he preferred was [eɪ] or
[æ]. Mackintosh, p. 15, records the word only with the vowel [æ],
which he marks as long because it is accented. Alexander, *Columbian
Dictionary*, records it only with [ɑɪ]. Cooper, *Notions*, II, 133, gives
[æ] as a characteristic New England pronunciation in *chamber, angel*
and *danger*, the rest of the country having [eɪ] in these words.

The word *drain* [dreɪn] still has a popular variant form [driɪn],
and this is noted as an error to be corrected by Dearborn, Staniford,
Webster, Johnson and Elliott, Jaudon, and doubtless by other early
grammarians. It seemed good enough to Webster, however, to be

included in the dictionaries of 1806 and 1807, where both spellings, *drain* and *dreen*, are recorded. But in the dictionary of 1828, the form *dreen* is dropped without comment. In the *Plymouth Records*, the spellings *drenes*, II, 35 (1710), and *drean*, II, 47 (1711), indicate a pronunciation with [iː].

The pronunciation of *James* as [dʒiːmz] still lingers in occasional dialectal uses, as in the rustic pronunciation of the name of the James River in Virginia. Its wider use in seventeenth and eighteenth century English is attested by frequent spellings, e.g. *Jeames, Dedham Records*, III, 59 (1639).

Cummings, p. 146, gives *scene* and *seine* as sounding alike, that is, both with the vowel [iː]. This is the only pronunciation for *seine* given by Worcester, both in his first edition and in the revision of 1859. It is given by Webster in his dictionary of 1828, and though the common pronunciation of the word now has [eɪ], the pronunciation with [iː] still appears even in some of the more recent American dictionaries. The *New English Dictionary* records only the pronunciation with the vowel of *sane* for *seine*.

In present standard American pronunciation the word *vase* has three pronunciations, [veɪs], [veɪz] and [vɑːz], and it would require detailed statistical investigation to determine which of the three is most common. The pronunciation with [ɔː] is now only humorous, but Walker remarked that the word was sometimes pronounced "by people of refinement," with the *a* like *aw*, but this," being too refined for the general ear, is now but seldom heard." The refined pronunciation with [ɔː] was merely the eighteenth century way of producing the effect of the continental *a*, and is like other similar words, for example, *eclat*, noted above under the discussion of [ɑː]. The eighteenth century pronunciation [vɔːz] thus stands for its day in the same position as [vɑːz] for the present. The naturalized English pronunciation would be [veɪs] or [veɪz]. Sheridan gives only [veɪs], but Walker says he has heard the word uniformly pronounced with the *s* like *z*. In his earlier dictionaries and in the dictionary of 1828, Webster gives only [veɪs]. Freneau rimes *vase* with *face*, p. 110, *place*, p. 111, and *race*, p. 120. The traditional pronunciation is undoubtedly [veːs], and the analogy of words like *chase, erase, base,* etc., tends to establish this pronunciation in a very strong position.   The word, however, is often a parlor or polite word, and thus is subject to change according to the whims of fancy. The modern predilection for [ɑɪ] as a cultivated pronunciation accounts for the present frequent pronunciation [vɑɪz].

For *raisin,* Webster, *Dissertations,* p. 116, says a pronunciation *reesin,* i.e. [ˈriːzn] is "very prevalent" in two or three principal towns in America, but he prefers the pronunciation with [eɪ] on the ground of "derivation, analogy and general custom."   Staniford, p. 67, gives *reasons* for *raisins* as an impropriety, and the pronunciation is mentioned by other grammarians.   Sheridan and practically all the other dictionaries except Walker, give only [eɪ] as the vowel in the word, but Walker, p. 26, declares that *"raisin,* a fruit, is pronounced exactly like *reason,* the distinctive faculty of man."   From Walker the pronunciation passed into many other books written under his influence, for example, Cummings, p. 145.   In support of his pronunciation, Walker, under the word *raisin,* cites the pun in Shakspere, *Henry IV,* Part I, Act II, Sc. IV, in which Falstaff declares that if reasons were as plenty as blackberries, he would give no man a reason upon compulsion.   This he thinks proves that *reason* and *raisin* were "pronounced exactly alike in Shakspere's time" and that Sheridan's pronunciation of *raisin* "as if written *ray-sn,* is not only contrary to the most settled usage, but destructive of the wit of Shakspere."   The pun does not of course prove that this word regularly had [iː] in Shakspere's day, for if the pronunciation with [iː] had only been occasional, the pun would still have been permissible.   There is also the other probability that *reason* could be pronounced with [eɪ] in Shakspere's time, a kind of pronunciation still surviving in Irish English.   A similar pun occurs in *Winter's Tale,* II, III, 91, where *beat* must be pronounced with [eɪ] to justify the pun on *baits.*   But whatever the antiquity of the pronunciation of *raisin* with [iː], its popularity in America, as Webster says, was probably limited to several urban localities.

For *naked*, Fowle, *Companion to Spelling Books*, p. 119, records
the variant vulgarism *necked*, which is still widely current in popular
speech.

(7) [iː] as in *feet*

Sheridan, p. 59, mentions as one of the peculiarities of Irish
pronunciation the use of [eː] for [iː] in words like *tea*, *sea*, *please*,
deceit, *receive*, etc., and this has always been one of the common
marks of Irish English as employed by dialect writers in America.
Early examples will be found abundantly in the speech of Teague
O'Regan in Brackenridge's *Modern Chivalry*. But the pronunciation
was formerly current also in American cultivated speech. Webster,
Dissertations, p. 114, notes that *deceit, conceit, receipt*, "are generally
pronounced by the eastern people," that is, the people of New
England, as *desate, consate, resate*. He calls this an error for the
correct pronunciation with [iː], and adds that this latter is "the practice in England, in the middle and southern states, and, what is
higher authority, analogy warrants the practice." The presence
of the pronunciations *resate, consate, desate* in New England in the
eighteenth century can scarcely be accounted for on the ground of
Irish influence, but they are to be explained, as were the cases of
[ɪ] for [ɛ] noted above, as survivals from earlier British usage common
both to American and Irish English. For the origin and distribution
of the sound in England, see Wyld, *History of Modern Colloquial
English*, pp. 209 ff. Jespersen points out, *Modern English Grammar*,
I, 337, that Irish agrees in this respect with the dialects of southwestern England, represented, for instance, by Fielding in spellings
like *maneing* for *meaning*, *bate* for *beat*, and by Hardy in spellings
like *mane* for *mean*, *spaik* for *speak*, *clane* for *clean*, etc. Numerous
examples are given by Kruisinga, *A Grammar of the Dialect of West
Somerset*, p. 155. We seem to have here, then, another instance
of agreement between the characteristic speech of New England
and the southwestern dialects of the English of the mother country.

The spellings of the town records often indicate a pronunciation
[eː] where present English has [iː]. Thus in the *Watertown Records*

we find *spake*, p. 17 (1648), p. 92 (1667), for *speak; resaights*, p. 116 (1673), *resaite*, p. 122 (1674), for *receipts, receipt; naythur*, p. 114 (1672), p. 135 (1677), for *neither; aythur*, p. 114 (1672), p. 122 (1674), for *either*. In the *Duxbury Records* the name *Peabody* is frequently spelled *Pabodie*, p. 5 (1642), *Paybodie*, p. 38 (1683), etc. As these records are printed in modern spelling, except the proper names, they offer little evidence for pronunciation. In the *Plymouth Records* occurs the phrase *for brach of law*, I, 169, for *for breach of law*. For *either, neither*, however, the spelling *ither*, I, 193, *nyther*, II, 168, indicate a pronunciation with [aɪ]. In the *Dedham Records*, IV, 48 (1662), and so often, *receive* is spelled *recaiue*. In the *Groton Records*, the spelling frequently indicates a pronunciation [eɪ], as in *lauing*, p. 64 (1681), p. 74 (1682), for *leaving; rasin* for *reason*, p. 65 (1681); *pase*, p. 71 (1682), for *peace; sason*, p. 72 (1682), for *season; ayther*, p. 74 (1682), for *either; spachy*, p. 75 (1682), *spashy*, p. 76 (1682), *spashie*, p. 91 (1685), for *specie; dasant*, p. 77 (1682), for *decent; lagully*, p. 77 (1683), and so often, for *legally; trat*, p. 79 (1683), for *treat; sats*, p. 79 (1683), for *seats*, and so often; *Dackins sate*, p. 80 (1683), for *deacon's seat; resaigt*, p. 86 (1683), for *receipt; resaiued*, p. 86 (1683), for *received; what*, p. 88 (1684), p. 91 (1685), for *wheat; sased*, p. 88 (1684), for *seized; plase*, p. 91 (1685), for *please; Dackn*, p. 92 (1685), for *deacon; prach*, p. 103 (1691), for *preach*. For *creek*, however, the *Groton Records* write *crick*, p. 74 (1682). In the *Huntington Records*, the spelling *ither*, p. 39 (1662), *ithar*, p. 86 (1663), and *nither*, p. 164 (1670), indicate a pronunciation with [aɪ] for *either, neither*. In the *Easthampton Records* occur *complately*, I, 53 (1653), for *completely; spak*, II, 402 (1698), for *speak;* but for *creeks* the form *cricks* occurs, I, 3 (1648). In Green, *Three Military Diaries*, p. 105, occurs the spelling *spakeing* for *speaking*. The spelling for *neither* is *nither*, p. 98, which probably indicates a pronunciation with [aɪ]. In the *Norwalk Records* we find *sedge or crick-thatch*, p. 101 (1707), and *crick*, p. 103 (1709), for *creek*. In the *Southold Records, crick, krick, crike* occur frequently, as at I, 298 (1674), 313 (1673), 378 (1683), etc.; in the *Hempstead Records, crick* is the spelling at I, 151 (1663), I, 294 (1674), etc. But the records do not indicate a pronunciation which would make *creek* rime with *break* and probably [eɪ] never occurred in this word. In the *Hempstead Records*, the spellings very frequently indicate a pronunciation [eɪ] for words that now have [iː], as in *paece* for *piece*, I, 168 (1665); *faete* for *feet*, I, 190 (166); *recaived* for *received*, I, 147 (1672); *aech* for *each*, I, 142 (1663); *strack, straeck* for *streak*, I, 183 (1665). The spelling *naither*, I, 98 (1661), *ayther*, I, 153 (1664), *aythor*, I, 268 (1669), indicate [eɪ] in these words. The spelling *eyther*, I, 15 (1654), might be meant for either [eɪ] or [aɪ], but certainly not for [iː]. For *creature* the spelling *craeter*, I, 100 (1661), indicates a pronunciation ['kreɪtər]. In ordinary dialectal use this was shortened and lowered to the pronunciation commonly indicated by *critter* in literary transcriptions of dialect.

Mackintosh, p. 45, gives *cheap, fear, year, meat*, as having either [iː] or [eɪ], but the following he marks only with [eɪ]: *leap, threap* ("to rebuke," described by the *New English Dictionary* as now only Scottish and northern dialectal usage, and probably a part of Mackintosh's Scottish tradition; it is not recorded in Webster's early dictionaries, though it appears in the dictionary of 1828, marked there as "local"), *bear, pear, tear, swear, wear, sweat, threat, treat, treatise, treaty, deaf, heaven, measure, jealous, zealous, pheasant, pleasant, pleasure, quean, treasure*. The pronunciation of *measure, pleasure, treasure* with [eɪ] may still be heard dialectally. But *beach, beast* and *heath*, according to Mackintosh, have [iː]. On page 46 he gives *conceit, conceive, seize* as having either [iː] or [eɪ,] but *either, neither, leisure* as having only [iː]. These divisions in usage seem to be arbitrary. On page 27, he gives a number of other words which now have [iː] as having [eɪ], e.g., *edict* (with the *t* silent), *equal, sequel, idea, real, ere, adhere, revere, severe*, etc.

Bradford, pp. 19–28, says that *veil, veal* and *vale* are pronounced alike, and *waive* (i.e. *wave*), and *wean*. His statement seems to mean that *veal* and *wean* had the vowel [eɪ]. Some words with this pronunciation are marked by the early grammarians as improprieties. Thus Dearborn, p. 134, corrects *bacon* for *beacon*, and this word appears also in the lists of Staniford and of Elliott and Johnson.

Dearborn and Staniford both give *bate* for *beet* as an impropriety;
and Dearborn, p. 134, gives *bahold* for *behold*, and Staniford, p. 66,
gives *consate* for *conceit*. In the Jack Downing papers by Seba
Smith, New York, 1859, p. 52, Beacon Street in Boston is given
in the Down East dialect as Bacon Street. Cummings, p. 156,
mentions *beacon* and *bacon* as likely to be confused. Ussher, pp
95–96, gives *bates* for *beets* as an impropriety.

The rimes of the New England poets of the eighteenth century
indicate rather a free use of pronunciations with [eɪ] in words which
later took [iɪ] in general speech. Thus we find the following in
Dwight's *Conquest of Canaan: proclaim: stream*, p. 13; *beam: name*,
p. 20; *sway: sea*, p. 22; *stray: sea*, p. 253; *sea: away*, p. 304; *forsake:
speak*, p. 19; in *Greenfield Hill, sea*, riming with *convey*, pp. 52, 168,
with *obey*, p. 97, with *sway*, p. 168; *tea: away*, p. 49; *gleam: flame*,
p. 71; *flame: beam*, p. 72; *stream: flame: came*, p. 99; *neat* riming with
state, p. 141, and *great*, p. 119; *complete: great*, p. 152. In Barlow's
Columbiad, sea rimes with *way*, pp. 42, 68, *day*, p. 296, *sway*, p. 380;
state: meet, p. 378; *haste; east*, p. 105; *James, streams*, p. 172; *heave:
wave*, p. 169. In Ladd occur the rimes *retreat: great*, p. 27; *seat:
debate*, p. 73; *besieged: raged*, p. 73; *vailed: concealed*, p. 85; *mead:
strayed*, p. 118; *speak: break*, p. 150; *meads: shades*, p. 155; *face:
peace*, p. 136. The following have been noted in Trumbull: *seas:
base*, I, 57; *uneasy: crazy*, II, 83; *deceit, fate*, II, 138; *way: sea*, II,
190; *ceased: waste*, II, 197. In view of the statement of Webster
that this was a local New England pronunciation, it is interesting
to observe the following similar rimes in Freneau, for as Freneau was
unusually careful in riming, his rimes may be taken as satisfactory
evidence that the pronunciation was also current in the Middle
States. Freneau rimes *sea(s)* with *raise*, p. 22, with *way*, p. 36,
with *sway*, p. 145, with *lay*, p. 168; *brain: unseen*, p. 22; *tree: lay*,
p. 104; *name: dream*, p. 115; *meet: great*, p. 140; *waiting: debating:
eating*, p. 335.

In *Heroes of the Lake*, New York, 1815, *flame* rimes with *stream*,
pp. 13, 46, with *gleam*, p. 52; *meet* rimes with *fate*, p. 29; *main* with
stream, p. 36; *again* with *scene*, p. 9, and *breaks* with *streaks*, p. 9.

In the proper name Beatty, Beattie, the pronunciation with [eɪ] still remains, though ['biɪtɪ] seems to be gaining.

For *either*, *neither*, the most general present pronunciation in America is ['iːðər], ['niːðər], though ['aɪðər], ['naɪðər] are also heard and are sometimes cultivated as refined pronunciations. The third pronunciation ['eɪðər], ['neːðər] is limited to dialectal speech. All three of these pronunciations are historically derivable from the Old and Middle English forms of the words according to regular phonetic principles. They represent, therefore, variant developments of the same words which have survived in different degrees. Franklin's transcription for *either*, p. 301, shows that he pronounced the vowel with a sound equivalent to the present [aɪ]. Webster, *Dissertations*, p. 114, gives the vowel [aɪ] as the common New England pronunciation, but he reprehends this as an error of the same kind as *desate*, *consate*, *resate*, for *deceit*, *conceit*, *receipt*. In his dictionaries, both the two earlier dictionaries and the dictionary of 1828, he records only [iː] as the vowel in these words. In this he is in accord with Sheridan, Walker, and most of the other dictionaries. Worcester, however, gives the pronunciation with [aɪ] as a second form, and quotes the statement of Smart, that between [iː] and [aɪ] in *either*, "there is little, in point of good usage, to choose." The pronunciation with [aɪ] seems at present to be gaining slightly, perhaps through the influence of British speech of the southern type, in which this is the prevailing form. But in northern England and in America generally, the pronunciation with [iː] is by far the more common.

Dunlap, in *The Father*, Act II, a play first performed in 1789, has the spelling *n'ither* to indicate one of the dialect features in the speech of the Yankee maidservant Susannah. This evidently means ['naɪðər], and it apparently suggested a rustic Yankee pronunciation to a New York audience of the time. The presence of *either*, *neither*, with [aɪ] in New England, and also in southern British English, is another indication of the direct dependence of the former upon the latter.

In the word *leisure* pronunciations with [iː] and [ɛ] are now current in standard usage and it would be difficult to determine which is the more common. Webster, *Dissertations*, p. 116, says that the pronunciation with [ɛ] is the most general in America. In the interest of analogy, he prefers the pronunciation with [iː], but he does not dogmatize. In the dictionary of 1828 he gives both pronunciations. Worcester, however, recognizes only the pronunciation with [iː], and in this he has the support of most of the earlier dictionaries, including Sheridan and Walker. On the side of authority and of the analogy of spelling, the pronunciation with [iː] holds the stronger position, but the pronunciation of words like *measure, pleasure, treasure*, has always afforded a powerful support to the pronunciation with [ɛ].

The word *plait*, Walker, p. 26, says ought to be pronounced like *plate*, a dish, and "pronouncing it so as to rhyme with *meat* is a vulgarism, and ought to be avoided." The American dictionaries are generally in accord with Walker, and it is only in the latest edition of Webster, the *New International*, that the statement is reversed and [pliːt] is said to be "perhaps" more common than [pleɪt]. There can scarcely be any question that this is now the case when the word is used in the sense of a fold, or to fold; it is then commonly pronounced [pliːt] and spelled *pleat*. When it is used in the sense of a braid of hair, or to braid hair, etc., it is commonly pronounced [plæt] and may be written *plat*, though in this sense the old spelling *plait* also persists. The situation in America is therefore the same as in British usage, where, according to the *New English Dictionary*, under the word *plait*, "as a spoken word, *plait* is obsolete," its place being taken either by *pleat* or *plat*. Staniford, p. 69, gave *pleet* as a vulgarism for *plait*, and Webster, in his first two dictionaries, of 1806 and 1807, gives both forms *plait* and *pleet* for the word. Elliott and Johnson, p. 30, give *plete* as an error for *plait*. In the dictionary of 1828, the form *pleet* disappears entirely, along with many other details of the earlier dictionaries which were discarded as being too local or provincial. The discarded pronunciation has in this case crowded out the preferred pronunciation [pleɪt], though the latter lingers in the dictionaries and as a dictionary pronunciation. Cobb, p. 165, gives *plait* as sounding only like *plate*, and similar purist authority for [pleɪt] can be found in books down to the present day.

For *really*, Dearborn, p. 137, lists *raley* as an improper pronunciation. The same pronunciation is recorded by other early grammarians, for example, Ussher, pp. 95–96, both for *really* and *real*, and it is often indicated, by a variety of spellings, as a feature of rustic New England pronunciation. It is common in Haliburton's representation of the speech of Sam Slick. But it must have been general American popular usage, for it is frequently recorded in Longstreet's *Georgia Scenes*, e.g., p. 163, where it is spelled *rayly*. The pronunciation thus described probably varied between ['reɪlɪ], [reɪl], and ['reɪlɪ], [reɪl]. It must be taken as a survival of an older English pronunciation in which, at least in this word, [eɪ] had not been raised to [iː]. For examples of this pronunciation in British speech, see Jespersen, *Modern English Grammar*, I, 369. In present standard speech the vowel of *really, real* is not commonly [iː] but [ɪ], the words being pronounced ['rɪəlɪ], [rɪəl]. But Jespersen's statement that spellings like *raley, railly*, were meant to indicate only the lowering from [iː] to [ɪ] cannot be accepted. In present popular speech the syllabic quality of *l* in these words is often not recognized, *really* being a disyllable, and *real* a monosyllable. When pronounced in this manner, the vowel is not lowered, but the words are heard as ['riːlɪ], [riːl].

The pronunciation of *creek* as [krɪk] already mentioned is still widely current in colloquial and dialect speech. It is recorded as early as Bradford, pp. 19–28, who gives *creek* (of the sea) and *crick* (in the neck) as pronounced alike, and it is indicated still earlier by the naïve spelling of the town records, given above. The pronunciation [krɪk] is the only one recorded by Webster in his dictionary of 1828. Worcester, however, in 1830, gives only [kriːk]. A similar double pronunciation appears in the word *sleek*, which has developed a spelling *slick* to accord with the popular pronunciation. Webster, 1828, records *slick* as "the popular pronunciation of *sleek*, and so written by some authors." Cobb, pp. 168–172, lists *krik* for *creek* as an impropriety.   Perry, *Only Sure Guide*, p. 27, spells *sleek* as *slick*, but says *slick* is pronounced [sliːk].

The pronunciation of *leap* as [lep] is frequently recorded by the earlier phoneticians as an Irishism.   It was approved, however, by Sheridan, and its presence as a survival in American speech is indicated by the rhyme in Samuel Low's *Poems* (1800), p. 30:

> "A vale, replete with snow, betrays his steps,
> Incautious in the fatal depth he leaps."

(8)   [oː]   as in *stone*

When Colonel Crockett returned to his friends in the West after his memorable visit to New England, among other notable discoveries, he reported that people in that strange land said *stun* when they meant *stone*.   Many of them still do—or if their vowel in the word *stone* is not exactly the same as the vowel of *stun*, it is often so like it that the casual hearer perceives no difference between the two. But undoubtedly various shadings occur of the vowel which is ordinarily [oː] or a slightly diphthongized variant of this vowel, [oʊ], in standard speech.   In a great many words [oː] is "shortened and slightly advanced, in rustic New England speech," says Grandgent, p. 217.   Now [oː] is usually described as a mid back vowel with lip rounding, and the vowel of *son*, *some*, etc., is also a mid back sound, though the part of the tongue elevated in forming this sound lies a little in front of back position, best described as half-back.   The vowel of *son*, *some*, etc., is not rounded, and the vowel which Grandgent describes seems to be the vowel of *son*, *some*, with the lip rounding of the vowel of *stone*.   "This vowel," continues Grandgent, "is used by educated New England speakers in about fifty words and their derivatives, and it certainly prevails in the cultivated usage of this region in *Polk, polka, whole*, and probably in *both, folks, Holmes, most, only*, and some others."   Whitney, p. 216, says that in his pronunciation the sound is restricted to *none, whole, home, stone, smoke, folks, coat, cloak, toad, throat*, and that he has heard most often from others the same sound in *bone* and *boat*.

Forms like *hum* for *home,* *hull* for *whole,* *unly* for *only* are occasionally met with in regions outside New England, but only in dialect speech, and apparently always in the wake of New England migration. For the word *shone,* however, both [ʃɔn] and] [ʃʌn] are still to be met with in cultivated speech, though [ʃoːn] is much the more common form. Walker declared that in *shone* "the short sound of *o* is by far the most usual among those who may be styled polite speakers," and the pronunciation still has considerable dictionary authority.

The divergences in earlier New England usage are well illustrated by the criticisms of Holmes, in his *Rhymed Lesson (Urania),* a juvenile poem written in the second quarter of the nineteenth century:

> "Learning condemns beyond the reach of hope
> The careless lips that speak of sŏap for sōap;
> Her edict exiles from her fair abode
> The clownish voice that utters rŏad for rōad:
> Less stern to him who calls his cōat a cŏat.
> And steers his bōat, believing it a bŏat,
> She pardoned one, our classic city's boast
> Who said at Cambridge mŏst instead of mōst,
> But knit her brows and stamped her angry foot
> To hear a Teacher call a rōōt a rŏŏt."

It is apparent from these instances cited by Holmes that only one to the New England manner born might have hoped to steer safely among the many difficulties in the use of *soap, road, coat, boat, most,* and similar words.

Writing of diphthongs, among which he included long *o,* Willard, p. 15, makes an unusually acute observation with respect to the pronunciation of long *o* in New England. He remarks that long *o* "begins with a sound, which is never heard alone, except in the New England pronunciation of such words as *whole, home,* etc., which they pronounce shorter than *hole, comb* and *bone.*" Modern phoneticians frequently record the diphthongal long *o* as [ɔo] or even [ʌo], a rising diphthong, and evidently some such pronunciation as this was in Willard's mind.

In his *Dissertations*, p. 84, Webster remarks that "*o* is some-times shortened in common parlance, as in *colt*," but he adds that "the distinction between *o* in *coal* and *colt* seems to be accidental or caused by the final consonant, and not sufficiently settled or impor-tant to require a separate consideration." It will be noted that Webster does not reject the shortened vowel as an impropriety. In his *American Spelling Book*, p. 13, he even says that as *a* in *late* makes short *e* in *let*, and *e* in *feet* makes short *i* in *fit*, so also *o* in *hone* makes short *o* in *home;* and later, p. 48, in his spelling lists, he gives the following words as containing a short vowel: *none, stone, home, bolt, jolt, boult, dolt, moult, coat, dost.* These words are all in one group with no others and are supposed all to have the same vowel. But Webster does not recognize the short vowel in all words of this class, for on p. 47 he gives *oat, boat, doat, float, tone, loam*, and others, as all containing [oɪ].

Some of these shortenings of [oɪ] are reprehended by the earlier grammarians. Thus Dearborn rejects *shun* for *shone*, p. 114, and *hum* for *home*, p. 136, as improprieties. Johnson and Elliott, p. 30–31, give *hum* and *stun* as vulgar errors for *home* and *stone*. Stani-ford, pp. 68–70, gives *hum* for *home*, *shun* for *shone*, and *stun* for *stone*, as vulgarisms. Welcome-here Dix, a comedy Yankee charac-ter in Paulding's *Noble Exile* has many pronunciations like *cluss* for *close, whull* for *whole* and other similar New Englandisms.

The rimes of the poets give some indication of the extent to which the shortened vowel passed current in speech. Thus *home* rimes with *come, Anarchiad*, p. 74; in Dwight, *Conquest of Canaan, shone* rimes with *won*, p. 3, *road* with *flood*, p. 2. In *Greenfield Hill, zone* rimes with *fun*, p. 37, *throne* with *undone*, p. 77, *own* with *un-done*, p. 77, with *fun*, p. 161, *alone* with *come*, p. 41. In the *Colum-biad* one finds numerous similar rimes, e.g., *throne* with *sun*, pp. 29, 99, 103, 105, 115, *zone* with *sun*, pp. 68, 335, *shone* with *sun*, pp. 77, 83, 146, *known* with *sun*, p. 97, *own* with *sun*, p. 106, *moan* with *sun*, p. 126, *stone* with *shun*, p. 146, *smoke* with *took*, p. 234, *abodes* with *floods*, pp. 55, 104, *roam* with *come*, p. 228. In Humphries *shone* rimes with *sun*, p. 171, *alone* with *Washington*, p. 177, *home* with *come*, p. 31, 39, 179, *strove* with *above*, p. 186, *dome* with *come*, p. 164, *flowed* with *blood*, p. 13. In Trumbull *moan* rimes with *sun*, I, 33, *own* with *won*, I, 43, *stones* with *sconce*, I, 102, *broke* with *shook*, I, 118, *bones* with *once*, II, 18, *alone* with *one*, II, 26, *groan* with *done*, II, 70, *shone* with *one*, II, 183. Besides these there are in Trumbull, as in other poets, many rimes like *throat* with *shout*, I, 116, which indicate a shortened vowel for *throat*, see the discussion of the diphthong [ɑʊ]. In Ladd, *shone* and *sun*, p. 71, rime, and in Hitchcock, p. 145, *home* and *gum*. Of rimes of this type, practically none have been found outside the writings of New England poets.

The earliest example of this shortening which the writer has come across is in the *Hempstead Records*, I, 263 (1669), where we read that the cowherd agrees "that he shall make it his hull im ployment to ceep the said heard this next insuing Sommer." Note that *summer* is spelled with *o* and *whole* with *u*, though both had the same sound. The value of *o* as [ʌ] was of course well established in words like *son*, *some*, *love*, etc., and doubtless this value accounts for the fact that spellings like *hum*, *hull*, for *home*, *whole*, are not frequently met with in seventeenth-century records, even when they are naïvely spelled, for if *some* could be [sʌm] obviously *home* could be [hʌm] without change of spelling. It is probable therefore that pronunciations with the shortened vowel were more frequent than the record of spelling indicates.

For *gold*, usage formerly varied between [goːld] and [guːld], but the latter has now disappeared except as the proper name *Gould*. Sheridan recognized only the pronunciation [guːld]. Walker records both [oː] and [uː] in the word, but regrets that the second of these two pronunciations has grown "much more frequent than the first." He disapproves the pronunciation [guːld] on the ground of its irregularity, but notes that [goːld] is still used by the poets, as shown by their rimes, and that "solemn speaking, particularly the language of Scripture, indispensably requires the same sound." Webster notes that *gold* is differently pronounced "by good speakers" as *gold* or *goold*, *Dissertations*, p. 131, and though he prefers the former because of its conformity to analogy, he does not altogether reject the second pronunciation. In the dictionary of 1828 he gives only [goːld] as a main pronunciation, though he remarks that the pronunciation *goold* "is still retained by some people." By this time, however, the pronunciation with [uː] was passing rapidly out of use, and Worcester records only [goːld]. A number of the early grammarians record [guːld] as an impropriety, mainly on the ground of its violation of analogy, an objection strong enough in the end to bring about the extermination of this form of the word.

A similar pronunciation was that of [ruːm] for *Rome.* This pronunciation had ancient and respectable authority to support it. Walker thought the vowel of *Rome* was "irrevocably fixed" as the same as that of *move, prove,* and authorities both earlier and later than Walker could be cited. The writer of the *British Grammar,* p. 13, pronounced *Rome* like *room,* and this pronunciation is recorded in the several books of Granville Sharp. It is the pronunciation also indicated by Lindley Murray. In fact the pronunciation [ruːm] had so much authority back of it at the end of the eighteenth century that one wonders how the pronunciation [roːm] ever survived, still more how it became the only existing pronunciation. But the principle of survival of the fittest seems best to explain the situation. Both pronunciations were undoubtedly current, but variation in usage in so familiar a word must have been felt to be intolerable, and if one of the two forms must give way, the one most likely to yield was that which conformed less exactly to the normal expectation aroused by the written and printed form of the word. Webster puts the case for and against with his customary good sense. He notes that *Rome* is "very frequently pronounced *Room,* and that by people of every class," *Dissertations,* p. 119, but also that "there are many good speakers" who pronounce the word with [oː]. "It seems very absurd," he continues, "to give *o* its first sound in *Romish, Romans,* and pronounce it *oo* in *Rome,* the radical word. . . . A great proportion of people in America have restored the analogy of pronunciation in giving *o* its first sound in *Rome;* and a desire of uniformity would lead us to extend the practice."

One finds occasional rimes like *doom: Rome*, Honeywood, p. 113, in the poets, but they probably indicate only an occasional and rapidly disappearing pronunciation. As this word was a proper noun and was not commonly included in the dictionaries, analogy was free to operate without let or hindrance from the dictionaries.

The pronunciation of *yeoman* with the *o* silent was advocated by some early grammarians. Thus the author of the *British Grammar*, p. 19, gives *eo* as sounding short *e* in *jeopardy, leopard, yeoman*. Webster indicates the same pronunciation in his *American Spelling Book*, p. 59, and this is the pronunciation given for the word by Elliott and Johnson, and by Alfred, pp. 55, 94. But in his first two dictionaries, as in the dictionary of 1828, Webster gives only the pronunciation with [oː], the *e* being silent. This is now the only pronunciation heard either in England or America. Webster was fond of the word and liked to speak of the New England yeomanry, but in reality, *yeoman* and *yeomanry* have never been since the colonial period genuinely popular words in America. During the colonial period one frequently finds the word *yeoman* in documents and records, where it is used interchangeably with *farmer, planter*, or *husbandman*, but the word has long been current only as an historical or legal term and corresponds to no genuinely native traditions. It has, however, been transferred to naval use, where it still survives as an official title. The former diversity in British pronunciation is indicated by Walker, who says that "Sheridan, Scott and Buchanan pronounce the word as if written yeman," Kenrick as if written *yumman*, but W. Johnston, Perry, Entick and Fry pronounce it as if written yōman, and this only is the pronunciation which Walker approves. Mackintosh (1797), p. 46, records both a pronunciation with [oː] and one with [ɛ] as permissible. Mennye (1785), p. 57, gives *yeoman* as having the same vowel as *mother*, that is [ʌ].

A distinction is commonly made in the dictionaries in the pronunciation of *hoarse* and *horse, coarse* and *corse*. Words spelled with *oa* are supposed to be pronounced with [oː], and words like *horse, corse*, with [ɔ]. The distinction is one that is rarely maintained in practice, either in American or British speech. It is observed occasionally by some speakers who make a special effort to do so, but ordinarily *hoarse* and *horse* are pronounced alike, with the vowel [ɔ]. The *New English Dictionary* still makes the distinction, but in Michaelis-Jones, *A Phonetic Dictionary of the English Language* (1913), p. 190, both words have the same phonetic form. How long this identity has obtained, it is difficult to say, for if the later dictionaries do not accurately record the facts, it is still less likely that the earlier ones do. Walker distinguished between *hoarse* and *horse*, but not between *coarse, corse, course*, all of which are said to have had [oː]. Walker also distinguished between *port* and *sort*, the former of which is said to have had [oː], the latter [ɔ]. Under the word *sort*, Walker notes an affected pronunciation of *sort* to rime with *port*, but the affectation, he continues, "seems confined to a few in the upper ranks of life, and is not likely to descend to their inferiors, as it does not appear to have made any progress among correct and classical speakers." Walker also gives *forge* as containing [oː], but *gorge* as containing [ɔ]; *form* has [ɔ] except when it means a seat, or a class in school, when it has [oː]; *horde* has [oː], but *horn* has [ɔ]. It would seem from Walker's statements that the situation was very unsettled in his day, that many words written *o* before *r* which before had had [oː] were coming to be pronounced with [ɔ]. The contrary process, that is the pronunciation of *sort* as [soːrt] he notes specially as exceptional and as an affected refinement not likely to make its way. The same conditions must have existed in America. Staniford, p. 66, gives *korse* as a vulgar pronunciation for *coarse*, and Dearborn's correction, p. 136, of *kose* for *coarse*, implies a correct pronunciation [koːrs]. The pronunciation [koːs] still survives in southern, especially negro dialect. Webster, *American Spelling Book*, p. 47, gives the following as containing [oː]: *shorn, mourn, course, coarse, hoarse, oar, soar, gourd*, and others like these, and the following, p. 49, as containing [ɔː], *for, form, storm, born, corn, corse, morn, cord, lord, horse, corpse*, etc. As to the length of the vowel, Webster remarks in a footnote that the sound in *for, form*, etc., might perhaps have been better given as [ɔ], but though uncertain, he decides in favor of [ɔː]. It should be noted that

Staniford gives *koard*, meaning [koːrd] as a vulgarism for *chord*, p. 66, and *noarth*, meaning [noːrθ] as a vulgarism for *north*, p. 69. It is probable that the attempt to distinguish between the pronunciation of *hoarse* and *horse* was kept up by the grammarians to some extent because of the spelling. Words that were spelled with two letters for the vowel sound, such as *course, coarse, hoarse, oar, soar, door, floor, board*, etc., were felt to be more appropriately pronounced with [oː], whereas for words written with *o* alone, [ɔ] was felt to be sufficient. Of course, words written with *o* followed by *r* and a final *e*, like *more, sore, tore*, would also belong to the first class. But whatever the theory may have been, by the beginning of the nineteenth century the distinction between [oː] and [ɔ] in these words tended to become confused or to disappear and all of them to be pronounced with [ɔ].

Jespersen, *Modern English Grammar*, I, 365, notes the pronunciation of *forecastle* as ['foːksl] as indicating the survival of the older pronunciation of *fore-* with [oː]. The same thing may be observed frequently in southern dialect speech, especially negro speech, in America, where words like *fourteen* become ['foːˈtiːn], *force* becomes [foːs], *court* becomes [koːt], *short* becomes [ʃoːt]. Words in which standard speech has [ɔ] before *r* final, also have [oː] in southern dialect speech, as in *door, floor*, etc., pronounced [doː], [floː], etc. "One must admit, however," says Read, "The Southern R," in *University Bulletin*, Louisiana State University, Vol. I, No. 2, p. 7, "that Southerners of high culture may sometimes be heard to pronounce such words as *door, floor* respectively like *doe, flow*." He adds the anecdote that "the brilliant orator, Senator Daniel of Virginia, is said to have asked on one occasion whether Senator Hoar (*hoe*) was on the floor (*flow*). 'No,' replied one of Daniel's colleagues, laughing at the Southerner's pronunciation, 'Senator Hoar (*hoe*) will not return to the floor (*flow*) until half-past four (*foe*)'."

All these words may be pronounced with the *r* silent in standard speech also, but the vowel remains [ɔ] unchanged, except that it may be lengthened, *court*, for example, being pronounced [kɔːt], or perhaps with a slight glide vowel before *t* [kɔːɪət], sufficient to distinguish the word from *caught* [kɔːt].   Standard pronunciation with the *r* silent is thus a later development than Southern dialect pronunciation, the latter developing from the pronunciation [oː] for *o*, *oa*, *ou* before *r*, the former from the sound [ɔ], which the lexicographers were only beginning to record at the end of the eighteenth century.   That the Southern dialect forms began to appear early is evident from Dearborn's correction *kose* for *coarse*, noted above, and that they were also formerly present in the North as well as the South is equally probable.   What seems to have happened, in this case as in others, is that an early common dialect tendency has been eliminated in the North, but has maintained its existence in the popular speech of the South.

The pronunciation of words of this type with [oː] or some similar sound apparently accounts for a number of rimes in the poetry of the eighteenth century on words which could scarcely be made to rime in present English.   Thus rimes like *mourn; urn*, Freneau, pp. 28, 114, or *turn: mourn*, pp. 11, 27, 109, 160, or *turn: scorn*, p. 61, would scarcely have been made so frequently as they appear in the poetry of Freneau, and also other of his contemporaries, if the vowel of *mourn, scorn* had been [ɔ].   More likely it was a higher sound and more front, approximately [oː].   Even so the rime with *urn*, *turn* would not be very close, unless the vowel of *urn, turn* may be assumed to have been also higher, that is approximately [ʊrn], [tʊrn].   It is manifestly reasoning in a circle to say that the vowel of *mourn, scorn* must have been [oː] because the vowel of *urn, turn* was probably [ʊ], but on other grounds there is reason for thinking that the vowel of *urn, turn, burn, return* had not been completely assimilated in the eighteenth century to the vowel of *fern*, and was still maintained as a distinctive sound, probably [ʊ].   The words which commonly rime with these words in *u* are *mourn, borne, morn*.   According to Webster's rulings, *mourn* and *borne* would have [oː], but *morn* would have [ɔ].   Whatever the pronunciation of the poets may have been in actual speech, in their rimes they have treated *mourn* and *morn* as though they were pronounced alike, and the probability in this instance is that they pronounced *morn* with [oɪ] to satisfy the exigencies of rime.

In Green, *Three Military Diaries*, 1775–1779, p. 102, *mourn* is spelled *moorn*, a spelling which indicates a vowel different from that of *morn*, probably a high close [oɪ].

(9) [ɔ], [ɔɪ] as in *autocrat, awe*

One of the notable marks of present American English is the frequent occurrence of an unrounded [ɔ], scarcely distinguishable from [ɑ], in words written with *o*, as in *not, god, cost, soft, coffee, frog*, etc. Usage varies in these words between [ɔ] and [ɑ], and sometimes [ɑ] slightly lengthened, even appears for [ɔɪ], as in *caught* [kɑt], indistinguishable from *cot, cough, bought* [kɑf], [bɑt]. The pronunciation of *not, god*, etc., with [ɔ] is more common in New England than elsewhere in America. The pronunciation with [ɑ] is not recorded by the British phoneticians as now current in cultivated speech in England, but for America it may be said to be, in a large group of words, the general pronunciation. The differences in usage in America are notable, however, and are not easily reducible to rules. In general, it may be said that *o* before continuant consonants is more likely to be pronounced as [ɔ] than it is before stops. Thus for *cost, soft, broth, fond, bond, long*, a pronunciation with [ɔ], or even [ɔɪ], is perhaps more general than one with [ɑ], though statistics on the point would be needed to determine this point finally. And yet, though *fond, bond*, would be commonly [fɔnd], [bɔnd], *beyond* is apparently more frequently heard as [bɪ'jɑnd]. Likewise one observes a strong tendency to pronounce *o* as [ɔ] in closed syllables before *g*, as in *dog, log, hog*, etc., but before other stop consonants, as [ɑ]. But here again the differences in practice are varied and unsystematic.

The early American grammarians and dictionary makers, and for that matter the late ones too, record only [ɔ] for their so-called short *o*. It is true that one readily becomes sceptical of the value of these older dictionary statements when one observes that even the American dictionaries of present English likewise make no record whatever of such pronunciations as [hɑt], [gɑt], [nɑt] for *hot, got, not,* etc., and yet nothing is more certain than that these pronunciations are now, and for many years have been, widely used in American speech.   The presence of the sound seems to have been recognized as far back as Webster, who says, *Dissertations,* p. 110, that "it is a custom very prevalent in the middle states, even among some well-bred people, to pronounce *off, soft, drop, crop,* with the sound of *a, aff, saft, drap, crap.*"   He adds that this seems to be a foreign and local dialect, and "cannot be advocated by any person who understands correct English."   At another place, p. 383, he limits this pronunciation to the descendants of the Scotch Irish in America.   Webster is not altogether clear in his statement here, since "the sound of *a*" might be [æ] or [ɑ].   It obviously would not be [eː], and if it had been the sound of *a* in *fall,* Webster would not have been moved to comment on it.   The question is then, did Webster mean to indicate a pronunciation [æf], [sæft], [dræp], [kræp], or [ɑf], [sɑft], [drɑp], [krɑp]?   Dearborn gives *crap, drap* as improprieties for *crop, drop,* and Elliott and Johnson so characterize *saft* for *soft.*   Staniford, pp. 67, 68, has *drap* as a vulgarism for *drop,* and *map* for *mop.*   Some of these words occur in other similar lists, especially *crop* and *drop.*   In Royall Tyler's *The Contrast,* first performed in 1787, the provincial Yankee Jonathan speaks of "a drap of cyder with a pepperpod in it."   But these citations do not, unfortunately, clear up the question whether the sound intended by the spelling with *a* is [ɑ] or [æ].   In the case of *crop, drop,* the pronunciation [kræp], [dræp] are still to be heard in dialect speech and one might infer from this fact that the sound rejected as an impropriety in these words in the eighteenth century was the same.   The pronunciations [kræp], [dræp] are also recorded as dialectal survivals in southwestern England (see Wright, *English Dialect Grammar,* under *crop, drop,* and Kruisinga, *A Grammar of the Dialect of West Somerset.* §§151, 152), and the American and the British dialect forms probably go back to the same source.   It is extremely improbble, however, that a jump was made in the pronunciation of these words from a vowel [ɔ] to a vowel [æ] without any intermediary stages, the most obvious of which would be [ɑ]. The [ɔ] was first unrounded to [ɑ], and this sound in the closed syllable then fronted to [æ]. The process is illustrated by the word *strop*, still current, especially in the compound *razor-strop*, as a variant of strap, and by the words *stomp*, *tromp*, dialect variants of the verbs *stamp*, *tramp*. It seems probable that these spellings are merely occasional records of a variation between [ɔ] and [ɑ], passing even at times into [æ], which was much more widespread than the spellings themselves indicate. One is not surprised to find the early grammarians paying little attention to the pronunciation [ɑ] for [ɔ], for the unrounding of [ɔ] was a change slighter than they were accustomed to note. A stray indication, therefore, such as the listing by Elliott and Johnson, p. 31, of *vamit* as incorrect pronunciation of *vomit*, becomes unusually significant.

The variation between [æ], [ɑ] and [ɔ] appears also in the early *Watertown Records* in the proper name which is now commonly spelled Knapp. This appears in the spelling *Knop*, p. 17 (1648), but also as *Knap*, p. 49 (1656), the more common spelling being *Knop*. The proper name *Knapp* is written *Knop* in the *Groton Records*, p. 16, and so often throughout these records. By origin this proper name is the same as the common noun *knap*, meaning hill, as in *The First Century of the History of Springfield*, II, 176 (1685), *to the first Pine Tree upon the knap or Hill*. For examples of the variation between *knap* and *knop* in this word, see the *New English Dictionary*, under *knap*. The word still survives in British local and dialectal use, as in Mistover Knap, in Hardy's *Return of the Native*. See also the *New English Dictionary* under *nap*, the raised surface of cloth, for variations between *nap* and *nop* in this word.

In the *Lunenburg Records* (1719–1764) the proper name *Spafford*, *Spaffard*, a variant of *Spoffard*, occurs frequently. In the same records, pp. 223, 235, occurs *Ardeway* for *Ordway*. In the *Huntington Records*, *morrow* is spelled *marrow*, p. 30 (1660), p. 227 (1676), and *long* is spelled *lang*, p. 40 (1662).

Often in the *Hempstead Records,* as at I, 164 (1665), *crapt, crap* appears for *cropped, crop,* meaning to cut, as in marking cattle or horses. Perhaps the spelling *hears* for *horse, Hempstead Records,* I, 176 (1665), should be taken as indicating a pronunciation [hɑrs] or [hærs]. The word is ordinarily spelled in these records with *o,* but an early pronunciation with [ɑ] is indicated by the popular colloquial use, still current, of *old hoss* [oɪld haɪs] as a term of familiar address.

Webster's statement that [ɑ] for [ɔ] was characteristic of the speech of the Scotch-Irish in America finds support in Brackenridge's picture of the dialect of Teague O'Regan, an American in the making, in *Modern Chivalry.* Besides other Irishisms like *baste, mate, ate, clane, plane, plase,* etc. for *beast, meat, eat, clean, please,* Teague uses such pronunciations as *harse* for *horse, tratting* for *trotting, aff* for *off* (I, 174), *affer* for *offer* (II, 138), *acrass* for *across* (I, 169), *crass* for *cross, langer* for *longer, anest* for *honest* (I, 166).

But here again the statement that these pronunciations of words with *o* as [ɑ] in American English were derived directly from Irish English is much less credible than the supposition that American and Irish English coincided because of their common inheritance from a common origin. That [ɑ] for *o* was sometimes heard in England in the seventeenth century is manifest from the fact that it is satirized in the speech of Lord Foppington in Vanbrugh's *Relapse* (1696). Lord Foppington speaks the affected English of a beau, and in speech his special affectation is indicated by such spellings as *stap* for *stop, packet* for *pocket, rat* for *rot, Tam* for *Tom, Gad* for *God, pasitively* for *positively, manstrous* for *monstrous, passible* for *possible, Lackets* for *Lockets, praper* for *proper, nat* for *not, fand* for *fond, far* for *for, a-clack* for *o'clock, bax* for *box, resalve* for *resolve.* Vanbrugh also writes *a* for *o* before *r,* as in *tartures* for *tortures, lard* for *lord,* and for *o* as the first elements of what is now the diphthong [au], but which ordinarily in the seventeenth and eighteenth century had as its first element a sound much nearer to [ɔ]. Thus we have *raund* for *round, pawnd* for *pound, crawn* for *crown, tawn* for *town, haw* for *how, sprauts* for *sprouts.* There can be no question but that

Vanbrugh intended to represent by these various spellings a pro‑
nunciation [ɑ] for the usual value of *o* as [ɔ], and though this trick of
speech was utilized ·as one of the traits of a foolish, affected noble‑
man, there is no reason to suppose that Vanbrugh invented it. On
the other hand, it could not have been very general in cultivated
speech, for then it would not have been marked enough to serve
as an affectation. It is retained in Sheridan's *Trip to Scarborough*,
which Professor Matthews has characterized as "a deodorized adapta‑
tion of Vanbrugh's *Relapse*."

In *The Politician Outwitted* of Samuel Low, New York, 1789,
the same pronunciation, though not consistently indicated in the
text, appears in the speech of Worthnought, an affected New York
fop. "He is positively a very eccentric bady," says Worthnought,
Act IV, Sc. II, "and there is a small tincture of a barbarous sart
of wit in what he says; but it wants an immensity of correction, an
infinitude of polishing; he is a mere son of nature, everything he
says is expressed in such a Gathic, uncouth, Anti-Chesterfieldian
style; and as for his dress, it is pasitively most prepasterously clownish
and original." All this is pretty clearly imitated from Vanbrugh,
but whether imitated or original, the passage shows that the pro‑
nunciations indicated by such spellings as *bady*, *Gathic*, were at least
not general at the time, and on the other hand were credible enough
when they were heard.

A little later, however, in the *Madmen All* of J. K. Paulding,
written about 1800, the stage Englishman, Huskisson Hodgson,
uses such pronunciations as *impawsible*, Act II, Sc. v, for *impossible*
with supposedly ludicrous effect. To the native of New York or
Philadelphia, with whose speech Paulding was most in sympathy,
such pronunciations may have been ludicrous, but they could
scarcely have been so in New England. Huskisson Hodgson is a
broad comedy Britisher of the haw-haw type, as the following
passage will show, formerly popular on the American stage, but
his words are interesting as showing what seemed to a New
Yorker of the early nineteenth century to be absurdities of
speech:

"HODG. A churming day we have had, Miss Garafeliaw [Gara-
felia]; it reminded me —ah—ah—of the last mawning I spent
with the—ah—Duchess of Devonshiawr. She was a par-
ticulaw—aw—aw—friend of mine, and we felt quite—ah—
ah—melancholy at pawting.

GARAF. Indeed, Mr. Hodgson? I was not aware you were so
familiar with the Duchess.

HODG. Oh, deaw—yaas—yaas. I was staying at her—her
cawstle. I met her in the garden before breakfast. —'A
churming mawning, Mr. Hodgson,' said she. 'Yaas'—said
I—'vawstly so, your grace.' And then I went into breakfast,
where we had—auh—auh—some very foine Dutch herrings—
which makes me remember it."[1]

In the present English dialects in England, [ɑ] frequently occurs
for *o*, as it does in American speech. Thus [ɑ] is recorded for *o* in
bottom for southeast Kent, and east Devonshire, for *box* in southeast Kent, for *broth* in Dorset and east Devonshire, for *cot* in southeast Kent, for *follow* in northern Ayrshire, for *cross* in northwest
and east Oxfordshire, Sussex, east Dorset, and north Devonshire,
see Wright, *English Dialect Grammar*, p. 73. The change of *o* to
[ɑ] extends over a still wider area when *o* is followed by *p*, and [ɑ]
is found also for *o* before *ft*, *st*, and other combinations. In some
of these, present American use has generally [ɔ], and in others usage
varies between [ɔ] and [ɑ], with variation also in the quantity of the
vowels. But the presence of [ɑ] for [ɔ] in present British dialect
speech is another indication that one need not go to Irish speech to
explain its presence in American speech. Wyld, *History of Modern
Colloquial English*, pp. 240 ff., gives examples from the days of
Queen Elizabeth and earlier.

For *beyond*, New England popular speech sometimes has [bɪ'jɛnd].
This is mentioned as an incorrect pronunciation by Elliott and
Johnson, p. 30. Its presence in earlier cultivated speech is attested
by the rime *beyond: end* in Trumbull, I, 19. For various forms of

---

[1] See the discussion of this type of pronunciation by Richard Grant White,
Words and Their Uses, pp. 60–62.

beyond, yon, yonder in present dialect speech, see the indexes to
Dialect Notes. In Fowle, *Companion to Spelling Books*, Boston,
1843, p. 118, *beyend* is given as a vulgarism.

The second syllable of the word *because* was formerly often pronounced with [eɪ], as in the speech of Humphrey, a back-country
servant in Samuel Low's *The Politician Outwitted*, New York, 1789,
or in the *Letters of J. Downing . . . to Mr. Dwight,* New York, 1834,
p. 25 and elsewhere. This pronunciation is usually indicated by
the spelling *becase* and is commonly corrected by the early grammarians. Its widespread and early occurrence throughout New England is indication that the pronunciation was not originally an
Irishism in American speech, though now it would usually be regarded as a feature of Irish dialect. The presence of the vowel [eɪ]
in this word is to be explained by analogy to the substantive *case.*
In John Easton's *Narrative* (1675) the form *cause* does not appear
either as noun, verb, or in the compound *because*, but instead the
form of the word is consistently *case*, as on p. 30, "we have Case to
think **yᵗ** was the great Case of the war against us." And for the
conjunction, see p. 22, "and sum others wear but Sudierners [so-
journers] with Philip becase removed by the English having got
their land." The word *causes* in the title of this work is the editor's,
not the author's word.

Another variant sometimes recorded is [bɪˈkʌz], but this latter
pronunciation might readily arise in the word by reason of its unstressed position.

The vocalization of the consonant *h* in Old English *dohter* has
resulted in Modern English *daughter* with [ɔ]. An older variant
form is occasionally recorded in which the consonant was not lost
but was replaced by [f]. This appears in some early American
spellings, as in the *Huntington Records, dafter*, p. 8 (1657), p. 25
(1660) and so often. *Southold Records*, I, 308, has *dafters.* In
Hempstead Records, I, 192 (1665), also p. 208 (1665), occurs *boeft*
for *bought.* The scribe who wrote this made most vigorous efforts
to be phonetic, spelling *Jamaica* as *geameacooe, colored* as *coelleread*,
I, 192, and though one may not be quite sure what these spellings

mean, one can at least be sure that they were rich in intention of meaning. In *Hempstead Records*, I, 230 (1666), *dafter* also occurs. In Easton's *Narrative* (1675), occurs *thoft* for *thought*, p. 15, and *boft* for *bought*, p. 15, p. 25.

(10) [uɪ] as in *boot*

The most notable development in Modern English of [uɪ], usually derived in the case of native words from Middle English [oɪ], has been the tendency of [uɪ] to shorten in certain words into [ʊ] and even into [ʌ]. Thus *rood*, *good*, and *blood* all go back to Old and Middle English forms with [oɪ], but appear now in Modern English with three different vowels, [ruɪd], [gʊd], [blʌd]. These three vowels are all clearly recognized by the early phoneticians and are recorded by Wesbter in the main in the same words in which they occur in present English. An exception is the word *sugar*, which Webster, *American Spelling Book*, p. 104, pronounces *shoogar*, but which now generally has [ʊ]. There are other words, also, in which usage is now divided between [uɪ] and [ʊ] and in which it has long been divided. Walker, p. 35, declared that the only words written *oo* that have [ʊ] are *wool, wood, good, hood, foot, stood, understood; blood* and *flood* rime with *mud; soot* is vulgarly *sut*, riming with *but, hut,* etc., but should have *oo*, as in *boot;* and *door, floor*, have [oɪ] in England, but [uɪ] in Ireland. To Walker's list of words with [ʊ], Webster, *American Spelling Book*, p. 51, adds many others, his examples being *root, foot, shoot, book, cook, hook, look, took, brook, crook, flook, rook, shook, wood, good, hood, hoof, roof, loof, soon, hoop* (of a cask), *coop, poop, wool*. He also pronounces *croup* as [krʊp], and he makes a distinction between *hoop* (of a cask), pronounced [hʊp], and *hoop* ("to cry out, but more commonly spelt whoop"), pronounced [huɪp]. The pronunciation of *shoot* as [ʃʊt] is continued even in the dictionary of 1828. This is corrected by Worcester, 1830, to [ʃuɪt], but Worcester changes Webster's [ʃʊk] also to [ʃuɪk], the former change coinciding with present use, the latter being contrary to it. Similar variation may be observed in other words of this group, e.g. *root*, which Webster records as [rʊt] and Worcester as [ruɪt]. Both pronunciations occur in present English, as they doubtless have occurred in cultivated speech for the past hundred years and more. It will be observed that Webster's list of words with *oo* pronounced [ʊ] is considerably larger than Walker's, and no doubt there was a growing tendency in this direction, at least in New England, in the late eighteenth and early nineteenth centuries. Thus even words like *broom, room, spoon,* etc., were sometimes pronounced [brʊm], [rʊm], [spʊn], etc., and such pronunciations may still be heard, though they are rare and the influence of spelling now seems to be decisive against them. Other words in which the same variation occurs in present English are *aloof, boot, coop, Cooper, food, groom, hoof, hoop, Hooper, nook, proof, rood, roof, rook, rooster, root, soon, soot, spook, woof.* For *soot* the form [sʌt] is also very generally current in colloquial speech, though it is now without dictionary authority. In the *Compendious Dictionary,* 1806, Webster gave the word as either *soot* or *sut,* but in the dictionary of 1828 he records only [sʊt]. Nares, *General Rules,* p. 76, gives *oo* as *u* short, that is [ʌ], in *blood, flood, soot.* In *put,* he recognizes both [pʊt] and [pʌt], p. 38, but prefers the latter. Mennye (1785), p. 58, gives *foot, soot* as having the vowel of *mutter,* the same as in *flood, blood,* but *brook, cook, good, wood, wool, stood,* etc., have [ʊ], and *bloom, goose,* etc., have [uɪ]. In his list of words sounded alike, p. 91, he gives *rough, ruff, roof.* Bradford, pp. 19–28, in his list of words different in spelling but sounded alike, has *rough, ruff, roof; sun, son, soon, swoon; stood, stud;* these are presumably to be taken as only a few illustrations of what was a much more general feature of his pronunciation.

Some of the early grammarians record corrections for words in this class. Thus Dearborn lists as improprieties, *huff* for *hoof,* p. 136, *ruff* for *roof,* p. 138, and *spunful* for *spoonful,* p. 139. To these Staniford adds *shuck* for *shook,* p. 80, *sut* for *soot,* p. 70, and the reverse of the usual change, *soople* for *supple,* p. 70. Jaudon, p. 214, adds *tuck* for *took* as an impropriety. In the dialect of Jack Downing, see *Letters,* New York, 1834, p. 78, among other New Englandisms like *stun* for *stone, eend* for *end,* we find *ruff* for *roof.*

The spelling *ruff* might indicate either a vowel [ʊ] or a vowel [ʌ], but either would have been regarded as a departure from the standard form [uː]. Ussher, pp. 95–96, records *huff* for *hoof*, *ruff* for *roof*, *spunful* for *spoonful*, *sut* for *soot*, as improprieties.

Occasional early naïve spellings indicate a pronunciation with [ʌ] for *oo* in words which no longer retain this sound. Thus we find *fut*, *futt*, *Plymouth Records*, I, 267 (1698), for *foot*, and *tuck*, ibid., I, 228, for *took*. The spelling *fut* for *foot* occurs also in the *Lancaster Records*, p. 231 (1725). In the *Hempstead Records*, I, 185 (1666), occurs *futt* for *foot*, and occasionally elsewhere in these records. *The Song of the Minute Man* (1777) has *tuck* for *took*.

After lip consonants the tendency towards [uː] was strengthened, and one occasionally meets with spellings like *booshel*, *boolet*, in *Watertown Records*, p. 38 (1651), for *bushel*, *bullet*. In the *Hanover Records*, as on p. 121 (1793), *Fuller* is sometimes spelled *Foolar*. But in general the lip consonants have not prevented the lowering of [uː] to [ʊ] in standard speech, though they seem to have prevented the sound from passing into [ʌ].

Webster's pronunciation of *croup* as [krʊp] is no longer current and was given up by Webster himself in the dictionary of 1828. There are two words spelled alike, *croup*, and both pronounced [kruːp], one meaning the rump of a horse, the other a disease of the throat. From the former has come the word *crupper*, which indicates a probable pronunciation [krʌp] for this word.

The pronunciation of *wound* to rime with *sound* Webster faithfully defended even to the last ditch in the dictionary of 1828. In the *Dissertations*, p. 133, he opposed the pronunciation with [uː] as a modern pronunciation. "I say modern; for in America *woond* is a recent innovation. . . . But were *woond* the universal practice in Great Britain, this should not induce us to lay aside our practice for a foreign one. . . . Will not the Atlantic Ocean, the total separation of America from Great Britain, the pride of an independent nation, the rules of language, the melody of English poetry, restrain our rage for imitating the errors of foreigners?" On various other occasions Webster defended the pronunciation [wɑʊnd], and no

doubt it was widely used in his day. It is attested by the rime
wound: sound, Conquest of Canaan, p. 55, and Staniford, p. 72, rejects *woond* as an affected pronunciation. The word is always [wɑʊnd]
in Freneau, see pp. 169, 170, 187, etc. But [wuːnd] could not have
been an uncommon pronunciation, even in New England, for if it
had been unknown, Webster would not have preached against it.
Indeed Webster, *American Spelling Book*, p. 52, calls it "the fashionable pronunciation."

If it occurred still more commonly in the Middle States than
in New England, as is extremely probable, one need not explain
its dominance as due to American "rage for imitating the errors
of foreigners." Sheridan and Walker both gave the vowel as [uː]
and Walker says that though the word is sometimes pronounced
to rime with *sound*, "this is directly contrary to the best usage."
Good dictionary authority could be found for both pronunciations
in the later eighteenth century, and if usage was divided in America
at that time, it was so because American speakers had brought
with them to the new continent a divided practice. That the two
pronunciations were later reduced to one, and that not the one that
Webster advocated but the pronunciation of Walker, was probably
due in some measure to the authority of the latter. But the pronunciation [wɑʊnd] died hard. It was recorded, as a second choice,
by Worcester (1830). It may still be heard in American cultivated
speech, sometimes as a consciously preferred pronunciation.

The word *rout(e)*, a way, a routine journey, is now pronounced
[rɑʊt] only in very colloquial English, as in speaking of a milk rout(e),
or a mailcarrier's rout(e). Webster's *New International Dictionary*
(1916) says that [rɑʊt] is still common in the United States, prevailing in some localities, but that [ruːt] on the analogy of the French
pronunciation, is now displacing it. Walker, p. 36, preferred the
pronunciation with [uː], but remarked that the word was "often
pronounced so as to rhyme with *doubt* by respectable speakers."
In the dictionaries that passed under Webster's own supervision,
only the pronunciation with [ɑʊ] is given, and this also is Worcester's
choice. The later and present preference for [ruːt] is partly due to the

spelling *route*, partly perhaps to increased knowledge of French, and partly also to the use of the term in the more dignified and often international vocabulary of steamship and railway travel. Lyman Cobb, p. 166, gives *route* and *rout*, "tumultuous crowd," as sounding alike.

The anglicization of *tour* [tuːr] to rime with *tower* is now restricted within the limits of popular or illiterate English and is not recorded in the dictionaries. But Benezet, pp. 147–154, gives *tour* (journey) and *tower* as sounding alike, and the same statement is even made by Lyman Cobb, p. 167. Mennye, p. 91, also equates *tour* and *tower*.

For *oo* before *r* the early orthoepists generally give [oː], in *floor*, *door*, though the vowel actually spoken before *r* was probably somewhat lower and more open than [oː], and for other words with a lip consonant followed by *oo* before *r*, e.g. *poor*, *boor*, *moor*, they give [uː]. Yet a pronunciation with the same vowel as in *door* was also current in words of this second group, pronounced to rime with *pore*, *bore*, *more*, etc. This pronunciation still lingers, especially in the South and Southwest (see citations in *Dialect Notes*, under *poor*, *pore*, the only one of the words popularly current in America). Its presence in Dwight's pronunciation is attested by the rimes *lore*: *poor*, *Conquest of Canaan*, p. 70; and *door*, *Greenfield Hill*, p. 34, *store*, pp. 35, 140, *more*, p. 127, all riming with *poor*. Bradford, pp. 19–28, gives *pore*, *poor*, *pour*, *power*, as all pronounced alike. In the *Watertown Records*, p. 161 (1670), *poor* is spelled *pore*. The *Song of the Minute Man* (1777) gives *poure* for *poor*.

The division in usage arose early, see Jespersen, p. 367, and it has been persistent. Emerson, *Boston Hymn*, rimes *poor* and *more* and *poor* and *war*. Whittier, *Maud Muller*, rimes *door* with *poor*, and Jespersen cites Tennyson's rime *store*: *poor*: *more*.

For *moor* the two pronunciations with [uː] and with [oː] also persist, the former being much the more common, though in the proper name *Moor(e)* the latter is not infrequent, even with the spelling unchanged. Walker, p. 35, says that *moor*, a black man, is regular "in polite pronunciation, and like *more* in vulgar. *Moor*, a marsh, is sometimes heard rhyming with *store;* but more correct speakers pronounce it regularly, rhyming with *poor.*"

As a common noun *boor* has never been a popular word in America and thus has generally been made to conform in pronunciation to the spelling and the analogy of the usual value of *oo.* As a proper noun, however, the word *Boor, Boer* became popularized during the Boer War, and it then assumed the two forms with [uː] and with [oː], reflecting the same division of usage as appears in *poor, moor,* though the pronunciation with [oː] was of course encouraged by the Dutch spelling Boer. Bradford, pp. 19–28, gave *boar, boor, bore* as all pronounced the same.

For *your, yours,* likewise, two forms, one with [uː], the other with [oː] [ɔː], have long been current. Dwight has the rime *shores*: *yours, Conquest of Canaan,* p. 68.

Likewise for *sure* the same variation in pronunciation is attested by Dearborn's citation of *shoar* as an impropriety for *sure,* p. 138, a pronunciation that still survives. Dearborn also lists *shoar* as an impropriety for *sewer,* a drain. But Webster in his dictionary of 1806, records *shore* as a variant of *sewer* in good standing. In his dictionary of 1828, he retracts, however, saying that *sewer* is "corruptly pronounced *shore* or *soer.*" Under *sewer,* Walker gives the word with [oː], both in the sense of one who sews and of a passage for water, but adds that in the latter sense the word is "now corrupted to shore." Cummings, p. 154, gives the spelling *sewer,* but pronounces the word as though it were spelled *shore.*

In present English *your* and *sure,* pronounced with [oː], [ɔː] are characteristic marks of certain negro and southern dialects, but this pronunciation, especially for *your,* is likely to be heard elsewhere and also in cultivated speech. Grandgent, p. 218, says in New England it is "frowned upon everywhere but in Boston, where yɔəz = *yours* is very common."

For *chew* a frequent popular pronunciation has *chaw.* Walker says that *ew* is sometimes pronounced like *aw* in the verb *to chew,* but this is "gross and vulgar." Under the word *chew,* he gives both *tshoo* and *tshaw,* but says "the latter pronunciation is grown vulgar."

Nares, *General Rules*, p. 63, gives [tʃɔː] for *chew* as the only proper pronunciation. Most of the early American grammarians correct this pronunciation, and evidently it was a pronunciation of wide occurrence. Dearborn, p. 134, gives *chow* as an incorrect pronunciation of *chew*. Staniford, p. 66, gives both *chaw* and *chow*, as pronunciations to be corrected. Jaudon, p. 213, also mentions *chaw*. In *Eine nuetzliche Anweisung*, p. 38, [tʃɔː] for *chew* is the only pronunciation recorded. Both the forms *chaw* [tʃɔː] and *chow* [tʃoɪ] were formerly in general use, and abundant illustrations will be found in the *New English Dictionary* under these forms. Both *chaw* and *chew* are entered as in good use by Alexander, *Columbian Dictionary* (1800), who was simply following Perry. The double forms *chew*, *chow*, are in origin similar to the forms *shew*, *show*, *shrew*, *shrow*, *strew*, *strow*, in which the double development is due to original Old English forms with diphthongal stressed vowels, *eo*, *ea*, the latter forms with [ju] developing on the basis of the element *e* of the diphthong, followed by *w*, the forms with *aw*, *ow* developing on the basis of the second element of the diphthong. In all instances usage has generalized on one or the other of the double forms, *chew*, *shrew*, *strew*, in the one case becoming the accepted standard forms, and *chow*, *chaw*, *shrow*, *strow* persisting only as dialectal or archaic poetic forms, while in the other, *show* has become standard and *shew* exists either only as a spelling or as an archaic pronunciation.

The pronunciation [juː] or [ɪuː] for [uː] in *to*, *too*, *do*, etc., is one of the continually recurring marks of the rustic New Englander in the comedies of the latter eighteenth century, see further under [juː]. The following stanza from the *Song of the Minute Man* illustrates this and several other colonial pronunciations:

> "Now tew oure Station Let us march and randevuse with pleasure
> we have been like Brave minut men to sarve so Great A Treasure
> we let them se amediately that we are men of mettle
> We Jarsey Boys that fere no nois will never flinch for Battle"

"This was writ," as the author relates, "att Boundbruck March 13th A D 1777," the author evading the difficulties of punctuation by omitting punctuation altogether.

(11) [juː] as in *music*

The orthographic representation of this sound is *u*, as in *music*, *ew* as in *few*, *iew* as in *view*, *eau* as in *beauty*. In the initial position, after [k], and after lip consonants, present American usage uniformly has the sound [juː] for orthographic long *u* and its equivalents. After *l* and *r*, the sound is rarely [juː] except occasionally in conscious speech, but commonly [uː], as in *lute* [luːt], *Luke* [Luːk], *rude* [ruːd], *rule* [ruːl]. But after *d, t, th, n*, and *sh, s, z*, usage varies widely in present practice, some speakers pronouncing *duty* as ['djuːtɪ], others as ['duːtɪ], some pronouncing *nude, new* as [njuːd], [njuː], others as [nuːd], [nuː], etc. Academic and dictionary authority is strangely opposed to the pronunciation of [uː] in all the words of this latter group, and it is often characterized as a mark of vulgar or illiterate speech, in spite of the fact that it is and has long been widely current in the speech of persons of undoubted cultivation and education. Lord Frederic Hamilton, in his volume of recollections, *The Days Before Yesterday* (1920), recalls that Gladstone "had certain peculiarities of pronunciation; he always spoke of 'constitootional' and of 'noos.'" Gladstone must have shared this 'peculiarity' with many others. In present American English one finds a similar divided use which is explained by the history of this sound in America. Whitney (1874) declared, p. 220, that in his pronunciation the vowel of *tube, new* and other words which he mentioned was frankly and unmistakably the same as the vowel of *food*, etc.

Both Sheridan and Walker make a good deal of the diphthongal quality of "long u," a sound which they analyze into the two elements [i] and [u]. But Webster waged an unending feud against this diphthongal sound in most of the words in which Sheridan and Walker said it occurred, and his hostility to it undoubtedly arose from the fact that it did not occur in that common New England pronunciation of his day for which Webster felt such high respect. He did acknowledge in the *American Spelling Book*, p. 12, that "in a few words it [the letter *u*] answers the purpose of the consonant *y* before *u*, as in *union, unanimity,* which are pronounced *yunion, yunanimity,*" but this value of *u* as [juː] was strictly limited to words with *u* in the initial position. He acknowledged also that "long *u*" when it closed a syllable, as in *due,* was a diphthong, "composed of its simple sound found in *truth,* and the sound of *oo.*" This latter statement apparently means nothing more than that there is slightly more lip rounding at the end of [uː] than at the beginning. But elsewhere he explains away more explicitly what is commonly meant when one speaks of the diphthongal character of "long *u.*" The sound is not composed, he says, *Dissertations,* p. 85, "of *e* and *oo.* We do not begin the sound in the position necessary to sound *ee,* as is obvious in the words *salute, salubrious, revolution;* but with a greater aperture of the mouth and with a position perfectly easy and natural. From that position we pass to the position with which we pronounce *oo,* and there close the sound." Webster's meaning here is not altogether clear, for his description might mean a diphthongal sound [ʊuː] or [ʌuː], though it could not mean anything like [iuː] or [juː]. Nor are his illustrations with *u* after *l* decisive, because in this position "long *u*" has always shown a strong tendency to be pronounced as [uː]. But what Webster says of *u* after *l,* he would say also of *u* after other consonants. Speaking of the word *fuel, Dissertations,* p. 159, he declares that "in this word, as also in *new, brew,* etc., we do not hear the sound of *e* except among the Virginians, who affect to pronounce it distinctly, *ne-ew, ne-oo, fee-oo.*" Even the diphthongal quality described above is more a matter of theory with Webster than of observation, for he says, p. 85, that though *u,* considered by itself, may be diphthongal, actually and in combination with consonants, it is but the mark of a simple sound or vowel.

Webster was so evidently in earnest in his endeavor to indicate certain distinctions in the value of *u* besides [juː] that some care must be taken not to do him injustice. He certainly rejected the sound which is now [juː], not only in words like *flute, abjure, truth,* which are neither pronounced, he says, *fleute, abjeure, treuth,* nor *floote, abjoore, trooth,* but he rejected it also in *mute, pure,* which he says are improperly pronounced *meute, peure* by those of the first rank in Great Britain and by some "fashionable speakers" in America. But what is this sound which he prefers and which is neither *eu* nor *oo*? "However obscured by affectation in the metropolis of Great Britain and the capital towns of America," this correct sound is still preserved, says Webster, p. 152, "by the body of the people in both countries. . . . Ask any plain countryman, whose pronunciation has not been exposed to corruption by mingling with foreigners, how he pronounces the letters *t, r, u, th*, and he will not sound *u* like *eu*, nor *oo*, but will express the real primitive *u*. Nay, if people wish to make an accurate trial, let them direct any child of seven years old, who has had no previous instruction respecting the matter, to pronounce the words, *suit, tumult, due*, etc., and they will thus ascertain the true sound of the letter. . . . Illiterate persons therefore pronounce the genuine English *u* much better than those who have attempted to shape their pronunciation according to the polite modern practice." From all this comment, two inferences may be drawn, first that Webster's sound for *u* in *truth, tube, duke*, for *ew* in *few, eau* in *beauty*, etc., was always the same, a sound which he did not like to represent by the spelling *oo* because this spelling indicated an excessive lip-rounding. His "long *u*" must have been therefore practically the sound current now in *rule, truth*, etc., that is the sound [uː]. It is probable that words like *rood, brood, food*, etc., were pronounced with greater lip rounding in Webster's day than they are in present English. The second inference is that though this pronunciation was current in New England, it was open to the suspicion of being a provincial or rustic pronunciation, or at least a local pronunciation, when it was compared with the usage of the rest of the country.

The comments of James Carrol, *The American Criterion* (1795), on this sound are interesting. Carrol remarks, p. 24, that "*u* has the long sound *oo* when it is immediately preceded by *d, l, n, r, s*, or *t*, and is at the same time followed in the same syllable by a single consonant and a silent *e* final; as in *duke, Luke, nude, rude, tune*," etc. *Duty, luminous, numerous* are given as pronounced "dooty, loominous, noomerous," etc. In a note, p. 25, however, Carrol adds "I would remark here, that the dialect of the southern states, is an universal exception to this part of the rule. For, when *p*, *l*, *n*, *r*, *s*, *t* or *z* precedes *u* in the same syllable, they sound it like *eoo* or *yu*; thus, *duty*, *luminous*, *tune*, they pronounce *dyuty*, *lyuminous*, *tyune*." Carrol based his book upon New England pro. nunciation, which he says, p. 25, "I prefer to every other English dialect." He remarks in his Preface, p. iii, that "the pronunciation of the southern states of English America is almost as different from that of the New England states, even among the learned, as any two dialects of the language of any illiterate nation can be supposed to be."

Webster stood by his guns faithfully, and even in the dictionary of 1828 insisted on the pronunciation of *u* which he had defended forty years before. "Equally inaccurate," so he says in the Introduction to his *American Dictionary*, "is the definition of the diphthongal *u*, or long *u*; which these writers [Sheridan and Walker] allege to consist of the sounds of *e* and *oo*, or *yu*. It has this sound indeed in *unite*, *union*, and others; but this is a departure from the proper sound of this character, as heard in *cube*, *abuse*, *durable*, *human*, *jury*. These words are not pronounced *keeob*, *obeoose*, *deoorable*, *heooman*, *jeoory*. The effort to introduce this affected pronunciation is of most michievous tendency. The sound of *e* is not heard in the proper enunciation of the English *u*, and for that reason, it should not be so stated on paper, nor named *yu*; as the error naturally leads to a corrupt pronunciation. . . . But this is not the whole evil; this analysis of *u* has led orthoepists to give to first or long *u*, two distinct sounds, or rather to make a diphthong and a vowel of this single letter. Thus they make it a diphthong in almost all situations, except after *r*, where they make it a vowel equivalent to *oo* or the French *ou*. They represent *u* as being equivalent to *ew*, that is, *e* and *oo*, in *cube*, *tube*, *duty*, *confusion*, *endure*, pronounced *kewbe*, *tewbe*, *dewty*, *confewsion*, *endewre*, but in *brute*, *fruit*, *rude*, *intrude*, *ruby*, they make *u* equivalent to *oo*; thus *broote*, *froot*, *roode*, *introode*, *rooby*." Webster acknowledges that after palatals and labials before *u* there is a natural tendency to insert an *e*, and this same cause "has given rise to the pronunciation of *e* before the vowel in such words as *guide, guard, kind, guise*. This is precisely similar to the vulgar pronunciation of *cow, gown, county, town*, etc., that is, *keow, geown, keounty, teown;* a pronunciation formerly common in New England, and not yet wholly extinct. This vicious pronunciation, in all words of this kind, whether countenanced by men of low life or of fashionable life, ought to be carefully avoided, as the slender sound of *e*, in such cases, gives a feebleness to the words utterly inconsistent with that full, open and manly enunciation which is essential to eloquence." As it happens, the explanation which Webster gave of the origin of the diphthongal pronunciation of *u* is historically incorrect, but even if it had been correct, it is easy to see how such insistence upon theory and such disregard of practice as Webster here exhibits should have brought upon him the charge of narrow-minded pedantry. What Webster says with respect to usage cannot have been true. He was particularly attentive, he declares, during his stay in England, "to the public speakers of England, in regard to the point, and was happy to find, that very few of these made the distinction here mentioned. In that country as in this, the long *u* has a uniform sound after all the consonants." One cannot reject the suspicion that Webster heard for *u* the sound which he wanted to hear. It is probable that usage is less divided today than it was a hundred years ago. The authority of the dictionaries, grammars and teachers has so consistently favored the diphthongal pronunciation of *u* and rejected Webster's pronunciation that even in New England the latter is now less common than it was formerly. Worcester's dictionary of 1830 fully recognized the value of long *u* as [juː] in *tube, tune, pure, lute*, etc., and as [uː] only after *r*, and the later editions of Webster of course adopted this pronunciation. Fowle, *Common School Speller*, Boston, 1842, p. 90, says that "the great fault of New Englanders and their offspring is pronouncing the *u* as if it was *oo—magnitoode, institoote*, etc."

The two main historical sources for Modern English [juː] are

(1) native words which in Old English contained a front vowel followed by *w*, as in *niwe*, "new," the *w* later vocalizing and thus foɪming a diphthong with the preceding vowel; and (2) French words with *u*, as in *pure*, the vowel being first a simple but much rounded vowel in French, which later passed into a diphthongal quality. The diphthongal quality of the vowels of these words, both native and French, is established for as early as the sixteenth century, see Wyld, *History of Modern Colloquial English*, pp. 242–244, but usage in them varied for a long time. Since the diphthong might develop merely into [uː] whether the word was a native word or French, obviously words with original [uː] might be attracted to the class of words in which [juː] tended to become the prevailing form. In New England rustic speech considerable confusion arose between words which historically have [uː] and those with [juː]. Thus the words *to, do* were pronounced [tjuː], [djuː], see Grandgent, p. 224. Lowell transcribed *bruised* as *breused*, and *smoothed* as *smeuthed*. Pronunciations like [spjuɪn] for *spoon*, [skjuːl] for *school* are occasionally indicated in literary transcriptions of dialects. Staniford, p. 69, gives *nune* as a vulgarism for *noon*, and pronunciations like *tew* for *to, dew* for *do*, etc., are recorded. In Lindsley's *Love and Friendship* (1809), a comedy, the two Yankees, Captain Horner and Jonathan, his man, among other dialect pronunciations, are made to say *dew* for *do, tewe* for *to, too, two, glew* for *glue, threwe* for *through, scheuner* for *schooner*. This confusion probably goes back at least to the seventeenth century. In the *Southold Records*, I, 29 (1655), we find *tew* for *two*.

Lowell's comment on the rustic New England pronunciation of "long *u*" in his day scarcely conveys definite impressions to the ear. "Our 'uplandish men' retain," he says, in the preface to the *Biglow Papers*, "the soft or thin sound of the *u* in some words, such as *rule, truth* (sometimes also pronounced *truth*, not *trooth*), while he says *noo* for *new*, and gives to *view* and *few* so indescribable a mixture of the two sounds, with a slight nasal tincture, that it may be called the Yankee shibboleth." If the soft or thin sound of *u*, of which Lowell speaks, was the sound which he indicated by the spelling *trooth,* not only the uplandish man, but also the citizens of the hub of the universe ordinarily had that sound in words like *rule, truth,* in Lowell's day. More probably, however, Lowell meant to describe by the terms soft and thin a diphthongal sound which gave to *rule, truth* a pronunciation similar to that represented by the spelling *nune* for *noon,* that is, [rɪuːl], [trɪuːθ]. By the spelling *truth* he probably meant to indicate [trʊθ]. Holmes, in *A Rhymed Lesson (Urania),* comments on the New England pronunciation of *view* as follows:

> "But school and college often try in vain
> To break the padlock of our boyhood's chain:
> One stubborn word will prove this axiom true,—
> No quondam rustic can enunciate *view.*"

In *Elsie Venner,* Chapter VIII, he declares that the "unspellable pronunciation of this word is the touchstone of New England Brahminism." As a rustic and un-Brahmin pronunciation, Holmes spells the word *v'oo,* which apparently meant [vuː]. But the correct pronunciation, too subtle to indicate, Holmes characterizes, Chapter XXXII, as one of the elements of success in life. A pronunciation of *view* as [vɪuː] may still be heard in the speech of the older generation in New England, the first element of the diphthong being distinctly vocalic, short and unstressed, the second being only slightly rounded. Remembering how unwilling the discoverers of fine distinctions in speech are to agree that anyone else can quite precisely get the sound they have in mind, one hesitates, out of respect for the ghost of Dr. Holmes, to say that this present pronunciation of *view* in New England speech is the same as the subtle one which Holmes so greatly admired, but one may at least assume with some confidence that the two were much alike.

In the present dialects [ɪuː] may sometimes be heard instead of [juː], but the statements of the earlier orthoepists are not precise enough to enable one to tell how early a distinction between [ɪuː] and [juː] existed. The more the stress was shifted to the second element of the diphthong, the more consonantal the first element would become. The descriptions of "long *u*" as composed of *e* and *oo* cannot be taken as altogether adequate, though so far as they go, they indicate a pronunciation [ɪuɪ]. On the other hand the phonetic spelling *yu* was probably an attempt to indicate [juɪ].

In the unstressed syllable, [juɪ] sometimes is weakened, as one would expect it to be always in the New England pronunciation of *u*, but the weakening of [juɪ] to [ə] has not persisted in any form of cultivated American speech. Walker, p. 23, described *sing-e-lar*, *reg-e-lar*, *par-tick-e-lar*, as an "incorrect pronunciation . . . which prevails, not only among the vulgar, but is sometimes found in better company . . . but nothing tends more to tarnish and vulgarize the pronunciation than this short and obscure sound of unaccented *u*." Under the word *figure* Walker speaks of a "delicate" and a "coarse" pronunciation of words like *figure*, the delicate of course having [juɪ] the coarse [ə]. Webster in the dictionary of 1828, indicated his pronunciation of *figure* by the spelling *fig-ur*, which would be Walker's coarse pronunciation. He writes also *val-u* to indicate the pronunciation of *value*. In the Introduction to the Dictionary, he specially insisted that the unstressed vowel of *volume* must be short, and declares that he has never heard the word pronounced *volyume*, as Walker and others had given it, "either in England or America." But these pronunciations which Webster defends were certainly local New England pronunciations and elsewhere were characteristic of uncultivated speech. But even in New England they must have been more than questionable at the time Webster's dictionary of 1828 was published, for Worcester in his first edition of 1830 records only the pronunciation with [juɪ] in words like *figure*, *value*, *volume*, etc. The rimes of the poets do not offer any evidence for the pronunciation of *u* in the stressed syllable, for a rime like *due; too* would have satisfied the eighteenth-century ear, and for that matter many contemporary ears, whether *due* were pronounced with [uɪ] or [juɪ] in the unstressed syllable. However, such rimes as the following from Trumbull illustrate the characteristic value of *u* as a simple vowel in eighteenth-century New England speech: *failure: valour*, I, 48; *ague: Carthago*, I, 50; *peril: ferule*, I, 62; *Venus: genius*, I, 140; *figure: bigger*, I, 62. Freneau, p. 302, has the rime *solemn:*

volume. Staniford, p. 66, gives *continner* or *continyew* as vulgar pronunciations for *continue*, the pronunciation *continyew* being characterized as an "affected vulgarism."

As late as the *Elementary Spelling Book*, New York, 1843, p. 145, Webster gave the following pairs of words as being pronounced alike: *imposter* and *imposture; gesture* and *jester; tenure* and *tenor; valley* and *value; century* and *centaury.* As the name for the letter *w* [double ju], [double juː] Webster, *Elementary Spelling Book*, p. 15, gives the name *oo* [uː], which is in accord with his pronunciation, since he regularly pronounced "long *u*" as [uː], or a sound very similar to this.

The word *lieutenant* seems to have been pronounced very generally throughout the seventeenth and eighteenth centuries as *lef-* or *levtenant, lif-* or *iivtenant.* The spellings of the New England town records for these two centuries almost always indicate these pronunciations with *f* or *v* before *t*, and there can be no doubt that this was the common colloquial pronunciation. The pronunciation may be still be heard in America, but rarely compared with [lju'tɛnənt] or [lu'tɛnənt]. In England, however, it remains in general use, preserved probably by conservative military tradition. By origin the *f* or *v* is merely a consonantizing of the second element of the diphthong [juː]. Webster acknowledged this pronunciation neither in his earlier dictionaries nor in his dictionary of 1828. He must have been familiar with it, but probably rejected it because it was not in harmony with the spelling of the word. Walker remarked that "this word is frequently pronounced by good speakers as if written Livtenant." "The difference between the short *i* and short *e* is so trifling," he adds, "as scarcely to deserve notice: but the regular sound, as if written *Lewtenant*, seems not so remote from the corruption as to make us lose all hope that it will in time be the actual pronunciation." From this one infers that in Walker's day *Lewtenant* was not yet the actual pronunciation. As to American usage, Coxe, *A New Critical Pronouncing Dictionary*, 1813, p. 36, remarks that "*leftenant* prevails most generally, but *lew-tenant* appears to be becoming more popular." This doubtless was a fair statement of the case. In his first edition, Worcester, p. xiv, observes that "the pronunciation of *lieū-těn'ant* is supported by respectable authority and is deserving of countenance, as it is best conformed to the spelling of the word; yet, where it would appear stiff and affected, one of the other forms, *lif-těn'ant*, *liv-těn'ant*, or *lev-těn'ant* is to be preferred." Accordingly in the body of the dictionary Worcester authorizes only *lieū-těn'ant* as the formal pronunciation of this word. In the revision of 1859, however, he reversed his position and gave *lev-těn'ant* as the preferred pronunciation, probably led to do so by the influence of British usage. In this instance Worcester did not show his usual discretion, for by the middle of the century there could have been no doubt that the pronunciation now current had established itself as the normal pronunciation for this word in America.

(12) [ʌ] as in *sun*

This sound is a lowered and unrounded form of earlier [u] or [ʊ], written *u* in *sun, shut*, *o* in *come, some*, and of earlier [uː], written *oo* in *blood, flood*. Just how early these lowerings took place it is difficult to determine because of the inexactness of the earlier descriptions. The lowering of [u] as in *come* was much earlier than the lowering of [uː], but this latter change was well under way, at least in southern English, by the middle of the seventeenth century. In northern English the rounded vowel persisted longer and is still to be heard in the Scotch pronunciation of words like *come, some*, etc., as [kʊm], [sʊm], etc. This rounded sound may have continued in America, but the evidence to prove that it did, is slight. The rimes of the poets, if they could be accepted at their face value, would indicate a pronunciation [kʊm], [blʊd], [flʊd], etc., for a number of words, but rimes like *food: blood*, Dwight's *Columbiad*, pp. 75, 96; *good: blood*, pp. 82, 112, 145; *doom: come*, p. 203; *floods: woods*, p. 54, are so likely to have been merely convenient eye-rimes that one hesitates to attach much weight to them in the absence of confirmatory evidence. Franklin's transcriptions for the vowel of words like *some, such, rushing*, indicates a sound which can have been only [ʌ], as he describes it, "*um, un*, as in *umbrage, unto*, etc., and as in *er*." This is Webster's "short *u*," as in *come, love, sir, bird, her, American Spelling Book*, p. 25. In the *Dissertations*, p. 85, Webster remarked that "the sound of *u* in *tun* is a separate vowel, which has no affinity to any other sound in the language." The affinities of [ʌ] are not such as Webster would have recognized, with his habit of referring all vowels to [eɪ], [iɪ], [oɪ] or [uɪ] as prototypes, but one can infer at least that Webster was right in not connecting [ʌ] with [u].

For a few words with [ʌ], variants are occasionally recorded by the grammarians for correction, and some of these still persist in dialect speech. Thus *kivver* for *cover* is corrected by Dearborn, p. 136, also *sitch* for *such*, p. 138, *ingyons* for *onions*, p. 136, *shet, shot*, for *shut*, p. 43. These or similar words, e.g., *jist* for *just*, are mentioned by other grammarians, but the list was never large and the words probably never had much vogue in cultivated speech. In the *Hanover Records, adjust* is spelled *adjest*, p. 110 (1792), and so often, and *justice* is spelled *Gestiss*, p. 116 (1792). In *Plymouth Records*, II, 20 (1708), the spelling *jedged* occurs for *judged*. In Green, *Three Military Diaries, just*, adverb, is spelled *jest*, p. 89, and the adjective also is so spelled, p. 97. The spelling *civer-lid* occurs in the *Southold Town Records*, I, 215 (1675).

Cooper, *Notions*, II, 132, remarks that in New England "by a singular corruption, the word *stone* is often pronounced *stun*, while *none* is pronounced *noane*, or nearly like *known*. The latter is almost a shibboleth, as is *nothing* pronounced according to the natural power of the letter, instead of *nuthing*." He adds further that "it is not too much to say that nine people in ten, in New England, pronounce *does, dooze*, when the mere power of the letters would make it nearer *doze*." He mentions also that "even in Boston" and in the speech of "men of education and manners," he has heard people say *he shew me that*, for *he showed me that*." In all these cases analogy and the influence of spelling, unusually strong in New England, undoubtedly determined the pronunciation.

The word *put* besides its general form with [u] has a specialized pronunciation [pʌt] as a term in golfing. The variations in the pronunciation of *put* are the same as those in *roof, soot,* etc., discussed under [uː]. A speaker who pronounced *foot* as [fʌt] might pronounce *put* as [pʌt]. In the little poem about the mountain and the squirrel, called *Fable,* Emerson rhymed as follows:

> "Talents differ; all is well and wisely put;
> If I cannot carry forests on my back,
> Neither can you crack a nut."

Emerson was not always exact in riming, but in this instance it seems he would have avoided the rhyme *put* and *nut* unless he had thought that *put* as [pʌt] was a permissible variation.

(13) [ə], [ʌɪ] as in *bird*

The two sounds indicated at the head of this section must be considered together because they occur in the same words in the pronunciation of different speakers. The words are those spelled with *e, i* or *u* before *r* final, or *r* followed by a consonant, as in *her, pert, fir, flirt, cur, curt.* Words spelled *ea* before *r* and a consonant have either [ɑː] as in *heart, hearth,* or the vowel sounds under discussion, as in *earl, earth, yearn,* etc. The words spelled with *ea* have in general had the same history as words spelled with *e, heart, hearth* being of the same type in development as *sergeant,* and *earl, earth, yearn,* etc., of the same type as *term, verse,* etc. An occasional spelling with *y* as in *myrrh* is to be considered merely as a variant of *i.* Some words spelled with *o* are also to be included in this list, the *o* in these words being an orthographic equivalent of *u,* as in *worth, word, work.*

The sound [ʌɪ] occurs in these words in the speech of those persons who do not pronounce their *r*'s. The vowel in this pronunciation is similar to the vowel of *cut,* but is slightly higher and considerably longer and more tense, as will be observed by comparing *cut* [kʌt] with *curt* [kʌɪt]. The sound [ə] occurs in the speech of those persons who are said to pronounce their *r*'s, and it is consequently the pronunciation of by far the larger proportion of speakers in

America. The pronunciation with [ʌɪ] is limited to certain regions on the Atlantic seaboard, and to the speech of other persons who have been trained to speak with what is commonly called the Eastern pronunciation.

The quality of the vowel [ə] is peculiar in that it is the only vowel sound in standard American speech in which the point of the tongue is elevated above the lower teeth. The sound differs from [ʌɪ] mainly in that the point of the tongue, instead of being pressed against the backs of the lower teeth, as in [ʌɪ] and all other vowels, is tilted up and back until it almost touches the roof of the mouth, and it may be called therefore the reverted vowel. In other words, the tongue position for r is approximately assumed even while the vowel is being pronounced. All that is necessary to change [ə] into [r] is a slightly further raising of the tongue which will bring it into such close contact with the roof of the mouth as to produce the audible friction from the current of air as it passes out of the mouth which constitutes the special quality of [r] as a consonant. The question is still much discussed whether or not in American speech this further raising really takes place, that is, whether or not there is a consonantal [r] in such words as *dirt, fur, her,* at all. If there is not, then a word like *dirt* would be simply [dəɪt], in the speech of those who are said to pronounce their r's, the vowel being merely the reverted vowel lengthened. The writer is convinced, however, that ordinarily in the speech of those Americans who may be said to pronounce their r's, the reverted vowel is followed by a slight consonantal frictional element which can be designated only as [r]. This point is of more importance, however, in connection with [r] than with the vowel, and it will be discussed more at length under the treatment of that consonant.

Though *e, i, u,* have the same sounds in present English when they occur before r final or r followed by a consonant, such was not always the case, and for historical treatment, it is advisable to take each of these vowels separately. For *e* in words of these kinds, Sheridan generally recorded a pronunciation [ɛ], except for *e* in *her, hers,* which he records as having the same vowel as the *u* in *but,* that is, [hʌr], [hʌrz], and for *e* in *merchant* and derivatives he records ['mærtʃænt]. But he does not carry through this latter sound, as one might expect him to do, in words like *mercy, person,* etc. He has [klærk] for *clerk,* but ['klɛrdzɪ] for *clergy,* showing that his grouping was not consistent. Under the word *merchant,* Walker notes that Sheridan pronounced this word like *march.* "About thirty years ago, this was the general pronunciation," says Walker, but now "is become gross and vulgar." The only words that retain this pronunciation, according to Walker, are *clerk, sergeant,* and a few proper names. It should be observed that Walker misinterprets Sheridan in that he ascribes the vowel [aː] to Sheridan's pronunciation of *merchant, clerk,* etc., in which Sheridan really intended [æː]. Undoubtedly this [æː] frequently became [aː], as in the still surviving British pronunciation of *clerk, Derby,* and various other words, and in the word *sergeant,* which is the only word in American speech in which *e* before *r* and a consonant is pronounced [aː]. But though *e* followed by *r* and a consonant, continues Walker, is no longer equivalent in polite speech to *a* followed by *r* and a consonant, it has not returned to the proper sound of *e,* by which he means [ɛ], but all such words "have acquired a sound of *e* which they never had before, and which, though a feebler and a shorter sound, conduces to the simplicity and regularity of our pronunciation." Yet in the body of his dictionary Walker records words like *servant, service,* etc., as having the short sound of *e,* that is [ɛ]. His difficulty here was apparently that he had not quite made up his mind to accept the feebler and shorter sound which he had ascribed to *e* in words of this type. In the dictionary, p. 13, after noticing that *marchant, sarvice, sarvant,* for *merchant, service, servant* were heard only "among the lower order of speakers," he adds that though the proper names *Derby, Berkeley* still retain the old sound, as if written *Darby, Barkeley,* "even these, in polite usage, are getting into the common sound, nearly as if written *Durby* and *Burkeley.*" "As this modern pronunciation of the *e,*" he concluded, "has a tendency to simplify the language by lessening the number of exceptions, it ought certainly to be indulged."

These concluding remarks of Walker are specially significant, and they show that, as Walker judged it, the general tendency of words with *e* followed by *r* or *r* and a consonant, was to take on pronunciations very similar to those which they have today. That this tendency was not completed, however, is shown by Walker's reference to this sound of *e* as a "modern pronunciation." This can only mean that it had but recently come under Walker's observation, for in London speech, which was not the standard that Walker followed, it seems to have been completed long before Walker wrote. Perry, in his *Royal Standard English Dictionary*, records what he calls the "common sound," the sound of *u* in *buck*, both for *e* before *r* and for other vowels in this position. In his *Sure Guide*, pp. 22, 27, 32, which preceded the dictionary, he indicated the vowel which he describes as like the vowel in *buck* or in *her*, as occurring in all the places where one today could expect it to occur, for *e* followed by *r* and a consonant, and even for *were*, for *i* followed by *r*, as in *fir*, *sir*, *stir*, or by *r* and a consonant, as in *dirge*, *bird*, etc., for *o* followed by *r* and a consonant, as in *word*, *worse*, etc., for *u* as in *burn*, *curse*, etc., for *ea* as in *pearl*, *learn*, *search*, etc. The only exception he makes is in the word *girl*, which is marked in the dictionary as being pronounced [gærl]. But *virgin*, *virtue*, *gird*, *girth*, and all the other words with *i* followed by *r* and a consonant have the "common sound." The common sound could scarcely have been the vowel of *buck*, as Perry describes it, though this description was as near as one could expect him to come. Even today professional students of language speak of the vowel of *burn* as the same as that of *but*, and of the unstressed vowel [ə] as in *about*, as the same as the vowel of *but* (see Lounsbury, *English Spelling and Spelling Reform*, 1909, p. 131). It seems altogether probable that the vowel Perry had in mind for his "common sound" as it appeared before *r* was either [ʌː] or [ə], the sounds which it has in present English.

This common sound of *u* in *buck* must have been present in certain forms of popular speech long before Perry recorded it in his *Sure Guide* or his *Dictionary*. It is in fact clearly indicated in American use by many spellings of the seventeenth century in the town records. In the *Groton Records* one finds *furst*, p. 12 (1664), for *first*, and so often; *thurty*, p. 76 (1682), for *thirty*, and so often; *wur*, p. 82 (1683), for *were*; *pursin*, p. 93 (1686), for *person*; *confurmed*, p. 92 (1685), for *confirmed*. For *first* the spelling *forst*, p. 72 (1682), also occurs. But besides and contemporary with this pronunciation, the pronunciation of *e* before *r* and a consonant as [æ], [ɑ] is also clearly indicated by the spelling *clark*, p. 7 (1662), and so often, though also often *clerk*; *detarmen*, p. 12 (1664), for *determine*, and so often; *sargin*, p. 64 (1681), for *sergeant*, and so often; *larning*, p. 65 (1681), for *learning*; *hard*, p. 72 (1682), for *herd*, and so often; *confarmed*, p. 75 (1682), for *confirmed*; *sartify*, p. 82 (1683), for *certify*; *Garshom*, p. 93 (1686), for *Gershom*, and so often, but also often *Gershom, Gurshom*; *parsin*, p. 82 (1683), for *person*, and so often. The spelling *atarney*, p. 90 (1683), for *attorney* shows that sometimes words which historically should not have had two forms were confused with words like *term, person*, etc., pronounced with the so-called common sound and also with [æ], [ɑ]. The spelling *querter*, *Groton Records*, p. 120 (1701), for *quarter*, was probably intended to indicate a pronunciation of the word with [æ] or [ɛ].

In the *Watertown Records* similar divergent spellings occur. One finds *hur*, p. 15 (1647), for *her*, and so often; *survice*, p. 59 (1658), for *service*; *burds*, p. 97 (1669), for *birds*, and so often; *shurts*, p. 110 (1671), for *shirts*; *furst, thurd*, p. 111 (1671), for *first, third*; *wurk*, p. 114 (1672), for *work*; and very frequently in unstressed syllables, spellings like *ordured, mastur, aftur, naythur*, etc. The spelling *fur* p. 141 (1679), for *for* evidently indicates an unstressed pronunciation of the word. But on the other hand, spellings like *confear*, p. 119 (1674), for *confer*; *parson*, p. 93 (1668), for *person*; *starling*, p. 148 (1680), for *sterling*, are not infrequent, indicating that usage varied in words of this type between the common vowel and [æ] or [ɛ].

The spellings of the *Plymouth Records* are so confused that they offer little help in determining the precise pronunciation intended, though they show clearly enough that the pronunciation of the type of words under discussion was very unsettled. Thus we find *terns*, I, 235 (1694), for *turns; gerle*, I, 12, for *girl; tirme*, I, 295, II, 1, for *term; terret*, II, 21 (1708), for *turret; retern*, II, 27 (1709), for *return; Tirke*, II, 35 (1710), for *Turkey; squerels Rock*, II, 66 (1710), for *Squirrels Rock;* besides these of course occur frequent spellings like *clarck, clark* for *clerk, parson* for *person*, etc. The pronunciation of *far* with the common vowel is indicated by the spelling *furr*, as in the phrase the *furr eare*, I, 211 (1686), or the *nar eare . . . and fur eare*, I, 2, *the near ear and the far ear*. This pronunciation still survives in dialectal use, and it merely reflects the double development of Middle English *fer(re)* into [faːr] and [fər], like *parson* and *person*. The pronunciation [naːr] for *near*, indicated by the spelling the *nar eare*, may be explained as derived from Middle English *ner*, with a short vowel, though the usual form is *neer*, with a long vowel, which would regularly give later [iː]. Or it may be simply by analogy to *far*.

In the *Huntington Records* occur such spellings as *sturling*, p. 61 (1664), for *sterling; Bud*, p. 212 (1675), 227 (1676), for *Bird; durt*, p. 317 (1681), for *dirt*. For *sirrah* occurs the spelling *sarra*, p. 226 (1676), which means a pronunciation ['særə] or ['sɛra]. This pronunciation was insisted upon for this word by lexicographers and grammarians as late as the early nineteenth century, when the word passed out of use.

In the *Southold Records*, I, 470 (1658), occurs again the spelling *furr* for *far*. As was pointed out above, it is a regular development from Middle English *ferre*, which could as readily undergo a double development as *person* and *parson, clerk* and *clark*, etc. The proper name which usually appears as *Terrell* in the *Southold Records*, is written *Turril*, II, 164 (1699). On the other hand, one finds *Garle*, II, 179 (1698), and *gairle*, II, 180 (1698), for *girl*, and the proper name *Herbert* is *Harbert*, II, 41 (1685). And for the proper name which might and frequently did become *Purcell*, one finds *Paresall*, II, 179 (1698) and frequently, and a variant of this *Parshall*, II, 266 (1690), etc. In the *Hempstead Records*, I, 22 (1657), one finds *purmit* for *permit, pur Aker* for *per acre*, II, 33 (1657), *ox pastur* for *ox pasture*, I, 91 (1660), *thurd* for *third*, I, 162 (1665), but *ferst* for *first*, I, 104

(1662), and *thard* for *third*, I, 153 (1664), *thurty* for *thirty*, I, 178 (1665), *surtifi* for *certify*, I, 232 (1670), *porson* for *person*, I, 270 (1670), and *aformed*, I, 271 (1666), for *affirmed*. Other spellings which indicate a pronunciation retaining the older [ɛ] in these records are *hard* for *herd*, I, 92 (1660), *parsun, parsons*, for *person, persons*, I, 92 (1660), *heard* for *herd*, I, 93 (1660), *taremes* for *terms*, I, 93 (1660), *shert* for *shirt*, I, 65 (1658), *bearth* for *birth*, I, 300 (1675), *farme, confarmation* for *firm, confirmation*, I, 212 (1665), *wirmes* for *worms*, I, 236 (1667). In *Hempstead Records*, I, 187 (1669), occurs the spelling *har* for *her*. This is a very rare spelling and doubtless represented a rare pronunciation. When *her* is not spelled in the usual way it is spelled *hur*, and this orthography accords better with the commonly recorded seventeenth-century pronunciation than the spelling *har*.

The variation in pronunciation accounts for the spelling *varse*, p. 84, *virs*, p. 85, for *verse*, in Green, *Three Military Diaries*. No doubt the writer pronounced the word [vɛrs] or [værs], since his normal spelling appears in words like *sarv*, p. 91, *larn*, p. 94, *sarch'd*, p. 95, *farmness*, p. 104, for *firmness*, words with *e*, *i*, and *a* followed by *r* and a consonant all being pronounced with [æ], [ɛ]. So also in *Easthampton Records*, where *Gerdiner*, II, 32 (1695) and often, for *Gardiner*, *peart*, II, 321, and often, for *part*, *ere*, II, 101 (1681), for *are*, *Sarge and cersey*, II, 90 (1680), for *serge and kersey*, all are to be pronounced with [æ], [ɛ], in some words passing over into [ɑ]. The first name of *Perley Buck* in the *Hanover Records* is variously spelled, *Perley, Parley, Pearley*, see the index of the Records for examples; and from the several pronunciations indicated by these spellings would develop at least two well-established later pronunciations, ['pərlɪ] and ['pɑːrlɪ].

This unsettled state of affairs is reflected in the remarks of the early commentators. In his *Dissertations*, p. 105, Webster criticized the "very common error, among the yeomanry of America, and particularly of New England," of pronouncing *e* before *r* like *a*, for example, *marcy* for *mercy*. Webster thinks "this mistake must have originated principally in the name of the letter *r*, which, in most of our school books, is called *r*," that is [ɑːr]. "This single mistake," says Webster, "has spread a false pronunciation in several hundred words, among millions of people," and in a few instances, as in *clerk, sergeant,* it has become general among polite speakers. To remedy this evil, Webster proposed to give the name *er* to the letter *r*, to be pronounced [ɛr]. In reality the mere name of the letter *r* could have had no effect upon a vowel preceding it, and Webster's proposed new name for *r* was doubly futile. The pronunciation of *e* as [ɑ] before [*r*] was of course due to a confusion of the development of [ɛ] with that of [æ] before [r], the latter regularly becoming [ɑ] and remaining so in present standard speech. The spelling with *e*, however, was a strong argument against the pronunciation [ɑ] and those words with earlier *e* that became established with the pronunciation [ɑ] have all taken the spelling *a* in America, with the single exception of the word *sergeant*. In his first edition, 1830, Worcester recorded both [klɑːrk] and [klərk] for *clark*, but only ['sɑːrdʒənt] for *sergeant*. But in the revision of 1859, p. 12, he remarked that in this country "it is very common to pronounce these words, more in accordance with their orthography," as [klərk], ['sərdʒənt], though in the body of the dictionary he retained [ɑː] as the preferred pronunciation in both words. Since *clerk* has become universally [klərk] in America, *sergeant* remains the only word in which *e* before *r* and a consonant may be pronounced [ɑː]. Thus the proper names *Marcy, Darby, Clark, Barclay,* are all spelled with *a*, also often *sergeant* when it is the proper name *Sargent*. But the most significant part of Webster's comment is to come. He notes that "some fine speakers" in order to avoid "this disagreeable singularity" of pronouncing *e* as [ɑ], "have run into another extreme, by pronouncing *e* before *r*, like *u, murcy*." This is an error, says Webster, and "the true sound of the short *e*, as in *let*, is the correct and elegant pronunciation of this letter in all words of this class." He reprehends, *Dissertations*, p. 126, the pronunciation of *heard* as *hurd*, calling it an affected pronunciation of the "fashionable world," current only in the "capital towns." The coincidence between Webster and Walker, between whom there could have been no exchange of opinion, is very good evidence that *e* before *r* final and *r* followed by a consonant was generally tending at the end of the eighteenth century to be pronounced in cultivated use as it is in present English.   Walker calls the pronunciation modern, and Webster describes it as an extreme custom of "some fine speakers"; these statements mean merely that the new pronunciation was clearly set apart from the vulgar pronunciation with [ɑ], and had not yet supplanted the traditional and conventional pronunciation with [ɛ].   Walker expresses himself more charitably towards the innovation than Webster.   The latter, however, could not put out of his mind's eye the printed letter, *e*, and his refusal to allow any pronunciations like *murcy*, for *mercy*, was due to their "disagreeable singularity," as was his refusal to allow [ɑ] for *e*. He remits the rigor of his theory in only two words.   The word *sergeant* he allows to be pronounced *sarjent*, and *her* as *hur*.   In the several lists of the *Spelling Book*, *e* followed by *r* is always found in groups of words containing [ɛ], and popular pronunciation like *marcy*, *parfect*, for *mercy*, *perfect*, are corrected.   These pronunciations with [ɛ] were still adhered to in the dictionary of 1828, but by this time they must have seemed extremely artificial.   Even the *Elementary Spelling Book*, of 1843, makes no provision for any other sound than short *e* [ɛ] for *e* followed by *r* and a consonant, and apparently all such words as *term*, *fern*, *stern*, *perch*, *terse*, etc., were to be pronounced [tɛrm], [fɛrn], [stɛrn], [pɛrt], [tɛrs], etc.   This faithfulness to the letter persists in a slight degree even today, especially among professional teachers of elocution, but it is doubtful if [tɛrm], [fɛrn], etc., are ever heard as natural pronunciations.

Though Webster seems to have been, in this case, unjustifiably conservative, undoubtedly the pronunciation [ə] for *e* before *r* made its way into general cultivated use but slowly.   Apparently it was unknown to Duponceau, p. 251, who thinks the only debatable point in the pronunciation of the two words, *herd*, *merchant* is whether the vowel is to be taken as [æ] or [æ:].   And yet it seems to have been undoubtedly Franklin's pronunciation, not only for *e*, but also for *i* before *r* and a consonant.   Franklin had only one symbol for the sound in *some* and the sound in the first syllable of *about*, that is for [ʌ] and [ə], but this symbol he used for the vowel *i* in *whirlwind*, p. 300, *first*, p. 302, for *e* in *uncertain*, p. 302, *servant*, p. 302, for *ea* in *learning*, p. 301 (though he has [ən'lernd] for *unlearn'd*, p. 303, which may be an oversight), for *u* in *occurs*, p. 301, and for *o* in *words*, p. 302. The sound in these words Franklin described as "a very short vowel, the sound of which we would express in our present letters thus, *uh:* a short, and not very strong aspiration," p. 297. It will be remembered that Perry as early as 1775 in his dictionary, and still earlier in his *Sure Guide*, had recorded the "common sound" as definitely fixed in London speech. And Franklin's usage corresponds to that indicated by numerous spellings of the early town records.

The statements of Willard, an unusually careful observer, are worth noting, to show how these distinctions and differences lingered. He says, page 12, that "*e* before *r* in *serve, serpent*, and the like, is to have the same kind of sound, which it has in *berry*, but it is to be nearly twice as long. It is not to be pronounced like *u* in *surly*, nor like *a* in *Sardis*, nor like *a* in *care*." For *girl* he prescribes the pronunciation with [ɛ], as in *serve*, but *bird* has the "common sound" of *i*, that is the vowel of *burst*. In a later list, pp. 152–154, he gives [ɛ] as the sound of *e* or *ea* before *r* as the rule, and sometimes of *i, y* before *r*. Thus *fir, myrrh, gird, girl, mirth, myrtle, virgin*, etc., are supposed to be pronounced with [ɛ], but exceptionally *stir, birch, dirge, thirst*, etc., with "the sound of *u* in *fur*." Such distinctions could obviously only be maintained by dogmatic instruction, and various other grammarians give evidence of the struggle which went on for a time between Walker and nature, until nature conquered. Thus Israel Alger, in his *Orthoepical Guide to the English Tongue*, Barnstable, Massachusetts, 1836, being a version of Perry's *Only Sure Guide* with a top-dressing of Walker, edited from Isaiah Thomas's edition of the former, remarks that "there is one peculiarity which distinguishes Mr. Walker's pronunciation from the vulgar, and which deserves notice, and that is the proper sound of short *e* before *r* . . . whereas in the common pronunciation, it has

been made to express the sound of short *u*," *merry* and *mercy* thus
having the same vowel. Cummings, p. 20, gives [klɑɪrk] as the proper
theoretical pronunciation of *clerk*, but adds that the sound of the
vowel is "commonly *clĕrk*," that is [klərk]. Earlier he had remarked,
p. x, that "those who are desirous of imitating Walker precisely
will find it necessary to pay great attention in giving the true sound
to short *e* before *r* lest it run into the sound of short *u*," as in *early*,
earldom.

The common vowel is clearly recognized by Worcester for both
e and *i* in his first edition of 1830. After discussing *a* and *o* before
r final and *r* followed by a consonant, he notes, p. xii, that in this
position *e*, *i* and *u* have also been affected by *r* in a way which he
says has not been taken into account by the orthoepists. In this
position, the vowels *e*, *i*, *u*, *y* "have all nearly or quite the same
sound, as will be perceived in the words *her*, *sir*, *fur*, *myrrh*, *herd*,
bird, *surd;* but their short sounds are widely different, when followed
by *r*, as well as by other consonants, as in *merry*, *mirror*, *Murray*."
These vowels, *e*, *i*, *u*, *y*, before *r* final or *r* and a consonant, "are
to be pronounced with as short a sound as they readily or naturally
receive in their respective situations; but they cannot, thus situ-
ated, be pronounced with their proper short sound without effort
or affectation." These statements are about as complete an identification of Worcester's pronunciation of *e* before *r* with that now
current as one could well expect in a phonetic description written
in Worcester's day. He recognized that the "peculiar character"
of the vowel sound in *her*, *herd*, etc., is caused by the *r*, but unfortunately he had at hand no exact vocabulary which would enable him
to describe the organic formation of this sound. The stress he lays,
however, upon the slightness of the vocalic sound is significant.
The 'proper' sounds of these several vowels as short sounds are
different from the 'common' sound, the former being preserved only
when *e*, *i*, *u* followed by *r* are further followed by another vowel,
as in *merry*, *mirror*, *Murray*. A fuller description had been given
by Walker, p. 13, with which Worcester was probably familiar and

with which he probably agreed. The *e* in *her*, said Walker, "is pronounced nearly like short *u*, and as we hear it in the unaccented terminations of *writer*, *reader*, etc., where we may observe that the *r* being only a jar, and not a definite and distinct articulation like the other consonants, instead of stopping the efflux of voice, lets it imperfectly pass, and so corrupts and alters the true sound of the vowel."

The rimes of the earlier poets often indicate a pronunciation which, at first glance, might seem to indicate that the pronunciation [ɑ] for *e* before *r* and a consonant, reprehended by all the grammarians and lexicographers as vulgar, was widely current also in cultivated speech. No doubt it was in some degree, since otherwise there would have been little point in correcting it in educational books. But since the spelling *a* before *r* and a consonant usually meant [æ] in the eighteenth and early nineteenth centuries, it is apparent that a rime like *arms: terms*, *Anarchiad*, p. 43, may have been a rime between [æ] and [ɛ], two sounds similar enough to satisfy the ears of most rimesters. On the other hand, the rime may have meant a rime between two exactly similar vowels, that is between [ærmz] and [tærmz]. The probabilities are in favor of this latter interpretation, and this means of course that when [ærmz] was ready to become [ɑrmz], [ɑɪrmz], [tærmz] might go the same way and become [tɑrmz], [tɑɪrmz]. Rimes of this kind are fairly frequent in the poets, e.g., *desert: heart*, *Conquest of Canaan*, p. 51; *part: desert*, p. 196; *search: march*, *Columbiad*, pp. 339, 344; *universe: mass*, Hitchcock, p. 70; *research: arch*, Humphreys, p. 38, *errant: warrant*, p. 198; *harness'd: earnest*, p. 229; *hearth: mirth*, p. 132; *errand: apparent*, Trumbull, I, 62; *vermin: chairman*, I, 67; *person: farce on*, I, 18; *alarming: sermon*, I, 33; *observe: starve*, I, 37; *warn 'em: concern 'em*, I, 119; *infernal: Arnold*, I, 153; *researches: marches*, I, 155; *verse: farce*, II, 13; *desert: heart*, II, 53.

The pronunciation of *i* before *r* final or *r* and a consonant began to show some tendency as early as the beginning of the seventeenth century to fall in with the pronunciation of *e* in similar positions, see Jespersen, *Modern English Grammar*, I, 319, but here again the identification of the two sounds took place only gradually. Walker's distinctions are somewhat elaborate. When *i* is followed by *r* and another consonant not in a final syllable, he says, p. 15, "it has exactly the sound of *e* in *vermin, vernal,* etc., as in *virtue, virgin,* etc.," a sound which he records simply as [ɛ], but "which approaches to the sound of short *u.*" When *i* comes before *r* followed by a consonant in a final syllable, "it acquires the sound of *u* exactly, as *bird, dirt, shirt, squirt,* etc." The only exceptions to this rule are *mirth, birth,* and *firm,* "where *i* is pronounced like *e,* and as if the words were written *merth, berth,* and *ferm.*" Walker should have added to his three exceptions another pronunciation which he records in the body of his dictionary, that of *girl,* as [gɛrl]. When *i* comes before *r* followed by a vowel, it preserves its "pure, short sound," as in *irritate, conspiracy,* etc., "but when *r* is followed by another consonant, or is a final letter of a word with the accent upon it, the *i* goes into a deeper and broader sound, equivalent to short *e,* as heard in *virtue,* etc. So *fir,* a tree, is perfectly similar to the first syllable of *ferment,* though often corruptly pronounced like *fur,* a skin. *Sir* and *stir* are exactly pronounced as if written *sur* and *stur.*" "The sound of *i* in this situation," Walker concludes, "ought to be more carefully attended to, as letting it fall into the sound of *u,* where it should have the sound of *e,* has a grossness in it approaching to vulgarity." It must be said, however, that Walker's rules did not provide a very secure defense against this danger of vulgarity; for if *sir, stir* may be pronounced *sur, stur,* why may not *fir* be pronounced *fur?*

The author of the *British Grammar,* p. 10, says that *i* is "sounded like short (u)" in *first, shirt, bird, third, dirt, flirt, thirty, thirsty,* etc., and he says nothing about *i* pronounced [ɛ] in words of similar spelling. "Some Writers," he remarks, "give the Sound of obscure (u) to (i) in *first, bird,* etc., but I think it preposterous to represent the obscure Sound of one Vowel by that of another, especially when we consider that these obscure Sounds can scarcely be communicated to, or distinguished by the Ear. For if we take for Instance the Word *Father,* and substitute *a, i, o, u* in the Place of *e* and still

pronounce the Word with its proper Accent and Cadence, it will
be difficult for the Ear to determine the Difference between Fáthar,
Fáther, Fáthor, Fáthur, and Fáthr without the (e)." But apparently
what troubles this writer is merely the designation of the sound, not
its quality. For *i* in all the word before *r* he apparently recognizes
only [ʌ]. For *e* before *r* in accented syllables when *r* is final or before
a consonant, he still has [ɛ].

Webster's groupings of words in his *American Spelling Book*
are made according to no principles that can be followed. On p.
51 he gives the following as having short *e* [ɛ]: *skirt, dirge, virge,*
firm, stirp, chirp, quirk, fir, myrrh; and on p. 52, the following as all
having short *u,* the vowel of *come: dirt, shirt, flirt, birt, squirt, kirk,*
bird, first, sir, stir, twirl, birch. On p. 60 he gives *circuit, firkin, dirty,*
stirrup, skirmish, squirrel, virgin as having short *u* in the accented
syllable; but though *virgin* has short *u, virtue,* p. 60, has short *e.*
If Webster's lists are based upon observation of actual spoken usage,
they offer a good illustration of the illogicality and lack of system
of practical speech; for why should *skirt* be pronounced with short
e, and *shirt* with short *u?* It is probable, however, that Webster's
hearing in this case was somewhat obscured by his theories of the
fitting. Doubtless he was striving to save as many words as possible
from what he must have regarded as the popular corruption of pronouncing short *u* for *i.* Duponceau, p. 252, makes a similar effort.
He records the same vowel in *fir, sir, third, bird,* as in *herd, merchant,*
and this in turn is the same vowel as the vowel of *carry, terrible,*
man, that is [æ]. He acknowledges that "the vulgar pronunciation"
of *fir, sir, third, bird,* and other words similarly spelt, is *fur, sur,*
thurd, burd, but adds, "I do not think it correct." But both Webster
with his [ɛ] and Duponceau with his [æ] were fighting a losing battle.
The pronunciation of *i* with the sound of *u* in *curl* had become so
general by 1830 that Worcester was enabled to record it in his dictionary without protest as the common American pronunciation.
This means that it must have been widely current for at least a
generation before. The older pronunciation with [ɛ] has practically
disappeared, the only word in which it is still heard being *girl,* some-

times pronounced [gɛrl]. This word is also sometimes pronounced [gærl], and this latter form, with the omission of the *r*, has given what is often written *gal* in literary transcriptions of dialect speech. With the *r* omitted in the pronunciation [gɛrl], a form [gɛl] results, which often appears in dialect transcriptions in the spelling *gell*.

Words with *i* before *r*, or *r* and a consonant, ordinarily represent an earlier form with *i* [ɪ]. In a few words, however, forms with earlier *e* [eː] have been more or less confused with words that had *i* [ɪ]. The regular later development of Middle English [eː] is [iː], but before *r*, this [iː] was commonly lowered and also usually shortened to [ɪ]. Thus the present phonetic form of a word like *fierce* is [fɪərs], or with the *r* silent, [fɪəs]. What one might posit as the regular phonetic development of this word would be [fiːrs]. The present orthographic representation of this original [eː] which became [iː] is *e* as in *here*, *ee* as in *deer*, *ea* as in *fear*, *ie* as in *fierce*, *pier*. These particular words with final *r* have retained the vowel as [iː] or [ɪ], but some of them and a few other words in which the vowel occurred before *r* and a consonant formerly varied in usage. For the words *fierce*, *pierce*, Sheridan gave only [fɛrs], [pɛrs]. Walker under *fierce* gives both *feerce* and *ferse*, the former indicating a pronunciation [fiːrs], with the vowel as yet unlowered. The first of these, he says, is the more general, and the second is heard chiefly on the stage, because on the stage, where passions are to be represented, a short vowel is better to denote "a rapid and violent emotion." Under *pierce* these opinions are said to apply also to that word. Perhaps all that Walker's reference to the stage means is that Walker had observed the pronunciation there more frequently than elsewhere, not because it did not occur elsewhere, but because at the theater the habit of observation was more assiduously cultivated. Webster, in the *American Spelling Book*, p. 51, gives *fierce*, *pierce*, *tierce*, as having [ɛ], the same vowel as *verse*, and as *skirt*, *firm*, etc. This pronunciation is retained even in the dictionary of 1828. Worcester in 1830 records *fierce*, *pierce*, with both pronunciations, [iː] having the preference. He records *tierce* also with both, [tɛrs] having the preference. In Worcester's revision of 1859 the pronunciation

[fɛrs] is omitted, but [pɛrs] and [tɛrs] are retained as second choices
for *pierce, tierce*. Webster in his *Dissertations*, p. 125, made a local
distinction. "In the middle and southern states," he says, "*fierce,
pierce, tierce* are pronounced *feerce, peerce, teerce*." But this he
regards as wrong, and declares that "the standard English pronunciation now is *ferce, perce, terce*, and it is universal in New England." If Webster's statement is correct, we have here another
indication that the general pronunciation in America has been derived
not from New England practice, but from that of the Middle States.
But both Webster and Worcester were doubtless conservative in
retaining the pronunciations [fɛrs], [pɛrs], and Webster especially
must have held on to it for theoretical reasons after it had ceased
to be general. If it had been general there is no reason why *fierce,
pierce*, should not have been developed in the same way as *verse*,
that is, have taken on the so-called common vowel. But [fərs]
and [pərs] are not commonly recorded as pronunciations for these
words. The pronunciations are mentioned by Nares, *General Rules*,
p. 66, who says, "I have heard *ie* pronounced like short *u* in *fierce,
pierce*, but I think very improperly." Nares mentioned Milton's
rime *pierce: verse*, L'Allegro, 138, but this of course may have been
[pɛrsɪvers]. A pronunciation [pərs], [pʌɪs] does exist, however,
for the proper name *Pierce, Pearce*, this being the normal development from [pɛrs], a pronunciation which conservative family tradition may have sustained in some special instances. The spelling
Parce, Lunenburg Records, p. 104 (1738), and so often, beside *Pearce,
Peirce* was apparently intended to indicate a pronunciation [pɛrs];
so also the spelling *Perce, Hanover Records*, p. 178 (1800).

The pronunciations [fɛrs], [pɛrs] are indicated by the rimes *fierce:
universe*, Humphreys, p. 54, 130, 133, *fierce: verse*, p. 142; *pierce:
verse*, p. 107, *pierce: verse, Columbiad*, p. 313; *fierce: disperse*, Trumbull, II, 83.

The word *beard* is given only as [bɛrd] by Sheridan, and only as
[biɪrd] by Walker. "*Beard* is sometimes, but erroneously, pronounced *beerd*," says Webster, *Dissertations*, p. 128. "General
practice," he continues, "both in England and America, requires

that *e* should be pronounced as in *were*, and I know of no rule opposed to the practice." The *e* of *were* was of course [ɛ]. This pronunciation is retained in the dictionary of 1828, but Worcester, 1830, gives only the pronunciation with [iː]. The pronunciation [ɛ] may still be heard in rustic New England speech, e.g., in *bearded barley* ['bɛrdɪd 'baːlɪ], and it persists also, with the vowel lengthened, in the proper name *Baird*, a variant of *Beard*. It is indicated by the rime in *beard him: scared him*, Trumbull, I, 61; perhaps by the rime *heard: beard*, *Columbiad*, p. 214, though of course the quality of the vowel in *heard* is open to question; and by the rime *prepar'd: beard*, Freneau, p. 232.

For *heard*, under the influence of the infinitive *hear*, Webster made a long but unavailing struggle to maintain the pronunciation [hiːrd]. "In the fashionable world," he says, *Dissertations*, p. 126, "*heard* is pronounced *herd* or *hurd*. This was almost unknown in America till the commencement of the late war; how long it has been the practice in England, I cannot determine. To most people in this country, the English pronunciation appears like affectation, and is adopted only in the capital towns, which are always the most ready to distinguish themselves by an implicit imitation of foreign customs. Analogy requires that we should retain our former practice; for we may as well change *feared*, *seared*, into *ferd*, *serd*, as to change *heard* into *herd*." Both Sheridan and Walker gave only the form [herd], and it is this form which has become universal in its modern development [hərd], the other having become impossible in cultivated speech.

The pronunciation [hiːrd] for *heard* is recorded a number of times in the rimes of the New England poets, as in *jeered: heard*, Trumbull, I, 21; *appear'd: heard*, *Conquest of Canaan*, pp. 1, 13; *heard: fear'd*, pp. 40, 90, 140; *heard: disappear'd*, *Greenfield Hill*, p. 100; *heard: appear'd*, Humphreys, pp. 8, 173, *rever'd: heard*, p. 180; *rear'd: heard*, p. 62. This last example is dubious since *rear* was often pronounced with [ɛ]. But the pronunciation [herd] is indubitable in Ladd's rime *bard: heard*, pp. 118, 151, 160; he also rimes *appeared: heard*, p. 63, but in his verse *appear* frequently rimes with words with [ɛ], as in *appeared: herd*, p. 74. Freneau's rimes *heard: appear'd*, pp. 151, 320, probably indicate a pronunciation [hiːrd].

The word *peart*, common still in dialect speech and often recorded in earlier New England dialect stories, is a variant form of standard present English *pert*, the latter going back to a pronunciation [pɛrt], the former to [piːrt]. Jaudon, p. 215, corrects *pearch* as an impropriety for *perch*, these forms being parallel to those of *peart, pert*.

In his corrections of provincial Irish pronunciations, Walker, p. x, says that the Irish pronounce the words *fearful, cheerful* with the same vowel as *fear, cheer*, that is, with [iː], whereas the correct and British pronunciation is ['fɛrfəl], [tʃɛrfəl]. In the body of the dictionary, under *cheerful*, he regrets the short vowel in this word and in *fearful* as irregularities, but says such irregularities cannot be entirely prevented and must be recorded when custom gives them "considerable currency," as it does in the case of *cheerful* and *fearful*. The pronunciation [ɛ] in *cheerful, fearful* might develop into the common vowel, and Worcester, *Fourth Book* (1834), records *furful* as an improper pronunciation for *fearful*, p. 300, and also *churfulness* for *cheerfulness*, p. 205. Webster does not record this distinction. Lowell, however, in his Yankee version of the opening lines of *Richard III* in the *Biglow Papers*, spells *fearful* as *ferfle*, and Grandgent, p. 239, interprets this as meaning the same vowel as in *hurt*. Walker makes another distinction, p. 29, which may be reflected in Lowell's version of rustic New England speech. He says that *ea* in *fearful* is "long when it signifies *timorous*, and short when it signifies *terrible*, as if written ferful." No such distinction now obtains in present speech.

The main question with respect to the value of orthographic *u* before *r* final or *r* and a consonant is when the *u* was lowered from the sound of *u* in *bush*, to the sound of *u* in *but*. On this point the earlier phonetic descriptions are very inadequate; they do not ordinarily recognize the difference, though it is probable that the lowering took place early in the modern English period. Still less satisfactory are the early descriptions of the special quality of the sound in words

like *fur, hurt,* etc. The statement usually made is that the sound
is the same as the sound of *u* in *but, hut,* etc. It is extremely improbable that it was so, especially when the *r* was distinctly pronounced.
With the *r* lost, the vowel may have remained approximately the
vowel of *but,* as it still is in this type of pronunciation. But with
the *r* sounded, physiological conditions would tend to cause a reverted vowel to be produced before the *r.* This might be only a
glide vowel, transitional between [ʌ] and [r], in which case the phonetic
form of a word like *hurt* would be [hʌərt]. A pronunciation like
this is possible, but would not easily be long maintained. The
natural tendency would be to revert the vowel completely, giving
[hərt], the current pronunciation for *hurt* in the speech of those who
pronounce their *r's.* What is here said of the vowel of *hurt* applies
also to the vowel of *dirt, term* and similar words, after the vowels of
these several types of words were reduced to the common sound
which the earlier phoneticians describe as the vowel of *hurt.* When
the *r* was pronounced, the vowel most probably was the reverted
vowel, when the *r* was not pronounced the vowel was merely [ʌɪ],
a long and tense vowel not unlike the sound of *u* in *hut.*

The development of an initial [j] before *e* followed by *r* is occasionally recorded, but was probably always limited to popular or dialectal
use. Bradford, pp. 19–28, gives *yarn, earn,* and *yern* (to compassion-
ate), as all having the same pronunciation. This would have been,
in his day, [jærn]. Mennye, p. 91, also gives *yarn, earn, yearn* as
pronounced alike. The pronunciation of *herb* as *yarb* perhaps falls
in the same class. The syllabic character of the *r* seems here to cause
first a diphthongal vowel preceding it, the first element of which
becomes consonantal through shifting of the stress to the second
element. Somewhat similar must have been the origin of the pronunciation *forbe-yarance* for *forbearance.* "The Colonel," wrote
John Esten Cooke, *An Old Virginian Gentleman,* in a newspaper
article, 1870, "is attached to old customs and observances. He
spells *honor* with a *u,* politics with a *k,* and says *thar* for *there,* and
forbe-yarance for *forbearance.*" Nares remarks, *General Rules,* p.
120, that "*r* does not perfectly unite with long vowels and diph-

thongs preceding it, but retains something of the sound of *er* or *ar*, hence it is that the monosyllabic *bare*, *bear*, and *hair*, sound very like the dissyllable *prayer*." But *prayer* obviously becomes genuinely dissyllabic only when the vocalic elements of the word are separated by a consonantal element. Some further examples of this consonantal development may be noted. In *Plymouth Records*, I, 2, *ear* is spelled *yeare*, and so often. In the dialect employed by Bret Harte, *here* is variously spelled with an initial *y*, as in *yar*, *Poetical Works*, p. 113, *h'yur*, ibid., 129. In Longstreet, *Georgia Scenes*, this is one of the constant features of the speech of uneducated Georgia whites, as in *yearly* for *early*, p. 128, *yearnest* for *earnest*, p. 160, *yea'th* for *earth*, p. 213. It occurs also in R. M. Johnston's Georgia Tales, as in *Mr. Absalom Billingslea* (1888), *yeth* for *earth*, p. 319, *yeares* for *eares*, p. 378, and so frequently in other words.

In New York City and vicinity, a diphthongal development has taken place in dialect pronunciation for the vowels *e*, *i*, followed by *r* and a consonant, especially an alveolar or dental consonant. This diphthong varies somewhat in quality but seems to be most commonly a sound best represented by [ʌɪ] or [əɪ]. According to Babbitt, *Dialect Notes*, I, 463 (1896), "the *r* has become a vowel, and forms with the preceding vowel a diphthong which is very close to the French sounds heard in *feuille*." The popular transcription of this dialect pronunciation is *oi*, as in *thoid* for *third*, *foist* for *first*, *Oiving* for *Irving*, etc. But the first element of the diphthong is ordinarily closer to [ʌ] than it is to [ɔ], and the diphthong seems most satisfactorily analyzed as composed of the vowel of *cut* followed by the vowel of *bit*, the two elements of the diphthong being about equally prominent. Historical evidence for the origin of this diphthong is lacking, and though statistics showing the extent of its use are not available, it is a matter of common observation in New York that the pronunciation is widespread and is making its way from the lower popular level to the general popular level. That it is of native origin and not due to Irish or other foreign influence, as is often supposed, is extremely probable. The difference between the very general Eastern American and British pronunciation of

first as [fʌɪst] and the New York pronunciation of the same word
as [fʌɪst] is not so great as to necessitate calling in a special explanation for the latter pronunciation.   Both pronunciations are due to
the absorption of the *r* into the preceding vowel, a process not dissimilar to that which changed [ɑ] to [ɔɪ] through the loss of *l* in words
like *talk, chalk,* etc.   Though the New York pronunciation cannot
be shown to be a survival from an earlier Yorkshire pronunciation,
it is of interest to note that a very similar development is present
in modern Yorkshire dialect speech.   According to Cowling, *Dialect
of Hackness* (Northeast Yorkshire), (1915), p. 33, original Middle
English *i* before *r* and a consonant has become a sound like the *o*
in Scotch *top, hot, nod,* etc., with the lips only slightly rounded, that
is, approximately [ɔ], and the *r* has been assimilated.   Among examples cited are *bird, birk, church, third, first, birth,* etc., which might
be transcribed for this Yorkshire dialect as [bɔd], [bɔk], [tʃɔtʃ], [θɔd],
[fɔst], [bɔθ], etc.   This, to be sure, is not precisely the sound which
appears in the dialect of New York, but it is not far from it, especially
if one may assume a slight vocalic survival of the *r*, giving the diphthongal [ɔɪ], as in [bɔɪd], [bɔɪk], [tʃɔɪtʃ], [θɔɪd], etc.   Historical connection between Yorkshire and New York, Long Island and New
Jersey was especially close during the seventeenth century when
this region came into the hands of the Duke of York and was commonly known in local documents as New Yorkshire.   Immigration
from Yorkshire into this region was probably greater than it has
ever been into New England, the town of Burlington, New Jersey,
named after the town Birdlington, pronounced Burlington, in Yorkshire, being notably a Yorkshire settlement.   Though not provable,
on the basis of the evidence at present available, the supposition
of direct historical connection between this feature of present New
York and Yorkshire dialect pronunciation is at least plausible.

(14) [aɪ] as in *ride*

This diphthong is a Modern English development from Old
and Middle English [iː].   The change began probably in the early

part of the sixteenth century, and in passing from a simple to a diphthongal sound, several stages are to be assumed. Owing to the imperfect description of the sound given by the early phoneticians, see Jespersen, I, 234, the exact character of these several steps cannot be determined. The general trend, however, was in the direction of lowering, first perhaps to [ɪi], then to [ei], [ɛi] and then from this stage "into some kind of [əi]," described as early as the middle of the seventeenth century. The constitution of the diphthong in present English is variously given by phoneticians, though it is most frequently described as made up of [a] or [ɑ] and [ɪ], the second element also having been lowered. In American pronunciation generally the first element is certainly nearer to [a] than to [ɑ], and a pronunciation occurs with the first element practically [æ], though it is relatively rare in America. Without entering further into the complicated general history of this diphthong, we may turn to examine the evidence for its pronunciation in the records of American speech.

In his transcriptions, Franklin has only one symbol for the [ə] of *about* [əˈbaʊt] and the [ʌ] of *some* [sʌm], and it is this symbol which he uses as the first element of the diphthong in question. He has also only one symbol for the vowel of *did* and the vowel of *deed*, which he uses as the second element of his diphthong. Franklin recognized the difference between the vowel of *did* and the vowel of *deed*, but he says that the "true sound" of *i* is as the vowel in *deed*, and this he seems to regard as the type sound to which [ɪ] should be subordinated. It is consequently not possible to say with precision what Franklin meant by his transcription, but if we recall his description of the sound which he prescribed for the unstressed vowel of *about* and for the vowel of *some* as "a very short vowel, the sound of which we would express in our present letters, thus *uh*," p. 297, we cannot go far wrong if we take his pronunciation of the diphthong to have been approximately [əi] or [əɪ], as in [bəɪ] for *by*, [dɪˈvəɪn] for *divine*, [əɪðər] for *either*, [əɪ] for *I*, etc. This implies a relatively light stress on the first element of the diphthong. According to Shewmake, *The English Language in Virginia*, this pronunciation still survives in the cultivated speech of Eastern Virginia.

Webster's description of the sound is very similar to Sheridan's. The latter says the diphthong "is composed of the fullest and slenderest of our vowels," that is of the vowel of *hall*, and [i], the vowel of *he*. Sheridan's description, p. 10, is detailed, and there can be no doubt that the sounds he heard here were [ɔ] and [i]. In his *Dissertations*, p. 84, Webster says that in pronouncing "long i," we begin the sound "nearly with the same aperture of the glottis as we do the broad *a* or *aw*. The aperture, however, is not quite as great. We rapidly close the mouth to the position where we pronounce *ee*, and there stop the sound." The description in the *American Spelling Book*, p. 12, is essentially the same. It is the same, also, as Webster's description of the diphthong represented by the spelling *oi, oy*, different spellings for the same sound, which is always composed, according to Webster, of broad *a*, that is [ɔː], and long *i* [iː]. This description likewise agreed with the description of *oi, oy* given in the *Dissertations*, p. 85. There can be no doubt that words like *fine* and *join* had the same, or approximately the same, vowel sound in the speech of many Americans at the end of the seventeenth century. The rimes of the poets are convincing evidence that this identity of sound in the two types of words still lingered in good use in America. But that this sound was [ɔː] combined with [iː] one could not be altogether sure without further evidence than Webster's. For even Webster did not stand by his own description. In the Introduction to the dictionary of 1828 he rejected Sheridan's analysis of "long-*i*" as made up of "broad *a* or *aw* and *e*," and denied that "long *i*" and *oi, oy* were pronounced alike. He rejected also Walker's statement that "this diphthong *i* is composed of the sound of the Italian *a*, as in *father*, and the sound of *e*." "The truth is," he concluded, "the mouth, in uttering *i*, is not opened as wide as in uttering *aw* [ɔː] or *à* [ɑː]; the initial sound is *not* that of *aw* or *à*, nor is it possible, by any characters we possess, to express the true sound on paper. The initial sound is not formed as deep in the throat as *aw* or *à*; the position of the organs is nearly, yet not exactly the same. The true sound can be learned only by the ear." The only facts that appear clearly from Webster's statements are that he approved neither [ɔ] nor [ɑ] as the first element of the diphthong. The sound that he did approve might have been [a], for which he had no symbol, or it might have been [ə] or [ʌ], sounds with which he was familiar but which he may not have been willing to recognize as diphthongal elements, and for which also he had no symbols.

Willard, p. 15, remarks that long *i*, "according to Mr. Walker, begins with the Italian sound of *a*," but that, "as generally pronounced in New England, however, the first sound of *i* is the same with *u* in *bur*." It is quite probable that several pronunciations of this diphthong were present in the eighteenth and early nineteenth century. Thus it may have been pronounced as [ɔɪ], as [ɑɪ], as [aɪ], as [əɪ], and as [ʌɪ]. It is not surprising that Webster found the diphthong hard to analyze. The same difficulty confronts the phonetician today, and it arises from the uncertainty of the character of the first element of the diphthong. In fact, except the first, all the forms of the diphthong just noted may be heard in present cultivated American speech. The first can also be heard in what is known as Irish English, as represented in dialect stories by such spellings as *foine*, *toime*, for *fine*, *time*, and approximately the same sound has been frequently observed by the writer as survivals of native rustic dialect in Connecticut.

The pronunciation of *oblige* with [iː] persisted as an old-fashioned pronunciation into the nineteenth century, and indeed even now is not altogether unknown. In Southern American English the word has taken a form, especially in negro dialect, which obscures its origin. The following citations will suggest the line of development: "but la'me! 't would o' been obliged to been found out," Longstreet, *Georgia Scenes*, p. 208; "Lord bless you man, don't try to get up! Lay still and take it!—you bleege to have it," *ibid.*, p. 63; "Dey'll git better—dey er bleeze ter git better, 'kaze dey can't git no wuss," Harris, *Chronicles of Aunt Minervy Ann* (1917), p. 40.

An older pronunciation of *sigh,* which now seems to have fallen completely out of use, ended the word with a consonant. Thus Hurry Harry in Cooper's *Deerslayer,* Cap. xv, speaks of *syth's and and lamentations.* Cooper's spelling with the apostrophe is probably intended to indicate a voiceless *th,* and this is the kind of *th* one would expect in this word, if one expected any. Forms with *f* are also recorded, see *New English Dictionary,* under the verb *sigh.* All these forms, *sigh, syth,* and *sife,* go back to a Middle English form typically represented in Middle English spelling by *sighen,* in which *gh* indicates a palatal or guttural fricative consonant similar to *ch* in German *ich, ach.* Ordinarily this consonant sound has been completely vocalized and united to the preceding vowel, as in the standard pronunciation of *sigh,* and in *right, light, eye, dry,* and hosts of other words. Sometimes, however, by a process of substitution according to which a slightly different sound is substituted for another so near like it that the ear may confuse the two, the original fricative has persisted, though not in its original value, since the consonant sound in German *ich, ach* has completely disappeared from the standard speech, but as the somewhat similar sound [f]. Examples of this are *enough,* by the side of archaic *enow, Goodenough, Goodnow* or *plum duff,* a variant form of *dough;* or *tough, rough,* which historically should not have a final consonant any more than *plough* or *bough.* The substitution of a *th*-sound for an earlier palatal or guttural fricative is less common, though undoubtedly that is what has happened in the case of *sigh.* The ease with which [f] and [θ] change places is illustrated by such frequent popular pronunciations as *fink* for *think, brof* for *broth, troth* for *trough,* etc. In the New Haven Records, p. 295 (1646), occurs the phrase *fetched a deep sight,* with *sight* for *sigh.* The pronunciation of *sigh* with a final [θ] is corrected by some of the early grammarians, for example, by Dearborn, p. 138, who lists *scythe* as an impropriety for *sigh.* One finds it occasionally also in early American fiction and drama, though always as a bit of dialect or colloquial color in speech. Walker has a long note under the word *sigh,* in which he condemns the pronunciation with a final consonant, expressly described as the consonant of *thin,* although this pronunciation "prevails in London" and is current on the stage. Sheridan spelled the word *sih* to indicate this pronunciation, and no·doubt the pronunciation of the word with some kind of continuant consonant following the vowel was not uncommon in cultivated speech during the eighteenth century. Nares, *General Rules* (1792), p. 106 says that *sigh* "is by some persons pronounced as if written with *th;* a pronunciation which our theatres have adopted."

For *China*, as the name of a country, Alexander, in his *Columbian Dictionary*, gives the pronunciation ['tʃaɪnə], but as the word for crockery ware, he pronounces the word differently, presumably with the vowel [eɪ]. Perry, whom Alexander usually followed, gives only the first of these pronunciations for both uses of the word. But the distinction made by Alexander was made by many others, for example, by Walker, who says that "this absurd pronunciation [of *China* as *Chainee*] seems only tolerable when we apply it to the porcelain of China, or the Oranges, which are improperly called China Oranges; but even in these cases it seems a pardonable pedantry to reduce the word to its true sound." Webster in the dictionary of 1828 has only [aɪ] as the vowel in *China*.

The pronunciation of *shire* with [iː], making the word rime with *shear*, was common in the seventeenth and eighteenth centuries. This is the pronunciation prescribed by Walker, p. 14, who notes it as the only instance in which *i* succeeded by final *e* does not take the value of the vowel of *eye*. Early American authorities often recommend this pronunciation, e.g., Ussher, pp. 95–96, Alfred, p. 150. But it seems not to have been Webster's pronunciation, for he mentions it neither in his earlier dictionaries nor in the dictionary of 1828. Worcester, in his dictionary of 1830, gives both the pronunciation with [iː] and the one with [aɪ], with the preference for the former, and this is repeated in the revision of 1859. The pronunciation with [iː] is indicated by the spelling *shear, Watertown Records*, p. 139 (1679).

(15) [aʊ] as in *house*

In origin this sound of present English is a diphthongal development from an Old and Middle English [uː], usually written *ou*, *ow*, in Middle English, but certainly the simple vowel [uː] until the beginning of the Modern English period. In analyzing the earlier diphthongal development of Middle English [uː], authorities in the sixteenth and seventeenth centuries describe what seems to have been [ou] or [ɔu], see Jespersen, I, 235. By the latter half of the seventeenth century, however, the descriptions "agree very well" with the sound now current. The precise analysis of the first element of the diphthong in present English is difficult, and the sound certainly varies a good deal, even among cultivated speakers. Most commonly in American speech, the first element is [a], the vowel of *father*, but in Southern speech it is not infrequently [æ], and so also in New England dialect speech. According to Primer, *Pronunciation of Fredericksburg, Va.*, p. 198, the sound of German *au*, as in *Haus*, is heard among a "select few" in Eastern Virginia, but the usual pronunciation is given as [ɛʊ], or with a slightly lowered quality of the first element of the diphthong, approximately [æʊ].

The change from [uː] to a diphthongal sound did not affect northern English and Scottish speech, and this explains the presence of [uː] in the present pronunciation of some northern proper names, for example *McDougal*, and in the word *uncouth*, borrowed by standard speech from the northern dialect.

Walker, p. xv, described the diphthong *ou*, *ow*, as composed of the French *â*, which would be [ɔː], and [uː], and says the "English sounds of *thou* and *now* may be expressed to a Frenchman by spelling them thâou and nâou." Sheridan's analysis of the diphthong had been the same. Yet other descriptions, cited by Jespersen, I, 236, show that this pronunciation could not have been universally established, and that besides [ɔu] the diphthong must also have been pronounced in the eighteenth century with a value approximating [au] or [ʌu]. The same divergence in usage doubtless existed in

America, though the early evidence points to [ɔu] as the prevalent pronunciation.

Webster, *Dissertations*, p. 86, describes the diphthong as "compounded of third *a* and *oo*." As Webster's third *a* is [ɔ] his statement implies that the older Modern English value of the diphthong as [ɔu] persisted in America down to the end of the eighteenth century. This inference is borne out by other evidence. Franklin regularly recorded the first element as [ɔ], as in *foul, flower*, p. 300, *our, down*, p. 301. Alfred, *The American Universal Spelling Book*, Staunton (Va.), 1811, says that "the pure diphthong sound of *ou* is made by uniting the sounds of broad *a* [ɔ] and middle *u* [ʊ]." But perhaps this description is only a literary survival, and may not have been based upon observation. The rimes of the poets given below, however, indicate a pronunciation [o] or [ɔ] for the first element of this diphthong as late as the second decade of the nineteenth century. Mackintosh (1797) described the sound of *ou* as in *bound, count*, etc., as being [o] followed by [u], the first element being the same as the vowel of *though, dough*, etc. And Mennye (1785), p. 91, gives *floor, flower, flour* as sounding alike, also *lower, lowr* (to frown), and *pour, pore, power*.

The rimes of the poets of the eighteenth and early nineteenth centuries abundantly testify to a pronunciation which was either [ou] or [ɔu]. Thus we find in Barlow such rimes as *brow: below, Columbiad*, pp. 51, 99, 112; *bough: snow*, p. 84; *crowd: strode*, p. 194; *howl: soul*, p. 285; and numerous rimes like *power: shore*, pp. 21, 25; *stores: powers*, pp. 29, 48; *towers: adores*, p. 112; *devour: gore*, p. 62; *hour: shore*, p. 161; *shores: flowers*, p. 312. In Dwight we find *bow* (verb): *below, Greenfield Hill*, p. 39; *pours: flowers*, p. 39; *brow: know*, p. 42; *woe: brow*, pp. 46, 87; *grows: brows*, p. 48; *devour: more*, p. 52; *scower'd: roar'd*, p. 67; *bestows: brows*, p. 76; *hour: restore*, p. 88; *plough: woe*, p. 152; *woe: now*, p. 154. In Trumbull occur the rimes *grown: town*, I, 7, 94; *down: own*, I, 11; *proud: road*, I, 57; *known: down*, I, 56; *throat: shout*, I, 16; *odour: powder*, II, 43; *grown: crown*, II, 49; *own: crown*, II, 68; *scowl: roll*, II, 172; *show: brow*, II, 172; *glow: brow*, II, 173; *now: below*, II, 191. Similar rimes are to be found

in other verse of the poets of the New England group.   They are
to be found also in Freneau, as for example, *door: bower*, p. 97; *more:
hour*, p. 115; *hour: shore*, p. 152; *power: more*, p. 200; *shore: power*,
p. 258; *down: crown: own*, p. 333; *prow: below*, p. 4.   Other examples
from the Middle States are the following from the poems of William
Foster, Salem, New York, 1805: *plough: snow*, p. 9; *boughs: shows*, p.
8; *plough: low*, p. 28; *shore: pow'r*, p. 46; *alone: known: town*, p. 48;
store: power, p. 48; *repose: boughs*, p. 49; and the following from
Heroes of the Lake, 1814: *now: foe*, p. 20; *know: bow* (verb), pp. 24,
61; *pour: shower*, p. 35; *now: low*, p. 36; *shore: power*, p. 47; *now:
below*, p. 53.

In several words some uncertainty in usage developed.   Thus
Walker, p. 36, points out that *pour* is "sometimes pronounced to
rime to *pore*, and sometimes to *power*."   He advocated neither
pronunciation, but one which gives the word the same vowel as
poor.   For *prowl* he prefers a pronunciation, p. 37, riming with *owl*,
agreeing with Sheridan, though he notes that others pronounce the
word to rime with *soul*.   Both pronunciations occur in the rimes
of American poets, [proɪl] as late as 1819, in Mead's *Mississippi
Scenery*, *prowl: stroll*, p. 18; *roll: prowl*, p. 52.   Nares, *General Rules*,
p. 82, gives *prowl* with [oɪ] and also *prow*, *prowess*.   He also gives
pour with [oɪ], p. 77, and says that *power* has the "proper" sound
of *ou*, *ow*.   Just what he meant by the proper sound of *ou*, *ow*, it
is impossible to say, since *ou*, *ow* often meant in the eighteenth
century [ou] as well as other sounds.   We cannot simply infer therefore, from a rime like Pope's *pour: shower*, in the *Messiah*, as Lounsbury does, *English Spelling*, p. 155, that Pope pronounced *pour*
with [ɑu].   His pronunciation of *pour* may have been in fact practically that of Modern English, and his pronunciation of *shower* different.

The older pronunciation of the diphthong as [ou], or even approaching [ɔu], remained well down into the middle of the century
in America.   Webster indeed recanted his earlier position on this
point, as given in his *Dissertations*, though the meaning of his later
statements is not clear.   In the *American Spelling Book*, p. 14, he

described the diphthong *ou, ow* as "composed of a sound peculiar to itself, and that of *oo*." In the Introduction to the dictionary of 1828, he specifically rejected Walker's, and his own earlier, analysis of the diphthong as made up of "broad *a*, or *aw*," and [uː]. "The broad sound of *a*," he says, "is not the initial sound of the diphthong; it is not commenced as deep in the throat, or with the same aperture as *aw;* it is a sound that can be learned only by the ear." In the absence of any more intelligible description, it would be futile to attempt to guess what sound Webster meant to prescribe for the first element of the diphthong.

Cummings (1822), p. 144, gives *power* and *pour* as alike in sound. Willard, *The General Class Book*, Greenfield, Massachusetts, 1840, whose first edition appeared in 1828, p. 15, says that in *ou, ow*, the first letter "has the same sound, which it has in *voice*, and the *u*, or *w*, the sound with *o* in *do*." "Thus to pronounce *cow* properly," he continues, "the same sound should be given to *cow* as if you were going to say *coy*, and if, instead of short *i* or *y*, you add the sound of *o* in *do*, the diphthong will be rightly pronounced. So, to pronounce *ou* in *sound*, you must begin as you would in pronouncing *soil*." He adds further in a footnote, that "many persons give to the *o* in this diphthong the Italian sound of *a* as in *car*, and what is unspeakably worse, many others give it the flat sound, as in *care*. Teachers should be very particular in requiring their pupils to give the broad sound to the *o* in all such words as *cow, sound, soil*, and *joint*." The value of *oi, oy*, he describes as being *o* with "the broad sound as in *north*, and *i*, or *y*, the short sound of *i* as in *pin*." "Some pronounce *oi* in many words in the same manner with natural *i*. *Oil* they pronounce *ile*, and *point, pint*, and *loin, line*. This is very old fashioned." The care with which Willard described what he takes to be the correct pronunciation of *ou* shows that this matter was of some importance as a question of usage in the early nineteenth century. Similar particularity is found in other grammars and reading books. William Russell, *Primary Reader*, Boston, 1843 , p. 32, gives *gâoon*, that is [gɑun], as an error for *gown*, which would be [gɔun] in his pronunciation. He points out, p. 26, that "the

common error in this sound [of *ou, ow*] consists in substituting the
sound of *a* in *far* for that of *o* in *orb* [for the first element] and prolonging unduly the first sound of the diphthong, causing a broad
and drawling sound; thus, *Pawnd, tawn,* for *pound, town.*" He
adds that "the local error of New England substitutes for the initial
sound of this diphthong, that of *a* in *at,* or of *e* in *met,* thus *Paund,
tawn,* for *pound, town.*"   Russell's description indicates with sufficient
clearness the difference between the present standard pronunciation
of the diphthong, which was just beginning to make its way at the
middle of the century, and the older pronunciation.   The present
English diphthong [au] or [aʊ] is a slow diphthong, with the two
elements of it prolonged and equally distinct.   This quality was
well described by Russell as "causing a broad and drawling sound,"
especially noticeable to ears accustomed to the older sound in which
both the [ɔ] and the [u] must have been short and rapidly pronounced.
With this latter sound in mind, it is not difficult to see why such
combinations as *own: crown* were regarded as adequate rimes in
verse.   As an earlier description of this sound, the statement of the
author of the *British Grammar* (1784) may be noted.   Describing
the diphthongal value of *ou, ow,* he says, p. 19, that "if we said *o—oo*
extremely quick, it discovers this Sound exactly; as *louse, mouse,
fowl, town,* etc., which are sounded quick *lo—oos, mo—oos, fo—ool,
to—oon.*"   This would be an adequate definition of the sound as
current in the eighteenth century in America and as persisting in
careful speech into the second quarter of the nineteenth century.
According to Shewmake, *The English Language in Virginia,* the
cultivated speech of Eastern Virginia still contains a pronunciation
uh—oo for *ou,* apparently a sound not widely different from that described by Russell.

(16) [ɔɪ] as in *join*

The eighteenth-century phoneticians are in essential agreement
in their descriptions of the elements of this diphthong.   The first
element they describe as being [ɔː] and the second as [iː].   So Walker,
p. xv, says "the diphthong oi or oy is composed of the French *â*

and *i;* thus *toy* and *boy* would be exactly expressed to a Frenchman by writing them *tâi* and *bâi,"* and Webster and others give essentially the same description. It is perhaps not necessary to take this description too literally. The distinction between [ɔː] and [ɔ] in the first element, and between [iː] and [i] in the second, is not one that earlier students would be likely to make, and it is altogether probable that the most common form of the diphthong in present English, [ɔɪ], has been its common form throughout the Modern English period.

The most interesting question in connection with [ɔɪ] turns on the older identification of words written with *oi* with words written with *i,* as in the rime *join: fine.* Such rimes could have originated in the first place, even as poetic licenses, only if the vowels of the two words were considerably closer together than they are in the present pronunciation of *join* and *fine* as [dʒɔɪn] and [faɪn]. Does this mean that the vowel of *join* or the vowel of *fine* was formerly different? As was pointed out under the discussion of [aɪ], the second of these suppositions is at least certain. During the seventeenth and eighteenth centuries the Modern English equivalent of Old and Middle English [iː] took on diphthongal forms that made a fairly close rime between that sound and the sound of *oi, oy* [ɔɪ]. But the vowel of *join* has also undergone change, and among its seventeenth-century forms must be counted a pronunciation [ʌɪ], see Jespersen, I, pp. 100, 329. In the course of development, therefore, the modern derivatives of Old and Middle English [iː] and of the sound represented by the spelling *oi, oy* in a number of new borrowed words tended to become approximately the same. Until the latter half of the eighteenth century it was good usage to pronounce words like *join* and *fine* with the same vowel. Towards the end of the century, however, the distinction between *boil* and *bile,* *toil* and *tile,* etc., became a mark of careful speech. Walker, p. 35, speaks of the pronunciation of *boil* like *bile,* etc., as "a very prevalent practice among the vulgar," but as something carefully to be avoided in polite speech. Most of the early grammarians and orthoepists in America agree in condemning the pronunciation of *oi* like *i,* though the custom must have been generally current in cultivated speech down to the very end of the century and have lingered on with old-fashioned speakers well into the nineteenth century. Benezet, pp. 147–154, in a table of words, "the same in Sound, but different in Spelling and Significance," gives such pairs as *bile, boil, file, foil, high, hoy* (a ship), *oyl, isle, I'll, ile* (the side of a church), *line, loin, rial* (a foreign coin), *royal,* without any expression of disapproval. So also Bradford, pp. 19–28, gives as pronounced alike *file* and *foil, hie, high* and *hoy* (a ship), *I'll, isle, ile,* and *oyl, imploy* and *imply, kind* and *coin'd, line* and *loin, mile* and *moil* (labor), *nice* and *noise, pint* and *point, tie* and *toy, tile* and *toil, vise, vice* and *voice.*

A great many naïvely spelled words of the early records indicate a pronunciation of words with *oi* as [aɪ], e.g. *implyment, Plymouth Records,* I, 84 (1666), for *employment; pint* for *point,* I, 284 (1700); *apinted* for *appointed,* I, 291 (1701). An example of the reverse, that is spelling *oi* in a word which etymologically had [aɪ], is found in the spelling *spoiles* for *spiles, Plymouth Records,* II, 259 (1728): "voted that the Land upon the point by the Bridge . . . be raised by setting up spoiles and filled up with sea Weed." Obviously if one wrote *point* and pronounced it [paɪnt], one might pronounce *spiles* and write it *spoiles.* In the *Watertown Records* one finds *implyed,* p. 114 (1672), for *employed,* and frequent labialized spellings like *apwint,* p. 139 (1679), for *appoint.* The spelling *loyable* for *liable* (1648), *Proceedings of the Massachusetts Historical Society,* New Series, II, 157, is apparently due to a confusion of *loyal* with *reliable.*

The pronunciation still exists in a few words in dialect speech, but has dropped completely out of cultivated speech. The difference in spelling was doubtless the most important influence in bringing about the separation between *i* and *oi.* The words with *i* may be said to have taken their normal course, but the spelling *oi, oy* as exceptional encouraged the special pronunciation [ɔɪ] for the words in which it occurs.

In a very considerable number of instances the older pronunciation of *oi* as [ʌɪ], which perhaps might also may be recorded as [əɪ′], occurred when the sound was followed by *l,* as in the stock examples *boil, spoil, oil, toil,* etc. It is not improbable that the presence of the lingual point consonant [l] had something to do with the modification of the [ɔɪ] diphthong in the direction of an [ʌɪ], [əɪ], [aɪ] diphthong. It is not improbable also that the pronunciation of words like *oil* as [ʌɪl], [əɪl] which is common in the popular dialect of New York City and elsewhere, is merely a survival from an earlier more general pronunciation. To the untrained ear, these words as thus popularly pronounced seem to have an *r* in them, and the New Yorker is said to pronounce *curl* when he means *coil*, and *coil* when he means *curl*. The ear of the person who makes such an observation is probably not greatly deceived, since the reverted vowel [ə] which he expects in *curl* often becomes merely [əɪ] with the complete loss of reversion of the point of the tongue accompanying the loss of the consonantal character of *r*.

Cobb, pp. 168–172, gives the pronunciation *kwate* as an impropriety for *quoit*, which he describes as being pronounced *kwoit*. The same correction was made by Webster (1783), p. 49. The pronunciation [kweɪt] still persists in dialectal use, see *Dialect Notes*, IV, 188. The older spellings of this word as recorded in the *New English Dictionary* are *coit* and *quait*, besides *quoit*. The spelling *quait* and the corresponding pronunciations were current in the seventeenth and eighteenth centuries, and the modern pronunciation [kweɪt] is merely a survival, though the spelling has become uniformly *quoit*. The etymology of the word is unknown, but according to the *New English Dictionary*, the variant spellings indicate a French origin.

One of the common features of uncultivated Southern pronunciation in America, especially negro pronunciation, is the form of the present participle of *going* with a [w] after the initial consonant and the vowel changed and lengthened, that is [gwaɪn], usually spelled *gwyne* in dialect stories. This pronunciation is merely a survival of a custom in speech which was formerly more general. It originated through the loss of the syllabic quality of the first of the two vowels in *going*, which from the nature of the vowel [o] naturally took the form of the lip consonant [w] when the vowel ceased to be purely vocalic. Exactly the same process accounts for the standard pronunciation of *choir* as ['kwaɪər], this word being derived from Latin *choru(m)*, through an Old French form *cuer*. The same explanation applies to the [w] in *quilt, quince, quiver*, and some other words, see Jespersen, I, 37–38. In the present British dialects, the form [gwaɪn] for *going* is general in the south Midland, southern and southwestern dialects, but not elsewhere, see Wright, *English Dialect Grammar*, pp. 91–92. It is a very plausible inference, therefore, that the pronunciation was brought over to America as one of those numerous features of early American pronunciation that can be traced to southern British origin. That the pronunciation was formerly current in New England as well as the South is evident from the inclusion of it in his lists of improprieties by the New England grammarian Dearborn (1795), who reprehends, pp. 114, 135, *gwyne* for *going*. Staniford (1797) also corrects *quile* and *quine* for *coil, coin*, p. 65. Jaudon (4th ed. 1828), who endeavored to purify Philadelphia usage, insistently corrects *gwoin* for *going*, p. 213. In the Jack Downing papers written by Seba Smith, the first appearing in 1830, Jack's grandfather, who was a soldier of the Revolution, is made to say *Burgwine* for *Burgoyne*. But by 1830 this was evidently a very old-fashioned pronunciation. In Alexander, *Columbian Dictionary* (1800), *coif, coit* are marked as pronounced *kwoyf, kwoyt*, though Perry, usually followed by Alexander, gives these words as [kɔɪf], [kɔɪt]. A similar development of [w] after *b* and before *oi* is mentioned by some early writers, for example, Nares, *General Rules* (1792), p. 74, who records *boil* pronounced *bwoile*, and *boy* pronounced *bwoy*.

That this pronunciation was very old is indicated by numerous early spellings. In Hazard, *Historical Collections*, II, 108 (1648), we find *apwoynted* for *appointed*, and p. 111, *pwoynte* for *point*. These spellings are in the *Records of the United Colonies*, which are written in a good standard official style and spelling throughout. In naïve spelling, the same pronunciation is indicated in the *Watertown Records* by *apwinted*, p. 113 (1672), *apwintted*, p. 115 (1673), *apwinting*, p. 122 (1674), *appwint*, p. 122 (1674), *apwint*, p. 139 (1679), *apwointed*,

p. 137 (1678). For *pie*, R. M. Johnston, in *Mr. Absalom Billingslea* (1888), p. 351, writes *p'wye* in central Georgia rustic speech.

Occurrences of this pronunciation in various regions of England, mostly southern, are noted by Wright, *Dialect Grammar*, §244, and also by Kruisinga, §300, in West Somerset.

(17) [dʒ] as in *judge*

The history of [dʒ] as developed from *d*, runs parallel to the corresponding voiceless [tʃ], see §25, developed from *t*, that is, [dʒ] results from the close combination of *d* with a succeeding front sound, written *i* in *cordial*, *soldiers*, *e* in *grandeur*, and *u*, representing an earlier diphthongal sound, in *gradual*, *individual*, etc. In the stressed syllable, as in *due*, *duty*, etc., the change of [d] to [dʒ] was never as general as in the unstressed syllable. Nor again does the change of [d] to [dʒ] seem to have been established as early as the change of [t] to [tʃ] in unstressed syllables, or ever to have been as generally diffused as the latter change. Apparently the influence of orthography has operated more effectively to retain the pronunciation of [d] before unstressed front sounds than it has to retain [t] in similar positions, cf. the pronunciation of such words as *obedient*, *gradient*, *expedient*, etc., with *quotient*, *question*, *nation*, etc.

Sheridan went only half way in his record of this sound. He gives it usually for *d* followed by *i*, as in *obedient*, *tedious*, *odious*, etc., but not in *cordial*, the second syllable of which he pronounced -*dyal*, and not for *d* before *u*, as in *gradual*, etc., which he marked as having [d] followed by the third sound of *u*, that is [ju]. But Walker accepts the pronunciation of *d* as [dʒ] not only in *tedious*, *odious*, *insidious*, etc., but also in *cordial*, *verdure*, *education*, "elegantly pronounced ed-jucation," and similar words. In the stressed syllable, however, e.g. *duke*, *reduce*, [dʒ] "cannot be too much reprobated." In advocating these pronunciations, Walker acknowledged that he was somewhat persuaded by theory. He does not pretend that the pronunciation of *tedious*, *odious*, *insidious* with [dʒ] is the "politest" pronunciation; "for the sake of analogy it were to be wished it were, but an ignorance of the real power of the letters, joined with a laudable desire of keeping as near as possible to the orthography, is apt to prevent the *d* from going into *j*, and to make us hear *o-de-ous, te-de-ious*, etc." For the sake of consistency, therefore, Walker would like to pronounce *d* as [dʒ] before all *-ious* endings; "nor should we forget that *India* comes under the same analogy, and ought, though contrary to reputable usage, to be pronounced as if written *Indyan*, and nearly as *In-je-an.*" In the word *tragedian*, which was the reductio ad absurdum of the opponents of the pronunciation of *d* as [dʒ], Walker of course permitted only *tra-je-de-an*, because [dʒ] in the third syllable would have led to an offensive "tautophany, or successive repetition of the same sound."

For *India, Indian*, the pronunciation with [dʒ] was formerly quite general in cultivated usage, but persists now only as an archaic dialectal pronunciation of *Indian*. Jaudon, p. 214, gives *Westingies* as an impropriety for *West Indies*.

Webster has a combined attack on *d, t* and *s* preceding *u* pronounced as [dʒ], [tʃ], and [ʃ], as in *education*, pronounced *ejucation*, *nature* pronounced *natchure*, and *superior* pronounced *shuperior*, *Dissertations*, p. 147 ff. These pronunciations he thinks did not prevail "before the period of Garrick's reputation on the stage." He quotes with approval the statement of Kenrick, *Rhetorical Grammar* (1773), p. 32, that it is "a Metropolitan pronunciation, supported by mighty fine speakers," and infers from this that it is modern and local, even in Great Britain. "But the practice has prevailed at court and on the stage for several years, and the reputation of a Garrick, a Sheridan and a Siddons, has given it a very rapid and extensive diffusion in the polite world." The pronunciation, however, as Webster views it, rests upon a mistaken notion of the value of *u*, which should not be a diphthong but a simple vowel. But he rejects it not only on the ground of theory, but also of usage. "I have been personally informed," he says, *Dissertations*, p. 170, "and by gentlemen of education and abilities, one of whom was particular in his observation, that it is not general, even among the most eminent literary characters in London. It is less frequent in the interior counties, where the inhabitants still speak as the common people do in this country. . . . But whatever may be the practice in England or Ireland, there are few in America who have embraced it, as it is explained in Sheridan's Dictionary. In the middle and southern states, there are a few, and these well bred people, who have gone far in attempting to imitate the fashion of the day. Yet the body of the people, even in these states, remain as unfashionable as ever, and the eastern states generally adhere to their ancient custom of speaking, however vulgar it may be thought by their neighbors." In a note Webster remarks that "the late President of Pennsylvania, the Governor of New Jersey, and the President of New York college, who are distinguished for erudition and accuracy, have not adopted the English pronunciation." At the risk of being unduly long, a further quotation may be made from Webster, illustrative both of his ways of thinking and of the pronunciation of his day. "In pronunciation be very cautious of imitating the stage," he warns in his *Essays*, p. 401, "where indeed nature *should be represented*, but where in fact we find too much strutting, mouthing, rant, and every kind of affectation. The modern pronunciation of our language on the English stage iz, beyond mezure, affected and ridiculous. The change of *t, d,* and *s* into *ch, j,* and *sh,* in such words as *nature, education, superstition,* originated in the theatrical mouthing of words; and iz, in language, what the stage-strut iz in walking. The practice haz indeed spred from the stage among our polite speekers, who have adopted it, az peeple do other fashions, without knowing why." Except for the naïve notions of the power of dictionaries and the stage in originating and establishing the practical customs of speech, Webster's statements fairly represent the facts, which were that for *d, t, s* before unstressed *u,* an older pronunciation retained in the latter eighteenth century the ordinary value of these letters as [d], [t] and [s], and that this pronunciation persisted as a very general pronunciation in New England, but that the more modern pronunciation, and the general pronunciation outside of New England, tended to give these letters the value of [dʒ], [tʃ], and occasionally [ʃ] before unstressed *u* [ju]. But the pronunciation *shuperior* for *superior*, and so in all compounds with *super-*, though advocated by Sheridan, seems never to have gained wide currency. It is not recorded by Walker and probably appeared only sporadically, whether in British or American speech. It is not mentioned by Staniford, pp. 66–68, who in his list of "affected vulgarisms" includes not only [tʃ] for [t] in words like *creature, fortune*, etc., but also pronunciations like *jewbus, jewty, individjewal* for *dubious, duty, individual*, and who would not have failed to mention *shuperior* for *superior* if such a pronunciation had been at all current in his day.

(18) [f] as in *far*

A pronunciation of the word *after* as though it were spelled *arter* is mentioned as an impropriety by the early grammarians, e.g., Dearborn, p. 133, Elliott and Johnson, p. 30–31, and is frequently indicated in literary transcriptions of New England dialect speech. It may still be heard in rustic New England speech, not only in the word *after*, but also in *daughter*. The *gh* in *daughter* was formerly pronounced as [f], and this pronunciation persisted down to the beginning of the nineteenth century, though the normal form established in the eighteenth century had the *gh* silent. Yet Timothy Dwight, writing in 1810, in the *Memoirs of the Connecticut Academy of Arts and Sciences*, I, 372, remarks that "*gh* is now either quiescent, or converted into the sound of *f; as in daughter, laughter*." Though it might seem at first thought and from the evidence of the orthography that we have here a phonetic development of [f] into [r], the inherent improbability of such a development makes it impossible to accept it. There is no phonetic reason why [f] should become [r]. A simpler explanation is that the [f] disappeared before [t] in *after*, as the sound has regularly done in *daughter, slaughter*, etc., that the preceding vowel was lengthened, and then as the tongue approached the position for [t] was reverted, thus producing what the ear commonly takes to be [r]. The same explanation applies to such dialect forms as are sometimes spelled *arsk, larf, larst*, for *ask, laugh, last*. The spelling may be not merely an orthographic device to indicate the quantity of the preceding vowel as [ɑɪ], but it may indicate also a change in quality, due to the reverting of the point of the tongue as it approaches the position of [s], [t].

The pronunciation of the *ph* of *nephew* varies in present speech between [f] and [v], the former being much the more general. In England the latter is said to be more general. Sheridan and Walker both gave the consonant as [v]. Webster gave it as [f] in his earlier dictionaries, as well as in the dictionary of 1828. Worcester in the dictionary of 1830, gave only [v]. Other American authorities vary in the same way, in the main giving [f] as the value of *ph*, except a few now and then, e.g., Alfred, p. 51, who calls special attention to the word as containing [v]. Historically, the sound to be expected would be [v], since the word goes back to an Old English word with *f* intervocalic, the value of which would have been [v]. The spelling with *ph* was at first merely an orthographic variation, supposedly an improvement, introduced by persons who thought the word should be made to look something like Latin *nepos*. The spelling *ph*, how-ever, regularly has the value [f], and American speech, with its great deference for spelling, has tended to establish this sound in *nephew*. Mackintosh, p. 74, recorded *ph* as having the value of [v] in *phial nephew* and *Stephen*. He also declares, p. 56, that *f* in *if* always has the sound of [v]. This seems like a hard saying. For *phial* the common spelling now is *vial*.

In *Hempstead Records*, I, 210 (1667), *off* is spelled *oft*, as in *a crop on the oft eare*. This is an instance of the adding of a stop consonant after a continuant, as in the popular pronunciation of *once, twice*, as *oncet, twicet*, etc., an organic phonetic process established in stand-ard English in *against, amongst*. It occurs after various continuants, and in these records *townd*, as at I, 100 (1661), is very frequent for *town*. In the *Watertown Records*, p. 83 (1664), occurs *proft* for *proof*.

A pronunciation of *lieutenant* as though spelled *leftenant* is now but rarely heard in America, though common in England and espe-cially so in army circles. The pronunciation was formerly current also in America, and the spelling of the early town records frequently indicates it. Thus in *Plymouth Records*, I, 2, we find *Leiftenant*, and so very frequently, though the spelling *lieutenant* also occurs. The accepted spelling was always *lieutenant*, and the greater harmony between this spelling and the now conventional pronunciation has been the determining cause in establishing the present standard pronunciation of America.

(19) [h] as in *home*

In the *Southold Town Records*, I, 1 (1651) and very frequently throughout these records as late as the eighteenth century, one finds *home* spelled *whome*. This might be merely an imitative spelling suggested by *who, whole*. It occurs so continually, however, and in the writing of so large a number of different persons, that one can scarcely doubt that it represented an actual pronunciation. It is found also in the *Hempstead Records*, as at I, 25 (1657). In the *Hempstead Records*, I, 159 (1664), not only is *home* spelled *whom*, but *oats* is *wootes*, and on the other hand, *whomsoever* is spelled *homsoever*. In the *Easthampton Records*, I, 14 (1651), *whome* occurs for *home* and elsewhere frequently. Moreover, the spelling *w'ome*, *Southold Records*, I, 291 (1665), is as clear proof as one could look for that the word was pronounced with a labial rounding. Wright, *English Dialect Grammar*, indicates a distribution of this rounded pronunciation in British dialects from Somerset to Yorkshire. In origin it may be compared with the labial rounding in *one*. It appears in *Smithtown Records*, p. 37 (1707), when *whod* is written for *hood*.

The records do not indicate that at any time or in any region was the loss of *h* [h] in words with this sound in the initial position, or the addition of *h* at the beginning of words with initial vowels, familiar to all in Cockney speech, current in American use. Occasionally one finds *an* used before words beginning with *h*, as in *Southold Records*, I, 18 (1653), *ffower acres and an halfe*, which indicates a silent or very weak *h*. But when one recalls the extremely naïve and phonetic character of much of the documentary material of the seventeenth and eighteenth centuries in America, one may be assured that if initial *h* had been frequently lost where it etymologically belonged, or added where it did not belong, one would find these pronunciations abundantly illustrated in spellings. In fact, however, the spellings do not indicate these pronunciations.

In contemporary dialectal use, the pronoun *it* in the form *hit* has been observed in various regions, see the indexes to *Dialect Notes*. The form *hit* is in all probability a direct survival from Old English *hit*.

Words with initial *h* are often recorded in dialect speech with a spelling *y*, as in Sherwood, *A Gazeteer* (1837), *yearb* for *herb*, *year* for *here*, *hyether* for *hither*. See also under (13) [ə], for a similar development before *e*, *ea* followed by *r*.

(20) [k], [g] as in *carter, garden*

The pronunciation of *k*, *g* in words like *carter, garden*, with a glide sound between *k*, *g* and the succeeding vowel is a well-known characteristic of present Southern, especially of Virginian, speech. It is to a considerable extent disappearing now under present day leveling influences, but can still frequently be heard, both in cultivated Virginian speech, and in the negro's naïve imitation of cultivated speech. In its origins the pronunciation was due to the development of a palatal glide between the palate consonants *k* and *g*, and the succeeding low vowel *a*. The same pronunciation arose also in words like *kind, guide*, in which the letter *i* stands for a diphthongal sound, the first element of which is approximately the same as the vowel of *carter, garden*. The glide sound thus developed became really more consonantal than vocalic, and the phonetic representation, therefore, of words like *carter, garden* in Virginian speech ordinarily would not be [kɪ'ɑːtə], [gɪ'ɑɪdn], but [kj'ɑːtə], [gj'ɑɪdn]. The vowel [ɑː] in words like *carter, garden*, etc., was a development of the late eighteenth century, the earlier vowel being [æː]. The consonant [k], [g] preceding [æː] would naturally be more front than it would be if the vowel it stood before were [ɑː]. What apparently happened, therefore, was that the front value of [k], [g] before earlier [æː] persisted for a while, even after [æ:] became [ɑ:], and this palatal consonant was thus considered to have changed the succeeding vowel into a diphthong.   In words with [k], [g] before present [aɪ] a similar explanation accounts for pronunciations like [kjaɪnd], [gjaɪd], etc. The present diphthong [aɪ] goes back to a Middle English and early Modern English high front vowel [i:].   This vowel developed into a sound which Elizabethan phoneticians describe as [eɪ], and this [eɪ] later became still lower, assuming several slightly varying forms which may be represented by [ʌɪ], [ɑɪ], [aɪ].   But the palatal quality of [k], [g] which was determined by its position before the earlier [i:], [eɪ] was carried over for a while in the eighteenth-century pronunciation of words like *kind, guide,* even after the vowel following [k], [g] had become a low vowel.   Rapidly, however, the initial [k], [g] adapted themselves to their changed surroundings, becoming relatively back palatal or guttural consonants as compared with their earlier values, and pronunciations like [kjaɪnd], [gjaɪd] then automatically disappeared.

The pronunciation as it appears now in Southern American speech is thus merely a local survival from a time when this pronunciation was not only more general but was also highly commended as an elegant accomplishment in speech.   It was approved by Walker, who remarks, p. 12, that "when *a* is preceded by the gutturals, hard *g* or *c*, it is, in polite pronunciation, softened by the intervention of a sound like *e*, so that *card, cart, guard, regard,* are pronounced like *ke-ard, ke-art, ghe-ard, re-ghe-ard.*"   Walker also notes that "this sound of the *a* is taken notice of in Steele's *Grammar,* p. 49, which proves it is not the offspring of the present day."   The same approval is given, p. 21, to long *i* after [k], [g].   "This *sky, kind, guide, guise, disguise, guile, beguile, mankind,* are pronounced as if written *ske-y, ke-ind, gue-ise, disgue-ise, gue-ile, begue-ile, manke-ind.*"   "At first sight," continues Walker, " we are surprised that two such different letters as *a* and *i* should be affected in the same manner by the hard gutturals *g, c,* and *k;* but when we reflect that *i* is really composed of *a* and *e,* our surprise ceases; and we are pleased to find the ear perfectly uniform in its procedure, and entirely unbiassed by the eye. From this view of the analogy we may form judgment of the observation of a late writer on this subject, that '*ky-ind* for *kind* is a monster of pronunciation, heard only on our stage.'—Nares' *Orthography*, p. 28."[1] Nares, however, does not mention the pronunciation of a glide sound after *k, g*, before [ɑɪ] as in *carter, garden*, and apparently it was unknown to him, since otherwise he would certainly have spoken of it. But the pronunciation was probably only beginning to make its way in the third quarter of the eighteenth century. So long as *a* before *r* final or *r* and a consonant remained [æɪ] as it certainly did throughout the greater part of the eighteenth century and among some speakers to the end of the century, there would have been no occasion for the development of a glide sound after [k], [g]. With the change of [æɪ] to [ɑɪ], however, the physiological conditions were present which might lead to the development of a glide sound between [k], [g] and [ɑɪ]. When Walker describes this as a polite pronunciation, his statement is perhaps equivalent to saying that by his time [æɪ] in words like *carter, garden*, etc., had become an old-fashioned pronunciation. The "polite" pronunciation apparently did not live long as an approved ornament of cultivated speech. The authority of Walker helped to keep it alive as a prescription of the books until the middle of the nineteenth century, but it seems never to have been a deep-rooted popular pronunciation. It was, moreover, too wide a departure from the conventions of spelling to make way against that powerful regulator of the language.

It may be remarked in passing that Walker has considerably stretched a point in calling in the authority of Steele in defense of his pronunciations *ke-ard* and *ke-ind*. One would not expect to find these pronunciations as early as the beginning of the eighteenth century, for the vowel of *card* certainly and probably also the vowel of *kind* were at that time still sufficiently high and front not to call for the development of a glide sound before the preceding consonant and the vowel. And in fact Steele, or whoever it was who wrote

[1] The original title of Nares' work was *Elements of Orthoepy*, but a new title page was printed in 1792, changing the title to *General Rules for the Pronunciation of the English Language*. The book was otherwise not changed.

the grammar commonly ascribed to him, mentions none of the words like *card* and *kind*, nor had he in mind the pronunciation of such words characteristic of the late eighteenth century. All he says is that "[y] is often subjoin'd to the Guttural Consonants [c], [g] when a Palatine Vowel follows; for *can, get, begin,* etc. sound as if they were written *cyan, gyet, begyin,* etc., for the Tongue can scarce pass from these Guttural Consonants to form the Palatine Vowels, but it must pronounce [y]. But it is not so before the other Vowels, as in *call, Gall, go, Gun, Goose, come,* etc.," *Grammar of the English Tongue,* 4th ed., London, 1721, p. 50. The phonetic situation thus described by Steele is not only different from the one implied by Walker's pronunciation of *card, kind,* but its interest lies also entirely in the field of theoretical phonetics, not in that of practical usage.

Webster notes this pronunciation of *kind, sky,* etc., as fashionably current in America in his day, but he connects with it, as in his opinion having the same origin, a feature of rustic New England pronunciation, that is the pronunciation of the present English diphthong [ɑu] in *cow, power,* as if written *kiow, piower.* "There is a vulgar singularity in the pronunciation of the eastern people," he says, *Dissertations,* p. 106, and by eastern people he means the people of New England, "which is very incorrect, and disagreeable to strangers; that of prefixing the sound of *i* short or *e,* before the dipthong [sic] *ow;* as *kiow, piower,* or *peower.* This fault usually occurs after *p, c* hard, or those other consonants which are formed near the seat of *ee* in the mouth, or in passing from which to the succeeding vowel, the organs naturally take the position necessary to pronounce *ee.* But the most awkward countryman pronounces *round, ground,* etc. with tolerable propriety." The presence of a glide sound after [k] in *cow* might reasonably be said to have been due to the consonant, but this explanation seems scarcely to apply to *power,* or words like *bound, found,* or words like *out, ounce,* etc., without initial consonant but with this same peculiarly New England quality of the vowel. That this was in Webster's day only a rustic pronunciation in New England would also lead one to regard it as arising merely from the well-known high quality of the first element

of the vowel in that locality, discussed under the sound [au], and
not as due to the influence of a preceding consonant upon the vowel.

The pronunciation of words like *kind, sky, guide*, with a glide
sound after the initial consonant Webster describes as being a very
modern imitation of "the English stage pronunciation." "This
is the same barbarous dialect, as the *keow* and *veow* of the eastern
country people. Yet, strange as it may seem, it is the elegant pronunciation of the fashionable people both in England and America.
. . . It is presumed that the bare mention of such barbarisms will
be sufficient to restrain their progress, both in New England and
on the British theater," *Dissertations*, p. 109. Curiously enough,
Webster does not mention the pronunciation *cart, garden*, etc., with
a glide sound after the initial consonant, though this was really
parallel to the fashionable eighteenth-century pronunciation of
kind, sky, guide, etc. His failure to mention it is perhaps due to the
fact that Nares had not mentioned it, but its presence in America
is attested by Staniford, p. 66, who notes it for correction. In the
dictionary of 1806, p. xiii, commenting on the different pronunciation
of *u* in *pure* and *rude*, Webster declares it to be "an egregious mistake
to suppose that this unavoidable modification of the vowel changes
the sound of it to that of another letter." "Much less," he continues, p. 14, "ought this modification of sound to be considered
as a new vowel sound. It is this blunder which has introduced
the sound of *e* before *i* and *y* in *sky, kind, disguise*, etc., *skey, keind,
disgyise* . . . but good speakers should be careful not to fall into
this error. *Skey* and *kyind* are precisely the faults which distinguish
the vulgar of New England, in *keow, geown* . . . but whether in
the vulgar of New England or in the court and stage of England,
it is, as Nares, in a passage cited by Walker, declares, a 'monster
of pronunciation.'" The same reasoning and examples are repeated
even in the dictionary of 1828, though to words of the types of *cow*
and *kind*, Webster now adds *guard*. The pronunciation of *guide,
guard, kind, guise*, with *e* before the vowel he condemns together
with the diphthongal pronunciation of *u* in *mute, pure*, etc., and
declares that it is "precisely similar to the vulgar pronunciation of

cow, gown, county, town, etc., that is, *keow, geown, keounty, teown;* a pronunciation formerly common in New England, and not yet wholly extinct. This vicious pronunciation, in all words of this kind, whether countenanced by men of low life or fashionable life, ought to be carefully avoided; as the slender sound of *e,* in such cases, gives a feebleness to the words utterly inconsistent with that full, open and manly enunciation which is essential to eloquence." These statements of Webster's are a strange mixture both of errors of fact and of judgment.

Staniford, pp. 66, 68, gives both *keard, keeind* as "affected vulgarisms" for *card, kind.*

The word *huckleberry* in this form is peculiar to America. The British, and the original, form of the word is *whortleberry.* The change of [t] to [k] before [l] is not illustrated in many English words of standard speech, but it has been frequently noticed in the speech of children, see Jespersen, I, 353. The earliest recorded instance of *huckleberry* in the *New English Dictionary* dates from 1670, and this is the earliest citation in Thornton's *American Glossary.* Webster does not include the word, either in his earlier dictionaries or the dictionary of 1828. In the latter he has only *whortleberry* and makes no mention of *huckleberry.* In Worcester's first edition, *huckleberry* did not appear, but it is inserted in the revision of 1859, citing Dr. Bigelow as authority. Alfred, p. 116, gives only the spelling *whortleberry* and says the word is pronounced *hurtlberry,* not *huckleberry,* a statement which of course proves that it was pronounced in the latter way. Cobb, pp. 168–172, also gives *huckleberre* as an improper pronunciation of what should be *hwurtleberre* in pronunciation, *whortleberry* in spelling. The only popular form is now *huckleberry.*

The word *perfect* in standard Modern English has a spelling pronunciation. In Middle English the word was spelled *parfit, perfit,* etc., with no consonant *c* [k] before the final consonant. This spelling was taken from French, from which the word was immediately derived. Later, however, the spelling of the word was revised to bring it more into accord with its ultimately Latin etymology, and thus it came to be written *perfect*. In time the spelling affected the pronunciation and the older pronunciation disappeared. Occasional survivals in America are indicated, however, by the spelling of the early town records. Thus in *Huntington Records*, p. 463 (1686), one finds *perfitt* for *perfect*, and so often in these records. In the *Groton Records*, p. 10 (1663), occurs *perfeted* for *perfected*.

(21) [ŋ] as in *sing*

The only point of importance in the pronunciation of this consonant is concerned with its quality in final unstressed position. Very commonly in present familiar speech, and so almost universally in the popular dialects, the final consonant in words like the present participles *walking, reading, fighting*, etc., is the simple nasal sound [n]. The vowel before the [n] is also generally omitted, the [n] becoming syllabic. The informal dialect pronunciation of a word like *fighting* would therefore be ['faɪtn], the formal and theoretically standard pronunciation would be ['faɪtɪŋ].

Is this informal pronunciation a recent and growing corruption of a fuller form, or is it a survival from earlier pronunciation, held in check by the conventions of cultivated speech and now, under the influence of the written and printed forms of the language, more or less disappearing from cultivated speech? Every reader of eighteenth-century English verse knows that the weakening of the ending *-ing* is not infrequently reflected in the rimes of the time, especially in poems on somewhat light subjects, which readily take on the color of colloquial speech. Wordsworth's rime *sullen* and *culling*, in the *Ode on the Intimations of Immortality*, Stanza IV, will also be recalled. In Wordsworth's *Ellen Irwin* occurs the stanza:

> "Proud Gordon, maddened by the thoughts
> That through his brain are travelling,
> Rushed forth, and at the heart of Bruce
> He launched a deadly javelin!"

In Coleridge's *Imitation from Ossian, blooming* rimes with *the dreary vale of Lumin*.

Similar rimes in early American verse indicate that the weakened ending was then much more general than it is in present cultivated colloquial speech. Thus the following rimes in Trumbull's verse were apparently intended to give merely a light and familiar touch to the verse: *pleasing: treason*, I, 6; *lie in: prophesying*, I, 7; *pressings. Hessians*, I, 7; *pursuing: ruin*, I, 17; *proceeding: Eden*, I, 19; *brewing. ruin*, I, 20; *fitting: Britain*, I, 46; *retreating: beaten*, I, 141; *scanning. Buchanan*, II, 19; *sporting: fortune*, II, 75. Similar rimes occur in the other poets of the time, e.g. in Humphreys, *bewitching: kitchen*, p. 196; *slump in: jumping*, p. 198; *falling: all in*, p. 198; *Helen: telling*, p. 208; in the *Anarchiad, seeking: Deacon*, p. 44; *right in: inditing*, p. 109; *open: copying*, p. 111; *sparing: share in*, p. 113; *session: wishing*, p. 113.

It is true, however, that these rimes occur almost exclusively in light or satirical passages. Dwight, in *Greenfield Hill*, p. 127, in a rather serious passage has *wishing: permission*, but this is exceptional. The presence of *g* in the spelling of words ending in unaccented *-ing* must always have led careful or academic speakers to think of the syllable as ending in something more than [n]. The ending *-ing* has also grammatical value as determining part of speech or a particular function of the verb, and this again keeps the full form of the word clear in the minds of analytic speakers. Yet in spite of this mental disposition in favor of [ŋ], in unreflecting speech the ending has constantly tended to take merely the form [n], though this latter pronunciation practically never is recorded in spelling, except in reproductions of illiterate or dialect speech. When Elliott and Johnson, therefore, equate such words as *coffin* and *coughing*, or *garden, guardian, guarding*, as sounding alike, pp. 20, 21, though the spelling does not show it, the obvious intention is to indicate a weakening of the ending *-ing*. Perry, *Royal Standard English Dictionary*, p. 19, says that "some orators pronouncing *g* at the end of words; as, *loving;* and others say it should be silent; as, *speaking*," the pronounciations intended evidently being ['lʌvɪŋ] and ['spiɪkn], though the text does not indicate this by any change of spelling. Walker, p. 49, justifies a pronunciation *singin* for *singing*, but permits the pronunciation only in participles formed from verbs ending in *-ing*, as *sing, ring*, etc. But *writing, reading* and *speaking,* he says, "are certainly preferable to *writin, readin*, and *speakin,* wherever the pronunciation has the least degree of precision or solemnity." One infers from the statement that *writin, readin,* and *speakin* were preferable, or at least customable, wherever the pronunciation was not precise or solemn. Dearborn, p. 136, lists "*in* for *ing* at the end of words" as an impropriety.

Numerous spellings in the earliest town records indicate a pronunciation of words in final *-ing* as though spelled *-in, -en*, e.g. *Norwalk Records*, p. 43 (1654), *meten, insuen*, for *meeting, ensuing; grindin* for *grinding*, p. 69 (1678), and many other spellings like these. In *Plymouth Records*, I, 192, and often, occurs *heren pond* for *herring pond; shillins* for *shillings*, I, 188; *Clampudden*, I, 305, for *Clampudding; accordin* for *according*, II, 258; etc. Variant spellings with *-in, -en* and *-ing* are almost always met with in the records in proper names like *Belden, Belding; Conklin, Conkling; Loren, Lorein, Lorin, Loring; Gowen, Gowin, Goin, Going* (*Lunenburg Records*); *Irvin, Irving; Holden, Holding; Cummins, Cummings; Darlin, Darling; Goodwin, Goodin, Gooding*, etc. In many instances, as in *Belden, Belding*, two formations become standardized and are now felt to be two separate names. In the common nouns *tarpaulin, tarpauling, leggins, leggings* two standard forms are now in use.

The reverse process, the pronunciation as [ŋ] of an unaccented consonant which should be merely [n] according to spelling and etymology, is examplified in but a few words, especially *garden* and *kitchen*. Pronunciations like *garding, kitching* are due to the analogy of words which legitimately have the ending *-ing*. The form *garding* for *garden* is the most common of all the words of this type, and in Scottish English it was raised to the level of a literary word. Examples of these literary uses are cited in the *New English Dictionary* under *garden*. Dearborn, pp. 136, 138, cites *linning, sarting, sovering*, as improprieties for *linen, certain, sovereign*. In *Watertown Records*, p. 107 (1671), *childering* occurs for *children;* as also *Norwalk Records*, p. 61 (1673). In *Huntington Records*, p. 186 (1672), occurs *ruings* for *ruins*. In *Lunenburg Records*, p. 110, the proper name *Robinson* is spelled *Robbingson*. In the *Hanover Records*, p. 92 (1790), *certain* appears as *certing*.

A plural of *house* with a weak ending, that is *housen*, was popularly current in New England as late as the close of the eighteenth century. In the local town records one often finds the word *housing* used when a collection of buildings is referred to, as in *Plymouth Records*, I, 276 (1700), *dweling housing*, meaning dwelling houses. This may be merely a participial noun formed from *house*, but more probably it is the archaic plural *housen* pronounced with the final [ŋ] that appears also in popular speech in *garden, linen*, etc.

Only an academic interest attaches to Webster's characterization in the Introduction to the Dictionary of 1828, of such pronunciations as *ingk, ungkl, kongkord, kongkorse, kongkubine* as "odious vulgarisms" and corruptions for *ink, uncle, concord, concourse, concubine*. In all these words Webster would pronounce [n] and not [ŋ], that is [ɪnk], ['ʌnkl], etc., and in words generally of this type, e.g. *sink, tinker, twinkle*, etc., he indicates only a pronunciation with [n]. But these prescriptions certainly indicate merely what Webster thought ought to be, not what was. His characterization of them as "odious vulgarisms" could not have been based upon observation of actual speech; it reflected only Webster's exaggerated respect for conventional spelling.

In some contemporary urban dialects, a pronunciation of [ŋ], stressed and unstressed, as [ŋk], as in *king*, pronounced [kɪŋk], etc., has entered through foreign, especially Yiddish, influence. The same pronunciation is indicated as an early and native development in English by the spelling *Sprinkfield* for *Springfield*, Hazard, *Historical Collections*, II, 110 (1648), and elsewhere often in these documents. This older pronunciation has not survived, however, and there is no evidence for a general pronunciation [ŋk] for [ŋ] in present English except where there is probability of foreign influence. In the unstressed syllable this pronunciation is indicated by the spelling *payingc* in *Easthampton Records*, I, 32 (1653). In *Norwalk Records*, p. 41 (1653), *shinckles* for *shingles* occurs a sufficient number of times to indicate that the spelling represented a genuine pronunciation. In the *Huntington Records* for the proper name *Ingersoll*, the variants *Inkersol, Inkerson* also appear. Examples of this pronunciation occur in sixteenth-century British records, e.g. Cavendish, *Life of Wolsey*, 1557, p. 97, writes *hankyng*, for *hanging*, Queen Elizabeth in 1548, writes *brinkinge of me up*, and *our brinkers up*, see Wyld, *History of Modern Colloquial English*, p. 290. Instances of the pronunciation of [ŋk] for [ŋ] in modern British dialects are cited by Wright, *English Dialect Grammar*, p. 274, very widely distributed in *anything, nothing*, but present also in other words. "In parts of Lancashire, Cheshire, Derbyshire, when dialect speakers try to talk 'fine' they generally substitute [ŋk] for [ŋ] in all present participles and verbal nouns ending in -ing." "The same thing," adds Wright, "can often be heard among educated speakers in those parts."

The explanation of the pronunciation of [ŋ] as [ŋk] is similar to that which accounts for the tendency to add [t] after [s] as in *against*, and in popular *oncet, twicet* for *once, twice*, and *d* after *n*, as in *sound* from earlier *soun*, and in popular *gownd, drownd* for *gown, drown*. The supposition is that after a continuant consonant, in order to bring the continuant definitely to a close, a stop consonant is developed, the particular stop being the one which lies nearest in organic formation to the continuant which it terminates.

(22) [r] as in *car, cart*

The situation with respect to the pronunciation of *r*, as it is commonly conceived, is that before vowels all speakers pronounce their *r*'s, but that Eastern and Southern speakers omit *r* when it is final and before another consonant, speakers in all other regions of the country pronouncing it in these positions. There can be no question but that consonantal *r* has disappeared from typical Eastern and Southern speech when final or before another consonant, but it is not so certain that speakers in other regions of America actually pronounce a consonantal *r* finally and before other consonants.

Instead they may in some instances only modify the quality of the vowel preceding the *r*, lifting and reverting the point of the tongue as one does in pronouncing [r] even while the preceding vowel is being produced, but not lifting the point of the tongue so high as to cause an actual contact between the tongue and the palate, by which means alone a consonantal *r* could be produced.   A word like *car*, in this manner of pronunciation, would consist only of the initial consonant followed by the reverted vowel, which to the average observer's ears produces the impression of being [r]; and a word like *cart* would consist only of the initial consonant, followed by the reverted vowel, which in turn would be followed by the final consonant.   In the speech of those persons who are said not to pronounce their *r*'s, *car* would consist of the initial consonant, followed by a vowel not reverted, and *cart* would consist of the initial and final consonants with a vowel, not reverted, between them.   Although in neither case would a genuine consonantal [r] be pronounced, the difference nevertheless between a pronunciation with a reverted vowel and one with a vowel not reverted would be so great as to lead most observers to say that in the former pronunciation the *r* was pronounced, but in the latter it was not.   If one were analyzing present pronunciation in detail, one would therefore distinguish three types of pronunciation, that in which no [r] is pronounced and the vowel is not reverted, that in which no [r] is pronounced and the vowel is reverted, and that in which a fricative consonantal [r] is pronounced, with or without reverting of the preceding vowel. For practical purposes the speakers of the second and third types may be grouped together, constituting those who are said to pronounce their *r*'s as against those of the first group, who do not pronounce their *r*'s.

The two most interesting points in the historical consideration of [r] are first, the time of disappearance of [r], and second, the geographical division which in America limits the loss of [r] final and before consonants to the East and South.

The statements of the early observers with respect to [r] are ordinarily not very discriminating.   Thus Webster, *American Spell-*

ing Book, p. 15, says "*r* has always the same sound as in *barrel*, and is never silent." This is very dogmatic, for *r* certainly was often silent in the speech of Webster's day. Webster objected to the name of the letter *r*, "that is, *ar*," because it "has led the common people to pronounce *mercy*, *service*, etc. *marcy*, *sarvice*." To correct this error, he re-named the letter *er* [ɛr], *American Spelling Book*, p. 27. Later, however, he gave up the vain attempt to change the name of the letter. In his *Dissertations*, p. 110, he remarked that "some of the southern people, particularly in Virginia, almost omit the sound of *r* as in *ware*, *there*. In the best English pronunciation, the sound of *r* is much softer than in some of the neighboring languages, particularly the Irish and Spanish; and probably much softer than in the ancient Greek. But there seems to be no good reason for omitting the sound altogether; nor can the omission be defended on the ground, either of good practice or of rules. It seems to be a habit contracted by carelessness." One detects here in Webster's statements a certain qualifying cautiousness which leads one to believe that [r] was not heard finally and before consonants in the New England speech of Webster's day as universally as Webster's remarks in general would indicate. With the grammarian's reverence for the letter, Webster would certainly prescribe a [r] wherever the spelling gave him the slightest warrant for hearing one.

Some of the early grammarians acknowledge a silent *r* in a few words. Mackintosh, p. 62, gives *r* as silent in *harslet* and *worsted*, but in no other words. Mackintosh, however, explicitly refused to recognize what he regarded as the unjustifiable corruptions of spoken language and on this ground might have insisted on the presence of [r] even when he did not hear it. Moreover, he was by origin a Scotchman, and *r* was not lost in northern British speech. In *Eine nuetzliche Anweisung*, p. 25, *r* is said sometimes not to be heard, the examples given being the words *horse*, *marsh*, *marshy*, *partridge*. In Peyton, *Les Elemens de la Langue Anglaise* (Philadelphia, 1794), p. 23, *r* is said to be silent in *harsh*, *marsh*, *marshy*, *harselet*, *partridge*. These words, however, all belong to small and

special classes.   Some eighteenth-century grammarians also give
r as silent in *Marlborough*, see Horn, *Untersuchungen*, p. 17.   But
in the main the grammarians, early and late, have been as dogmatic
as Webster in their statements.   Thus Alfred, p. 9, who presumably
represents Southern speech, says that "*r* always has the same sound,
and is never silent."   A more discriminating early nineteenth-century observer is Willard, p. 21, who first makes the traditional dogmatic statement that "r is never silent," but then proceeds as follows:
"In the beginning of a word, and when it comes between two vowels,
as in *rag* or *very*, it has a great deal of sound; but when it comes
before a consonant, as in *harm*, or *bird*, it has very little sound.   After
several vowels, however, it is heard almost as a distinct syllable,
thus *hire*, *more*, and the like are necessarily pronounced like *higher*
and *mower*, while *feared*, *corn*, etc., differ little in pronunciation from
fe-ud and *caw-un*."

More trustworthy, because less conscious, evidence for the loss
of [r] is afforded by some of the rimes of the earlier poets.   Apparently [r] disappeared first in cultivated speech before continuants,
especially the continuant [s], and this disappearance gave rise to
certain forms of words without *r* which are still common to popular
speech in all regions of America, both those regions in which [r] is
pronounced before consonants and those in which it is not.   Thus
cuss is a survival from *curse*, *pussy* from *pursy*, *passel* from *parcel*,
pusly from *purslane*, *fust* from *first*, *hoss* from *horse*.   The two words
in which Mackintosh recognized the loss of *r* were *harslet* and *worsted*.
The early grammarians frequently reprehend *skase* for *scarce*, e.g.,
Lyman Cobb, pp. 168–172, and Webster in his dictionary of 1828,
mentions *scase* as a popular pronunciation for *scarce*.   The form
cose for *coarse* also appears in the list of corrections made by the
early grammarians.

Examples of rimes which indicate a loss of [r] before [s], sometimes before [n], are abundant in early American verse.   Thus in
the *Anarchiad* we find the rimes *curst: trust*, p. 19, *learn: man*, p. 47.
This second rime, with the [r] silent in *learn*, would be a perfect rime
according to New England pronunciation of the time, since the

vowel of *learn*, with [r] pronounced or not, would be [æ], [ɛ]. In the *Columbiad* we find the rime *first: dust*, p. 64. In the poems of Trumbull occur the rimes *nurse: us*, I, 47; *just: worst*, I, 95; *nurse: house*, I, 144; *first did: hoisted*, I, 109; *check first: breakfast*, I, 147. Examples in the works of Humphreys are *first: trust*, pp. 34, 170; *lust: thirst*, p. 42; *disgust: accurst*, p. 61; *dust: first*, p. 164; *accurst: dust*, p. 183; *check first: breakfast*, p. 196; *across back: horse back*, p. 196. In the *Poetical Works* of David Hitchcock occur the rimes *lust: curst*, pp. 26, 104; *thus: curse*, p. 32; *occurs: thus*, p. 51; *just: first*, p. 51; *lust: first*, pp. 52, 96, 110, 114; *earth: wrath*, p. 65, *earth* being pronounced [æɪθ]; *universe: mass*, p. 70, with ['junɪvæs] as the pronunciation of *universe*; *trust: first*, p. 98, 126; *fuss: curse*, p. 127; *worst: lust*, p. 158; *durst: unjust*, p. 54; but only one rime in this poet indicates a loss of [r] before a stop consonant, *thought: resort*, p. 84. In the poems of Freneau occur *dust: thirst*, p. 8; *just: first*, p. 55; *dust: nurs'd*, p. 108; *worst: dust*, p. 136; *first: just*, p. 359; in the verse of Foster occur *loss: corse*, p. 34; *cross: horse*, p. 97; *morning: dawning*, p. 122; in that of Honeywood, *dawn: thorn*, p. 35; *dust: first*, p. 69; *dust: worst*, p. 95. The rime *hear: idea*, Honeywood, p. 105, is dubious, since it may indicate either that the final *r* of *hear* was lost or an [r] was added at the end of *idea*.

Inasmuch as occasions for riming words with *r* before other consonants than [s] with words that had no *r* occurred as abundantly as those of the type of *first: dust*, the prevalence of rimes of this second kind and the almost complete lack of rimes of the first kind is good evidence that *r* was commonly lost, even in cultivated speech, in the eighteenth century before [s] but not before other consonants. There is another indication that this loss of [r] before [s] was an early development completed in cultivated speech before the general loss of [r] before consonants and finally in New England and Southern speech. Words like *curse, first* may have in present speech three phonetic forms, the popular form [kʌs], [fʌst], the Eastern pronunciation [kʌɪs], [fʌɪst], and the General pronunciation with reverted vowel, [kərs], [fərst]. The last pronunciation is of course the one in which the [r] is said to be retained; the second is the one customary

in cultivated Eastern speech for all words containing a vowel written
i, e, u before *r* and a consonant or *r* final.   There is a very great
difference in social connotation between the popular pronunciation
[kʌs] and the Eastern pronunciation [kʌɪs].   The vowel in [kʌɪs]
is not only longer than the vowel of [kʌs] but more tense and higher.
In usage the difference is that between an approved and a contemned
standard.   It is plain, therefore, that we have here two stages of
development, an earlier which affected *r* before *s*, and which is represented in present English only by popular survivals, and a later which
affected *r* before all consonants or *r* final, represented in the cultivated Eastern type of pronunciation of all words of this class.   That
the loss of *r* before *s* antedated the general loss of *r* is indicated likewise by several other popular survivals.   Thus for *parcel* the present
cultivated pronunciation of the Eastern type is ['paɪsl], but a popular
form ['pæsl] as in a *passel of fools*, must come from the time when *a*
before *r* was still [æ].   So also the popular expletive *massy sakes*,
a contracted form of *for mercy's sake*, contains the older form [mæsɪ]
for *mercy*, instead of the present cultivated form, which would be
['mʌɪsɪ] in the Eastern type of pronunciation.

Several words with *r* before *sh* [ʃ] belong in the same group.   A
frequent popular pronunciation of *harsh* as [hæʃ] or [hæɪʃ], exactly
as though written *hash*, in New England and elsewhere, represents
the older pronunciation of [æ] for *a* before *r*.   Webster in the speller
of 1783, p. 46, spells *harsh* with the *r* silent and groups the word with
cash, dash, gash, etc.   In the edition of 1787, the *r* is not marked
silent, and the word is grouped with *arch, march, parch,* etc.   In
Baltimore there is a native pronunciation, with local flavor, of the
first word in the name *Marsh Market Place* as [mæʃ], though the *a*
in *Market* is always [aɪ].   Bradford, pp. 19–28, give *harsh, hash* and
marsh, mash, as being alike in sound.   He defines *mash* as "the hole
of a net."   Eliott and Johnson, pp. 19, 21, 22, 24, in a list of words
having nearly the same sound include *burst* and *bust, durst* and *dust,
harsh* and *hash, marsh, mash* and *mesh* (of a net), pronunciations
which are not denounced as reprehensible.   Seba Smith, in *My
Thirty Years out of the Senate* (N. Y. 1859), p. 25, has a spelling *ha'sh*

for *harsh*, in Maine dialect pronunciation. Cummings, p. 156, says that *marsh* and *mash* are likely to be confused. A spelling of *hash* as *harsh*, in Low, *The Politician Outwitted*, New York, 1789, Act II, Sc. ii, is probably to be taken also as an indication of the pronunciation [hæʃ] for *harsh*. The word is spoken by Humphrey, a rustic, who says, "Well, if the case lies there, that settles the harsh, d'ye see?" The earliest example of the idiom *to settle the hash* in the *New England Dictionary* is for the year 1825. Thornton has an American example for 1807 and another for 1824. The word was perhaps unfamiliar in a written form to the author of the play from which the above quotation is made, who therefore equated it with the word he knew as [hæʃ], that is *harsh*. Joel Chandler Harris, *Mingo* (1884), p. 132, records [hæʃ] for *harsh* in the speech of whites in Georgia. He also has [hæθ] for *hearth*, p. 163; so also Sherwood, *A Gazeteer* (1837).

An early loss of *r* before *l* is indicated in the word *girls*. This word, pronounced with the so-called 'common sound' of *e, i, u,* before *r*, has given the current present pronunciations [gərl], [gʌɪl]. In the eighteenth century, *i* before *r* was frequently pronounced as [ɛ], giving the pronunciation [gerl], or with the *r* silent, a pronunciation frequently indicated by the spellings *gel, gell*. But *i* before *r* was also at times pronounced in the same way as *e* before *r*, that is, either as [ɛ] or as [æ]. This latter sound often developed into [ɑɪ], as in *servant, service*, etc., pronounced *sarvint, sarvice*, etc. In *girl*, however, the vowel did not go beyond [æ], giving a pronunciation formerly widely current and still persisting in popular speech, which is commonly indicated by the spelling *gal* [gæl].

On the whole, the early grammarians pay little attention to the loss of *r* in their rules for correcting errors in English, which may mean either that the facts had escaped their observation or that the loss of *r* had not become prevalent. The former of these alternatives is the more probably true. But Dearborn, pp. 136, 138, gives *kose, skase*, as improprieties for *coarse, scarce*. Staniford's corrections, pp. 55–70, include *awkud* for *awkward*, *beth* for *birth*, *chawcoal* for *charcoal*, *chip* for *chirp*, *hash* for *harsh*, *mash* for *marsh*, *pawnger* for *porringer, safon* for *saffron*. Elliott and Johnson, pp. 30, 31, correct only *coase* for *coarse* and *noath* for *north*. Jaudon, pp. 213, 214, gives *hoss, skase* as improprieties for *horse, scarce,* and *funiter* as an impropriety for *furniture*. Cummings, p. 156 ff., gives the following as likely to be confounded: *alms* and *arms, balm* and *barm; burst* and *bust; calk* and *cork; colonel* and *kernel; durst* and *dust; farther* and *father, furze* and *fuzz; marsh* and *mash.*

Yet a few years later the loss of *r* before consonants and finally is so fully indicated in the corrections of William Russell that one cannot escape the conclusion that it had become much more general by the beginning of the nineteenth century than the earlier grammarians would lead one to suppose. Russell distinguished, *Sequel,* p. 29, between a "hard r," initial or before a vowel, and a "soft r," final or before a consonant. Walker, p. 50, claims to have been the first to make this distinction, though he calls the two kinds of *r* rough and smooth. The rough *r* he describes as formed "by jarring the tip of the tongue against the roof of the mouth near the fore teeth," and this *r*, he says, is the characteristic *r* of Irish speech. But his description is really a satisfactory account of the ordinary trilled or fricative *r*, common in certain positions as well in British as in Irish speech. The smooth *r* he says is "a vibration of the lower part of the tongue, near the root, against the inward region of the palate, near the entrance of the throat," and this *r* is the one which "marks the pronunciation of England." One might suppose that Walker meant to describe as the characteristic English, or soft *r*, a deep guttural or uvular *r*, yet certainly this was not the kind of sound he had in mind. His statement is a good illustration of the fact that even conscientious observers have often failed to perceive the character of what Walker calls a soft *r*, for his soft *r* was practically not a consonant at all. "In England," he says, "and particularly in London, the *r* in *bar, bard, card, regard*, etc., is pronounced so much in the throat as to be little more than the middle or Italian *a*, lengthened into *baa, baad, caad, regard;* while in Ireland the *r*, in these words, is pronounced with so strong a jar of the tongue against the fore part of the palate, and accompanied with such an aspiration or strong breathing at the beginning of the letter, as to produce that harshness we call the Irish accent. But if this letter is too forcibly pronounced in Ireland, it is often too feebly sounded in England, and particularly in London, where it is sometimes entirely sunk." Walker concludes that "provided we avoid a too forcible pronunciation of the *r*, when it ends a word, or is followed by a consonant in the same syllable, we may give as much force as we please to this letter at the beginning of a word, without producing any harshness to the ear. Thus *Rome, river, rage,* may have the *r* as forcible as in Ireland; but *bar, bard, card, hard,* etc., must have it nearly as soft as in London."

These remarks of Walker's have been quoted because the description he gave of London speech doubtless applies equally well to Eastern American speech of the early nineteenth century. When therefore a professional teacher of elocution, such as Russell was, classed the omission of the sound of *r* as an error, as for example, *waw, fah, stah, ala'm, retu'n, depa't, depa'tshu,* in Russell's spelling, for *war, far, star, alarm, return, depart, departure,* he was obviously objecting to the accomplished facts of the speech of his day in the interests of a theory made up mainly out of respect for spelling. As Russell was Scotch by birth, it may be that in his own speech he retained a stronger *r* final and before consonants than was customary in southern British English. But teachers of speech in general continued, and still continue, to put it down as a rule that *r* is always to be pronounced, even though in reality they pronounced no *r;* and the current dictionaries likewise fail to recognize the existence of a type of pronunciation with the [r] omitted. This is the less to be expected in American dictionaries, since the greater respect generally accorded to the Eastern type of speech as an approved standard would supposedly lead the dictionaries to indicate a preference for not sounding *r* final or before consonants. In the case of no sound, however, has the tyranny of spelling been so powerful as in [r].

There remain the interesting questions, why did the sound of *r* final and before consonants come to be generally omitted in Eastern and Southern American speech at the end of the eighteenth century and why was it not omitted in other types of American speech? Was the loss of [r] due to the influence of British upon American speech? Was the loss of [r] in the South, as it is so frequently said to have been, an effect of the relaxing influence of climate upon speech, or of the influence of negro English upon cultivated English? To these questions fairly positive answers can be given. In the first place, there is no probability that the loss of [r] in the South has a different explanation from that which explains the loss of [r] in New England. So far as negro influence is concerned, though it is probable that negro speech has in some instances modified the speech of educated white persons, there is no historical evidence whatever to show that Southern speech acquired its present pronunciation with [r] omitted finally and before consonants through imitation of the imperfect imitation by ignorant negroes of the speech of cultivated white speakers. The negroes omitted their *r*'s because they heard no *r*'s in the speech of their white superiors. Since the negroes were entirely dependent upon hearing in learning the sounds of speech, their sounds could not be affected by the visual impressions of spelling, and for this reason their pronunciation of words with *r* final or before consonants may seem broader, may seem fuller and franker, than that of educated white speakers. Even this difference, however, is likely to be an illusion on the part of the critical hearer, who is inclined to hear the speech of educated persons in terms of conventional spelling but of uneducated persons in terms of illiterate spelling.

The loss of [r] in typical Southern speech must have been due to the same causes as the loss of [r] in New England speech. In the lack of any positive evidence to show that this feature of American speech was the result of imitation of British speech, one must assume the contrary. The burden of proof certainly falls on him who would maintain that American speech between the close of the Revolution and the War of 1812 was so respectful of English example that it took over so marked a feature of pronunciation as the one under consideration. Even if it had been, however, it would still be necessary to show by what direct means of communication the English custom was transmitted to America. It could not have been through

Walker's dictionary, the first book on pronunciation that circulated widely in America, since Walker's dictionary appeared only in 1791, whereas Webster's observations and the corrections of grammarians like Staniford and Dearborn show that the pronunciation without [r] was already current in America. It should be noted also that Webster, who never lost an opportunity to reprehend any trait of speech that had a British flavor, says nothing about the omission of [r] as being characteristically British.

The only reasonable conclusion is, therefore, that the loss of the [r], both in America and in England, was a natural and early change in language which took place in popular speech unaffected by learned or standard influences. Later, when questions of standard came up for discussion, the matter of the omission of [r] was noticeable and seemed important. Now it happened that both in England and America the weakening and disappearance of [r] as a final sound and before consonants was particularly noted at about the same time, that is, at the end of the eighteenth century. Are we to see in this an actual coincidence in historical development, or merely a coincidence in the critical record of historical development? Undoubtedly the latter, for one can scarcely conceive that any inherent necessity in the nature of the English language should cause two such widely separated branches as British and American English to develop at a given moment in the same ordained way. It is a further coincidence, moreover, that when British writers began to select one form of British speech as an approved standard, the form chosen was a type of southern English as contrasted with northern English. For this choice the historical reasons were deep seated and compelling, the leading position of the speech of London having been fairly established since the end of the fourteenth century. But this commendation of an approved standard should not lead one to suppose that all British speech was, or thereby became, uniform. The loss of [r] final or before consonants never has been as marked a characteristic of northern as of southern British English. The parallel between British and American speech in the loss of [r] is due therefore to the emergence of a feature of southern dialect speech in England in the approved standard of British speech and in the approved standard of New England and Southern speech. If this explanation is correct, the loss of [r] final and before consonants is another indication of the close connection between the earliest American speech and the southern type of speech in England. To make this supposition quite convincing, however, one must be assured that the weakening of [r] in America was really an older dialectal phenomenon, a trait of speech which did not develop on American soil in the eighteenth century, but one which went back, as a common inheritance of both British and American speech, to an early colonial custom in America. To prove that this was so, one must turn to other evidence than that of sophisticated grammarians and explicit critics of speech. With them the obsession of the correct spelling has always been so powerful that it renders doubtful their statements concerning the phonetic value of *r*. The naïve spellings, however, of the early town records indicate a loss of *r* which must have been much more general than the mere numbers of spelling with *r* omitted might lead one to suppose. For though the early town clerks were not often specially trained in the keeping of official records, they were nevertheless not illiterate. The mere willingness to enter upon the task of keeping records implies a certain amount of literacy, and upon one who has had literary experience at all, the consonant framework of words is likely to make very definite impressions. For this reason spellings without *r* when they do occur are unusually significant. So also are spellings in which a silent *r* is inserted where it does not etymologically belong.

Some of the spellings of the *Groton Records* are *Mos*, p. 27 (1669), for *Morse*, and so frequently; *fouth*, p. 110 (1693), for *fourth; clack*, p. 123 (1703), for *clerk; woned*, p. 129 (1706), for *warned; proposhans*, p. 102 (1690), for *proportions*. In the *Plymouth Records*, the spelling *Bostorn*, I, 228 (1694), II, 185 (1717), and a number of times elsewhere, for *Boston*, indicates a habit of treating *r* as a silent letter. This is the same device as the spelling *Linkhorn* which appears in the genealogical discussions of the family of Abraham Lincoln. The spelling *Linkhorn* means ['lɪŋkən] as the spelling *Bostorn* means ['bɔstən]. In *Washbon*, I, 217, for Washburn, the *r* is omitted. In the *Dedham Records* the spelling *Mertcalfe*, III, 146 (1657), for *Metcalf* is to be noted. One finds also *Barstow* spelled *Bastow*, III, 204 (1652). In the *Huntington Records*, the spelling *Bud*, p. 212 (1675), 227 (1676), for *Bird* occurs a number of times. In Green, *Three Military Diaries*, 1775–1779, *horses* is spelled *hoses*, p. 86; *alarmed* is spelled *alam'd*, p. 91, and *accursed* is spelled *acused*, p. 96. The proper name *Coos*, pronounced ['koːɔs], is spelled *Cohors*. In the *Watertown Records*, for *Parson* the spelling *Passen*, p. 19 (1649), frequently occurs, also *Passam*, *Passon;* for *Parkhurst* one finds *Parkhust*, p. 44 (1655); also Parkis, p. 136 (1678), and other similar forms; for *Barsham, Bersham, Barsum* occurs the spelling *Bassum*, p. 45 (1665); for *Morse, Mors, Morc*, the spelling *Moss* is found, p. 54 (1659); for *Whitacars, Whiticurs* [Whittaker], etc., one finds *Whittacus*, p. 97 (1669) *Wittacius*, p. 97; *Whetycus*, p. 99, etc. In *Springfield Records*, the first name of *Born Van Horn* appears as *Bon*, II (1715), as *Baun*, II, 456 (1729). The second name is spelled *Van Horeen*, II, 315 (1710), evidently in an heroic attempt to retain the *r*. In *Lancaster Records*, the spelling *northen* for *nothing* occurs, pp. 231, 232 (1725). In *Springfield Records*, *Hathaway* is spelled *Harthaway*, p. 257 (1733). In the *Easthampton Records*, I, 93 (1655), one finds *horsers* for *hawsers*. Ussher, *Elements of English Grammar* (1803), spells *chamber* as *charmber*, p. 95, to indicate a quality of the accented vowel. Whatever the vowel may have been that he strove to indicate, there can be no doubt that his *r* was silent and merely intended as a mechanical clue to the pronunciation of the vowel. In the *Lunenburg Records*, p. 142 (1749), *master* is spelled *marster*, apparently to indicate a vowel [aː]. In the same records the spelling *Calton*, p. 148 (1751), occurs as a variant for *Carleton*. Likewise in the *Hanover Records* one not only finds *r* frequently omitted where it historically belongs, but also frequently added where it does not belong. Thus we find *propotion*, p. 90 (1790), and so often, for *proportion; poter*, p. 91 (1790) and elsewhere, for *Porter; lebity*, p. 117 (1792), for *liberty; incoporateing*, p. 117 (1792), for *incorporating; Roges*, p. 120 (1793), for *Rogers; Talton*, p. 203

(1803), for *Tarlton*. The proper name *Fobes* occurs only three times
in the *Hanover Records*, p. 63 (1786), p. 81 (1789), p. 111 (1792)
always in reference to the same person. The only spelling found in
the Records is *Fobes*, though the name intended was undoubtedly
Forbes. As the name was very uncommon in the community, it
apparently had not established itself in the clerk's mind in a conventional form, and he therefore merely put it down as it sounded
to his ear. In *Southold Records*, II, 41 (1685), occurs *notherly* for
northerly, and II, 352 (1691), *Haughton* for the name regularly spelled
Horton in these records. A silent *r* seems to be written in *wartering*
for *watering*, II, 193 (1704).   In the *Hempstead Records*, I, 168 (1665),
one finds *geoge* for *George*, *buttorck* for *buttock*, I, 174 (1665), *pasneg*
for *parsonage*, I, 227 (1666), *Chals* for *Charles*, I, 250 (1668). Perhaps
more significant are the many examples of the use of *r* merely as a
silent symbol to indicate the value of a preceding vowel, a custom
which could have arisen only after *r* had established itself as a silent
letter.   Examples are *pertition*, p. 93 (1790), and a number of times
elsewhere; *methord*, p. 96 (1790), for *method; surfitiant*, p. 97 (1790),
for *sufficient; marsters*, p. 97 (1790), for *masters; equiverlent*, p. 100
(1791), for *equivalent; serfitiant*, p. 111 (1792), for *sufficient; covernent*, p.
115 (1792), for *covenant; Havern*, p. 237 (1808) for *Haven*. In Green,
Three Military Diaries, [ə] is written *er* a number of times, as in
oppersit, p. 84, for *opposite; rezerlution*, p. 85, for *resolution: feler*,
p. 88, for *fellow; famerly*, p. 95, for *family; arrers*, p. 95, for *arrows;
follar*, p. 96, for *follow*.

To the difficult question why *r*'s are pronounced in the Western
or General type of pronunciation and not in the Eastern and Southern
in America, only a theoretical answer can be given. A large part
of the settlement of the West was the result of migrations from New
England, yet even the New England communities of the West did
not maintain the pronunciation without *r*, still felt to be locally
characteristic of New England. In New England, especially in
Eastern Massachusetts, and in the South in Virginia, conservative
tradition, more or less unbroken, especially in the South, was strong
enough to preserve the pronunciation without *r* which the culti-

vated speech of both regions inherited from the same type of speech
as that which has produced London and southern British speech.
But it should be noted that New England speech, in this respect
as in many others, is not now and probably never has been completely uniform.   Between the Connecticut and the Hudson a speech
exists which is noticeably different from that of eastern Massachusetts
and the seaboard generally, and in this speech the pronunciation
of *r* final and before consonants is a common feature.   Now it was
just from this region that large numbers of New Englanders, perhaps
the larger number, departed from their old homes to try new fortunes in the Central and Western States.   All New England emigrants, therefore, did not carry with them an *r*-less pronunciation.
Moreover, the Western population from the beginning was extraordinarily mixed, Scotch, Irish, and northern British being mingled
with the descendants of those who were of southern British origin.
These latter must soon have fallen into the minority, and their
speech in consequence have been modified to bring it into harmony
with that of their neighbors.   Perhaps also formal instruction in
the schools and the habit of reading have not been without influence
in the Western pronunciation of *r*.   New England has also had its
schools and its readers, but students of language are frequently
called upon to observe that only in unsettling social circumstances,
such as migration, do forces which may long have been present
exert their full power.

(23) [s], [sk], [ʃ] as in *see, scheme, she*

A pronunciation of *s* as [ʃ] in *sure* and *sugar* has been current
through the modern period.   The same pronunciation was sometimes recorded for *suet,* as in *Eine nuetzliche Anweisung,* p. 26.   In
the *Watertown Records,* p. 40 (1654), *ensuing* is spelled *inshuinge.*

In the unstressed syllable *s* sometimes becomes [ʃ], as in *Hempstead Records,* I, 167 (1665), *witneshth* for *witnesseth,* I, 172 (1665),
wittnesh for *witness.*   In these records, the proper name *Pearsall*
appears as *Parshall,* I, 249 (1668), and the form *Parshall* occurs fre-

quently in the *Southold Records*. In *Groton Records*, p. 120 (1701), *overplus* appears as *overplush*, and this is not an infrequent pronunciation of the word. The pronunciation probably arises in unstressed syllables through lack of clear articulatory definition of the difference between [s] and [ʃ]. Thus a word like *prejudice* caused naïve writers and doubtless also naïve speakers great difficulty, appearing in such spellings as *prejdich, Hempstead Records*, I, 202 (1668), *preddich*, I, 157 (1664), besides various others that stand nearer to the conventional form of the word. In his dictionary of 1806, Webster recorded *cutlas* as *cutlash* or *cutlass*, but in the dictionary of 1828, the form *cutlash* was dropped.

On the other hand, *sh* before *r* sometimes becomes *s*. Fowle, *Common School Speller*, p. 165, reprehends "a very faulty pronunciation of words with *sh* as *srill, srink*, etc."

A final continuant like *s* frequently is brought to a close by adding a stop consonant, *t*, which etymologically has no justification. An example of this which has become established in standard English is *against*, and a very common one in popular English is found in the pronunciation *oncet, twicet*, etc. ,for *once, twice*. That this natural phonetic development easily took place in earlier periods when the restraint exercised by the authority of conventional spelling was not strongly felt is evident from such forms as *overplust* for *overplus, Groton Records*, p. 60 (1680), *cumpeste* for *compass, Southold Records*, I, 177 (1649), *unleste* for *unless, Southold Records*, I, 433 (1655). So *t* is added to *cliff* in *clifft, Southold Records*, I, 122 (1675), and to *orphan* in *orphants, Hempstead Records*, I, 59 (1658). A very frequent form of *town* in the *Hempstead Records* is *townd*.

For *schedule*, a learned word, various pronunciations have prevailed. At present in America the only pronunciation is ['skɛdjuːl]; in England the first syllable is more commonly [ʃɛd-]. An older pronunciation favored [sɛd-]. Mackintosh, p. 74, gives *schedule, schism* as having *ch* mute. Cobb, p. 159, prescribes *sed jule* as the proper pronunciation.

In certain words subject to Dutch influence the spelling *sch* occurs sometimes for words which ordinarily have *sc*. Thus the name

Scudder appears as *Schudder*, *Southold Records*, I, 181 (1659); *Scadden*, *Scadding* appears as *Schadden*, *Hempstead Records*, I, 54 (1658), and *Scott* as *Schott*, *Hempstead Records*, I, 63 (1658). In many personal names the value of Dutch *sch* has persisted as [sk] as in *Schuyler*, *Schuylkill*, *Schermerhorn*, *Schenck*, and others, but when a Dutch spelling *sch* is easily assimilated to a German word with *sch*, or an English one with *sh*, the Dutch word has usually become [ʃ], as in *Schurman*, pronounced as though written *Sherman*. The spelling *sch* with the value of [sk] also appears in a number of place names in the United States, some being Dutch spellings of Indian names, as in *Schaghticoke*, *Schenectady*, *Schenevus*, *Schodack*, *Schœneck*, *Schoharie*, *Schooley*, *Schroon*. These places occur in New York or New Jersey where Dutch settlements formerly existed. Only a knowledge of local practice, however, would enable one to tell how *Schaal* in Arkansas, or *Scheding* in Nebraska, or *Scholten* in Missouri, are to be pronounced.

(24) [θ], [ð] as in *thing, that*

The character of this sound is such that it may easily be mistaken by the ear for other sounds somewhat closely related to it in organic formation. Thus a spelling *Hildretch*, *Southold Records*, I, 309 (1673), for *Hildreth* shows a confusion of [θ] and [tʃ]. For *bequeathe* one finds *becueffe* in the *Hempstead Records*, I, 162 (1665), *bequefe*, p. 230 (1666).

For *th* a pronunciation [t] is not infrequently recorded by early spellings, as in *Ester*, *Southold Records*, I, 235 (1664), for *Esther*, *Dority*, I, 406 (1684), for *Dorothy*. For *panther* a popular form *panter*, *painter* is fully illustrated by Thornton, though his earliest citation is for 1803. In the *New Haven Records*, p. 97 (1643), *Winthrop* appears as *Wintrop*.

A complete loss of the consonant is indicated by the spelling *Sohold* for *Southold*, *Southold Records*, II, 1 (1696), a kind of loss which writers of sea tales in dialect often record in *sou'-west*, for *south-west*, etc.

(25) [tʃ] as in *nature*

The groups of words here to be discussed consist first of those words in which *t* followed by *u* in an unstressed syllable has become [tʃ], as in present English *future, nature*, etc., and second those in which *t* followed by *u* in a stressed syllable has become [tʃ], as in *tune*, by some speakers formerly pronounced [tʃuɪn]. The pronunciation in the second of these groups was never as general as the pronunciation in the first and is to be regarded as an extension of the first. The development of *t* followed by *u* into [tʃ] results from the close combination of the consonant with the [j] which constitutes the first element of the sound [ju]. It follows, therefore, that this development could take place only if the letter *u* were pronounced with diphthongal value, and with the main stress in the diphthong on the second element. In this matter of the pronunciation of *u*, however, the greatest diversity of usage prevailed during the eighteenth century and earlier, and in consequence the greatest diversity of usage in the pronunciation of words like *future, nature*, etc. The tendency of [t] to develop into [tʃ] before [ju] undoubtedly began in the seventeenth century, but it was not until the eighteenth century that opinion on the subject became critical and acrimonious. Then, as so frequently happens, two different pronunciations which had grown up in the main unconsciously, were brought into clear consciousness by the advocates of theories of standard speech, one group elevating pronunciations like ['fjutʃər], ['neɪtʃər] as the only possible correct speech, and condemning ['fjuɪtər], ['neɪtər] as vulgar, and the other group doing just the reverse.

Sheridan and Walker were the first important advocates of *t* pronounced [tʃ] before [ju]. But Sheridan went further than Walker, pronouncing *t* as [tʃ] not only before *u* of unstressed syllables, but also before *u* in stressed syllables. Walker, p. 55, expressly rejects pronunciations such as "*tshootur, tshoomult, tshoomour*, as Mr. Sheridan writes them"; and he rejects also *tootor, toomult, toomour*, "as they are often pronounced by vulgar speakers." The only pronunciation he permits for *tutor, tumult, tumour* is one which he represents by the spellings *tewtor, tewmult, tewmour,* etc. So far Walker's prescriptions agree in the main with certain types of present usage and no doubt describe accurately a custom of cultivated speech in England in the latter eighteenth century. Under the word *nature,* Walker acknowledges that "there is a vulgar pronounciation of this word as if written *natur,*" but adds that it "cannot be too carefully avoided."

But Walker goes on to say that this pronunciation of *t* as [t∫] "extends to every word where the diphthong or diphthongal sound commences with *i* or *e.* Thus *bestial, beauteous, righteous, frontier,* etc. are pronounced as if *best-cheal, beaut-cheous, right-cheous, front-chier,* etc., except in the terminations of verbs and adjectives, which preserve the simple in the augment, without suffering the *t* to go into the hissing sound, as *I pity, thou pitiest, he pities,* or *pitied, mightier, worthier, twentieth, thirtieth,* etc. This is agreeable to the general rule, that forbids the adjective or verbal terminations to alter the sound of the primitive verb or noun." Here Walker seems to have been ridden more or less by a theory, for the analogy which he illustrates as operating in verbs and adjectives might operate just as well to preserve the head form in words like *beauteous, bounteous,* etc., and in fact the only word of this type in which *t* has regularly become [t∫] is *righteous.*

Turning to American speech, one finds, as was to be expected, that the line of division between the pronunciation of *t* as [t∫] and as [t] before *u* was parallel to the line of division between the pronunciation of *u* as [ju] and as [u]. In other words, one finds that when this question became of conscious interest in the latter eighteenth century, pronunciations like *nater, futer, creater,* etc., were current in New England speech, in old-fashioned speech and in uncultivated speech as survivals, but that elsewhere the cultivated pronunciation in such words was as it is in present English. The pronunciation *nater* is one of the constantly recurring marks of the speech of the rustic Yankee who appears so frequently as a stock comic character in the dramas, novels and realistic sketches of the last quarter of the eighteenth century and the early nineteenth cen-

tury. Yet the pronunciation was not limited to rustic New England
speech, and in defense of it, Webster was exceedingly earnest. He
was convinced of course that the *u* in words like *nature, rapture,*
etc., *Dissertations,* p. 156 ff., had no diphthongal value, and therefore thinks it to be as reasonable to pronounce *tumble* as *tshumble*
as to pronounce *nature, rapture,* as *natshur, raptshur.* In fact, Webster insists that a pronunciation like *tshun, tshurn, fatshal, immortshal,*
for *tun, turn, fatal, immortal,* is "actually heard among some very
respectable imitators of fashion; and is frequent among the illiterate,
in those states where the *tshn's* are most fashionable. . . . When
a man of little education hears a respectable gentleman change *t*
into *tsh* in *nature,* he will naturally be led to change the same letter,
not only in that word, but wherever it occurs. This is already done
in a multitude of instances, and the practice, if continued and extended, might eventually change *t,* in all cases, into *tsh.*" Webster's
statement of the facts here is probably as untrue as his statement
of theory. There is no likelihood at all that pronunciations like
tshun, tshurn for *tun, turn,* were frequent, or even occasional, whether
among fashionable or illiterate speakers. The sounds of speech
very rarely develop under the direction of spelling, even in the relatively highly conventionalized speech of modern times. But the
significant inference to be drawn from Webster's remarks is that
the pronunciations with [tʃ] were the fashionable pronunciations
and the ones that people imitated when they took pains to imitate
any. "I am sensible that some writers of novels and plays," says
Webster, *Dissertations,* p. 158, "have ridiculed the common pronunciation of *creatur* and *natur,* by introducing these and similar
words into low characters, spelling them *creater, nater.* And the
supporters of the court pronunciation allege, that in the vulgar
practice of speaking, the letter *e* is sounded and not *u.*" But this
is again a quibble about spelling, and Webster concluded that "the
true sound of *u* in *creature, nature, rapture, legislature,* etc.," is the
same as the vowel in the second syllable of *liar, elder, factor,* and
that the consonant is of course simply [t]. The pronunciation with
[tʃ] seems to him "barbarously harsh and inharmonious," *Disserta-*

tions, p. 162.   But that the pronunciation [tʃ] was a growing one
in Webster's day is further indicated by his remark, *Dissertations,*
p. 170, note, that "there are many people, and perhaps most of them
in the capital towns, that have learned a few commonplace words,
such as *forchin, nachur, virchue,* and half a dozen others, which they
repeat on all occasions; but being ignorant of the extent of the practice, they are, in pronouncing most words, as vulgar as ever."   This
pronunciation of *t* as [tʃ] seemed to Webster fraught with very deep
and wide significance.   "A man of great soul," he exclaims, "would
sooner imitate the virtues of a cottage, than the vices of a court;
and would deem it more honorable to gain one useful idea from the
humble laborer, than to copy the vicious pronunciation of a splendid
court, or become an adept in the licentious principles of a Rochester
and a Littleton."

The principles here laid down Webster consistently maintained,
even in the dictionary of 1828.   Throughout all this period, however, Walker must have represented a much more faithful record
of the facts of American speech than Webster, and this difference
between Webster and Walker was one of the main reasons why, before
the appearance of Worcester, Walker was so generally preferred to
Webster as a guide to pronunciation.   Worcester's first edition
accepts in general Walker's pronunciation, though it does not recognize [tʃ] in *beauteous, frontier.*   Later editions of Webster followed
Worcester, or at least agreed with Worcester, in recognizing what
must have been since the beginning of the nineteenth century an
accomplished fact in American pronunciation.   The influence of
spelling, however, has always been powerful in words of this type,
and one still hears occasionally a defense in theory, though very
rarely an illustration in practice, of a pronunciation of words like
nature, rapture, etc., with the *t* sounded according to its ordinary
value.   This deference to spelling led Webster, even in his latest
dictionary, to record the pronunciation of *t* followed by *i*, as in *nation,
position,* as though it were really pronounced as a *t*, that is ['neɪtɪən],
[po'zɪtɪən].   There can be no question, however, but that in actual
speech in Webster's day, such words were universally pronounced

with [ʃ], or that *t* in words like *nature, future* was all but universally pronounced [tʃ]. On this point Webster was extraordinarily stiff-necked, and the greatest concessions he ever made were those in his *Elementary Spelling Book* (1843), where he declares that *natshur, jointshur,* though a pronunciation common both in England and America, is not "the most elegant." Without explicitly giving up his old pronunciation, he adds, p. 135, that the pronunciations *nate-your, jointyur,* "though a departure from the rules of the language, by prefixing the sound of *y* to *u* short, is at present fashionable, among elegant speakers." This "anomaly" he would limit to twenty-seven words of two syllables, of which he gives a list. The half-hearted pronunciation indicated by the spellings *nateyour, jointyour,* was but a creation of the study, intended to satisfy a theory of what the proper pronunciation should be.

Some of the early spellings of the town records indicate a pro-nunciation with [t] before unaccented *u,* as *futor* for *future, Norwalk Records,* p. 56 (1669) and so often, and perhaps *natuer* for *nature,* p. 58 (1670), has the same significance. In the *Easthampton Records,* I, 129 (1657), *torture* is spelled *torter.* In the *Groton Records,* p. 107 (1693), *pastures* is spelled *pastors,* and many other words like this. In the *Watertown Records,* p. 81 (1663), *future* is spelled *futer.* In Green, *Three Military Diaries,* p. 87, *spiritual* is spelled *sperital;* p. 88, *lecture* is spelled *lecter;* p. 91, *natural* is spelled *natteral.* The spelling *stooped* for *stupid,* p. 88, indicates clearly the value which this writer gave to all his so-called long *u*'s. Examples of this kind of naïve spelling are numerous throughout the seventeenth and eighteenth centuries, but because of the comparatively strict conven-tionalization of spelling, direct records of the pronunciation of *t* before *u* as [tʃ] are not readily found. But the rustic pronunciation indicated by the spellings *nater, creatur,* which Webster notes as early as 1789 and which appear frequently in the representation of comic New England characters in the drama of the last quarter of the eighteenth century, could serve only as contrast to the polite pronunciation with [tʃ] if the latter had been well established. A broad comedy situation in *The Politician Outwitted* (1789), by Samuel

Low, Act I, Sc. ii, turns on the pronunciation of *future* by a rustic as *futer*, mistaken by a gentleman for French *foutre*. It should be remembered that in rustic pronunciation, the accented vowel of *future* would also be a simple vowel and not diphthongal.

On the other hand and in agreement with Webster, we find that Franklin in *actually*, p. 303, and in *natural, naturally*, p. 301, records only a [t] and the inference is that generally in his pronunciation *t* has remained as [t] before *u*. Many of Trumbull's rimes indicate the same pronunciation, e.g. *slept on: Neptune*, I, 14; *desperater: nature*, I, 16; *gestures: Protesters*, I, 21; *torture: order*, I, 80; *certain: fortune*, I, 91; *adventures: Centaurs*, I, 102; *traitor: nature*, I, 157; *future: accoutre*, I, 171; *martyr: departure*, I, 176; *satire: nature*, II, 50; *addressed her: gesture*, II, 52; *victors: pictures*, II, 64; *chatter; nature*, II, 149. In Freneau occur the rimes *lecture: conjecture: spectre*, p. 154; *sweeter: creature*, p. 222; *dissenters: adventures*, p. 357; *oyster: moisture*, p. 289. Daniel Humphreys, *Compendious American Grammar* (1792), p. 25, rimes *neuter* and *future*. In the poems of Hitchcock (1806), the rimes *later: nature*, p. 122, and *nature: legislator*, p. 129, probably indicate a stray survival of the pronunciation of *nature* as *nater* after this pronunciation had disappeared in other words of this type.

The grammarians in general have little to say about the pronunciation of *t* as [tʃ], though Staniford (1797), pp. 66, 67, 71, reprehends *creachur, forchune, forchunate, fuchur, chune*, as "affected vulgarisms" for *creature, fortune, fortunate, future, tune*, without indicating precisely the character of the pronunciation which he preferred. The grammarians often have lists of words pronounced alike but spelled differently, and these lists occasionally give indications of survival of the older pronunciation, as when Bradford, pp. 19–28, equates *centaury, century*, and *centry* (a guard), *gesture* and *jester*. Timothy Dwight, *Travels*, I, 468, reprehends the pronunciation with [tʃ], remarking that "several of the most fashionable people [of Boston] have lately, and I think unhappily, adopted the harsh anti-English pronunciation of the vowel *u*, foisted upon the language by Sheridan, and derived from the brogue of his native country."

Mennye (1785), p. 68, has an unexpected reversal of the usual criticism, making the pronunciation with [tʃ] a mark of vulgar rather than of refined English. He says, "We are told, that *virtue* when rightly pronounced, sounds *vertshu:* If I form a just idea of the direction here given, I confess, I have often heard the word thus pronounced by a British private soldier, or an English country boor, but never by a good speaker, either in England or America." Perhaps all that one is justified in inferring from this criticism is that Mennye, in 1785, was not familiar with the pronunciation of *virtue* with [tʃ] in cultivated speech.

A curious reflection from the divided pronunciation of *t* as [t] and [tʃ] is found in the pronunciation *Massatusits* for *Massachusetts*, reprehended by Dearborn, p. 137. It would seem that only speakers who customarily pronounced *t* in words like *nature*, etc., would have thought of pronouncing *ch* as *t*. The pronunciation may have had a historical existence, however, as evidenced by the spelling *Mattatuhsetts, Southold Records*, II, 88 (1699).

The pronunciation of the preterite of *catch* as though written *cotch*, still current in illiterate speech, is due to the analogy of the infinitive and present forms, from which [tʃ] is transferred to the preterite *caught*. The pronunciation *cotch* is corrected by Dearborn, Bingham, and other early grammarians. Jaudon, p. 213, gives *kotch, sot, fotch*, as improprieties for *caught, sat, fetched*.

The word *stomacher* is not now in common use and perhaps was never strictly a popular word, like *coat, hat, dress*, and other names of familiar parts of apparel. It is a derivation from *stomach*, and should therefore be pronounced with [k] for *ch*. Early authorities, however, pretty generally agree in giving a different sound, perhaps to avoid a supposedly indelicate connotation of ideas. Walker describes the word as pronounced *stum-mid-jur*. Webster and Worcester give [tʃ] for *ch*, and some of the early grammarians, e.g., Alfred, p. 93, correct the pronunciation with [k] as an impropriety. Nowadays, since the word has become mainly an eye-word, most persons, if compelled to pronounce it, would pronounce it with the same consonant as in *stomach*.

In some words of classic or supposedly classic origin, *ch* was sometimes pronounced [k] where later English has [tʃ]. Thus Benezet, p. 147, gives *Calais* and *chalice, card* and *chard* (to dress wool), *cart* and *chart* as the same in sound but different in spelling and significance. These words are also found in other similar lists.

In *Groton Records*, p. 107 (1693), *chimney* is spelled *schimney*, which apparently means that the initial consonant was pronounced [ʃ].

(26) [v] as in *vessel*

Americans nowadays are familiar with the pronunciation of *v* as [w], and the reverse, of *w* as [v], only as examples of British humor in Dickens and similar writers. Nowhere in America does the exchange between [v] and [w] persist as a general native dialect survival, though of course it may be heard occasionally in the speech of individuals and in the speech of foreigners who have acquired only an imperfect command of English. Formerly, however, the pronunciation of *v* as [w] was not only present, but even widely current in America. "The pronunciation of *w* for *v* is a prevailing practice in England and America," says Webster, *Dissertations*, p. 112, and adds that "it is particularly prevalent in Boston and Philadelphia," where many people say *weal, wessel* for *veal, vessel.* Curiously enough, he did not find this pronunciation in Connecticut. "Vast numbers of people in Boston and in the neighborhood use *w* for *v;* yet I never once heard this pronunciation in Connecticut." Webster opposed the pronunciation on the ground that since the several letters usually have distinct value, the value of *v* being regularly [v], "every person should resign his peculiarities for the sake of uniformity." Benezet, in his *Pennsylvania Spelling Book*, pp. 147–154, the second edition of which appeared at Philadelphia in 1779, gives *weal* (good) and *veal, vile* and *wile* as pronounced alike. In *Watertown Records*, p. 128 (1676), *victuals* is spelled *wittalls;* and in *Groton Records*, p. 52 (1675), *provisions* is spelled *prowisions.* In the *Hempstead Records*, I, 135 (1694), *voted* is spelled *woatted.*

Several of the grammarians note this pronunciation as an impropriety. Elliott and Johnson, p. 31, correct *winegar* and *wessel* for *vinegar* and *vessel*. Bingham, *The Young Lady's Accidence*, Boston, 7th Edition, 1793, gives the following sentences, p. 53, for correction: *The wessel lays at the voff*, and *I cotch a werry bad cold*. Staniford, p. 71, gives *wagabone (vagabond)*, *weal (veal)*, *winegar (vinegar)*, *wandue (vendue)*, *wenzen (venison)*, *varb* or *werb (verb)*, *wirtue* or *virtchew (virtue)*, *wolum* or *volyum (volume)*, *womit (vomit)*, *wote (vote)*, *woige* or *wige (voyage)*, all as vulgarisms. Jaudon, p. 216, gives *weel* as an impropriety for *veal*. A little jest of Franklin's turns on the pronunciation of *vice* with [w] for *v*. In the "Petition of the Letter Z," *Works*, ed. Sparks, VI, 304, the letter asks to be restored to the word *wise*, where his place has been filled by "a little, hissing, crooked, serpentine, venomous letter, called *s*, when it must be evident to your worship, and to all the world, that W, I, S, E, do not spell *Wize*, but *Wise*."

The pronunciation is frequently indicated by R. M. Johnston in his representation of the rural speech of central Georgia, in his *Mr. Absalom Billingslea* (1888), as for example, *ewents*, p. 22, *insiniwation*, p. 25, *adwise*, p. 46, etc. Johnston was a conscientious and painstaking observer of dialect, and this pronunciation of *v* as [w] must be taken as a genuine local survival, not as merely a literary echo from Dickens or other British humorous writers.

Where does this pronunciation come from? It is not probable, as Jespersen, I, 385, has pointed out, that the exchange of *w* for *v* and of *v* for *w* was ever systematic. Probably an intermediate sound was formed, between [v] and [w], a sound somewhat like the *w* in German *schwester;* "this would strike those accustomed to a strict distinction between [w] and [v]," says Jespersen, "as something different from the sound expected in each word, and they would naturally interpret the intermediate sound as the wrong one in each case." This may have been so, but it is noteworthy that the pronunciation of what was taken to be [w] for [v] seems to have been much more common than the reverse. There are no examples in present British dialects, see Wright, *Dialect Grammar*, p. 206, of initial *w* being changed to [v] before a following vowel, though in

some dialects initial [wr] has become [vr].   On the other hand, initial
v pronounced [w] is recorded by Wright, p. 227, for Buckingham-
shire, Norfolk, Suffolk, Essex, Kent, and Sussex, in pronunciations
like *wenter, witlz, wiksn, konwē, -wai*, for *venture, vittles, vixen,
convey*.

A British critic of American speech, in the *Monthly Mirror*, March,
1808, quoted by Cairns, *British Criticisms*, p. 37, says that "Americans of a liberal education very commonly use the *v* for the *w*";
but no examples of words are given, and undoubtedly what the
critic meant was that *w* was used for *v*.

The presence of the pronunciation [w] for [v] in America is not
to be accounted for as due to admiring imitation of British speech.
The pronunciation in England seems never to have been a refined
or elegant pronunciation, like *kyind* for *kind*, or *future* with *t* pronounced as [tʃ].   It is probable that it occurred in England and
America as an inheritance from an older common stock.   There
is no record, according to Jespersen, of the occurrence of [w] for [v]
in England before the latter part of the eighteenth century, see
Jespersen, I, 385.   It is mentioned in 1787 as a London vulgarism,
and Walker (1791), p. xii, speaks of the "pronunciation of *v* for *w*, and
more frequently of *w* for *v*, among the inhabitants of London,
and those not always of the lower order," as a blemish of the first
magnitude.   Pegge (1803), p. 76, cited by Jespersen, says that "the
most striking and most offensive error in pronunciation among the
Londoners, I confess, lies in the transpositional use of the letters
w and *v*."   The distribution of [w] for [v] in the present dialects of
England suggests that the pronunciation arose in popular speech
in southern and midland regions, and thus seemed to the grammarians, when they became critically conscious of it, specially local-
ized in London.   As a feature of southern dialect in Britain, one
would expect the pronunciation of [w] for [v] to appear also in America,
especially in New England, among other survivals of British dialect.
And the citations given above from the town records, which antedate
Jespersen's earliest citations by a century, show that such was in
fact the case.   On the other hand, the pronunciation seems never

to have been popular and general, even in New England. Webster's statement that it occurred chiefly in Boston and Philadelphia leads one to infer that it was an urban pronunciation, probably augmented along the natural lines of intercourse between London and the larger cities of America. Its almost complete disappearance from American dialects would also be accounted for on the supposition that it was never a genuine and widely distributed popular custom, though perhaps the spelling in itself would sufficiently account for the feeling that to pronounce *v* as *w*, or *w* as *v*, was an unpardonable error.

The pronunciation of *vat* with initial *f* [f] indicated by the spelling *fats* for *vats*, *Dedham Records*, V, 72 (1678), *Hempstead Records*, I, 59 (1658), is of interest because it shows the persistence in America of the ordinary midland and northern form of the word, the pronunciation *vat* of standard English being supposedly an exceptional borrowing from the southern dialect. On the whole one might expect that the voicing of initial *f*, *s*, which is so marked a feature of the dialect of southwestern England, would appear frequently among the other southern characteristics of the speech of the earlier settlers of New England. But if initial *f*, *s* were often [v], [z] in America, the fact does not appear either from the statements of critical students of speech or from the naïve spellings of the uncritical.

(27) [ʍ] as in *when*

The pronunciation of words like *wheat*, *where*, *when*, etc., varies in America between [ʍiːt], [ʍɛɪr], [ʍɛn] and [wiːt], [weɪr], [wɛn], both pronunciations occurring in all regions and at all levels of speech, though the former is the more common. Especially when relatively lightly stressed, initial *wh* is likely to be pronounced as [w]. Academic authority is usually strongly opposed to this pronunciation, though the difference between [ʍ] and [w] is not great enough to force itself upon the attention of any except critical observers. The British phoneticians record [w] as the current pronunciation of *wh* in present southern standard British speech, and Jespersen, I, 374, remarks that the pronunciation of *wh* as [w] is not "nowadays regarded as nearly as 'bad or 'vulgar' as the omission of [h] and is, indeed, scarcely noticed by most people." In Michaelis-Jones, *A Phonetic Dictionary of the English Language* (1913), all *wh*-words are entered under [w] and they are generally so treated by the British phoneticians. How long the pronunciation [w] for *wh* has existed in English speech it is difficult to say, though it is probably older than the earliest references to it, which date from the beginning of the eighteenth century. Walker, p. xiii, mentions as one of the faults of Londoners "not sounding *h* after *w*." This pronunciation occurs, he says, "particularly in the capital, where we do not find the least distinction of sound between *while* and *wile*, *whet* and *wet*, *where* and *were*, etc." Apparently it has always been more common in southern British speech than in northern, and its presence in America is probably to be counted as one more of the many characteristics which American English has inherited from southern British. In Perry's *Royal Standard English Dictionary*, the first edition of which appeared in 1778, the pronunciation [w] for *wh* is explicitly recorded as standard, according to Perry's notions of standard, which were derived from the observation of London speech. All of Perry's words with *wh* are spelled with the *h* silent. In the early American editions of Perry, as in the fourth Worcester edition, 1796, this treatment of *wh* is taken over without modification or comment. Timothy Dwight, *Travels*, I, 468, speaking of the people of Boston, declares that "like the inhabitants of most other large cities, they often omit the aspirate in words beginning with *wh*, pronouncing, for example, *wheat* and *wharf*, *weat* and *warf*, etc." For this pronunciation Dwight expressed no positive disapproval, though the implication is that it was not current in Connecticut speech.

The pronunciation was not infrequently corrected by the early American grammarians. Thus Staniford, p. 72, gives *wich* as a vulgarism for *which*, and Jaudon, p. 216, corrects *wen*, *warf* for *when*, *wharf*. His correction of *wheel* for *we'll*, p. 216, indicates that with some speakers the attempt to avoid the voiced sound for *wh* led to the pronunciation of the voiceless sound for *w*.

The spelling *wich* for *which, Hempstead Records,* I, 33 (1658), may be taken as indicating a pronunciation [w] for *wh.*   It should be noted, however, that the spelling *w* for *wh* is extremely rare, even in the most naïvely spelled documents, a fact which leads one to suspect that *wh* was not commonly pronounced [w].

UNSTRESSED SYLLABLES

A constant tendency in the English language, from Old English times to the present day, has been to treat with slight respect the unstressed syllables of words. This has resulted in many instances in the complete loss of unstressed syllables, especially inflectional endings, and in the obscuring of the phonetic quality of such unstressed syllables as remain. Standard American use is now approximately uniform in its treatment of these surviving unstressed syllables, though in certain local forms of speech, instances may still be found of an older and formerly more general custom with fairly heavy accent on certain final syllables. Thus in New England, pronunciations like ['tɑʊ'ɛl] for *towel,* ['loː'ɛl] for *Lowell,* ['bɑɪs'kɪt] for *basket,* ['æd'ɪd] for *added,* etc., may still be heard. This type of pronunciation is somewhat elaborately indicated by Winston Churchill in one of the characters of his *Dwelling Place of Light* (1917). The character is a person of pure New England ancestry, of a stock "rooted there since the seventeenth century." His speech is described as a "dialect precise but colloquial," p. 2, and his lips are "moulded for the precise formation that emphasizes such syllables as *el,*" p. 4. When asked how many generations had passed since the settling of the first of the family in New England, "'Seven,' said Edward, promptly, emphasizing the last syllable," p. 5. Reading aloud "in his precise voice," Edward is described as "emphasizing admirably the last syllable of the words 'Russian,' 'vessels,' and 'Japan,'" p. 30. On another occasion he uses the word *civil,* and is described as pronouncing "that word 'civil' exquisitely, giving equal value to both syllables," p. 53.

247

When one examines the historical records one becomes convinced that since at least the seventeenth century considerable variation existed in the English pronunciation of these final unstressed or half-stressed syllables, especially syllables ending in *l, n.* Dwight, *Travels*, I, 468, complains that the people of Boston make "the language, in itself too rough, still rougher, by a violent junction of consonants which in spelling were separated. Dissyllables accented on the first, and terminating the last with a liquid, particularly with *l, n,* or *m,* they pronounce in such a way as to leave out the sound of the vowel. Thus Sweden, Britain, garden, vessel are extensively pronounced *Swed'n, Brit'n, gard'n, vess'l.*"

Cummings, however, whose first edition appeared in 1819, says that "the sound of *en* and *on* final in certain words is extremely disagreeable, and ought to be carefully avoided, as in pard'on, gold'en, gard'en, etc. The last syllable of these and similar words, is frequently pronounced like the monosyllable *den* or *don;* whereas the true sound is very similar to the nasal or last part of the sound of the letter *n,* when pronounced alone; and is correctly heard in the word doz'en," p. x. "This corruption," he adds, "is of modern growth, and may by some be thought too slight to deserve notice." But the pronunciation seemed important to many commentators of the middle decades of the nineteenth century. Willard, p. 215 ff., gives a list of words in which final unaccented vowels are to be pronounced like *i* in *pin* or *y* in *beauty,* his list including *fluid, carriage, college, knowledge, fossil, hostile, marvel, minstrel, model, novel, servile, sterile, juvenile, puerile, villain, furnace, lettuce, circuit, condit, profit, prophet,* etc. But a pronunciation like ['mɔdɪl] for *model,* or ['prɔfɪt] for *profit* is possible only if one gives the final syllable more stress than is now customary in these words. Willard distinguishes the above group from one in which he permits final vowels to be pronounced like *u* in *alum,* or *e* in *after.* In this latter group, p. 232, are included *ballad, synod, carol, legal, cymbal, symbol, viol, vial, balsam, column, phantom, felon, vigilant, surplus, acre, altar, centre, lunar, lustre, murmur, forward, bulwark, apron, saffron, stubborn,* etc. It is apparent from these lists that Willard's judgments were more or less influenced by spellings. M'Intyre, *The Southern Spelling Book*, 1833, also gives directions showing that in certain words unaccented [ə] was to be avoided. Thus he declares that *palace* is to be pronounced *pal lis; facile*, spelled *faccile*, is *fas sil*, p. 31; *malice* is *mal lis*, p. 34; *terrace* is *ter ris*, p. 42; *furnace* is *fur nis*, p. 59; though *menace* is given as *men ace*, p. 41, and *preface* as *pre fas*, p. 42. These last two are obviously examples of spelling pronunciations.

As late as 1895 a competent observer in New England legislated against unstressed [ə] in certain final syllables. According to Grandgent, *Die Neueren Sprachen*, II, 449 (1895), "Philadelphia, New York City, and some parts of the West and South," often substitute [ə] for [ɪ] in final syllables, as in *goodness* ['gʊdnəs] for ['gʊdnɪs], *honest* ['anəst] for ['anɪst], *I've got it* [aɪv gat ət] for [aɪv gat ɪt], *palace* ['pæləs] for ['pælɪs], but "in the rest of the country this pronunciation is regarded as extremely vulgar." If one excluded Philadelphia, New York City and parts of the West and South, the rest of the country would seem to have been mainly New England. Grandgent returns to the subject later, in *Old and New*, Cambridge, 1920, p. 143, but his defense of [ɪ] when one might have [ə] is now qualified. He notes that [ə] has encroached upon [ɪ], "*possible* being now usually pronounced in America with the middle vowel of *probable*, *enough* with the initial vowel of *about*." "The distinction between these sounds," he continues, "has become one of the niceties of careful diction; it is much more generally observed in New England than elsewhere in America. Particularly offensive to the ear of the old-fashioned Yankee is the same substitution in final syllables —'goodnus' for *goodness*, 'ahnust' for *honest*, 'nakud' for *naked*, 'stahp ut' for *stop it*." If the old-fashioned Yankee of which Grandgent here speaks does really pronounce [ɪ] in all these unstressed syllables, and if he would be deeply grieved to hear [ə] in them, this would be merely another illustration of the fact that people, when they begin to think about themselves, are ever inclined to take their own traditional inheritances, no matter how popular or undistinguished in origin, and make of them marks of special distinction.

In the Report of a Joint Committee on the Subject of a Phonetic English Alphabet, New York, 1904, made by a representative body of American scholars, difficulty was expressed in disposing of this unstressed and obscured vowel. The quality and extent of obscuration, it was remarked, p. 12, "vary somewhat with the style of the discourse, the idiosyncrasy of the speaker and the nature of the neighboring consonants, but it always tends in one of two directions: either towards the *i* of *pin*, as in the second syllable of *added, honest, captain, message, menace,* and in the first syllable of *example, refer, eject;* or else toward the *u* in *but,* as in the second syllable of *sofa, moment, Robert, separate, ebony, guttural,* or in the first syllable of *about, mature, attack, political, tureen.*"

The naïve spellings of the early records prove that the pronunciation of a clear [ɪ] or [ɛ] in unstressed syllables goes back to the seventeenth century. In the *Groton Records,* p. 64 (1681), occur spellings like *grantid, uotid* (voted), *chargis, catill, ratid, hundrid, chosin, uisibell* (visible). In the *Hempstead Records* very numerous spellings like *beadille,* I, 16 (1657) for *beadle, alwise,* I, 22 (1657), for *always, comforttabell,* I, 95 (1660), for *comfortable, abell,* I, 102, (1661), for *able, powndeg,* I, 27 (1657), for *poundage, liabell,* I, 27 (1657), for *liable, muttell,* I, 229 (1666), for *mutual,* indicate a tendency towards relatively heavy stressing of final syllables. In the *Plymouth Records, takein,* I, 216 (1719), for *taken, gravill,* II, 5 (1705), for *gravel, vallied,* I, 215 (1698), for *valid,* illustrate the same tendency. In the *Springfield Records, cattayle,* I, 156, *cattell,* I, 164, for *cattle, Morgin,* I, 416 (1676), for *Morgan, Aprel,* I, 416 (1676), for *April* may be noted. In *Hazord,* II, 108 (1648), *siuell, ciuell,* for *civil* occurs. In the *Watertown Records* one finds *singell,* p. 130 (1677), for *single, cassell,* p. 118 (1673), etc., for *castle,* and *childering,* p. 107 (1671), for *children* would be possible only if one gave the final syllable a fairly heavy stress. The same is true of *ruings* for *ruins, Huntington Records,* p. 186 (1672).

Perhaps in this group should be included the pronunciation of final unstressed *a* as [ɪ] instead of [ə]. The latter is now the only standard pronunciation, a final unstressed [ɪ] occurring only in words written with *i*, as in *Missouri, Cincinnati*. In popular use, however, [I] is common in *Cuba, Martha*, etc. The spelling *Sary* for *Sarah* indicates the pronunciation in *Watertown Records*, p. 81 (1663). For Billerica the spelling *Bilericy* occurs in the *Groton Records*, p. 79 (1683). For *Rebecca* the spelling *Rebeccy* occurs in *Dedham Records*, V, 192 (1686). Benezet, p. 147, Mennye, p. 91, Bradford, pp. 19–28, all give *Barbara, Barbary* and *barberry* as sounding alike.

The later convention was as it is formulated by Fowle, *Common School Speller*, 1842, p. 80, who says that "*a* at the end of a word is pronounced like *uh* in *Messiah*," adding the particular caution that it should not be pronounced like *a* in *fate*. Yet Halleck, *Poetical Writings*, 1869, p. 47, rimes *Tuscarora* with *glory*, not facetiously, and old-fashioned speakers well on to the end of the nineteenth century would have seen nothing strange in this pronunciation. In the dictionary of 1806, Webster recorded *taffeta* and *taffety* as both good forms of this word, but *taffety* was dropped in the dictionary of 1828.

Variation in the stressing of final syllables has resulted, in some instances, in establishing in authorized use two forms of certain proper names, felt to be quite separate and distinct, though etymologically the same. Thus the name Littell is a variant form of Little, Bedell of Beadle, Cattell of Cattle, Brownell of Brownel, Purcell of Pearsall, Belding of Belden, Gooding of Goodin, Whiting of Whitin.

Though earlier stressing for some final syllables more heavily than is now customary is indicated by the records, the reverse is of course more commonly to be met with, that is, the pronouncing of final syllables less fully than spelling and convention warranted. For the unaccented syllable *-ing* most speakers nowadays would insist on a pronunciation [Iŋ], certainly in theory and on the whole with some consistency in practice. Dwight, *Travels*, I, 468, noted that the Bostonians of his day pronounced unstressed *ing* as *en*, "as *exceeden* for *exceeding, aspirin* for *aspiring*, etc." "This pronunciation," he continues, "I have remarked in most Englishmen

whom I have seen, and it may be the prevailing one in England."
The naïve spellings of the town records indicate this pronunciation
very frequently, as in the *Groton Records*, p. 64 (1680), *accordin* for
according, *finishin* for *finishing*, etc. It was undoubtedly formerly
a widespread pronunciation, both popularly and in cultivated speech,
and it has disappeared or tends to disappear from later standard
speech mainly through the influence of spelling.

For unstressed *u*, which now ordinarily has the sound [ju] in
standard speech, older pronunciations with [ə], [ɪ] occasionally survive and are mentioned by the older writers. Thus Mennye, p. 91,
gives *valley*, *value*, *volley* as sounding alike. The pronunciation
vally for *value* is frequently indicated in early literary transcriptions
of New England dialect. It is corrected by Ussher, pp. 95–96, who
cities *valley* as an impropriety for *value*. For *Matthew* the spelling
Mathy occurs in the *Hempstead Records*, I, 204 (1666).

Likewise the syllable *ow* was pronounced with weakened value,
and in his list of improprieties, Ussher includes *winder* for *window*.
This pronunciation is indicated in the *Huntington Records*, by the
spelling *medder* for *meadow*, p. 118 (1662), p. 122 (1668), p. 360
(1683), and often, and *widder* for *widow*, p. 206 (1673). Green,
Three Military Diaries, writes *feler* for *fellow*, p. 88, *arrers* for *arrows*,
p. 95; *follar* for *follow*, p. 96. These pronunciations are all familiar
in contemporary dialect use, but as the early occurrences show,
are not modern corruptions.

The sound which is still standard in the second syllable of *iron*,
pronounced as though written *iern*, is given by Peyton, p. 23, as
occurring also in *squadron*, *apron*, *citron*, *saffron*. Peyton, p. 12,
says that *i* is silent in *venison*, *ordinary*, *business*, *chariot*, *cousin*,
medicine, *spaniel*, *devil*, *evil*, *cavil*, *regiment*. The only one of these
words in which *i* may now be said to be silent, except when followed
by a syllabic consonant, is *business*. For *venison*, *medicine*, *regiment*
a trisyllabic pronunciation is now standard in American speech.

The words *guardian*, *champion* are now sometimes pronounced
as dissyllables with a stress on the second syllable, that is, as [ˈgɑːr-
ˈdiːn], [ˈtʃæmˈpiːn]. This is now only a popular pronunciation,

though formerly in good use. The proper name *Gardeen* seems to be a survival of the older pronunciation. The metre in Shakspere, as in *I Henry VI*, iii, iv, 19, indicates a dissyllablic proɪunciation for *champion* which probably had a long vowel and a stress in the second syllable. In the *Hempstead Records*, I, 291 (1672), the spelling *Champin* for the proper name usually spelled *Champion* probably indicates the same pronunciation. For the pronunciation *guardeen* for *guardian*, Thornton gives several examples, his earliest being for 1761. Webster (1783), p. 57, gives *guardeen* as an impropriety for *guardian*. It is indicated by the spelling *gardine*, *Southold Records*, II, 384 (1694), and *gardean*, *Lunenburg Records*, p. 70 (1731). R. M. Johnston, *Mr. Absalom Billingslea* (1888), p. 326, writes *g'yard-yeens* for *guardians* in nineteenth-century Georgian dialect.

A group of words in which present American usage varies to some extent, and in which it has long varied, consists of those with endings like *-ice, -ise, -ine, -ile, -ive*, preceded by a stressed syllable. Most commonly these words now have a short vowel in the final syllable, as in *active, practice, practise, agile*, and many others. But even in *agile* the final syllable is sometimes [-aɪl] and still more commonly in *reptile*. In *gentile* it is always [-aɪl] to keep the word distinct from *gentle*. This difference in use probably arose through an attempt to indicate in these final syllables the long quantity, genuine or supposed, of the Latin syllable from which the English is derived. The natural English tendency would be to make all vowels short in syllables like these in which an unstressed syllable follows a stressed one, and only a very positive theory could have maintained pronunciations like ['æktaɪv], ['præktaɪs] for *active, practise*. Walker, p. 191, though he recognized the difference in actual usage, put it down as a general rule that words of this kind have the *i* in the final syllable short. The only exceptions he allowed were *exile, edile, empire, umpire, feline, archives*, and the words *confine, supine, saline, contrite*, which sometimes have the accent on the first and sometimes on the final syllable, but always have the vowel long. Walker even extends his rule to native compounds and says that *otherwise* has the *i* "more frequently short." But Walker was here evidently ridden by a theory the opposite of the one which accounts for the [aɪ] in these final syllables.

In America Webster found this pronunciation with [aɪ] to be characteristic in certain words of New England. "In the eastern states," he says, *Dissertations*, p. 103, "there is a practice prevailing among the body of the people, of prolonging the sound of *i* in the termination *ive*. In such words as *motive, relative,* etc. the people, excepting the more polished sort, give *i* its first sound [that is, aɪ]. This is a local practice, opposed to the general pronunciation of the English on both sides of the Atlantic. . . . These reasons, with the authority of the most approved practice, should operate to discountenance the singular drawling pronunciation of the eastern people." He then adds that "the same reasons are opposed to another local practice of a similar nature in the middle states, where many people pronounce *practice, prejudice,* with *i* long. I know of no authority for this beyond the limits of two or three states; and it is clear that the practice is not warranted by any principle in the language." Webster's geographical distinctions here seem dubious. It is not probable that [aɪ] was limited in some words to New England and in others to the Middle States. Cooper, in the speech of Natty Bumpo, indicates a pronunciation with [aɪ] in *practysing, Pioneers,* chap. xxii; *fav'rite, Pioneers,* chap. xli; *reptyles, Mohicans,* chap. xix; *practyse, Mohicans,* chap. xxv; *reptyle, Pathfinder,* chap. v; *fav'ryte, Pathfinder,* chap. xxvii; *actyve, Pathfinder,* chap. xxviii; *natyve, Pathfinder,* chap. xxix; *actyve, cowardyce, representatyves,* from *Deerslayer, passim.* Some of these pronunciations still persist in popular speech, e.g. *favorite, cowardice,* and also frequently *genuine,* with the vowel of the final syllable long. It is the pronunciation indicated in rustic British speech in George Eliot's *Silas Marner,* chap. vi, "if you're prac*tising,* I wish you'd prac*tise* that."

INFLECTION AND SYNTAX

Within the modern period fewer changes have taken place in the English inflectional and syntactical system than in pronunciation or vacabulary. As for pronunciation, this is so much a matter of unconscious habit and imitation that changes continually take place in it without the speaker's being aware of them. The sounds of any speech are the least stable elements in it. Vocabulary, on the other hand, is so immediately and obviously the echo of changing activities that even the careless observer can see it gaining and losing before his very eyes. New objects call for new names, and old objects or ways of doing things become old-fashioned and no longer talked about. But inflection and syntax lie halfway between pronunciation and vocabulary in this matter of conscious control. New ideas and new objects do not call for new inflections or new syntactical arrangements, but merely for a further application of the old. On the other hand, inflections and syntactical forms are not as individual and unconscious as pronunciations, for the very reason that they must be manipulated and used with some realization of generalized value. In learning a word, one learns the pronunciation with the word, and that is the end of it. But in using an inflection in a particular word, for example, that of the plural number, one does so with the realization that one may want to use that inflection at another time with an entirely different word. One is not surprised to find, therefore, that the inflectional system as now used in America differs but little from that now used in England or from that used in both America and England in the seventeenth century.

One might suppose that the large mixture of foreign elements

255

in the general American population might have occasioned the introduction of some foreign forms of phrasing, but in fact nothing of this sort can be proved. The phrase *different than* is sometimes said to be a Germanism, but Fitzedward Hall, *Modern English*, p. 82, found it in Addison, Steele, DeFoe, Richardson, Miss Burney, Coleridge, DeQuincey, Newman, and others. It is scarcely worth while to collect American examples, as they will be found frequently in popular writing, and not always as inadvertences, now and then in careful writing. Cooper, *The Prairie*, chap. xxii, speaks of something "made by a very different power than such as belongs to your chiselling masonry." The following is from the New York *Times* (1920): "Did you know that most blonds have different temperaments than most brunets?—that to get along with a blond type you must act different than you would to get along with a brunet?" Instead of looking to German for an explanation of this construction, one must turn one's attention to something nearer home. The phrase is the result merely of popular contamination between two related but differing expressions, probably between *other than* and *different from*. Some uncertainty might also have have been felt as to the proper connective to follow *differ*, *different*, since good usage itself has been unsettled on this point. In England both *different from* and *different to* are permissible, though the former is the more general in England and the only standard form in America.

Another idiom said to have been of foreign origin but certainly native and popular, is the omission of the verb of motion *go* or *come* after auxiliaries, especially *want*. This is exactly parallel to German *Ich will hinein*, "I want to come in," but manifestly what occurs in one Germanic language may by common inheritance occur in another. And in fact constructions like this are found in English as far back as Anglo-Saxon. In American usage the idiom must therefore be regarded as a popular survival. It is mentioned by Carlton, *The New Purchase* (1843), p. 78, who uses the phrase, "she know'd we wanted over [i.e. wanted to cross a ferry] and so hollered naterally," adding in a foot-note, "I want in, I want out, etc., are pioneer forms of speech that are still not uncommon in certain regions of the Middle

West." After the lapse of nearly three generations this statement is still as true as it was in the early nineteenth century. One may hear "I want off here" almost any day of the year on almost any street car in almost any town of the Middle West. If the construction by origin were a foreignism, it would be an astonishing example of alien syntax finding its way into the very heart of popular use. Thornton gives an example under the word *go* of similar omission after *intend*, dated 1784, and under *happen*, several examples of the omission of *to be* or *to go*. The *New English Dictionary* gives further illustrations. How close this construction lies to the spirit of native idiom is illustrated by the lines from Robert Frost's *Mending Wall*, "Something there is that doesn't love a wall, That wants it down."

"We only know of one marked Teutonism current in America," declared Bristed, *The English Language in America*, p. 70, and his one example is "*hold on*, for stop (halt-an)," though this, he wisely concludes "may be only *indirectly* Teutonic." But of things that are indirectly Teutonic in this way, not one but thousands may be found in any form of English.

The tense forms of the English verb have always been the cause of trouble, and though they are now pretty definitely settled in cultivated speech, in popular speech a variety of uses occur which differ from those of cultivated speech. But even in the latter, practice is not altogether uniform. The preterite of *dive* is most commonly *dived*, but sometimes *dove*, as in Roosevelt, *Hunting the Grisly*, p. 111, "The little animal . . . dove into the bushes." The preterite of *glide* is commonly *glided*, but Shelley, *Revolt of Islam*, I, 48, wrote "And we glode o'er a pellucid plain." Both *glode* and *dove* are very general in popular speech. The past participle of *swim* likewise varies between *swam* and *swum*, of *sing* between *sang* and *sung*, of *drink* between *drank* and *drunk*. The variations in tense forms in the eighteenth century were still greater. Madam Sarah Kemble Knight, a Boston lady of education, in her *Journals* written in 1704, uses *begun* for *began*, p. 9, *see* for *saw*, p. 24, and elsewhere frequently, *riss*, that is *riz*, for *rose*, p. 49, *ridd* for *rode*, p. 61, *come* for *came*, p. 63.

On the frankly popular level, one finds a great variety of tense forms of the verb, many of which have never been accepted in conventional language. Thus the participles *done* and *seen* do duty both as participle and preterite. The preterite of *sneak* is often *snuk*, of *creep* is *crope*, of *weed* is *wed*, of *heat* is *het*. This last form is recorded in Webster in his grammar as good use, and undoubtedly *het* as the preterite of *heat* only just failed to be accepted into good general use. Staniford, p. 29, gives only *heat* as preterite and past participle of *heat;* p. 28, he gives *crope* and *creeped* as preterites of *creep,* and *clung* or *clang* as the preterites of *cling.* All these instances of variation in tense formation as they appear in older records and in present popular speech are explainable on the basis of the normal historical and psychological changes which take place in language. They are by no means merely a recent development, for even in the oldest recorded Anglo-Saxon forms of English, one finds verbs which supposedly ought to belong in one group attracted by analogy to another group. A few instances may be noted as they occur in older American records. In the *Huntington Records,* p. 90 (1664), *see* occurs for *saw,* and p. 319 (1681), *stop* for *stepped.* Of these last two forms *stepped* is the new and *stop* the old, being a direct survival from the Old English strong preterite *stōp.* In the *New Haven Records,* p. 23 (1639), *see* also occurs for *saw,* and so also in *Easthampton Records,* I, 70 (1654). This was one of the uses almost universally legislated against in the grammars of the eighteenth and early nineteenth century, and like *het,* probably barely escaped being included within the limits of conventional speech.

As the preterite of *show,* Green, *Three Military Diaries,* p. 97, has *shue,* and the spelling *shew* also occurs a number of times. The variation between *show* and *shew* is common in the infinitive and present, and the spelling *shew* still survives in England, though the word is pronounced as though written *show.* In the present stem, this variation is due to a double phonetic development, as in *strew, strow, shrew, shrow,* but the use of *shew* as a preterite seems to be by analogy to *grew, threw, knew,* etc. In these *Diaries,* p. 96, *forsted* occurs as the preterite of *force.* This suggests the present common popular *bursted* as a preterite of *burst,* the *-ed* of *bursted* being added to *burst* because the stem of *burst* already ends in a dental. In the case of *forsted* one must assume therefore a pronunciation of the present as *forcet*, the inorganic *t* being added here as in *oncet*, *twicet*, *against*, etc. The addition of an inorganic *d* after *n* in *drown* is frequent in the popular forms *drownd*, *drownded*, and it occurs in these *Diaries*, p. 95, *drown* being spelled *drownd*. Inorganic *d* is also added after *l* in *milds*, p. 86, for *miles*.

A variant of *might* as *mought* is illustrated by Thornton with examples beginning with 1821, when Dwight, *Travels*, IV, 281, described *mought* as a Cockneyism. Thornton's latest example is for 1857, and all of his uses occur in familiar or humorous writing. The form is very old in the English language and examples will be found in the *New English Dictionary* from the fourteenth century. It occurs not infrequently in the early town records, as in *Southold Records*, I, 468 (1657), "there mought come a tyme hee mought know hee was not;" or I, 468 (1657), "That they . . . mought peaceably enjoy the above granted privileges." Thornton also illustrates *sot* for *set*, beginning with 1776, *seen* for *saw*, beginning with 1796, *fit* for *fought*, American examples beginning with 1821, *hove* for *heaved*, beginning with 1770, *plead* [plɛd] for *pleaded*, beginning with 1774. He cites examples of *gotten* as past participle for *get*, beginning with 1796. In England, the form *gotten*, except as an adjective participle, as in *ill-gotten gains*, is archaic and dialectal, but in America the participle *gotten* is still commonly used, though *got* is also current and perhaps the more general form. In America *gotten* is merely a survival from older use, as in *Southold Records*, I, 474 (1659), "his share of what they had gotten in that weeke." Another American survival is the participle *stricken*, illustrated by Thornton with examples beginning with 1790.

A few other verb forms which may be noticed are *writnd* for *written*, *Watertown Records*, p. 146 (1679), p. 148 (1680); *cetched* for *caught*, *Southold Records*, II, 447 (1760); *cotch* for *caught* is frequently corrected by the early grammarians. The preterite of *come* in popular speech is often the same as the present, but a less frequent variant is used by Carlton, *The New Purchase*, where the form regularly given for rustic Indiana speech of the first quarter of the nineteenth century is *kim*. Wright, *Dialect Grammar*, records a form close to *kim* as occurring in the northern counties of England. Historically the preterite of this verb has had a somewhat troubled existence, and the form current in standard English, *came*, is not derived from the normal Old English form *cōm*, which should give *coom* in Modern English. The preterite *kim* is probably a phonetic variant like the popular pronunciation of *can* as [kɪm]. Analogy of a word like *climb* is also possible. In standard English this verb has only the preterite *climbed*, but popularly it has also *clum* and *clim*, parallel to the two popular preterites of *come*.

In present American use, the preterite of the verb *eat* is spelled *ate* and almost universally pronounced to rime with *mate*. A pronunciation to rime with *met* is sometimes heard, most commonly in uncultivated speech, but now and then also in cultivated speech. In England the pronunciation [et] remains in undoubted good use, and though the verb is always written *ate* in the preterite, it may be pronounced indifferently to rime with *mate* or *met*.

The old plural of *houses* with a weak ending, *housen*, was commonly current in America throughout the seventeenth and eighteenth centuries. It appears frequently in the town records, as in *Southold Records*, I, 282 (1670), "with all my housen there belonging to." In the *Lunenburg Records*, p. 109 (1740), the town voted that "thay Build two School Housen . . . that the School Housen be Borded and Shingled and the Loar floor be Laid Down and the Chimney be Built and the Housen under Pend [underpinned] . . . that thay Rase one Hundred and twenty Pounds to Buld the School Housen." The form *housen*, however, often developed into *housing*, just as *garden*, *kitchen* became *garding*, *kitching*, and perhaps this development was also furthered by confusion between the participial form *housing* from a verb *to house* and the noun *housen*. For in any case the word *housing*, whether participial or nominal, would have been popularly pronounced like *housen*. Thus we find in *Plymouth Records*, I, 276 (1700), *dweling housing* for *dwelling houses*, and in *Dialect Notes*, IV, 381, occurs an undoubted example of *housing* for *houses* in 1716.   The early grammarians often reprehend *housen* as an impropriety, as for example, Ussher, p. 95 (1803), who spells the word *howzen*.   This archaic plural was frequently employed in humorous or satirical accounts of rustic New England characters in early plays and novels.   Thus in *Haverhill*, by James A. Jones, New York, 1831, a romance placed in the years just before the Revolution, Aminidab, a New Englander, speaks, p. 253, as New Englandly as the author can make him: "A tarnation big ship, too, and owned by Elder Pollard, he that built the block of housen where Elder Hillyard has his darned great bookstore, and owns that unimproved tract of brush on the road to Hingham."

The use of *was* with *you* as subject is now a sure mark of uncultivated speech.   As such, however, it is merely a survival of a use which was formerly permissible in the best society and in the most dignified writing.   Hall, *Modern English*, p. 209, has collected some examples, the number of which could be greatly increased by examining more eighteenth-century writings.   The use was very general in America throughout the eighteenth century, as in the following passage from a highly literary exercise in the form of a letter of condolence, written by John Adams, *Works*, II, 76 (1759), to a friend whose house had burned down: "You regret your loss; but why? Was you fond of seeing or thinking that others saw and admired so stately a pile?"   At this same time, *were* was also used with *you*, being probably the more general usage, and by a curious reversal of the present state of affairs, *was* as the exceptional form seems often to have been regarded as the better or finer usage.

A much disputed point in present American speech centers about the question of *you all* as used in cultivated Southern American speech.   In this use the two words are practically taken together as one word, with the stress on *you*.   A voluminous newspaper discussion has developed on this question, which has not, however, much clarified it.   According to C. Alphonso Smith, *Uncle Remus's Magazine*, Atlanta, Georgia, July, 1907, reprinted in the *Kit Kat*, Columbus, Ohio, Vol. IX, No. I, January, 1920, the distinctive Southern use gives the phrase *you all* a collective plural sense: "in every case the use of *you all*, with the accent on *you*, implies in the mind of the speaker the consciousness of a group." Smith thinks that *you all* is never used as a singular in the South, and Joel Chandler Harris and Thomas Nelson Page agree with him. He believes that examples which one sometimes finds in books of *you all* as a singular are due to mistaken observation and to mistaken feeling for the idiom. Perhaps nothing is so dangerous in questions of language as the universal affirmative, unless it be the universal negative. That *you all* is never used as a singular in Southern speech is certainly contradictory to the writer's observation and to the testimony of many observant Southerners. That it should be used as a singular, even though originally it was a plural, is not strange, for *you* itself illustrates exactly the same transition from a plural to a singular meaning.

On a somewhat lower social level are the forms *we uns, you uns,* for *we* and *you*. These pronouns are not used anywhere in cultivated speech, as *you all* is in the South, but are characteristic of rustic, especially the mountain speech of the Blue Ridge. Examples will be found abundantly in the writings of Charles Egbert Craddock. By origin the phrase seems to be a compound of the pronoun with *ones, we ones, you ones,* in colloquial style weakening to *we uns, you uns*. A similar use of *young uns*, meaning children, from *young ones*, should be noted, see *Dialect Notes*, IV, 230, and the indexes to the several volumes.

The weakened colloquial form of the personal pronoun, third person plural, accusative, as in *I told 'em* for *I told them*, is to be explained either as having arisen from a phonetic weakening of *them* in unstressed positions, or as a direct survival from Old English *heom, hem*, in which the *h* would readily disappear, leaving only *em*. The latter explanation seems more probable, and it receives some support from the occurrence of early examples of the weakened form, as in the *Hempstead Records*, I, 138 (1663), "and if he cannot finde them yt day . . . the Owners shall keep the herd the next day, whilest Edward seek to find ym up or else look ym up themselves." Of course one is not surprised to find the standard form *them* and the weakened form *em*, here written *ym*, occurring at the same time and in the writing of the same person. The writer's speech may have been consistent, that is, he probably always said *em*, but his writing represents a mixture of two speech traditions, one visual and the other aural.

As the weakened form *'em* was the only form of *them* current in popular speech when the word stood in its customary position after its governing verb or preposition, the full form *them* was left for specialized uses, that is, it became the accepted form in the more emphatic position before the word with which it made a close syntactical combination. In this use the word became a strong demonstrative, used as an adjective, as in *them boys*, or merely as a pronominal subject, *Them is the boys*. Apparently these functions of *them* might just as well have been served by *those*, as they are in standard speech. Historically, however, *those* as plural of *that* has not had a stable history. The Old English plural was ðā, which should give *tho* in later English. The *s* was added apparently by analogy to the common plurals of nouns, but the form *those* did not become established until the latter part of the fifteenth century. It is probable that the popular use of *them* as a demonstrative arose in this unsettled period and has persisted ever since. Examples of *them* as a demonstrative will be found in the *New English Dictionary* in reputable writings for as early as 1596, though the construction is characterized as now only dialectal or illiterate.

The contracted form *ain't*, whether used with a singular or plural subject, is now definitely not acceptable in careful cultivated speech. It is very widely current in illiterate speech, in general colloquial speech, and perhaps in some communities it may be heard even on higher levels. It has always been only a form of the spoken language and has never made its way into formal literary use. Formerly, however, it was not so reprehensible in colloquial style as it has become since the schoolmaster and the dictionary maker have had their day. The dialog of the comedies of the Restoration shows that polite speakers did not then carefully avoid it. By the end of the eighteenth century, however, the critical judgment of the grammarians was finally registered against it. Staniford, p. 65, gives *ain't* for *are not* as a vulgarism, and from this time on the grammarians regularly legislate against it.

The colloquial contraction *don't* for the third singular of the negative of *do*, instead of *doesn't*, seems not to have attracted the attention of the early grammarians. Undoubtedly it has existed in colloquial speech for centuries, but the choice between *don't* and *doesn't* was probably too slight to engage the attention of students before the rise of the late nineteenth-century school of microscopical purists.

The so-called improper use of *shall* and *will* has been called the Irish difficulty. It might as well be called the Scottish and the American and the British difficulty, for nowhere where the English language is spoken does there exist complete harmony between theory and practice in this matter of *shall* and *will*. The supposedly correct differentiation of the uses of *shall* and *will*, not observed in Shakspere and the Bible, is characterized by Logan Pearsall Smith, *The English Language* (1912), p. 29, as "one of the most elaborate and wonderful achievements of the Genius of the Language in modern times." It is described as "so complicated that it can hardly be mastered by those born in parts of the British Islands in which it has not yet been established." Elaborate and wonderful this differentiation may be, but it can scarcely be called an achievement if it is realizable only in parts of the British Islands, nor can one think that the Genius of the Language, whatever that may be, would trouble itself to develop so elaborate a machinery to be utilized in so restricted an area. The truth is that the subtleties of *shall* and *will* are to be laid rather at the door of the theoretical grammarian than at that of the Genius of the Language. To follow the subtleties of the grammarian, one must have an elaborate guide book, such for example as the well thought out book of Sir Edmund W. Head, *Shall and Will*, 2nd edition, London, 1858. If language is a game, to be played by rule and with painful attention to "form," such an elaborate set of directions for *shall* and *will* as is set forth in this and similar treatises may not only be useful but necessary.

Few persons, however, in theory regard language in this liglht, still ewer in practice. If one looks to practice, especially to coloquial practice, one finds that at no time or in no place has usage been as definitely organized with respect to *shall* and *will* as the prescriptions of the grammarians require. Since the main questions in the use of *shall* and *will* arise in the first and second persons, it is manifest that literary use has less opportunity to determine these questions than it would have in the third person, for the reason that in formal literary style the first and second persons are rarely used except in reporting conversations. The appeal must therefore be to spoken language, and any observation of spoken language which is adequate must be made directly on the facts, not on more or less trustworthy literary interpretation of the facts.

The use of a distinctive auxiliary form for expressing the future is a comparatively recent development in all the Teutonic languages. Originally the Teutonic future was expressed merely by the present, which thus performed a double tense function. This is the method of indicating future time in the verb in Old English. Even in the Old English period, however, a phrasal tense, made up of *shall* and *will*, was tending to be used in a strictly future sense. This future sense was a development from older phrasal verb forms with *shall* and *will* in which the auxiliaries had other and more positively modal value than merely the tense idea of futurity, the primary sense of *shall* being obligation, of *will* being desire. Neither of these meanings has ever been lost at any stage of the language, the idea of futurity having been merely added to them. It is easy to see how the idea of futurity might develop from the original meaning of *shall* and *will*, for it may readily be supposed that what one desires to do, one soon will do, and also what one is obliged to do, one also soon will do. The whole story of *shall* and *will* is therefore a story of how the future idea was combined with certain other ideas in the use of verb phrases with *shall* and *will*. The transitions in sense in this development are often minute and subtle, and even today it is sometimes difficult to distinguish the several possible threads of a speaker's intention in the use of these phrases. General tendencies, however, seem perfectly clear. One is the tendency to use *will* as the generalized type form to express futurity, the phrases with *shall* being retained in mere specialized modal senses. "In American colloquial speech," says Curme, p. 520, "we are struggling for an absolute future without any respect to free moral agent or natural law, a future tense which only indicates simple future time, such as is found in the classical language: 'Doctor Morgan, will (future act) I ever get up?', Eggleston's *Circuit Rider*, p. 302. 'Patty, I tell you I am wretched and will (future condition) be till till I die,' *ibid.*, p. 290. This new American usage is the felicitous outcome of a long struggle of over seven hundred years. In England this same usage is also found in the second and third person, but the final stage in the development, its use in the first person, has not yet been reached." But England is not at one in this matter. The final stage has not been reached in cultivated and literary southern British speech, but elsewhere the evolution of *will* as a simple future has gone further, as far as it has gone in America. When the author of the passage quoted above says that the use of *shall* and *will* is so complicated that it can hardly be mastered by those born in parts of the British Islands in which it has not yet been established, he is reversing the order of progress. The line of development and extension has been in the direction of the use of *will* as a simple future, for the first as well as the second and third persons, and those regions or types of speech which retain *shall* in the first are merely holding on conservatively to an older form. This conservatism in England is characteristic of the speech of the south of England which in modern times has been elevated to the position of a standard cultivated speech. As soon, however, as one passes out of the circle of the archaic southern speech of England, one finds a much greater freedom in the use of *will* as a future auxiliary. What has happened in the case of *will* has happened in many other details of the history of English inflections, the northern and midland regions being the ones in which generalization of analogical type forms, for example the personal inflections of the present tense of the verb and the plural inflection of the noun, proceeded most rapidly and completely. The situation in America parallels that in England. In New England where the traditions of seventeenth-century southern British speech are most fully preserved, one can hear the so-called "proper" use of *shall* and *will*, even in uncultivated rustic speech. On this level it is merely a survival of an untutored popular speech habit. Outside New England, however, the use of *will* as a simple future, for first as well as second and third person, may be fairly described as the common speech habit, present not only in uncultivated speech, but also the prevailing use in cultivated speech when it is not consciously precise. The distribution of the "proper" use of *shall* and *will* in natural speech coincides pretty exactly with the occurrence of the Italian *a* in words like *half, past, glance*, etc. In Modern English both of these are direct survivals from the dialect uses of southern British English; they have acquired distinction in England as parts of that English which has been elevated to the position of a formal standard, and in the United States they were transplanted directly to New England and have thus shared in the general distinction which came to this first center of culture in America.

It would be a rash prophet who should attempt to foretell the future fate of *shall* and *will* in American speech. Will the formal prescriptions of the grammarians ever become strong enough to overcome the instinctive tendencies of popular speech? or will the mood of the purist ever become so softened that he will lay aside his ancient dogmas and distinctions, and will accept, even for literary practice, the customs which have established themselves as satisfactory in popular speech? One thing seems certain, that nowhere in America do we now have a large body of speakers who make the distinctions in the use of *shall* and *will* as futures in their familiar natural practice, from whom as a radiating center of social influence, the "proper" use of *shall* and *will* might spread and become general. Such a community of use may have existed in New England in the seventeenth century, but now exists neither there, nor in any center of transplanted New England culture. The conclusion is inevitable, therefore, that if *shall* is to be retained as a future form and *will* is to be checked in its tendency to acquire general value as a simple future, these results must be attained through conscious endeavor and education. The history of language does not afford reason for hoping that conscious endeavor can do much to alter or check a tendency widely present in instinctive natural speech. In the matter of *shall* and *will*, since the use of *will* as a simple general future, and of *shall* and *will* in other more specialized and logically colored modal senses, often subtle and difficult to analyze, does not imply any loss in the expressive powers of the language, it would seem an act of common sense on the part of the grammarian to take his stand on the side of the accomplished facts of popular speech.

A very frequent syntactical form of contemporary popular speech is that which puts an *a* before every present participle, especially after *go*, as in *to go a-fishing, bye baby bunting, daddy's gone a-hunting*, etc. In phrases like these, the construction is historical, the *a-* being a weakened form of the Old English preposition *on* in unstressed position, and *fishing, hunting,*etc., being originally verbal nouns which have been assimilated in form and, to a considerable extent, in feeling, to present participles. Starting with these phrases, however, the *a-* has been prefixed to genuine present participles, after forms of *to be* and other verbs, with the result that in popular speech almost every word ending in *-ing* has a sort of prefix, *a-*. That this was an old use is evident from the early town records, and certain passages of the *Hempstead Records*, I, 342 ff. (1675), have interest enough to deserve quotation as showing how fully the flavor of present popular speech was present in the language two centuries and a half ago. It seems that John Junnins, that is Jennings, agreed to cut wood for Mr. Robert Jackson, and Robert Bedell declared that "he herd John Junnins say he must Cut Mr. Jackson sum wood an severall days John Junnings Cum to his house an was ther gret part of the day with an ax," but in spite of the ax, John Jennings seems not to have definitely got down to the work of cutting wood. John Bedell likewise stated "that one day he went to Mill and John Junnins was at beatses [Bates's] and betty bedell said [that] when John bedell Cum from the mill he went to william thickstones an Junnins was there with an ax and John bedell asked him what he

was goin to dwo and he said to Cut wood for Mr. Jackson." Still
a third informant, Mathew Bedell, declared "that he was one day
in Gorgeis [George's] lot a weding an John Junnins Cume to the
fence to him about nine or ten aClock and smoked it with him an
Junnins said he was agoing to Cut wood for Mr. Jackson an a while
after Mathew bedell went to John smiths an Junnins was there a
smokin of it an from thence Junnins went to thickstones and from
thence to bedells and from thence to beatsis an from thence home
againe." This seems bad for John Jennings, though when Mathew
Bedell was asked "how he knew it to be trew then he said he was
tould so by others then it was dislicked of an No use mead of it."
Allowing for the slightly heightened color of fiction, the colloquial
ease of the following passage from Bret Harte's *Luck of Roaring
Camp*, p. 15, is just that of the seventeenth century tale of John
Jennings: "I crep' up the bank just now," said Kentuck one day,
in a breathless state of excitement, "and dern my skin if he wasn't
a talking to a jaybird as was a-sittin' on his lap. There they was,
a-jawin' at each other just like two cherry-bums."

The expletive *it* in the phrase *smoked it* and *a smokin of it*, in
the passage from the *Hempstead Records*, was customary seventeenth-
century usage. When Mrs. Rowlandson was taken prisoner by the
Indians and went to see King Philip, she tells in her *Narrative*, 1682,
ed. Nourse and Thayer, p. 24, how King Philip "bade me come in
and sit down, and asked me whether I would smoke it (a usual Com-
plement now adayes amongst Saints and Sinners) but this no way
suited me." The *New English Dictionary* gives other seventeenth-
century examples of *smoke it*. In the seventeenth century one
used *drink* as the verb with *tobacco* as its object in reference to smok-
ing, and examples of this usage will also be found in the *New English
Dictionary*.

A very general idiom in present low colloquial speech is the phrase
kind of with the value of a qualifying adjective or adverb, as in
He is a kind of art critic (that is, not exactly an art critic), *He kind
of hesitated and then laughed* (that is, he hesitated slightly). The
logical elements of this idiomatic phrase are not clear on the sur-

face, and the probabilities are that it is a composition of an older idiom.   A frequent form of it in early nineteenth-century use was *kindly*, as in "Well, you see, I kindly, you know, turned the conversation upon different sorts of wickedness," Paulding, *Westward Ho* (1832), I, 165; "I was so pleased . . . that somehow or other kindly, I couldn't harm him," *ibid.*, I, 175.   This survives in present dialectal use, as in "Hit kindly does a body good to break away from home-ties now and then," *Atlantic Monthly*, June, 1922, p. 758, in a sketch of Kentucky mountain life.   A connection of this word with Anglo-Saxon *gecyndelic* readily suggests itself, but more historical links are required to establish it.   The *New English Dictionary* does not record *kindly* in the sense illustrated above, and with respect to *kind of*, the dictionary merely says, without evidence to support the statement, that "the adverbial use arises out of the adjectival, cf. 'She was a mother of a kind to me,' 'she kind o' mothered me.'"   But this explanation is far from convincing.   The first example of *kind of* as a qualifying adverb in the *New English Dictionary* is for 1849.

The use of *real* as an adverb, as in *a real good sermon*, is now common in popular American speech, and has long been a mark of rustic dialect, especially in New England.   Thornton has American citations beginning with 1827, but the use must be much older and is probably British in origin.   It has never been current, however, in literary English.   The noun *plenty* used as an adjective stands on a somewhat higher level.   Phrases like *the deer are plenty in that region* may still be heard and even read in reputable writing, especially that of sportsmen.   Thornton has citations extending from 1796 to 1869.   The noun is said to be now nearly obsolete in England, and the *Century Dictionary* and the *New International Dictionary* describe it as now chiefly colloquial in America.

Writing in the mid-eighteenth century, Witherspoon, *Works*, IV, 467, comments on the use of the third person as a polite form of address in America.   "As I told Mr.—— for as I told you. I hope Mr.—— is well this morning. What is Mr. M——'s opinion upon this subject? This way of speaking to one who is present in the third person, and as if he were absent, is used in this country by way of respect. No such thing is done in Britain, except that to persons of very high rank, they say your majesty, your grace, your ladyship; yet even then the continuance of the discourse in the third person is not customary." This form of polite address, well established in German, Italian, Swedish and other Continental languages, seems never to have been extensively used in America, and Witherspoon's generalization was probably based upon rare and occasional instances. It may be, however, that he had observed it in Congressional or military use, where the forms of the third person in direct address still survive.

BIBLIOGRAPHY[1]

Adams, Daniel   The Thorough Scholar: or The Nature of Language   4th ed.
    Montpelier, Vt.   1817
Alden, Abner   Grammar made Easy   Boston   1811
—— An Introduction to Spelling and Reading   6th ed.   Boston   1813
Alexander, Caleb   Grammatical Elements   Boston   1793
—— The Young Ladies' and Gentlemen's Spelling Book . . . containing a
    criterion of rightly spelling and pronouncing the English language   Worcester
    [Mass.]   1799
—— The Columbian Dictionary of the English Language   Boston   1800
—— A Grammatical System of the English Language   6th ed.   Boston   1801
    ·Another edition   Rutland, Vt.   1819
Alfred, George   The American Universal Spelling Book   Staunton [Va.]   1811
Allison, Burgiss   The American Standard of Orthography and Pronunciation,
    and Improved Dictionary of the English Language   Abridged for the use of
    schools   Burlington, N. J.   1815
    This is the first edition of this work; "it is our next design," the author says,
    "to furnish the publick with the *American Standard* in a common octavo,
    without abridgment."   This larger edition never appeared.
Anarchiad, The, by Humphreys, Barlow, Trumbull and Hopkins   ed. Riggs
    New Haven   1861
    First published in parts in The New Haven Gazette in 1786–7, and in this
    volume first issued in book form.
Ash, John   Grammatical Institutes   Philadelphia   1788
    This is merely an American reprint of a British book which first appeared
    in 1766.   A number of other editions appeared in America, at different
    times and places, usually without credit to the original edition.
Barlow, Joel   Hasty Pudding, in Todd's Life of Barlow   New York   1886
    Hasty Pudding was written in 1792–1793.
—— The Columbiad   Philadelphia   1807
    An enlarged version of the Visions of Columbus   1787
Bartlett, John Russell   Dictionary of Americanisms   Boston
    1st ed. 1848   2nd ed. 1859   3rd ed. 1860   4th ed. 1877
Beauchamp, W. M.   Aboriginal Place Names of New York   New York State
    Museum Bulletin 108   Albany   1907
Beltrami, J. C.   A Pilgrimage in Europe and America.   2 vols.   London   1828

---

[1] See Preface, pp. x–xi.

Benezet, Anthony The Pennsylvania Spelling Book 2nd ed. Philadelphia
1779
    Benezet was a Philadelphia school teacher, of French extraction; he was
    born in France in 1713, and came to Philadelphia in 1731, where he died in
    1784. The first edition of his Spelling Book appeared in 1776.
Bingham, Caleb The Young Lady's Accidence 7th ed. Boston 1793
—— The Child's Companion 11th ed. Boston 1805
Bokum, Herman Introduction to the Study of the German Language Phila-
delphia 1832
    The German and English Interpreter, by the same author, is merely the
    Introduction with a different title.
Bowditch, N. I. Suffolk Surnames London and Boston 1861
    Not a scientific but a picturesque treatise.
Brackenridge, H. H. Modern Chivalry Philadelphia 1851
    Descriptions of American manners and customs written in the latter part of
    the eighteenth century.
Bradford, William The Secretary's Guide New York and Philadelphia 1728
    This is the 4th ed.; the first edition was made "above thirty years" before.
Braintree Records (1640–1793) ed. S. A. Bates Randolph, Mass. 1886
Bristed, C. A. The English Language in America Cambridge Essays, pp·
57–78 London 1855
British Grammar Printed by Nathaniel Coverly for John Norman, and sold
    at his Shop, near the Boston-Stone Boston 1784
    No author's name is given. On p. 77 the author speaks of his "English
    Dictionary, which has the Accent and Quantities marked on the alphabetical
    Words throughout." On pp. xxvii–xxx is a short preface, following the
    main preface, "To the Teachers of Youth in America," but nothing definite
    is said about American speech, which is regarded merely as a branch of
    British speech. The British Museum catalog cites a London edition of 1762,
    and gives the Boston edition of 1784 as of Boston, Mass.
Bryant, F. E. On the Conservatism of Language in a New Country
    Publications of the Modern Language Association, XXII, 277–290 (1907)
Burhans, Hezekiah The critical pronouncing spelling-book Philadelphia 1823
    Burhans published several other similar books.
Cairns, W. B. British Criticisms of American Writings 1783–1815
    University of Wisconsin Studies in Language and Literature, No. 1 Madison
    [Wis.] 1918
Carlton, Robert [Baynard Rush Hall] The New Purchase Princeton 1916
    First edition, 1843; the book describes pioneer life in Indiana about 1820
    and is rich in detail.
Carpenter, W. H. Dutch Contributions to the Vocabulary of English in America
    Modern Philology, VI, 53–68 (1908)
Carrol, James The American Criterion of the English Language; containing
    the Elements of Pronunciation New London 1795

Clapin, Sylva   New Dictionary of Americanisms   New York   1902

Cobb, Lyman   A just standard for pronouncing the English Language   Ithaca, N. Y.   1821

—— A critical review of Dr. Webster's series of books for systematick instruction in the English language   New York   1831

—— Cobb's orthographer and orthoepist; containing concise principles of pronunciation   New York   1835

Columbiad, *see* Barlow

Comly, John   English Grammar made easy to the Teacher and Pupil   2nd ed.   Philadelphia   1805

—— A New Spelling Book   Philadelphia   1854
The copyright is dated 1842. There were numerous editions, the earliest in the Congressional Library being the edition of 1817.

[Cooper J. F.]   Notions of the Americans, picked up by a Travelling Bachelor   Philadelphia   1828

Cowling, G. H.   The Dialect of Hackness (north-east Yorkshire)   Cambridge [Eng.]   1915

[Coxe, Richard Smith]   A New Critical Pronouncing Dictionary of the English Language   By an American gentleman   Burlington, N. J.   1813
Cushing, *Anonyms*, p. 450, attributes this dictionary to Coxe, and it is so catalogued by the Congressional Library and other libraries.

Cummings, J. A.   The Pronouncing Spelling Book   3rd ed.   Boston   1822
The date of copyright of the first edition was 1819.

Curme, G. O.   Has English a Future Tense?   Journal of English and German Philology, XII, 515–539 (1913)

Dearborn, Benj.   The Columbian Grammar   Boston   1795

Dedham Records   ed. D. G. Hill   Dedham, Mass.
Vol. III (1636–1659)   1892
Vol. IV (1659–1673)   1894
Vol. V (1672–1706)   1899

De Vere, M. Schele   Americanisms   The English of the New World   New York   1872

Dexter, F. B.   The History of Connecticut as Illustrated by the Names of her Towns   Proceedings of the American Antiquarian Society, New Series, Vol. III (1885), pp. 421–445

Dialect Notes   Publications of the American Dialect Society
The publications began in 1889, and four volumes have been published, the current volume being the fifth.

Dilworth, Thomas   A New Guide to the English Tongue   Philadelphia   1770
This was one of many American reprints of a well-known British spelling book.

Douglas-Lithgow, R. A.   Dictionary of American-Indian Place and Proper Names in New England   Salem, Mass.   1909

Dunlap, Fayette   A Tragedy of Surnames   Dialect Notes IV, 7–8 (1913)

Duponceau, Peter S.   English Phonology; or an essay towards an Analysis and Description of he component sounds of the English Language

Transactions of the American Philosophical Society, Vol. I, New Series, pp. 228–264 Philadelphia 1818

Duxbury Records (1642–1770) Plymouth, Mass. 1893
Not of much linguistic value, because the records have been printed in modern spelling, except for proper names.

Dwight, Timothy Conquest of Canaan 1785
—— Greenfield Hill New York 1794
—— Travels in New England and New York [1796–1815] 4 vols. New Haven 1821–1822

Easthampton (L. I.) Records
Vol. I (1639–1679) Sag Harbor 1887
Vol. II (1679–1701) Sag Harbor 1887

Easton, John A Narrative of the Causes which led to Philip's Indian War (1675) Prepared from the Originals by Franklin B. Hough Albany, N. Y. 1858

Eine nuetzliche Anweisung oder Beyhuelffe vor die Teutschen um Englisch zu lernen
Germanton [sic] bey Christoph Saur 1762
The rules of pronunciation are said, p. 41, to be taken from Thomas Lediard's Grammatica, 1725. The book is more important for the student of the pronunciation of German in Pennsylvania than for the student of English.

Elliott, John, and Johnson, junr, Samuel A Selected pronouncing and accented Dictionary 2nd ed. Suffield [Conn.] 1800

Elwyn, Alfred L. Glossary of Supposed Americanisms Philadelphia 1859

Emerson, B. D. The National Spelling-Book and Pronouncing Tutor Boston 1829

Emerson, O. F. The Ithaca Dialect, in Dialect Notes, I, 85–173 (1896)
Treats only the phonology of Ithaca, New York, but the completest dialectal study that has been made for any region in America.

English Dialect Dictionary, edited by Joseph Wright 6 vols. Oxford 1898–1905

Entick's New Spelling Dictionary Revised, Corrected and Enlarged by William Crakelt London 1787
The first edition of John Entick's Spelling Dictionary appeared in 1764.

Ewing, James The Columbian Alphabet Being an Attempt to New Model the English Alphabet Trenton 1798

Farmer, John S. Americanisms, Old and New London 1889

Follen, C. T. C. A Practical Grammar of the German Language 3rd ed. Boston 1837

Ford, Emily E. Notes on the Life of Noah Webster, edited by Emily E. F. Skeel 2 vols. Privately printed New York 1912

Foster, William C. Poetry on Different Subjects Salem [New York] 1805
Written under the signature of Timothy Spectacles.

Fowle, W. B. Common School Speller Boston 1842

Fowler, W. C. The English Language New York 1858
   "Abridged from octavo edition," which had appeared several years earlier.
Franklin, Benjamin A Scheme for a New Alphabet and Reformed Mode of
   Spelling with Remarks and Examples 1768
   Works ed Sparks (1838) Vol. VI, pp. 295–303
   Complete works ed. Bigelow (1887) Vol. IV, pp. 198–209
Fraser, Donald The Columbian Monitor New York 1792
Freneau, Philip Poems reprinted from the rare edition printed at Philadelphia
   in 1786 London 1861
Gannett, Henry The Origin of Certain Place Names in the United States
   Bulletin 258, U. S. Geological Survey Washington 1905
Grandgent, C. H. English in America Die Neueren Sprachen, II, 443–467;
   520–528 (1894)
—— From Franklin to Lowell A Century of New England Pronunciation Pub-
   lications of the Modern Language Association of America, XIV, 207–239 (1899)
—— Old and New Cambridge 1920
   Fashion and the Broad A, pp. 25–30 The Dog's Letter, pp. 31–56 New
   England Pronunciation, pp. 121–149
Gray, James Elements of English Grammar, deduced from the English language
   alone Baltimore 1818
Green, B. W. Word-Book of Virginia Folk-Speech Richmond, Va. 1899
Green, S. A. Three Military Diaries kept by Groton Soldiers Groton, Mass
   1901
   Especially Ames Farnsworth's diary, kept from April, 1775, to May, 1779.
Grimshaw, William An etymological dictionary; or, Analysis of the English
   language Philadelphia 1821 2nd ed. 1826 3rd ed. 1848
—— The Ladies Lexicon and Parlour Companion Philadelphia 1829
   Grimshaw also published The Gentlemen's Lexicon, or Pocket Dictionary
Groton Records (1662–1707) ed. S. A. Green Groton, Mass. 1880
Hall, B. H. A Collection of College Words and Customs 2nd ed. Cambridge
   [Mass.] 1856 1st ed. 1851
Hall, Fitzedward Exemplifications of False Philology New York 1872
—— Modern English New York 1873
Hanover Records (1761–1818) Hanover, N. H. 1905
Hargreaves, Alexander A Grammar of the Dialect of Adlington (Lancashire)
   Anglistische Forschungen, 13 Heidelberg 1904
Harrison, J. A. Negro English, in Anglia Vol. VII, pp. 232–279 1884
Harte, Bret Poetical Works Boston 1883
   Poems written in the sixties and seventies.
Hay, John Complete Poetical Works Boston 1916
   The Pike County Ballads appeared in 1871.
Hazard, Ebenezer Historical Collections Philadelphia Vol. I, 1792 Vol.
   II, 1794
   State papers and other documents, mainly of the 17th century, printed in
   the old spelling.

Hazen, Edward   The Speller and Definer   Philadelphia   1835
Professes to follow neither Webster nor Lyman Cobb exactly in spelling.
Hazen published other English text books.

Hempstead Records   North and South Hempstead, L. I.   Jamaica, N. Y.
1896

Heroes of the Lake   New York   1814
Written in the autumn of 1813.

Higginson, T. W.   English Sources of American Dialect, in Proceedings of
American Antiquarian Society, New Series, IV, 159–166 (1886)

Hitchcock, David   Poetical Works   Boston   1806
Hitchcock was a shoemaker who wrote poetry.   He lived in Connecticut
until he was 20, then in Massachusetts.   He was 33 years old when his
poems were published.

Hoar, George, F.   The Obligations of New England to the county of Kent
[England], in Proceedings of the American Archaeological Society, New
Series, III, 344–371 (1885)

Hodge, F. W.   Handbook of American Indians North of Mexico   Bureau of
American Ethnology, Bulletin No. 30.   2 vols.

Honeywood, St. John   Poems   New York   1801
Honeywood died in 1798.

Horn, Wilhelm   Untersuchungen zur neuenglischen Lautgeschichte   Quellen und
Forschungen, 98   Strasburg   1905

Hull, Joseph   A Guide to the English Language   Utica [N. Y.]   1820

Humphreys, Daniel   The compendious American grammar; or Grammatical
institutes in verse   Portsmouth, N. H.   1792

Humphreys, David   Miscellaneous Works   New York   1804
The preface is dated 1790, and the works themselves were written during the
preceding twenty-five years.

Huntington (L. I.)   Town Records, including Babylon (1653–1688)   ed. C. R.
Street   1887

Jaudon, Daniel   The Union Grammar   4th ed.   Philadelphia   1828
On pp. 213–216 is a list of vulgarisms and improprieties.   The author is
mentioned by Carlton, The New Purchase, p. 90, as "the excellent and justly
celebrated Mr. Jaudon."

Jespersen, Otto   A Modern English Grammar
Part I, Sounds and Spellings   Heidelberg   1909
Part II, Syntax   First volume   Heidelberg   1914

Jones, Stephen   A General Pronouncing and Explanatory Dictionary of the
English Language
First Philadelphia Edition   Philadelphia   1806
A reprint of the fifth English edition, the first edition having appeared in 1798.

Kelley, H. J.   The Western spelling book, designed for common schools . . . with
the pronunciation of Walker's critical pronouncing dictionary   Cincinnati
1832

Kelly, H. [?] J.   The American Instructor   Boston   1825

Kittredge, G. L.   The Old Farmer and his Almanack   Cambridge [Mass.]   1920

Knight, Sarah Kemble   Journals (1704)   New York   1825

Krapp, George Philip   Pronunciation of Standard English in America   New York   1919

Kruisinga, E.   A Grammar of the Dialect of West Somerset   Bonner Beiträge zur Anglistik, 18   Bonn   1905

Kuhns, Oscar   Pennsylvania-German Family Names, in The German and Swiss Settlements of Colonial Pennsylvania, pp. 231–246   New York   1901

—— Studies in Pennsylvania German Family Names   Americana Germanica, IV, 299–341 (1902)

Ladd, J. B.   Literary Remains   New York   1832
Ladd was born at Newport, R. I., in 1764, and died at Charleston, S. C., in 1786.   He lived at Charleston only a year or two.

Lancaster Records (1643–1725)   ed. H. S. Nourse   Lancaster [Mass.]   1884

Legler, H. E.   Origin and Meaning of Wisconsin Place Names   Transactions of the Wisconsin Academy of Sciences, Arts and Letters, XIV, 16–39 (1903)

Letters of J. Downing, Major, to his old friend, Mr. Dwight   New York   1834

Livingston, Arthur   La Merica Sanemagogna   Romanic Review, IX, 206–226 (1918)

Long, Charles M.   Virginia County Names   New York and Washington   1908

Long, Percy W.   English Dictionaries before Webster   Bibliographical Society of America   Papers, Vol. IV, pp. 24–43 (1910)

Longstreet, A. B.   Georgia Scenes   Augusta   1835
Previously published "in one of the gazettes of the State."

Lounsbury, T. R.   The Standard of Pronunciation in English   New York   1904

—— The Standard of Usage in English   New York   1908

Lowell, J. R.   The Biglow Papers   Second Series   Boston   1885
First appeared in 1866.

Lunenberg Records (1719–1764)   compiled by W. A. Davis   Fitchburg [Mass.[1896

Mackintosh, Duncan, et ses deux Filles   Essai Raisonné sur la Grammaire et la Prononciation Angloise   Boston   1797
An intelligently and carefully written book, intended to aid Frenchmen in pronouncing English.

Manning, William   The Key of Libberty, written in the year 1798   ed. Morison   Billerica, Mass.   1922

Martin, M. E.   Origin of Ohio Place Names   Ohio Archaeological and Historical Publications, XIV, 272–290 (1905)

Matthews, Albert   Uncle Sam   Proceedings of the American Antiquarian Society, New Series, XIX, 21–65, also pp. 250–252 (1908)

—— On Early Discussions of Americanisms   Transactions of the Colonial Society of Massachusetts, XIV, 257–264 (March 1912)

Matthews, Brander   Americanisms and Briticisms with other essays on other isms   New York   1892

Matthews, Brander   Parts of Speech   New York   1901

Mead, Charles   Mississippian Scenery   Philadelphia   1819

Mencken, H. L.   The American Language   New York, 1919, x + 374 pp.   2 ed.
New York, 1921, xvii + 492 pp.   3 ed.   New York, 1923, ix + 489 pp.

Mesick, Jane L.   The English Traveller in America (1785–1835)

Miller, Alexander   A Concise Grammar of the English Language   New York
1795

Moore, G. H.   The Name "Columbia"   Proceedings of the Massachusetts
Historical Society, Second Series, II, 159–165 (1885)

Morgan, Jonathan   Elements of English Grammar   Hallowell [Me.]   1814

Murray, Lindley   An English Spelling Book   New York   1811
The 17th American from the 9th London edition, improved by the
author.

Nares, R.   General Rules for the Pronunciation of the English Language   London
1792

New English Dictionary,   edited by James A. H. Murray   Vol. I, A and B
Oxford 1888
Not yet complete, but nearing completion.   Often referred to as Murray's
Dictionary or the Oxford Dictionary.

New Haven Records (1638–1649)   ed. C. J. Hoadly   Hartford   1857

New York Sunday School Spelling-book   3rd ed.   New York   1826

Norton, C. L.   Political Americanisms   New York   1890

North and South Hempstead, see Hempstead

Norwalk Records   compiled by Edwin Hall   Norwalk   1847

Orbeck, Anders   Early New England Pronunciation as reflected in some Seventeenth Century Town Records of Eastern Massachusetts
Columbia University Doctor's dissertation, 1925, in manuscript.   The records
are those of Groton, Dedham and Plymouth.]

Paltsits, V. H.   The Classic Nomenclature of Western New York   Magazine
of History, XIII, 246–249 (1911)

Paulding, J. K.   Letters from the South   New York   1817

Paulding, J. K., and Paulding, W. I.   American Comedies   Philadelphia   1847
Written about 1800.

Pelham, William   A System of Notation; representing the sounds of alphabetical
characters by a new application of the accentual marks in present use: with
such additions as were necessary to supply deficiencies   Boston   1808   50
+ 296 pp.
An elaborate attempt at recording English phonetically.

Perry, William   The Only Sure Guide to the English Tongue   7th Worcester ed.
Worcester, Mass.   1793
This was a pronouncer and spelling book.   The American ed. was published
by Isaiah Thomas, who says it has been "carefully revised by Perry's Royal
Standard English Dictionary and corrected of the numerous errors which
are in all other editions both British and American."   The first British
edition was printed at Edinburgh in 1776.

—— The Royal Standard English Dictionary 4th American Worcester ed. Worcester, Mass. 1796
The 1st American Worcester ed. of Perry was dated Jan. 1, 1788. The 1st British ed. of Perry was in 1775.

Peyton, V. J. Les Élémens de la Langue Angloise Nouvelle Edition Philadelphia 1794
An American reprint of a British book, the first edition of which appeared in 1765. Peyton had published in 1756 Les Vrais Principes de la Langue Angloise.

Pickering, John A Vocabulary, or Collection of Words and Phrases which have been supposed to be peculiar to the United States of America Boston 1816

—— Essay on a Uniform Orthography for the Indian Languages of North America Cambridge 1820

Picket, Albert The Essentials of English Grammar . . . containing obvious definitions and rules for speaking and writing correctly Cincinnati 1829
Picket published several other similar books.

Plymouth Records
Vol. I (1636–1705) Plymouth 1889
Vol. II (1705–1743) Plymouth 1892

Pound, Louise Walt Whitman's Neologisms American Mercury, IV 199–201 (February, 1925)

Primer, Sylvester Charleston Provincialisms Phonetische Studien, I, 227–244 (1888)

—— The Pronunciation of Fredericksburg, Va. Pub. of Modern Language Association, V, 185–199 (1890)

Prince, J. D. The Jersey Dutch Dialect, in Dialect Notes, III, 459–484 (1910)

Read, W. A. The Vowel System of the Southern United States Englische Studien, 41, 70–78 (1909)

—— The Southern R University Bulletin Louisiana State University Feb. 1910

—— Some Variant Pronunciations in the New South Dialect Notes, III, 497–536 (1911)

Reed, P. I. The Realistic Presentation of American Characters in Native American Plays Prior to 1870 Ohio State University Bulletin Columbus, Ohio Vol. XXII, No. 26 1918

Ross, Robert The American Grammar or a Complete Introduction to the English and Latin Languages 7th ed. Hartford 1782
Nothing American about the book except the title and authorship.

Rusk, R. L. Literature of the Middle Western Frontier New York 1925

Russell, William Primary Reader 2d ed. Boston 1843
Russell was a teacher of public speaking, and his most ambitious book was The American Elocutionist.

—— Sequel to the Primary Reader Boston [1845]
A collection of texts for reading, with mispronunciations indicated.

Sharp, Granville Short Treatise on the English Tongue: being an attempt to render the Reading and Pronunciation of the same more easy to foreigners
First edition, 1767, issued later under the title An English Alphabet for Foreigners.
—— An English Alphabet for the Use of Foreigners 6th ed. London 1812
The first edition of this work under this title was in 1786.
—— The Child's First Book Improved
The edition used, in the Columbia University Library, is without the title page and preface.
Sheridan, Thomas A General Dictionary of the English Language London 1780
Sherwood, Adiel A Gazeteer of the State of Georgia Washington City 1837
The first ed. was 1829, but the interesting list of Provincialisms, pp. 79–82, appeared first in the third ed. of 1837.
Shewmake, Edwin F. The English Language in Virginia
Unpublished University of Virginia doctor's dissertation.
Shreve, Joseph The Spellers Guide Buffaloe, Va. 1824
Smalley, D. S. An American Phonetic Dictionary of the English Language . . . designed by Nathaniel Storrs . . . with an introduction by A. J. Ellis Cincinnati 1855
Smith, Seba My Thirty Years out of the Senate New York 1859
A collection of the Jack Downing papers, which first began to appear in 1830.
Smithtown Records ed. Pelletreau Smithtown, Long Island 1898
Song of the Minute Man (1777), from a broadside in the collection of the American Antiquarian Society Worcester, Mass.
Sonneck, Oscar G. T. Report on "The Star-Spangled Banner," "Hail Columbia," "America," "Yankee Doodle"
Library of Congress Report Washington 1909
Southold Town Records ed. J. W. Case Vol. I 1882 Vol. II 1884
Springfield Records First Century of the History of Springfield (1636–1736)
Vol. I Springfield, Mass 1898 Vol. II Springfield, Mass. 1899
Staniford, Daniel A Short but Comprehensive Grammar Boston 1797
—— The Elements of English Grammar 2nd ed. Boston 1815
Steger, Stewart Archer American Dictionaries Baltimore 1913
University of Virginia dissertation.
Suffield Records Documentary History of Suffield, by H. S. Sheldon (1660–1749) Springfield, Mass. 1874
Tandy, Jeanette The Cracker Box Philosophers in American Humor and Satire New York 1925
Thornton, Richard H. An American Glossary 2 vols. Philadelphia 1912
Thornton, William Cadmus: or a Treatise on the Elements of written language Philadelphia 1793
Prize dissertation which was honored with the Magellanic Gold Medal, by the American Philosophical Society, January, 1793

Discusses the powers of the characters and contains an "essay on. the mode of teaching the surd or deaf, and consequently dumb, to speak."

Tooker, W. W.   The Origin of the Name Manhattan   New York   1901

Trumbull, John   Poetical Works   Hartford   1820
Poems written "before and during the Revolutionary war."

Tucker, Gilbert M.   American English   New York   1921
An expansion of a chapter in Tucker's Our Common Speech (1895).

United States Geographic Board, Fourth Report, 1890–1916   Washington   1916
Decisions   July 1916   July 1918
A fifth report, containing decisions to July, 1920, is in process of publication.

United States Official Postal Guide   Washington   1917
Supplements published monthly.

Ussher, George Neville   The Elements of English Grammar   Haverhill [Mass.]   1803
An edition issued at Exeter, 1796, describes itself as the 2nd American edition.

Walker, John   A Critical Pronouncing Dictionary and Expositor of the English Language   London   1791

Ware, Jonathan   A New Introduction to the English Grammar, Composed on the Principles of the English Language exclusively   Windsor, Vt.   1814

Watertown Records (1634–1680)   Watertown, Mass.   1894

Webster, Noah   A Grammatical Institute of the English Language . . . Designed for the Use of English Schools in America   In three Parts   Part I   Containing a new and accurate standard of pronunciation   Hartford   1783
This is the first edition of Webster's spelling book.

—— Dissertations on the English Language   Boston   1789

—— Essays   Boston   1790

—— The American Spelling Book   Boston   1798   (17th edition)

—— Compendious Dictionary of the English Language   Hartford and New Haven   1806

—— Dictionary of the English Language Compiled for the use of the Common Schools in the United States   New Haven   1807

—— Letter to the Hon. John Pickering, on the Subject of his Vocabulary   Boston   1817

—— An American Dictionary of the English Language   New York   1828

—— The Elementary Spelling Book, being an improvement on the American Spelling Book   New York   1843

Whitman, Walt   An American Primer   ed. Horace Traubel   Boston   1904

Whitmore, William H.   On the Origin of the Names of Towns in Massachusetts   Proceedings of the Massachusetts Historical Society, 1871–1873   Boston   1873   pp. 393–419

—— On the Origin of the Name of the Town of Lexington, Mass.   ibid., pp. 269–276

Whitney, W. D.   The Elements of English Pronunciation   Oriental and Linguistic Studies, 2nd Series, pp. 202–276   New York   1874

[Willard, Samuel] The General Class Book By the author of the Franklin
    Primer and the Improved Reader 19th ed. Greenfield, Mass. 1840
    The copyright notice is dated 1828.
Williams, R. O. Some Questions of Good English New York 1897
Woodbridge, Wm. A Plain and Concise Grammar of the English Language
    Middletown [Conn.] 1800
Worcester, J. E. Comprehensive Pronouncing and Explanatory Dictionary of
    the English Language New York 1830
    Revised with important additions Boston 1859
Worcester, Samuel A Fourth Book of Lessons for Reading with Rules and
    Instructions Boston 1847
    The copyright date of this book is 1834.
—— A Third Book for Reading and Spelling 107th ed. Boston 1848
    Russell's American Elocutionist was the source from which Worcester took
    his discussions of pronunciation.
Wright, Elizabeth Mary Rustic Speech and Folk Lore London 1913
Wright, Joseph English Dialect Grammar Oxford 1905
Wyld, H. C. A Short History of English London 1914
—— A History of Modern Colloquial English London and New York 1920
Zachrisson, R. E. Pronunciation of English Vowels, 1400–1700 Göteborg 1913
—— Northern English or London English as the Standard Pronunciation Anglia
    XXXVIII, 405–432 (1914)

INDEX OF SUBJECTS AND NAMES

In entries containing references to both volumes, page numbers preceding the semicolon refer to Vol. I, those following the semicolon, to Vol. II. Otherwise when no volume is indicated, Vol I is to be understood.

INDEX OF WORDS

In entries containing references to both volumes, page numbers preceding the semicolon refer to Vol. I, those following the semicolon to Vol. II. Otherwise when no volume is indicated, Vol. I is to be understood. Old and Middle English words, all foreign words, and stems, prefixes and suffixes are in italics.

clef, 94
clergy, II, 168
clergyman, 147
clerk, 58, 120; 37, 38, 95, 168, 170, 171, 173, 176, 228
Cleveland, 224
clever, 74, 78
clevey, 94, 95
clevis, 94
clevy, 94
cliff, II, 232
clim, II, 260
climb, II, 260
climbed, II, 260
clinch, II, 114
cling, II, 258
clinkers, 116
cloak, II, 132
clo'es, 235
cloister, 342
cloisteral, 342
cloke, 342
close, II, 134
cloth, II, 40
clove, 161
clum, II, 260
clumb, 246
clung, II, 258
coach, 138
coach whip, 113
coak, 342
coal, 75
coal-hod, 76, 77
coals, 75
coal-scuttle, 76, 77
coarse, II, 137, 138, 139, 140, 220, 223, 224
Coasset, 179
Coast (the), 135, 223
coat, 38; 132, 133, 134, 240
Cocheco, 182
cock, 78
cock-tail, 143
coffee, II, 141
coffin, II, 214

Cohasset, 173, 179
Cohees, 179
Cohoes, 84, 85, 178, 179
cohog, 106
cohogle, 115
Cohors, 84; 229
cohosses, 84
coif, II, 200
coil, II, 199, 200
coin, II, 12, 200
coined, II, 198
coit, II, 200
coke, 342
cold snap, 153
cold spell, 153
cole-slaw, II, 45
college, 147; 248
colonel, II, 224
color, 349
colored, 162; 147
colored person, 162
colour, 349
coloured, 349
colourist, 349
colt, 38; 134
colt's tail, 143
column, II, 248
$c\bar{o}m$, II, 260
comb, II, 133
come, II, 134, 135, 164, 165, 179, 210, 256, 257, 259
Come Outers, 147
comfortable, II, 250
command, II, 58, 75, 84
commit, II, 115
common, 129
commutation, 139
commute, 139
commuter, 139
compare, II, 108, 110
compass, II, 232
compass key, 114
complete, II, 128
completely, II, 126
compost, II, 27

gwine, II, 10
gwineter, 249, 250
gwyne, II, 199, 200
gyanousa, 113
gyastacutus, 113

ha', 235
hab, 253
Hackensack Meadows, 81
had, II, 93
Haddam, 190
Hadley, 190, 191
Haerlem, II, 72
haet, 128
hail storm, 144
hainous, 342
hair, II, 52, 107, 109, 110, 111, 185
hait, 127
Haite, 202
half, II, 33, 38, 58, 61, 63, 64, 67, 74, 77, 82, 267
half alligator, 301
half horse, 301
hall, 147; 51, 54, 188
halt-on, II, 257
halve, II, 61
Hamburg, 171
hammer, II, 73
hammock, 81
hand, II, 52, 61, 83, 84
handmaid, II, 26
Handmaid (the old), 318
hands, II, 26
handsome, II, 26, 73, 74
hang, 141
hanging, II, 217
hanker, 95
Hannah, 38
Hannibal, 195
Hanover, 191
han't, II, 58
happen, II, 257
happy hunting grounds, 165
hard, II, 51, 58, 225
hardly, II, 50, 53

hard pan, 80
Hard Shell Baptist, 147
hardware, 132
hare, 39
harm, II, 58, 84, 220
Harmony, 183
harnessed, II, 52, 177
harp, II, 58
Harrison (William Henry), 214, 218
harry carry, 92
harsh, II, 219, 222, 223
harslet, II, 219, 220
hart, II, 58
Hartford, 59, 120, 190, 191
has, II, 76, 93
hash, 115; 222, 223
hasp, II, 58
hassoc, 338, 341
haste, II, 107, 123
hat, II, 11, 51, 54, 66, 75, 87, 240
hat, II, 42, 76
hatchet, 165
hate, 128; 44, 51, 54, 90, 108
Hatfield, 191
Hathaway, II, 229
haul, II, 51
haunch, II, 55, 77
haunt, 39, 95; 35, 36, 39, 55, 64, 67, 71, 74, 77, 78
haus, II, 192
have, 233; 76, 93, 95
have a person's scalp (to), 165
have a tearing time (to), 127
Haven, II, 230
haver, 79
Haverhill, 79, 190, 191; 25
Haverstraw, 79
havoc, 338; 70
haw, II, 42
Hawkeye, 222
hawser, II, 229
hay, 79
Hayes, 215
haying, 92
haying season, 92

West Indies, II, 202
west of the Alleghanies, 134
West Side, 223
wet, II, 12, 245
wet goods, 132
wether, 342
Wethersfield, 190
we uns, II, 262
whapperknocker, 110
whar, 241
wharf, II, 82, 245
what, II, 12, 39, 50, 67
whatever, II, 50
wheat, 92; 126, 244, 245
when, II, 244, 245
where, II, 72, 106, 108, 111, 244, 245
whet, II, 245
whether, II, 95, 116
which, II, 245, 246
whiffenpuff, 112
whifflepoof, 113
while, 79; 245
whine, II, 12
Whip-her-I-will, 111
whipperwill, 110, 111
whippoorwill, 105
whirl-wind, II, 175
whiskey, 140
whisky-john, 167
Whiteneck, 209
Whiting, II, 251
Whitney, II, 115
Whitsun-night, II, 27
Whittaker, II, 229
who, II, 206
whole, 38; 132, 133, 134, 135, 206
whole hog, 318
wholly, 38
whomsoever, II, 206
whorra, II, 48
whortleberry, 97; 212
whurr, 338
-wich, 210
Wickes, 203
wickieup, 163, 167

wickup, 167
wid (for *with*), 249, 250
widow, II, 35, 115, 252
widow-hunter, 358
widow's weeds, 102
width, II, 116
wiener wurst, 157
wifmen, 366
wigwam, 163, 167, 358
wild, II, 35
wile, II, 241, 245
Wilkes (John), 192
Wilkesbarre, 192, 193
will, II, 264, 265, 266, 267, 268
Willamette, 199, 200
Willimantic, 175
Willington, 197
Willow Creek, 185
Wilson (Samuel), 220
wilt, 94
wimen, 366
wimmen, 343, 344
wind, 146, 318; 99
wind-fal, 341
Windham, 197
window, II, 252
Windsor, 187, 190, 191
Windy City, 224
wine, 12
wing, II, 12, 102
Winnepauk, 174
winno-welver, 113
winter, 12
Winthrop, 203; 233
Wintonbury, 187
wire puller, 150
wire pulling, 150
Wisconsin, 177, 180, 222, 337
Wisdom, 185
wise, II, 242
wish, II, 12
wishing, II, 214
wit, II, 100
witch, II, 12
with, 249, 250; 28, 114